THROUGH THE EYES OF WOMEN: GENDER, SOCIAL NETWORKS, FAMILY AND STRUCTURAL CHANGE

IN

LATIN AMERICA

AND

THE CARIBBEAN

THROUGH THE EYES OF WOMEN: GENDER, SOCIAL NETWORKS, FAMILY AND STRUCTURAL CHANGE IN LATIN AMERICA AND THE CARIBBEAN

Edited by Cecilia Menjívar

School of Justice Studies
Arizona State University

de Sitter Publications

INTERNATIONAL STUDIES IN SOCIAL SCIENCE

Series Editor
S. Ishwaran

VOLUME 3

Edited by Cecilia Menjívar

THROUGH THE EYES OF WOMEN:
GENDER, SOCIAL NETWORKS, FAMILY AND
STRUCTURAL CHANGE IN
LATIN AMERICA AND THE CARIBBEAN

de Sitter Publications

Canadian Cataloguing in Publication Data

THROUGH THE EYES OF WOMEN:
GENDER, SOCIAL NETWORKS, FAMILY AND STRUCTURAL CHANGE
IN LATIN AMERICA AND THE CARIBBEAN.
EDITED BY CECILIA MENJÍVAR

ISBN 0-9698707-5-2

Volume 3 in International Studies in Social Science.
Print-ISSN 1497-9616
E-ISSN 1497-9624

Copyright 2003 by de Sitter Publications, Willowdale, ON, Canada. All rights are reserved. No part of this publication may be reproduced, translated, stored in a retrieval system, or transmitted in any form or by any means, electronic, mechanical, photocopying, recording or otherwise, without prior written permission from the publisher.

Authorization to photocopy items for internal or personal use is granted by de Sitter Publications provided that the appropriate fees are paid directly to de Sitter Publications.
Fees are subject to change.

Cover Photo used with permission of peterarnold.com.

de Sitter Publications
374 Woodsworth Rd., Willowdale, ON, M2L 2T6, Canada

http://www.desitterpublications.com
sales@desitterpublications.com

PRINTED IN CANADA

This book is dedicated to the women of Latin America, whose courage and resilience in the face of much adversity are sources of inspiration to us all.

Table of Contents

Chapter 1
Introduction
    Cecilia Menjívar 1-10

Chapter 2
Questioning Globalization: Gender and Export Processing in the
Dominican Republic
    Helen I. Safa 11-31

Chapter 3
Gender, Work, and Family in Cuba: The Challenges of the
Special Period
    Maura I. Toro-Morn, Anne R. Roschelle, and Elisa Facio 32-60

Chapter 4
Psychic and Somatic Vulnerability Among Professional Women in
Argentina as a Result of the Precarization of Labor Linked During the
Socioeconomic Crisis
    Susana Masseroni and Susana Sauane 61-83

Chapter 5
Women and Survival Strategies in Poor Urban
Contexts: A Case Study From Guadalajara, Mexico
    Rocío Enríquez Rosas 84-111

Chapter 6
Families on the Verge of Breakdown? Views on Contemporary
Trends in Family Life in Guanacaste, Costa Rica
    Sylvia Chant 112-151

Chapter 7
Households and Income: Ageing and Gender Inequalities
in Urban Brazil and Colombia
    Maria Cristina Gomes da Conceição 152-171

Chapter 8
Work, Gender, and Space: Women's Home-Based Work
in Tijuana, Mexico
    Silvia López Estrada 172-198

Chapter 9
Organizing a Space of Their Own? Global/Local Processes in a Nicaraguan Women's Organization
Jennifer Bickham Mendez 199-230

Chapter 10
Making Feminist Sense of Neoliberalism: The Institutionalization of Women's Struggles for Survival in Ecuador and Bolivia
Amy Lind 231-261

Chapter 11
Competition and Cooperation Among Working Women in the Context of Structural Adjustment: The Case of Street Vendors in La Paz-El Alto, Bolivia
Victor Agadjanian 262-288

About the Authors 289-292

Subject and Author Index 293-303

INTRODUCTION[1]

Cecilia Menjívar*

Economic restructuring has reshaped social, economic, and political systems around the world. With economic restructuring, there also has been a restructuring of daily life, including changes in consumption patterns, cultural practices, community and family networks, and household expenditures (Benería 1992). As Lind (this volume) observes, a defining feature of this restructuring is the introduction of specific neoliberal policies (e.g., privatization, economic liberalization measures, regional trade initiatives) and decreasing state expenditure in order to integrate (and "globalize") national economies, cultures, communication, and ideas at a historically unprecedented pace.

The conditions within which economic restructuring occurred in Latin America and the Caribbean had been shaped since previous decades. With the shortcomings of the predominant development model (Import Substitution), deteriorating terms of trade, and the oil crises, these economies needed help to repay their increasing external debts. Thus, in the early 1980s international agencies and the United States offered the possibility of debt restructuring, provided that the debtor countries conduct some structural adjustments (Enríquez 2000). Such adjustments were characterized by liberal reforms, decentralization, increased privatization of state-owned enterprises and the health system, shrinkage of the public sector (and accompanying lay offs of government workers), elimination of consumer subsidies, decreased social spending (particularly in education and health), and expansion of a market economy regulated by capital and commodities. Thus, while these policies were broadly conceived as fostering economic growth (and specifically as strategies to insure that the debtor countries repay their debts) (Enríquez 2000), they contributed to normalize the practice of flexible labor and to minimize basic workers' rights (Follari 1998; Weeks 2000).

In this new scenario, endorsed and implemented by the International Monetary Fund and the World Bank, the position of the state as a "social manager" has been diminished in favor of more "efficient" private enterprises. Harris (2000: 147-148), however, points out that in spite of the privatization of state assets throughout Latin America, the state still retains a considerable degree of power and an authoritarian governmental bureaucracy; it is its role in the economy that has been redirected away from serving the needs of the poor. In fact, Robinson (1998-1999) observes that structural transformations (and neoliberal reforms) in Latin America have simply provided the capitalist elite with the opportunity to reconstitute state and business institutions.

The impact of these reforms has been assessed in many ways and contexts. Assessments indicate the contradictory nature of the policies and their

---

* School of Justice Studies, Arizona State University Tempe, Arizona 85287-0403, USA.

unequal effects: they have not been felt equally in all regions or countries or even within the same countries. These reforms have had differential effects by gender, class, ethnicity, and race. For women, particularly poor women, reductions in public and social spending have translated into increased burdens in their efforts to care for their families.

Two important aspects of this economic restructuring have been women's increased responsibility for household maintenance and new forms of employment. Women everywhere in the world have always contributed to their households' subsistence from a young age; thus, what is new is not women's participation in the labor force per se, but the rate at which it has occurred, the forms it has acquired, and the context in which it has taken place. Women are now, increasingly, "breadwinners" on par with men (see Safa 1995) and this new position (and its perception) has reverberated throughout society. Women's increased responsibility as wage earners has impacted all spheres of women's and men's lives, from marital relations, to gender and generational dynamics in the home, to notions of family, to new forms of political and grass roots organizing that put women's interests at the center.

This volume examines the effects of neoliberal reforms on daily life in Latin America and the Caribbean, as seen through the eyes of women. There is already a sizable body of research that focuses on the effects of economic restructuring on women's daily lives. However, the contributions in this volume situate women in their sociocultural milieus, so that women's perceptions and assessments are examined through a lens that includes the lives of other women, men, and other members of the women's families, work settings, communities, and political and religious organizations. And although women in this volume are presented as social actors pursuing diverse personal goals, their experiences, views, and objectives are embedded within broader forces in the economy, polity, culture, and legal systems that organize their lives.

An important theoretical contribution of this volume is the complex examination of informal social networks—whether these are examined as sources of material or emotional support or as basis for political engagement—as they are situated in broader frameworks in the different contexts. While some contributions reveal the continued centrality of informal networks for survival and in the formation of a person's identity, others show the fragmentation and weakening of these ties in the context of limited material resources, as has been observed elsewhere (González de la Rocha 2001; Menjívar 2000; Roberts 1995).[2]

There are a few points that highlight the uniqueness of this compilation. First, the women's (and their families') lives are not assessed using only conventional (economistic) or "neutral" tools. Rather, this volume contains the voices, views, and subjective perceptions of those affected by the same policies implemented throughout the region. Second, the contributions focus on different spheres of life, from micro-processes within the family, to work and occupations, to community, and to political organizing, which reflect not only the disciplinary background and research interests of each of the contributors but also the breadth and depth of the effects of structural reforms. Third, all the contributions focus on recent situations, as the data on which they are based all come from the second half of the 1990s. Thus, this examination reveals the cumulative effect that neoliberal policies have had on the lives of the women and men in Latin America and the Caribbean. And in contrast to other research that has been carried out with a similar focus (c.f. Dwyer and Bruce 1988), in this volume we examine negotiations within the household as well as in the public realm of political participation.

The first three articles focus on work and what engaging in new forms of employment (as well as new forms of work organization) has meant for the lives of women as members of their households and families. In these contributions we gain a good understanding of the effects their employment and work conditions have had in their lives and in their family dynamics. The next four pieces examine these family dynamics, including notions of the family, living arrangements, and intergenerational support. And the last three contributions look at women's political and community organizing in the face of increasing economic constraints, as well as the potential that exists for this kind of political participation. Together, the contributions in this volume present a comprehensive analysis of how the global economy, through the state and other local actors, affects the daily lives of women, men, and their families. They allow us a glimpse into what it means to live in a context of the increased economic vulnerability unleashed by neoliberal reforms in the 1980s and exacerbated by globalization in the 1990s.

HIGHLIGHTS OF THE CONTRIBUTIONS

In the first piece, Safa examines the changes that globalization has brought to women in Villa Altagracia, a garment exporting community in the Dominican Republic, and the implications of their increased labor force participation on gender relations and family structure. Safa analyzes the links between gender and work globalization and shows how changes in the gender composition of the labor force have altered gender relations. As women have attained greater economic autonomy, these changes have undermined the myth of the male breadwinner. As in other areas of the world, the transformation from agroexporting to export manufacturing generated jobs for women in Altagracia, but it also affected male employment negatively, as sugar production and import substitution industries— where men predominated—declined. However, even though women dominate in the free trade zones, men predominate in the better-paid technical and managerial jobs and are increasing their numbers as operators as well. Thus, although the male breadwinner model has been substantially eroded at the household level, its reassertion can be seen at the public institutional level and in the masculinization of labor in export manufacturing and on pineapple plantations.

The increased economic and social independence among women as a result of their work in the free trade zones has unleashed a "crisis of masculine identity" (Chant 1999 cited in Safa, this volume), marked by men's concern about a loss in their own bases of security and authority in the household. Women now resist marriage and remarriage because there are fewer eligible men willing and able to support a family. Thus, an effect of these economic changes has been the increase in female-headed households, which is not new in the Dominican case, but its current trend is certainly noticeable. In this context, women rely on consanguineous relationships for emotional, domestic, and financial support. The case of Villa Altagracia shows how female heads pool resources from several sources to survive; and thus, it illustrates how globalization has contributed to reinforcing these ties. Safa warns us, however, that these ties have their limits because even kin support is predicated upon a minimal amount of resources.

Toro-Morn, Facio, and Roschelle, in their analysis of the Cuban case, also note the importance of extended networks. These have become even more crucial for survival amidst the severe shortages of food, medicine, and other household supplies resulting from the crisis in the Cuban economy during the Special Period. The Special Period resulted from the disintegration of the Soviet Union and Cuba's sudden integration into the global capitalist economy. Situating their analysis at the intersection of the state, the family, and the economy in the midst of profound socioeconomic changes, these authors examine how a state that once aimed to institutionalize gender equity, has given in to the demands of global capitalism. Unlike the other cases in this volume, Cuba is making the transition from a socialist to a capitalist economy—rather than from an agrarian to an industrial economy—and it has not entered the global economy via export processing zones. However, the dynamics in Cuba are similar to those in its Caribbean neighbors where the feminization of the labor market has occurred. Toro-Morn, Facio and Roschelle argue that traditional gender, race, and class hierarchies have been restored in both the public and private spheres in Cuba.

As a result of Cuba's economic restructuring during the Special Period, women and men have suffered from low wages, unstable working conditions, and unemployment, and must engage in *la búsqueda* (or search). This is a survival strategy that includes the formal and informal sectors but operates mostly as an underground economy. Within this context, Toro-Morn, Facio, and Roschelle find that women have been more negatively affected as they have engaged in low-wage, part-time, temporary work in the service sector and in typically female-classified occupations. Even college-educated women work as secretaries, waitresses, and hotel domestics in the tourist industry. Additionally, many have left secure professional jobs to open small businesses that cater to tourists or work in *jineterismo*, or prostitution (mostly catering to a foreign clientele), which had been almost eradicated by the revolution. Thus, Cuba's entrance into the global economy has unleashed a profound economic crisis that has contributed to undermine the gains of Cuban women as a result of the revolution.

Economic crises linked to globalization are not confined to countries undergoing post-socialist economic transitions. The following two contributions examine the effects of broad structural factors in a context on intimate processes, revealing how individuals wrestle internally with deteriorating living conditions. They both expose the deleterious effects of economic crises on social networks, among the poor as well as among middle-class professionals. The case of Argentina demonstrates that crises can arise in economies that are well rooted in capitalism and have achieved a high level of socioeconomic development. Masseroni and Sauane examine the effects that the recent economic crisis in Argentina has had on the subjectivity of highly educated middle-class women in urban Buenos Aires. Although the economic transformations brought about by neoliberal policies have affected many poor women and men, these authors demonstrate that these policies have had broader repercussions, profoundly affecting (as in the Cuban case) the lives of professional, highly educated women as well. The neoliberal economic model, which has included flexibility and deregulation of working conditions, has given rise to more precarious working conditions. This situation has affected all sectors of society, but Masseroni and Sauane focus on its effects on the professional sectors, especially professional women. For middle-class professional women, work means much more than simply earning an income, therefore, the deterioration in their working conditions and life in general has lead to high levels of stress and tension affecting their psychophysical health and their subjectivity. Previously feeling a sense of control, these professional women now feel that they are at the mercy of their managers and unable to change anything. Negative effects are manifested in these women's self-esteem and self-representation, their thinking process, and in their feelings and emotions. In the face of flexibility at work, unemployment, and ever more demands from management, these women also perceive their work-based social networks crumbling. This produces great anxiety, as they derive a great deal of their sense of self from these informal interactions.

At the other end of the region, Enríquez Rosas also examines the effects of economic crises on the subjectivity and informal social networks of the individuals who bear the brunt of these changes, focusing on poor, marginalized urban households in a suburb of Guadalajara. Enríquez Rosas argues that subjectivity is a key factor when examining poverty because it allows an understanding of the sociocultural dimension of what it means to be poor and the influence of family on the dynamics—expansion of or reduction—of poverty. Through the women's eyes, she observes that these households represent contradictory spaces where relationships of support and conflict coexist, and where gender and age affect distribution of resources and participation in decision-making. The Mexican economic crises, which have contributed to more irregular employment and to a decrease in resources due to cuts in public spending, have forced many women to work in jobs that do not pay enough to survive. Consequently, similarly to the Cubans depicted in Toro-Morn, Facio, and Roschelle's study, the women in Guadalajara spend their days searching for survival. This constant search leaves them no time for socializing, which has serious consequences for their informal networks and for their potential to organize politically. And, as in the case of the Argentine professionals in Masseroni and Sauane's study, work is central for poor women in Guadalajara. However, in contrast to the high status that work carries for the professional Argentine women, for the poor women in Guadalajara work is key for survival. In both cases, however, work is part of the women's identity, subjectivity, and an important component of their social worlds. For these women in Guadalajara, having access to a job also ensures the family's survival is key for reducing poverty (which the women equate with hunger) in the city.

Similar to the approach in Masseroni and Sauane's and Enríquez Rosas' studies, Chant also examines the subjective interpretations of individuals; only in this case she looks at the views about the family among low- and middle-class women and men in Guanacaste, Costa Rica. There, some perceive changes in the family as new and even more egalitarian domestic arrangements, but others view them as a "weakening of the family." While the many changes in Costa Rican family dynamics in recent years—e.g., increases in lone motherhood, female-headed households, out-of-wedlock births, and rates of divorce and separation—have caused concerns about "family breakdown," not everyone understands them in the same manner. Age and gender, Chant observes, shape people's different experiences and interests. She finds that older men see these changes as "family breakdown" more often than their female counterparts or younger people. Women and younger groups view recent changes in a more positive light, as prospects for enriching and enabling continuity in family life. Chant argues that the reasons behind these different views are linked to social, legal, and economic processes that have destabilized "traditional" gendered divisions of labor, power, and rights within Costa Rican households. In spite of concerns about changes in the family, however, Chant points out that the family is in a state of relative health, provided one does not focus solely on the conjugal bond or the nuclear family. For instance, the extended family remains strong and represents an important form of support for women and men. Among her study participants, there was a will to retain "the family," broadly defined, as this was perceived as an essential part of people's development.

Through an examination of kin networks and their potential as sources of support, Gomes da Conceição also looks at notions of the family. Similar to Enríquez Rosas, she also analyzes how gender and age affect the allocation of resources and decision-making as well as intergenerational relations and kinship networks. Gomes da Conceição compares elderly women and men in Brazil and Colombia and observes that within the context of economic restructuring, and consequent crises, new social policies assume that the community and family will take on the economic and affective support of older generations. However, Gomes da Conceição's analysis shows the limitations of the family to assume all the informal care and support that the elderly demand.

National policies shape the manner in which kin networks operate. In Brazil the universal pensions system allows the elderly to live alone, whereas in

Colombia public resources to support the elderly are rare, and co-residence of adults and elderly represent the main form of support to the elderly. Within these contexts, new economic and social policies that circumscribe the provision of social services, elderly women's and men's experiences differ. Since elderly women and men are all beneficiaries of the universal social security system in Brazil, they can either live in separate households or with their adult children, as their access to pensions make them more attractive for intergenerational exchanges. In Colombia, the elderly depend on adult generations for their survival and often do not have financial resources with which to reciprocate. Thus, they contribute with domestic work, which places elderly women at the center of these intra-domestic exchanges, reproducing gender roles through the final stages of the life course, and encouraging women to work without remuneration. However, if family members, even if they are of advanced age, cannot contribute to an impoverished household and cannot obtain institutional resources to survive, they can face exclusion. Therefore, within new scenarios of fiscal crises, cuts in public spending, and unemployment, the capacity of extended families to support their members and to pool resources together has declined.

López Estrada examines the integration of home and work in the lives of women workers. Based on a case study of home-based work in Tijuana, Mexico, López Estrada focuses on the contradictions of the women's productive and reproductive roles in their daily lives, which are manifested spatially and temporally in how their households are reorganized to accommodate paid work. Home-based work, one of many forms of self-employment in Tijuana, has increased in recent years in response to economic crises and restructuring, as men have lost their jobs and women cannot find suitable formal employment. Even though many women now engage in home-based work, there are diverse arrangements—both harmonious and conflictive—that women make in their homes. These different arrangements are linked to the women's social class, occupation, educational level, stage in the life course, family structure, and the broader circumstances of their individual lives. Similar to the Argentine women in Masseroni and Sauane's study, middle-class women in Tijuana work to realize their professional aspirations or to maintain their class status. And, just as the women in Guadalajara in Enríquez Rosas' study, working-class women in Tijuana work to help with their families' survival. In both cases, these home-based workers make complex, negotiated arrangements in the home in order to balance theirs and their families' lives. López Estrada argues that home-based work can be advantageous for women because it permits flexible schedules (and therefore affords them more control over their lives) and it can provide a basis for negotiating gender relations within the family.

Moving from the realm of family and the household to the political arena, Bickham Mendez focuses on the formation and organizational practices of the Working and Unemployed Women's Movement "María Elena Cuadra" (MEC) in Nicaragua. She provides us a lens through which we can understand the impact of neoliberal reforms on women, the gender dynamics within the mass organizations of the Frente Sandinista de Liberación Nacional (FSLN), and the Sandinista labor movement's failure to respond to the needs of women workers and unemployed women. Bickham Mendez examines how place-centered, locally constituted political identities articulate with transnational flows of ideas and organizational practices and discourses to shape actors' collective strategies. She finds that MEC members have reformulated feminist notions and adapted feminist discourses to coincide with their vision of how an autonomous women's organization should be organized. MEC also has obtained considerable financial support from richer donors, which reveals existing global inequalities even within the (generally more egalitarian) nongovernmental organizations (NGOs) based in the North. In Bickham Mendez' analysis, feminist ideas, strategies, and practices do not move in a unidirectional manner from North to South, nor do they mean the same for all women in the South. Important class differences operate among women who organize politically, not only between the North and the South but also within the South. For instance, Bickham Mendez highlights the uneasy relationship of MEC with other Nicaraguan feminist organizations and with international and Northern NGOs, elucidating the complex ways in which power operates through and within transnational organizational relations.

Continuing with an examination of women's organizations, Lind looks at the emergence and institutionalization of women's struggles for survival in Bolivia and Ecuador in the context of neoliberal development policies implemented in the 1980s and 1990s. Lind observes that although neoliberal policies have contributed to the economic hardship and cultural/racial/ethnic degradation that many poor women face, they also have opened new opportunities for women's organizations and strengthened some women's NGOs. Paradoxically, by exacerbating women's workloads and worsening their conditions, neoliberal reforms have contributed to institutionalizing women's struggles for survival. Like Bickham Mendez, Lind also notes the dependent relations between the women's organizations, NGOs, and international donors or government-sponsored development programs that impose limitations on women's organizations and sustainability. Like in the Nicaraguan case, as women's organizations learn the language and discourse necessary to obtain state and development contracts, they become financially dependent on the state and the international development community. Lind observes, however, that while neoliberal policies have contributed to legitimate women's community organizations, they also have institutionalized poor women's second-class "neighbor" status.

Lind also notes the complex effects that neoliberal policies have had on women's efforts to organize. Whereas these policies have institutionalized poor women's second-class "neighbor" status, they have brought gains for middle-class feminists, as some women's NGOs that the state subcontracts have benefited politically and financially. Also, under pressure from international organizations, the state has extended more responsibilities to women's organizations and, thus, middle-class feminists have acquired some power within the state and in public decision-making processes. However, Lind warns, the power that these organizations have gained might be temporary, as this can fluctuate with the political current of the day as well as with the objectives of the international finance and development communities at the moment.

While Bickham Mendez and Lind analyze the emergence and dynamics of women's organizations as responses to the conditions shaped by neoliberal reform, Agadjanian, in his analysis of work-based informal networks among street vendors in La Paz-El Alto, Bolivia, takes a step back and examines the potential for forming women's organizations. Urban street commerce, as a product of the informalization of Latin American economies, is primarily a woman's occupation. The extreme overcrowding and low, unpredictable profits that characterize this market niche create a complex dynamic of competition and cooperation among the women street vendors. Agadjanian argues that increased competition in the swollen marketplace, combined with the spirit of individual entrepreneurship and self-reliance promoted by the dominant class ideology, undermine women workers' collective strategies through alienating them individually and reinforcing compartmentalistic small-scale solidarities and alliances within them.

In sum, the contributions in this volume unveil the complex interactions within and outside the household (and those that link the two) as well as womens' perceptions, subjectivities, and objectives as members of their families, households, organizations, and communities. And, though all the pieces add to our understandings of the lives of people in Latin America and the Caribbean—through their contributions to theories used to analyze the conditions that affect people's lives—these contributions' potential to inform policy should also be acknowledged. In this light, the pages in this volume should remind the reader of the authors' commitment and dedication to improving the lot of women and their families in a region struggling with new economic, political, and social regimes.

NOTES

[1] I would like to acknowledge the critical help from several individuals in the organization of these special issues. My heartfelt gratitude goes to the twenty-seven reviewers who provided excellent comments to the contributors; to my research assistants—Kimber Williams and Carlos Posadas—who carefully read the entire manuscript; and to Mary Fran Draisker, in the Publication Assistance Center at Arizona State University, for her meticulous editing of several drafts.

[2] In fact, González de la Rocha (2001) points out that the "resources of poverty" model she developed based on household studies in the 1980s has been transformed into the "poverty of resources" model of the 1990s.

REFERENCES

BENERÍA, Lourdes.
    1992. "The Mexican Debt Crisis: Restructuring the Household and the Economy." In *Unequal Burden: Economic Crisis, Persistent Poverty and Women's Work*, edited by Lourdes Benería and Shelley Feldman. Boulder, Colorado: Westview Press.

DWYER, Daisy and Judith Bruce.
    1988. *A Home Divided: Women and Income in the Third World*. Stanford, California: Stanford University Press.

ENRÍQUEZ, Laura.
    2000. "The Varying Impact of Structural Adjustment on Nicaragua's Small Farmers." *European Review of Latin American and Caribbean Studies* 69:47-68.

FOLLARI, Roberto.
    1998. "Redemocratizar el Sistema Político." *Revista Paraguaya de Sociología* 35(102):153-160.

GONZÁLEZ DE LA ROCHA, Mercedes.
    2001. "From the Resources of Poverty to the Poverty of Resources: The Erosion of a Survival Model." *Latin American Perspectives* 28(4):72-100.

HARRIS, Richard.
    2000. "The Effects of Globalization and Neoliberalism in Latin America at the Beginning of the Millennium." *Journal of Developing Societies* 16(1):139-162.

MENJÍVAR, Cecilia.
    2000. *"Fragmented Ties: Salvadoran Immigrant Networks in America."* Berkeley: University of California Press.

ROBERTS, Bryan.
    1995. *The Making of Citizens: Cities of Peasants Revisited*. London: Arnold.

ROBINSON, William I.
    1998-1999. "Latin America and Global Capitalism." *Race and Class* 40(2-3):111-131.

SAFA, Helen I.
    1995. *The Myth of the Male Breadwinner: Women and Industrialization in the Caribbean*. Boulder, Colorado: Westview Press.

WEEKS, John.
    2000. "Have Workers in Latin America Gained from Liberalization and Regional Integration?" *Journal of Developing Societies* 16(1):87-114.

QUESTIONING GLOBALIZATION: GENDER AND EXPORT PROCESSING IN THE DOMINICAN REPUBLIC

Helen I. Safa[*]

ABSTRACT

This article questions the benefits of globalization for low-income women through an analysis of 1997 data on women export-processing workers in the Dominican Republic. Export processing has contributed to an increase in women's labor-force participation and their greater economic autonomy. But the percentage of men employed in export processing has also increased and efforts to improve working conditions through collective bargaining or other means are still weak. The increasing percentage of female heads of household, who rely heavily on extended kin for financial and emotional support, provides additional evidence of the erosion of the male-breadwinner model.

INTRODUCTION

Despite the vocal protests against the International Monetary Fund (IMF), the World Trade Organization (WTO), and the World Bank (WB), and despite all the evidence accumulating regarding the negative effects of globalization on women, especially in developing countries, globalization still generates enthusiasm among some neoliberal scholars. It is true that globalization has helped to bring unprecedented prosperity to the United States, and to some middle-class women who have risen to leadership positions in the government and private business. Globalization apparently has produced greater equality between educated middle-class women and men while creating greater inequality among women. Globalization reinforced the increasing participation of women throughout the world in the paid, nonagricultural labor force, but most of these women are confined to low-paying jobs, often in the informal sector, without protection, security or hope of mobility. For example, in Japan 70 percent of the 2.5 million part-time workers who have joined the labor force since 1995 are women, and one-fourth of these women are the main breadwinner (Kamo 2000). Despite its promise of greater economic prosperity for all, globalization has produced greater class, gender, and regional inequality. Why?

Globalization is based on "a movement toward a world economy characterized by free trade, free mobility of both financial and real capital, and rapid diffusion of products, technologies, information, and consumption patterns" (United Nations 1999:xv). The internationalization and fragmentation of production produces fierce competitiveness among developing countries seeking foreign invest-

---

[*] Department of Anthropology and Center for Latin American Studies, University of Florida, Gainesville, Florida 32611, U.S.A.

ment by maintaining a low level of wages and nonwage labor costs and high productivity. Cheap labor, thus, becomes a comparative advantage and women provide much of it. This feminization of labor characterized by flexible, casual, and informal work has led to a decline in full-time, permanent wage employment, among men as well as women, with lower rates of male labor-force participation, lower real wages, and higher rates of unemployment (Standing 1999). Some decline in occupational segregation and in the male-female wage gap in developed countries such as the United States may be as much a product of deterioration in male employment as the result of women's advances (United Nations 1999).

While purporting to be a universal economic model, the principles of globalization have been applied selectively. Capital flows from developed countries have been primarily directed to selected countries in East Asia (principally China), Central America, and the Caribbean, with a disciplined, highly productive but cheap labor force. While capital moves around freely, labor is restricted, and regulations on immigration to developed countries have been tightened. Tariff protection and subsidies to farmers in Europe and to the powerful sugar lobby in the United States are permitted, but not in less-developed countries, where they are considered a market rigidity. Budget cuts have reduced the scope and efficacy of the public sector, as water, electricity, telephones, railroads and even education and health care are privatized, thus, slashing services to the poor. Government budget cuts instigated by structural adjustment programs mandated by the IMF and the World Bank have sharply curtailed social spending on housing, nutrition, health, and education, either in absolute terms or on a per capita basis (United Nations 1999). As a result, many of the gains that were made in developing countries in the post-WWWII period in literacy, life expectancy, and the GDP have been eroded. The world's poorest people, defined as those earning U.S.$2 a day or less, now number three billion, nearly half the world's population (Kahn 2000).

This article cannot deal adequately with all the aspects of women and globalization, which include positive achievements such as the growth of an international women's movement and the recognition of women's rights as human rights. Because of time, and my own area of expertise, I shall confine myself to an analysis of gender and the globalization of work. However, I shall not deal only with the workplace, but also examine the implications of women's increased labor-force participation on gender relations and family structure. In a previous book entitled, *The Myth of the Male Breadwinner* (Safa 1995), analyzing women industrial workers in Cuba, Puerto Rico, and the Dominican Republic, I argued that the male breadwinner model, where the man is considered the principal provider in the household and women are at best supplementary wage earners, is being eroded with economic structuring resulting from globalization. As women bear increasing responsibility for basic household expenses, as a result of their increasing labor-force participation as well as the deterioration in male wages and employment, women acquire greater control over the household budget and basic decisions. Marital bonds have grown more fragile, often resulting in the formation of female-headed households.

It is difficult to prove statistically that women's increased economic responsibility has contributed to the formation of female-headed households in the Dominican Republic, which rose nationally from 21.7 percent in 1981 to 26.8 percent in 1996 (Báez 2000, cuadro 1:20). However, this article will show that changes in the gender composition of the labor force are contributing to changes in gender relations, undermining the myth of the male breadwinner, and giving women greater economic autonomy. The terms of "negotiating with patriarchy" are changing and, thus, contribute to the fragility of the conjugal bond.

However, I would argue that the Dominican low-income family has never centered on marriage or the conjugal bond, which has always been weak and unstable compared with consanguineous relationships between a mother, her children, and her female kin. Female-headed households have a long history in the Caribbean and should not be seen as pathological, but as an alternative, legitimate form of family organization (Safa 1999). As we shall see, female-headed households can function quite adequately, as long as the consanguineous ties that provide crucial financial, domestic, and emotional support are maintained.

This article presents additional data on the relationship between female employment, female autonomy and the formation of female-headed households in Villa Altagracia, a community in the Dominican Republic located thirty kilometers north of the capital of Santo Domingo. Villa Altagracia has undergone rapid change from sugar production to garment export processing, producing dramatic changes in the gender and age composition of the labor force and consequent gender relations. In 1997, with the assistance of Dominican colleagues and the support of the North-South Center,[1] we conducted short surveys with 157 women working in the free trade zone and fifty-five men who were former sugar mill workers, none of whom were randomly selected. The results of this survey are presented in Tables 1 and 2. However, in this article I shall focus on the in-depth interviews I conducted personally in this community with fifteen women workers in the free trade zone and with about five former sugar mill workers, as well as community leaders, Dominican factory personnel managers, and union representatives. In February 2001, I returned briefly to Villa Altagracia to examine changes that have taken place and interviewed some women workers and the new human relations staff at the large Korean plant, as well as the director of the Dominican Association of Free Zones (ADOZONA), representing free trade zone entrepreneurs. It may be easier to understand the changes that globalization has brought to women in free trade zones through the prism of low-income households in one community. The results, I would argue, have far greater applicability.

Export-Led Industrialization in the Dominican Republic

The Caribbean has long depended on exports for economic growth. The plantations established during the colonial period grew sugar, coffee, tobacco, and fruits for export to the mother country, including England, France, the Netherlands, and later in the United States. The long period of colonialism, which in the Hispanic Caribbean lasted until the nineteenth century and is still prevalent in Puerto Rico, weakened the sense of autonomy and the development of a national bourgeoisie. In addition, these were small states lacking great mineral wealth or other natural resources, and sharply divided by race and ethnicity, brought on by years of slavery and indentured labor. So many of the characteristics today associated with globalization can be found in the Caribbean historically, although even there economies have entered a new phase of globalization, in which multinational corporations, banks, and international lending agencies like the World Bank and the IMF rather than the colonial powers are playing a hegemonic role.

The Dominican Republic, where this study was conducted, has moved rapidly since 1960 from an agricultural economy based on sugar exports and import substitution industrialization to a service economy dependent on tourism, export manufacturing, and agribusiness. The country remained dependent on sugar exports until the early 1980s, when the United States drastically cut its sugar quota. The emphasis shifted to export manufacturing, and during the 1980s, the Dominican Republic became the leading garment manufacturer in the Caribbean Basin, producing mostly for the U. S. market.

Strong state incentives combined with tariff initiatives offered by the United States under the Caribbean Basin Initiative (CBI) and other programs, led to an employment boom in export manufacturing, where the mostly female-labor force expanded from 20,000 workers in 1980 to 182, 000 in 1997, when my study was conducted (Consejo Nacional de Zonas Francas de Exportación [CNZFE] 1998). Labor costs were also lowered during this period, due principally to currency devaluations mandated by structural adjustment, so that the real hourly minimum wage declined 62.3 percent between 1984 and 1990 (Fundación Apec de Crédito Educativo, Inc. [Fundapec] 1992:32). The hourly wage of U.S.$0.56 an hour in 1990 was one of the lowest in the Caribbean. Since then, wages have increased considerably, to a weekly average of DR$701.21 (about U.S.$44) in 1999, and are now reputed to be the second highest in the Caribbean area, after Costa Rica. (CNZFE 2000, cuadro 25). However, even these salaries cannot compete with the rising cost of living.

Though export manufacturing generated jobs for women, it had a dampening effect on male employment—due to a decline not only in sugar production, but also in import substitution industries, where men predominated. Domestic manufacturing has actually suffered a loss in employment and investment since 1980 (Itzigsohn 1997:51), and during this period, female labor-force participation rates grew at a higher rate than those of men (Itzigsohn 1997:58). Nevertheless, unemployment nationally continues to be higher for women than for men, whose average wage is much higher.

The Transformation of Villa Altagracia and Men's Response

In Villa Altagracia, where this study was conducted, the changes in the gender composition of the labor force have been even more dramatic. The town's economy had been dominated for forty years by a large, state-owned sugar mill, which closed in 1986 due to low prices, low productivity, and a cut in the U.S. sugar quota. A free trade zone took over the existing buildings, including a large, Korean-owned garment plant employing about 2,500 workers—mostly women— and two smaller plants.[2] Villa Altagracia, thus, presents in microcosm the changes from sugar production to export manufacturing that have taken place in the Dominican Republic since 1980.

Though it has been fifteen years since the closing of the sugar mill, Villa Altagracia never recovered from this blow, and continues to share many of the paternalistic aspects of a company town. The mill was not only the town's principal employer, but supported many social services such as sports clubs, health clinics, a pharmacy, schools, bus transportation to the capital for university students, and even caskets for impoverished residents. With declining budgets, municipal authorities have been unable to fill the gap, and public services are deteriorating. Despite violent protests by town residents, Villa Altagracia has severe shortages of electricity and potable water (the plants have their own generators), and the sewage system has fallen into disrepair, as the mill no longer maintains it. There is no garbage collection, and most streets are unpaved and in poor condition. With the continuing influx of people from surrounding rural areas, housing is at a premium, and in 1997, twenty families had been occupying a school after their own houses burned. Health problems are abound, including child malnutrition and a high incidence of AIDS. Though municipal authorities have approached them, the Korean-owned factory refuses to provide funds for town improvement, even for a street light at the factory exit, needed to prevent serious traffic accidents. The Korean management mingles little with town residents, and resides apart in the better housing once reserved for the mill's administrative elite, replicating the class hierarchy of sugar production.

In Villa Altagracia, unemployment is much higher among men than among women, particularly older, unskilled workers who could not find new jobs in the city, and according to one former mill worker, "some of them have died of hunger." He added, "Before the father worked and maintained his family, but now it is the children who work," implying a change in the age as well as the gender composition of the labor force.

Many of the former sugar mill workers we interviewed continue to reside in Villa Altagracia in the single family, frame houses ceded to them by the mill after it closed. Many of these former workers are over sixty and receive a modest pension of about eighty-five dollars a month from the mill which, combined with informal work as vendors, carpenters, and so on, provides them with an average monthly household income of about DR$284 (Table 1). Younger members of the household, especially daughters employed in the free trade zone, also contribute to this household income, but as long as they are living in the paternal home, they defer to the father's authority.

Table 1.
Former Sugar Mill Workers, Villa Altagracia, Males, 1997

Household Averages	Average
Persons per household	5.3
Workers per household	2.0
Persons working in free trade zones	0.6
Dependents per household	1.9
Nondependents per household	3.3
Household income (in DR$ per month)	$3,162
Average Household Income (DR$ per Month)	**%**
Less than $1,600	33.3
$1600–$3000	31.5
$3001–5,000	18.5
$5,001 and above	16.7
Current Household Contributions of Respondent	**%**
All	41.4
More than half	18.2
Half	10.9
Less than half	14.5
None	12.7
No information	1.8
Type of Household	**%**
Nuclear	63.6
Extended	34.5
Compound	0
Complex	0
One-person	0
No information	1.8
Are There Subheads?	**%**
Yes	9.1
No	87.3
No information	3.6
Respondent Is Head of Household?	**%**
Yes	10.9
No	89.1
	N
Number of Cases	55

Although they often live with children and grandchildren in extended households, ninety percent of these men claim that they are the head of the household, reflecting the importance of home ownership in this low-income community. Most started working at an early age, seldom going beyond fourth grade, and were working in lower level manual and technical jobs in the mill at the time the plant closed. Although they are even now better off than fieldworkers, men over fifty have a hard time finding jobs. As one fifty-three-year-old former mill worker noted, "No one wants to employ [someone] after forty-nine or fifty."

Some of these older men are very resentful of the independence which paid employment has conferred on women working in the free trade zone. Tomás at seventy-two has had seven children with three women, and is now raising his two youngest. He claims that women working in the free trade zones are a "disaster. They have to dress pretty, they have to go clean everyday, and they cannot even be touched." Men accuse the women of "having fun with men," of spending their money in bars and beauty salons and contributing little to the household economy. This stereotype appears to reflect men's resentment at the erosion of their authority and the shattering of a gender hierarchy in which men were in authority as principal breadwinners and women were, at best, supplemental wage earners.

Even relatively younger men like Tony, who formerly worked in the mill but now is a local schoolteacher, has had serious conflicts with his wife who works in the free trade zone. They have three children, aged two, four, and eleven, and he claims they get sick and "acquire another culture" as a result of his wife's employment. She often returns home late in the evening, and Tony objects to the "transculturation that she has experienced in the zone, to that vocabulary, to that form of behavior of the zone, which is not how she normally used to be." He has tried to "correct" her and says she has "improved," but he has not insisted she quit because they need the extra income, especially to cover the high rent. Rent has escalated as a result of the severe shortage of housing.

Younger men also commute to the capital of Santo Domingo to work, commuting daily and sometimes weekly. They work in construction, on the docks, or in other forms of manual labor. Some younger men are employed locally, driving taxis or buses, or their own or rented motor scooters, which are used to transport workers and food to the free trade zone. Many men have also migrated to the United States and Puerto Rico, leaving behind *de facto* female-headed households dependent on remittances. Remittances from Dominican residents in the United States are estimated to exceed U.S.$1 billion annually, and constitute a crucial source of foreign exchange, second only to tourism (Itzigsohn 1997:67). Men who migrate often forbid their wives to seek paid employment in the free trade zone, because of its "corrupting" influence, as in the case of Margarita, whom we interviewed as she was preparing to join her husband in New York City. Margarita was apprehensive about the move because she has never lived outside of Villa Altagracia, where she has many relatives, and because she speaks little English. Though they have been living apart for years, she remains quite subordinated to her husband, claiming: "I want to live at his side. If he comes here, very well, but if he is there, if I have to go, I'll go. That is, I want to live with him always." No other respondent emphasized the importance of the conjugal bond this strongly. She is even leaving her children with a sister because the U.S. consulate would not give them a visa immediately. Margarita and her husband were legally married in 1993, presumably to facilitate her entry into the United States, after several children were born. With the DR$2,000 (then about U.S.$146) he sent every two weeks, Margarita bought a house, which she and her family are fixing up to rent while he is gone. A study in Villa Altagracia by McClenaghan (1997) found that none of the women receiving remittances were formally employed, although several earned income through the informal economy. This helps to explain the female subordination that McClenaghan found, which is contrary to my findings.

Women Workers and Gender Relations

The Korean-owned garment plant has replaced the paternalism of the sugar mill with rigid factory rules emphasizing high productivity, tight discipline, and total obedience. They know they are by far the most important employer in the town, except for the two smaller plants, which pay less. The minimum weekly wage in 1997 was DR$447 per week, close to the national minimum wage, but with incentives and overtime, most workers made about DR$600 (US$50) per week. Incentives are paid for high productivity and perfect attendance. Absenteeism is severely penalized and more than two unexcused absences can lead to dismissal. Turnover is a major problem, because workers become exhausted from long, ten-hour workdays, and many women work nights if required. Workers complained that they are fired if they refuse to work overtime, which is especially difficult for young mothers who have not seen their children all day.

The fifteen young mothers we interviewed, all of them under thirty and employed primarily at the large plant and one of the smaller garment factories, reject completely the image of the irresponsible, promiscuous women that men in Villa Altagracia have painted of them. Many have children they support on their own with little or no assistance from the children's fathers. Maritza, at twenty-four, has been working in the free trade zone for nine years, and has a three-year-old child. The father of her child works and lives in the capital, and provides some money for schools and medicine, but Maritza lives with her parents. Single mothers who live with their parents or other relatives normally pay them a basic stipend to cover rent and food, while paying other expenses themselves, but this is still much cheaper than living on their own. Maritza also studies at night and just managed to finish her high school degree. Maritza claims most women in the free trade zone are working to support their children, and that it was more difficult for women when the sugar mill was in operation. In the past, Maritza says, men "worked and earned money for the home and did what they pleased, but now the woman works, she maintains herself, she dresses herself, it cannot be the same."

Paid work has given women a new sense of autonomy, as Glenda, a married women with a one year old child, notes: "When one works, one feels more liberated, to manage one's own money . . . One feels freer to do anything because it is your own money. But when you are maintained or they give you something, you have to be under the person who supports you." Her husband works in the free trade zone, but they cannot afford a home of their own, and live with his parents. Glenda's mother lives in New York City and she hopes that her mother's legal marriage to a U.S. citizen will enable her mother to bring Glenda and some of her other children as well. In the meantime, Glenda's mother regularly sends remittances to support her children, who live with their grandmother, as well as gifts for Glenda's baby, her first grandchild.

Extended families play a critical role in supporting women workers, especially single mothers, providing not only housing and other forms of financial support, but also child care for those who are employed. An analysis we conducted of the 1991 Demographic and Health Survey (DHS) demonstrated that though female heads of household earn less than male heads and have a much higher rate of unemployment, overall family incomes for the two types are nearly equal (Duarte and Tejada Holguín 1995). Apparently, female-headed households are able to raise their income through the contributions of other family members, which with globalization may include remittances from abroad. Extended families, which represented 40 percent of all Dominican households in 1991, often include subfamilies, usually single mothers living with their children in the homes of parent(s) or other relatives. Most of these single mothers who are subheads are young and have high levels of education and occupation, including professional and other white-collar jobs. As a result, female-headed families with subfamilies have higher incomes and a higher average number of working members than female heads living alone with their children, although we do not have the income figures on a per capita basis. The DHS survey is a nationally representative survey of all Dominican households and demonstrates that a higher proportion of middle strata incorporate extended families and subfamilies (Duarte and Tejada Holguín 1995:89-90), suggesting that this strategy is not confined to the poor.

Both nationally and in Villa Altagracia, the percentage of extended families is higher in female-headed households than in male-headed households (see Table 2). The Table also shows that extended families do have more working members, but in Villa Altagracia, female-headed households have lower average

Table 2.
Women Workers in the Villa Altagracia Free Trade Zone, 1997

	Households by Type of Headship		
Household Averages	All	Male	Female
Persons per household	4.56	4.71	4.24
Workers per household	2.25	2.49	1.76
Workers in free trade zone	1.41	1.41	1.42
Dependents per household	1.36	1.36	1.34
Nondependents per household	3.20	3.34	2.90
Household income (DR$ per month)	4,353	4,624	3,778
Average Household Income (DR$ per Month)	%	%	%
1600–3000	37.2	25.5	62.0
3001–5000	44.2	53.7	24.0
5001 and above	18.6	20.8	14.0
Current Household Contribution of Respondent	%	%	%
All	24.4	13.2	48.0
More than half	12.2	16.0	4.0
Half	35.3	40.0	24.0
Less than half	26.3	28.3	22.0
None	1.3	1.9	0.0
No information	0.6	0.0	2.0
Type of Household	%	%	%
Nuclear	68.8	74.8	56.0
Extended	22.3	16.8	34.0
Compound	3.8	5.6	0.0
Complex	1.3	0.9	2.0
One-person	1.9	0.0	6.0
No information	1.9	1.9	2.0
Are There Subheads?	%	%	%
Yes	4.5	0.9	12.0
No	91.7	95.3	84.0
No information	3.8	3.7	4.0
Respondent Is Head of Household?	%	%	%
Yes	34.4	3.7	100.0
No	65.6	96.3	0.0
Number of Cases	157	107	50
Percentage	100	68	32

monthly incomes and fewer average numbers of workers per households than male-headed households. Santa is the only wage earner in her grandmother's household, although the old woman has some income from a small coffee farm in the rural area. Santa has had three children by three different partners, none of whom provide any assistance, and her grandmother and aunt help to raise them. Santa is very grateful to her grandmother, noting: "It is because of my grandmother that things are not worse. Because my grandmother, thank God, lends a hand with the children."

In extended households, there appears to be an expectation that every adult will contribute in some way, but financial responsibility is flexible, adjusting to changing circumstances. Thus, Maria moved in with her parents and three brothers when the youngest of her three children became sick and she had to take care of him. Her husband is unemployed and does not live with them, but Maria had worked previously in the free trade zone and as a domestic in the capital. She claims her brothers do not complain about supporting her because she does the cooking and the housework (her mother is employed as a domestic in the city and only returns weekends). She says: "When I worked, they didn't work, and I gave to them." Now apparently it is her turn.

Mothers and daughters are especially flexible at exchanging roles, and reflect the strength of the mother-daughter tie in most Dominican families. Dominica, at forty-seven, has been in three consensual unions, and "raised her children [while] working in the factories." At her age, it would be difficult to find a factory job, so she stays home and watches her daughter's two children, aged two and four, while her daughter works in the zone, and also attends school every night until 10 P.M. Her daughter says she is lucky to have her mother's support, but Dominica claims: "I take care of her children and she studies at night. She is already in the second year of high school. If she really achieves something, then I also gain. I have to sit and take care of her children so that she can get ahead."

While the economic crisis has undoubtedly increased the importance of extended families, consanguineous kin have always played a major role in low-income households in Latin America and the Caribbean generally. Even in male-headed households, the strongest bond is often between mother and child and consanguineous kin, stronger than the conjugal tie, which is emphasized in the nuclear family (for example, Fonseca 1991; Safa 1974, 1995). Women often return to live with their parents if their husbands are unemployed, which puts additional strains on the marital bond. Raquel has two small children, aged one and three, and left her partner to return to live with her family when he could not find a job. She claims: "all Dominican men are bad . . . our grandmothers tell us." But unemployment has made men worse, because "if he doesn't get work, then he can't help. If you pressure him, he is resentful because he has no place to turn, to work." She also claimed some men do not try hard enough to find a job and are supported by their partners working in the zone. Even unemployed men, however, rarely look after children or do household chores, underlining the importance of female kin.

Labor Rights and Working Conditions in the Free Trade Zone

Globalization is also reflected in recent changes in labor conditions in the Dominican free trade zones, such as the growing percentage of men employed, the growing number of factories owned by Dominicans, and the new Labor Code of 1992. Since the early 1980s, the percentage of men employed nationally in the Dominican free trade zones has more than doubled to over 40 percent, and the percentage of male workers reached 45.7 percent in 1999 (CNZFE 2000, cuadro 21). In technical and administrative jobs, men outnumber women, and the average weekly salary in these higher level jobs is more than double that of an operator (CNZFE 2000, cuadro 25). In a study done in 1996, the average monthly salary in the free trade zones for women was U.S.$179 versus U.S.$250 for men. This occupational segmentation cannot be explained by educational levels, which in the free trade zones as well as nationally are now higher for women than for men. In 1991, 63 percent of women in the free trade zones had completed secondary school compared with 47 percent of men (Fundapec 1992).

This trend toward increasing male employment in export manufacturing has also been noted globally and can be partly explained by the diversification of the export product towards higher value added, and the increasing capital intensity of production technology (United Nations 1999:10). Diversification is evident in the Dominican Republic, where more men are employed in plants producing trousers, coats, and other heavier garments, where women's nimble fingers are not so advantageous as in the making of blouses and lingerie. Men resisted employment as operators in garment plants, because they identified this as "women's work" (Elson and Pearson 1981), but they have since redefined trousers and other heavy materials as suitable. The deterioration in male employment has also forced men to seek alternative forms of employment, as one man who had been working in La Romana, another Dominican free trade zone for eight years, described:

> Work in the free trade zone is no good . . . You work because you have to and because there is no other source of income . . . because the policies of managers are always to suppress, to squeeze you dry, when you want to demand your rights. Especially in this country, the laws are not carried out. The big fish eats the little fish.

Though Dominican workers are referring to the relationship between capital and labor, the phrase aptly characterizes the relationship between multinational corporations and the Dominican state also, and between big, powerful countries like the United States and small, vulnerable countries like the Dominican Republic.

Men are also replacing women in the Dominican agribusiness pineapple plantation that Raynolds (2001) studied in 1989 to 1990 and again in 1995. Initially the pineapple plantation could not recruit male labor because the wages were too low, but with growing competition and the need for greater productivity, management switched to a *contratista* or intermediary system that replaced the larger female labor force with mostly men. *Contratistas* hired through their patronage networks, which also kept labor in line and reduced the company's responsibility for labor. Men were paid not by the day but by the job, which men preferred and made them more productive, and their wages now matched what they could earn elsewhere. Women were confined to the packinghouse, which was considered "women's work." Here we see how a depressed job market along with company techniques to "Dominicanize" labor has resulted in a shift back to male labor, similar to what can be found in export manufacturing.

The *contratista* system in agriculture is similar to subcontracting in manufacturing, because it gives the semblance of "nationalizing" the operation, while control remains in the hands of foreign companies who dominate the export market and finances. In the free trade zones, as of 1999, 30 percent of the plants are owned by Dominicans (CNFZE 2000, cuadro 17), most of them being subcontractors of the United States and other foreign producers, who prefer to let Dominicans deal with labor problems and other troublesome issues. Subcontracting or joint ventures is again part of a global trend to reduce the visibility of multinational corporations and to meet increasing competition.

Increased male employment in Dominican export manufacturing (and possibly in agribusiness) also reflects added protection for women resulting from a new Labor Code issued in 1992. Under this code, pregnant women are entitled to three months of maternity leave at half pay, and neither they nor women with infants can be fired. Given the high rate of pregnancy among young women workers, the Korean-owned plant has also insisted on a monthly pregnancy test given to every female job applicant and to women workers, which violates national and international labor rights that are difficult to enforce.

The new Labor Code passed in 1992 under pressure from organized labor in the Dominican Republic and the United States, was designed to modernize a labor code passed by the dictator Trujillo, and to insure the right to collective bargaining for all workers. Since export manufacturing began in 1969, there was an informal prohibition on union activity in the free trade zones, and workers who were active in union activity lost their jobs, and were blacklisted from employment with other firms in the zones (Safa 1995). Women workers are still reluctant to speak of their participation in union activity and, until recently, were not well represented in the leadership of the union movement, a traditionally male preserve.[3] Workers are particularly happy at receiving an annual severance pay or *liquidación* from the plants, which they think is part of the Labor Code. Actually, employers introduced the annual severance pay as a way of reducing the costs of paying seniority on severance and other worker benefits and as a way of getting rid of "undesirable" workers. By terminating all workers each December, workers who are suspected of labor union activity or other "irregularities" will not be rehired.

Still the new Labor Code stimulated the emergence of about 100 new unions, organized by the newly formed National Federation of Free Trade Zone Workers (FENETRAZONAS), affiliated with the National Confederation of Dominican Workers (CNTD), the largest of the three major Dominican labor confederations. The CNTD has the support of the American Institute for Free Labor Development (AIFLD), which petitioned the U.S. government to retract the tariff benefits the Dominican Republic received under the Generalized System of Preferences because of violation of worker rights. Two export licenses were canceled, both in Asian firms. The Dominican Ministry of Labor also brought sanctions against several firms for code violations, which is unusual because in the past, worker complaints of mistreatment or unjust dismissal had generally been rejected in favor of management (Safa 1995). However, government sanctions led to accusations of bias in favor of organized labor against the Ministry by an official of ADOZONA, the powerful private sector Dominican free trade association, and they were later withdrawn (U.S. Embassy Labor Reporting Officer 1994-1995).

Protracted struggles ensued in which several hundred workers lost their jobs, including two union organizers in Villa Altagracia, who as of 1997 had not been reinstated, one of whom accused his labor confederation of lack of support. Of 114 unions registered in the free trade zones in 1995, by 1997 only eleven had signed collective bargaining agreements with management (U.S. Embassy Labor Reporting Officer 1998). The AIFLD withdrew its petition to the U.S. government, but the Union of Needletrades, Industrial and Textile Employees of the United States and Canada (UNITE) continues to support labor organizing in Dominican free trade zones.

Globalization has forced U.S. labor unions to become more international and to abandon the protectionist stance they supported earlier. In the spring of 1998, UNITE organized a tour of U.S. universities for three Dominican free trade zone workers, including two from the Korean-owned plant studied here, to convince students and administrators at several Ivy League universities to adopt codes of conduct which would prohibit the purchase of products made under unfair labor conditions (Kim 1998). This effort has now gone nationwide as the anti-sweatshop campaign spread to many U.S. universities, since students are important consumers of the sports apparel made in these plants. It has helped push most large U.S. apparel companies operating in the Dominican Republic into implementing codes of conduct in recent years, but they generally rely on self-monitoring for enforcement, and firms still harass and fire workers who try to form unions (U.S. Embassy Labor Reporting Officer 1998:7).

In a return visit to the Korean plant in 2001, the personnel manager had been replaced by three Dominican human relations officers who act as intermediaries between the workers and management, giving training and orientation sessions to new workers, mediating complaints, and so forth. These human relations programs are an attempt to modernize management techniques and implement codes of conduct, thereby reducing friction with labor without opening the door to unions.

Parity with the *North American Free Trade Act* (NAFTA) is another issue that has hurt the apparel industry in the Caribbean because apparel is not included in the trade benefits provided under the Caribbean Basin Initiative (CBI). Although some apparel from the Dominican Republic and other countries in the Caribbean Basin enter the U.S. duty-free, they are limited to garments made entirely from U.S. manufactured and cut fabric (Deere and Meléndez 1992). Competition with Mexico has increased as a result of the duty-free trade benefits the apparel sector enjoys under NAFTA, while Central American countries offer cheaper wages. Government and business leaders in the Dominican Republic and other countries covered by the CBI have sought a parity proposal that would give their apparel sector trade benefits equivalent to NAFTA. U.S. retailers such as J.C. Penney also favor such a proposal, because it would make their products cheaper to buy. However, this parity proposal is opposed by both the U.S. textile industry and the very U.S. unions that have assisted in labor organizing in the Dominican free trade zones, because of the threat parity poses to U.S. workers. Here we see how conflicting interests of U.S. labor, retailers, manufacturers, and their Dominican counterparts forestall a concerted effort to improve labor conditions among the region's workers.

The parity proposal was finally approved by Congress in October 2000, but retains the provision that garments be made entirely from U.S. fabric. While acknowledging this weakness, the director of ADOZONA, in 2001 claimed that Dominican entrepreneurs must work "in alliance" with U.S. manufacturers to compete with Asian manufacturers (like the Korean plant), whom both see as their chief rival. The director suggested that time is limited for Dominican apparel manufacturing, if in the year 2005, trade barriers are removed for China and it becomes a full competitor.

Dominican labor federations now also compete to organize free trade zone workers, since they represent one of the few growth sectors in the economy, though there are still few women union leaders. Competing labor confederations claim the pacts signed by FENETRAZONAS (the Federation of Free Trade Zone Workers affiliated with the CNTD—the National Federation of Dominican Workers) have not improved worker conditions, but it remains the only federation to have achieved a free zone collective bargaining agreement. The four chief labor confederations are characterized by intense rivalry and remain fragmented, chiefly because of ties to political parties (Espinal 1991).

Jacobo Ramos, the head of FENATRAZONAS, argues that parity must include a social clause that guarantees the rights of workers to organize and have a decent living, a provision that the AFL-CIO also supports. Ramos, who is also vice president of the International Federation of Free Trade Zones, speaks eloquently of the need for labor to internationalize in order to prevent conflicts between workers from the United States, the Dominican Republic, and Central

America. He admitted he has been attacked in the Dominican Republic for siding too closely with U.S. unions, who some argue wish to close Dominican factories and return them to the United States. Though Ramos agrees that labor conditions and wages in the Dominican Republic and the United States can never be equal, he points to the inadequacy of a neoliberal model supported by international organizations like the World Bank and the IMF, which is accelerating poverty in the Dominican Republic. Ramos adds: "Because when the labor force is sick, when the labor force is badly paid, when the labor force has no type of work conditions, no country can develop on this basis, no country." As this case eloquently documents, the internationalization of labor is much weaker than the internationalization of capital, and cannot adequately protect workers from the exploitation of multinational corporations.

CONCLUSION

As we can see from the above discussion, even the gains that Dominican women have made in terms of increased labor-force participation under globalization may be short-lived. In the free trade zones, men still predominate in the better-paid technical and managerial jobs, and are increasing their numbers as operators as well. Attempts to address women's concerns, such as paid maternity leave, may result in women losing their preferential status over men in some apparel sectors.

What we are witnessing here is a reassertion of patriarchy and more specifically the male breadwinner model at the public institutional level such as employers, labor unions, and political parties. The male breadwinner model has been substantially eroded at the household level, as our female informants testify. But in my book, *The Myth of the Male Breadwinner*, I maintained that this ideology still prevails at the public level of the workplace and the state. It can be seen in the resentment men in Villa Altagracia feel toward women working in the free trade zones, accusing them of being frivolous and even promiscuous. It can be seen in employers' preference for men in supervisory positions and in the reluctance of labor unions to support women's leadership. It also can be seen in the masculinization of labor in export manufacturing and on pineapple plantations.

Low-income women like free trade zone workers may suffer from greater subordination at the public level than middle-class women because they are subject to class (and possibly race) as well as gender subordination. The increasing participation of Dominican middle-class women in political life—where a quota system in political parties has brought forth more women candidates—and as professional career women (Brea and Duarte 1999) suggests that the women's movement has succeeded in opening some space for women as public citizens, especially if they do not face additional class and racial barriers. However, middle-class women along with low-income women continue to face patriarchy at home, where, as Benería and Roldán (1987) point out, both are engaged in a continuous process of negotiation for more autonomy, in which paid employment plays a critical role.

The widening gap between normative ideals of patriarchy and grassroots realities of greater female autonomy has produced what Chant (2000) calls the "crisis of masculine identity," marked by men's concern about growing economic and social independence among women and a loss in their own bases of security and authority within households. Globalization has helped to fuel this crisis, by increasing low paid jobs for women and weakening men's position in the labor market, particularly among more vulnerable segments such as the older former sugar mill workers in Villa Altagracia. As a result, women are resisting marriage and remarriage because the "marriage market" of eligible men willing and able to support a family has shrunk, contributing to the formation of female-headed households.

The tendency toward the formation of female-headed households may be particularly marked in countries like the Dominican Republic in which conjugal ties have always been weak and women have relied heavily on consanguineous relationships for emotional, domestic, and financial support. In her review of women-headed households worldwide, Chant (1997) confirms the importance of extended household strategies as a major survival strategy, often enabling female heads to resist becoming the poorest of the poor. Villa Altagracia provides dramatic examples of how extended families, particularly among female heads, pool their resources from several sources to survive. Globalization has now transnationalized these ties, with remittances coming to Villa Altagracia not only from husbands, but also from grandmothers working in New York garment plants, or grandfathers collecting social security payments accrued in the United States.

However, household strategies have their limits, as Gonzàlez de la Rocha (2001) demonstrates in a recent article analyzing the effects of the deepening of the economic crisis in Mexico in the 1990s. The exclusion of a large segment of the adult population from the formal labor market, particularly the young and as in Villa Altagracia, older, unskilled men who had been displaced from traditional sources of employment in agriculture and heavy industry, also reduces the possibilities of informal sector employment and other self-provisioning activities because people need money to engage in these activities. Even mutual aid among kin is predicated upon a minimal amount of resources, so that Gonzàlez de la Rocha argues that her former "resources of poverty" model (Gonzàlez de la Rocha 1994), which she developed from household studies in the 1980s, has now been transformed into the "poverty of resources" model of the 1990s. The response, both in Mexico and the Dominican Republic, has been massive migration to the United States, which accelerated markedly in both countries in the 1990s. The Caribbean has long lived on the export of its labor, but now under the effects of globalization, larger, more diversified economies such as Mexico's, are being forced to do the same.

Emigration from the Dominican Republic more than doubled between 1985 and 1989, when structural adjustment started, compared to the preceding five-year period, and in 1990-1991, the percentage of women exceeded men (Báez 2000, cuadro 1.8). By 2001, the Dominican population of New York City, still the predominant location, had doubled to 765,945. Why should people be leaving a booming economy that has been dubbed "the hottest in the Americas," with growth rates of 7 to 8 percent a year from 1996 to 2000? When Leonel Fernández—the American-educated Dominican who assumed the Presidency in 1996—made foreign investment a key concern, foreign investment tripled from 1997 to 1999 (reaching 1.4 billion in 1999). But growth slowed in 2001, and in the first quarter of that year, exports from the free trade zones declined 7.2 percent with a loss of 2,000 jobs (Economist Intelligence Unit 2001). With the continuing slowdown in the U.S. economy, especially after the terrorist attack of September 11, which has also contributed to a decline in remittances to the Dominican Republic, the Dominican economy is deteriorating again.

Foreign investment in the free trade zones is based on cheap labor, and if wages rise, they will go elsewhere, like Central America or Mexico. Competition from cheaper wages elsewhere has already contributed to a decline in apparel production in the Dominican Republic (though it still represents close to two-thirds of all export processing workers) and to an overall decline in employment in the free trade zones from 1998 to 1999; the total number of employees in 1999 totaled 188,174 (CNFZE 2000:Cuadros 23 and 24). Codes of conduct have been implemented internationally by large retailers like Wal-Mart and Gap, who worry about their image among liberal consumers, and have succeeded in improving some working conditions worldwide, but have done little to raise wages. And most factories on the global assembly line do not work with these large retailers. As the director of ADOZONA noted, the future of the garment industry "hangs by a thread" because quotas protecting smaller exporters like the Dominican Republic or Bangladesh are due to expire on January 1, 2005, at which time China and India, which grow their own cotton, are likely to capture more of the lucrative U.S. market (Bearak 2001:1).

Globalization then has increased inequality both between and within countries because it has benefited capital far more than labor. The 1990s Asian financial crisis, among countries considered the success stories of globalization, points out the enormous costs to domestic economies and workers of such a strategy. The downward push on wages and cuts in social services discourages the development of a viable domestic consumer market in developing countries like the Dominican Republic. As Robinson (1999:60) notes, "the new model of development by insertion into new global circuits of accumulation does not require an inclusionary social base," which means the populist base of democratic regimes can be economically excluded from the market. But democracy requires they be included politically, which has led many Latin American countries, including the Dominican Republic, to develop "social funds" like Pronasol in Mexico, targeting the poor with temporary relief programs without modifying the structural causes of their marginalization (Robinson 1999:66). Fear of explosive social unrest has also led international lending agencies to help fund these programs, and it remains to be seen whether popular uprisings, such as the Dominican Republic has witnessed in the past, can be avoided. Democracies in Latin America are facing a crisis of legitimacy, which social funds, labor codes of conduct, migration and remittances, and women workers and their household survival strategies cannot contain indefinitely.

NOTES

1   Some of the material in this article was published by the North-South Center at the University of Miami, with the title "Women Coping with Crisis: Social Consequences of Export-led Industrialization in the Dominican Republic" (Agenda paper No. 36, April 1999). I want to thank the North-South Center for funding this research project and Jeffrey Lizardo of INTEC in the Dominican Republic for his able research assistance.
    An earlier version of this article entitled "Women and Globalization: Lessons from the Dominican Republic" appears in a book entitled *The Spaces of Neoliberalism: Land, Place and Family in Latin America,* published by Kumarian Press, Bloomfield, Connecticut and edited by Jacquelyn Chase, 2002.

2   The smaller of these two plants, owned and operated by a Dominican, has since closed.

3   A national survey conducted in the Dominican Republic in 1997 found that only two percent of women are members of labor unions (Brea and Duarte 1999:51).

REFERENCES

BÁEZ, Clara.
    2000. *Estadísticas para la Planificación Social con Perspectiva de Género.* Santo Domingo, Dominican Republic: Fondo de Población de las Naciones Unidas, Programa de las Naciones Unidas para el Desarrollo, Secretaría de la Mujer.
BEARAK, Barry.
    2001. "Made in Squalor: Lives Held Cheap in Bangladesh Sweatshops." *The New York Times,* April 15, Late Edition—Final, sec. 1, p. 1, col. 4, Foreign Desk.
BENERÍA, Lourdes and Martha Roldán.
    1987. *The Crossroads of Class and Gender: Industrial Homework, Subcontracting, and Household Dynamics in Mexico City.* Chicago, Illinois: Chicago University Press.
BREA, Ramonina and Isis Duarte.
    1999. *Entre la Calle y la Casa: Las Mujeres Dominicanas y la Cultura Política del Siglo XX.* Santo Domingo, Dominican Republic: Profamilia.

CHANT, Sylvia.
    1997. *Woman-headed Households: Diversity and Dynamics in the Developing World.* Houndmills, Basingstoke Hampshire, England: Macmillan Press Ltd.
    ———. 2000. "Men in Crisis? Reflection on Masculinities, Work and Family in North-West Costa Rica." *The European Journal of Development Research* 12(2):199-218.

CONSEJO NACIONAL DE ZONAS FRANCAS DE EXPORTACIÓN (CNZFE), Secretaría de Estado de Industria y Comercio.
    1998. *Informe Estadístico 1997.* Santo Domingo, Dominican Republic: CNZFE.
    ———. 2000. *1999 del Sector de Zonas Francas.* Santo Domingo, Dominican Republic: CNZFE.

DEERE, Carmen Diana and Edwin Meléndez.
    1992. "When Export Growth Is Not Enough: U.S. Trade Policy and Caribbean Basin Economic Recovery." *Caribbean Affairs* 5(1):61-70.

DUARTE, Isis and Ramón Tejada Holguín.
    1995. *Los Hogares Dominicanos: El Mito de la Familia Ideal y los Tipos de Jefaturas de Hogar.* Santo Domingo, Dominican Republic: Instituto de Estudios de Población y Desarrollo.

ECONOMIST INTELLIGENCE UNIT.
    2001. "Country Profile, Dominican Republic." Retrieved July 18, 2001 (http://www.viewswire.com).

ELSON, Diane and Ruth Pearson.
    1981. "Nimble Fingers Make Cheap Workers: An Analysis of Women's Employment in Third World Export Manufacturing." *Feminist Review* 7:87-107.

ESPINAL, Rosario.
    1991. "Between Authoritarianism and Crisis-prone Democracy: The Dominican Republic After Trujillo." In *Society and Politics in the Caribbean,* edited by Colin G. Clarke. Houndmills, Basingstoke, England: Macmillans Ltd. in association with St Antony's College, Oxford.

FONSECA, Clotilde.
    1991. "Spouses, Siblings and Sex-linked Bonding: A Look at Kinship Organization in a Brazilian Slum." In *Family, Household and Gender Relations in Latin America,* edited by Elizabeth Jelin. Paris, France: United Nations Educational, Scientific and Cultural Organization (UNESCO).

FUNDACIÓN APEC DE CRÉDITO EDUCATIVO, INC. (Fundapec).
    1992. "Encuesta Nacional de Mano de Obra." Report prepared for Inter-American Development Bank. Santo Domingo, Dominican Republic: Fundapec.

GONZÀLEZ DE LA ROCHA, Mercedes.
    1994. *The Resources of Poverty: Women and Survival in a Mexican City.* Oxford, United Kingdom; Cambridge, Massachusetts: Blackwell.
    ———. 2001. "From the Resources of Poverty to the Poverty of Resources: The Erosion of a Survival Model." *Latin American Perspectives* 28(4):72-100.

ITZIGSOHN, José.
    1997. "The Dominican Republic: Politico-economic Transformation, Employment and Poverty." In *Global Restructuring, Employment, and Social Inequality in Urban Latin America,* edited by Richard Tardanico and Rafael Menjívar Larín. Coral Gables, Florida: University of Miami, Miami North-South Center Press.

KAHN, Joseph.
    2000. "The World's Bankers Try Giving Money, Not Lessons." *The New York Times,* October 1, Sunday, Late Edition—Final, sec. 4; p. 5, col. 1, Week in Review Desk.

KAMO, Momoyo.
    2000. "Proceedings of the Beijing Plus Five Global Feminism Symposia. Feminism and Globalization: Women 2000." New York City, June 5-8. Cosponsored by the Center for the Study of Women and Society, City University of New York (CUNY), Graduate Center; National Center for Research on Women; and the Japan Preparatory Committee, Year 2000 Project. Retrieved 12 July 12, 2002 (http://www.ncrw.org/initiatives/symposia.htm).

KIM, Carrie.
    1998. "Caps for Sale." *UNITE* 4(3):24-25.

MCCLENAGHAN, Sharon Olivia.
    1997. "Factory Work, Gender Relations and Political Identity in the 1990s: Villa Altagracia, the Dominican Republic." Ph.D. dissertation, University of Portsmouth, United Kingdom.

RAYNOLDS, Laura.
    2001. "New Plantations, New Workers: Gender and Production Politics in the Dominican Republic." *Gender and Society* 15(1):7-28.

ROBINSON, William I.
    1999. "Latin America in the Age of Inequality: Confronting the New 'Utopia.'" *International Studies Review* 1(3): 41-67.

SAFA, Helen I.
    1974. *The Urban Poor of Puerto Rico: A Study in Development and Inequality.* New York, New York: Holt, Rinehart and Winston.
    ———. 1995. *The Myth of the Male Breadwinner: Women and Industrialization in the Caribbean.* Boulder, Colorado: Westview Press.
    ———. 1999. "Female-headed Households in the Caribbean: Sign of Pathology or Alternative Form of Family Organization." *Latino(a) Research Review* 4(1-2):16-26.

STANDING, Guy.
    1999. "Global Feminization through Flexible Labor: A Theme Revisited." *World Development* 27(3):583-602.

U. S. EMBASSY LABOR REPORTING OFFICER, Santo Domingo.
    1994-1995. *Foreign Labor Trends: Dominican Republic.* Washington, D.C.: U. S.

Department of Labor, Bureau of International Labor Affairs, Office of Foreign Relations (OFR).

———. 1998. *Foreign Labor Trends: Dominican Republic.* Washington, D.C.: U.S. Department of Labor, Bureau of International Labor Affairs, Office of Foreign Relations (OFR).

UNITED NATIONS.

1999. "1999 World Survey on the Role of Women in Development. Globalization, Gender, and Work." UN document A/54/227. New York, New York: Division for the Advancement of Women, Department of Economic and Social Affairs.

GENDER, WORK, AND FAMILY IN CUBA: THE CHALLENGES OF THE SPECIAL PERIOD

Maura I. Toro-Morn,[*] Anne R. Roschelle,[**] and Elisa Facio[***]

ABSTRACT

It is within the context of the Special Period, the economic crisis that began in the early 1990s after the collapse of the Soviet Union and the tightening of the economic blockade by the United States, that we analyze work and family relations in Cuba. Although women made significant gains in the labor market after the Revolution, the Special Period has eroded many of these gains. Using interviews collected in Cuba, we document the struggles that women workers encountered in order to continue to support their families and stay in the labor market. The growth of jobs in the tourist sector has led to worker redistribution and occupational downward mobility, as workers moved from professional to less skilled jobs in the tourism industry with little opportunities for mobility. We also capture how the Special Period has impacted Cuban families. Despite state attempts to legislate gender equity within the family, patriarchy was never fully eradicated in the home. This failure of the revolutionary project has been exacerbated by the country's current economic crisis. The burden of this crisis has fallen more heavily on women who continue to shoulder the responsibility for household work and childcare.

INTRODUCTION

Recently, there has been an explosion of studies about gender and globalization (Acosta-Belen and Bose 1993; Benería and Roldan 1987; Beneria and Stimpson 1987; Chow and Berheide 1994; Ghorayshi and Belanger 1996; Leacock and Safa 1986; Lopez Springfield 1997; Marchand and Parpart 1995; Marchand and Runyan 2000; Moghadam 1998; Nash and Fernandez-Kelly 1983; Roy, Tisdell, and Blomqvist 1996; Safa 1995; Ward 1990). Feminist scholars have produced a vast literature illustrating how global restructuring has accelerated women's entrance into low-wage, labor-intensive jobs in the garment, electronics, and pharmaceutical industries in Asia, Latin America, and the Caribbean (Beneria and Roldan 1987; Nash and Fernandez-Kelly 1983; Safa 1995). Studies have also linked globalization to the feminization of migration around the world (Constable 1997; Freeman 1997; Hondagneu-Sotelo and Cranford 1999; Toro-Morn 1999 forthcoming). Not surprisingly, most of these studies tend to focus on developing capitalist economies, neglecting how these global processes similarly impact socialist countries (Moghadam 1995; True 2000). However, the increasing consolidation of the global economy has made it impossible for scholars to continue to ignore the social, political, and economic changes taking place in formerly socialist economies like Hungary, Poland, and East Germany, and in countries

---

[*] Department of Sociology and Anthropology, Illinois State University, Campus Box 4660, Normal, IL, USA.
[**] Department of Sociology, State University of New York at New Paltz, Jacobson Faculty Tower 522, New Paltz, NY 12561, USA.
[***] Department of Ethnic Studies, University of Colorado at Boulder, Ketchum 30, Campus Box 339, Boulder, CO 80309, USA.

like China and Cuba that have embraced capitalist economic policies while maintaining an ideological commitment to socialism. Our research contributes to this body of literature by focusing on Cuba, the most recent example of a socialist country undergoing a transition to a market economy.

In this article we examine how the economic and social policies introduced by the state during the period of economic crisis, known in Cuba as the Special Period, have affected Cuban men and women across a variety of social locations. Using interviews and fieldwork data, we document how the Special Period has led to a redistribution of workers throughout the labor force. This redistribution hit women workers particularly hard. Professional women have been redirected into occupations in the service sector that are low paying, part-time, and do not offer opportunities for mobility. Within the service sector, there has recently been an explosion of jobs in tourism. Although the state has promoted tourism as a strategy to deal with the economic crisis and as a way to secure a place in the global economy of world travelers, tourism has also introduced unexpected problems and created new class divisions. Subsequently, many of the gains women made in the labor force as a result of the Revolution have been severely eroded.

A strategy Cubans used to deal with the changing political economy is by engaging in a process that they call *la búsqueda* (the search). *La búsqueda* is a survival strategy that encompasses both the formal and informal economy, but operates mostly as an underground economy. For Cubans, *la búsqueda* literally means "the search" for well being, for survival, and most importantly, the search for U.S. dollars (USD). As one respondent told us "no one in Cuba can survive without dollars, *everyone* is engaged in *la búsqueda*." *La búsqueda* is a gendered process. Men and women participate in both formal and informal aspects of *la búsqueda,* often along traditional gender lines. Women and men sell crafts and musical instruments in Old Havana markets. Women supplement their meager salaries by selling candy, sandwiches, and making hats out of plastic bags, or *nylitos,* whereas men sell cigars. In this paper we document how *la búsqueda* has driven young Cuban women into the global assembly line of sex workers, or as it is known in Cuba, *jineterismo* (prostitution), which is a more insidious form of *la búsqueda*.

The Special Period has also placed Cuban families in a vulnerable position. After the Revolution, the Cuban state introduced the Family Code in an attempt to legislate social reproduction and to foster gender equity in the private sphere, but Cuban women continued to bear most of the responsibility for the second shift (Jennissen and Lundy 2001; Safa 1995).

During the Special Period Cuban women once again became overburdened with the bulk of reproductive labor in their homes. The animated verbal struggles we witnessed between women and men around the gender division of labor is indicative of the continued fight Cuban women have waged to transform patriarchal familial relationships. A return to more traditional gender roles and an unraveling of the social safety net is also occurring in other countries undergoing post-socialist economic transitions (True 2000).

Our research contributes to the literature on gender and globalization by focusing on the complex relationship between the Cuban state, the family, and the economy in the midst of profound socioeconomic changes. Cuba offers an important case study to examine how a state that once aimed to institutionalize gender equity through law and social policy, has succumbed to the demands of global capitalism. And, like other countries undergoing post-socialist economic transformations in which traditional gender, race, and class hierarchies have been restored, we illustrate how these hierarchies are being reconstructed in both the public and private spheres in Cuba.

THE UNFINISHED REVOLUTION: GENDER AND THE CUBAN SOCIALIST PROJECT

> *Arriving here this evening, I commented to a comrade that this phenomenon of women's participation in the revolution was a revolution within a revolution.*
>
> Fidel Castro

Feminist scholars and activists all over the world have kept a close eye on Cuba and the situation of Cuban women since the Revolution (Jennissen and Lundy 2001). As a result, an impressive body of literature exists that documents the contributions of Cuban women to the Revolution (Cole and Reed 1986; Catasus Cervera 1996; Smith and Padula 1996; Stone 1981), the efforts of the state to eradicate gender inequality in the workplace (Bengelsdorf and Hageman 1978; Fleites-Lear 1999; Lutjens 1995; Vasallo Barrueta 1998), and its continuous struggle to legislate gender relations in the home (Jennissen and Lundy 2001; Safa 1995). Clearly, the social and economic changes that the revolution introduced have been impressive (Parker 1999). As Bengelsdorf and Hageman (1978) stated two decades ago "one has only to talk to any 40-year-old Cuban woman, to watch her eyes as she discusses the difference between her life before 1959, and her life now, as she describes her pride in what she and her neighbors have seen come to pass around them, shaped by their own hands and their own efforts" (p.361). In this section, we offer a brief overview of the programs and efforts Cuban women have put forth in their attempt to address gender inequality within the context of the Cuban socialist project.

As Lutjens (1995) states, "Cuban policies for women since 1959 have reflected a strategy shared by all modern socialisms, one that stresses the incorporation of women into public life via participation in production and a legal equality of rights that extends well into the domain of private- or domestic-life" (p.102). In the aftermath of the revolution, Cuban women were mobilized to defend revolutionary goals and to carry out tasks aimed at raising the standard of living for the masses of Cuban people. For many of these women such activities were the first step out of the home into any kind of social or political life.

Although Fidel Castro had made some statements about women's equality prior to the declaration of socialism in 1961, the "woman question" was never part of the revolutionary struggle. It was with the creation of the Federation of Cuban Women (FMC) on August 23, 1960 that the "woman question" was first addressed. The FMC was created to bring women into the revolutionary process. The FMC organized masses of women, house by house, in the cities and countryside, to build the militias and the Committees for the Defense of the Revolution (CDRs). In addition, the FMC organized the drive against illiteracy, set up schools for peasant women, and established a network of childcare centers. Because the FMC was an organization led by and made up entirely of women, those women who had never before participated in politics or public life felt at ease in its ranks (Stone 1981). The FMC also provided a place where women could discuss the problems they faced as women and press for changes to alleviate these problems. As a result women obtained the right to an education, a job, paid maternity leave, childcare, and abortion on demand. In addition, the FMC was instrumental in the elimination of prostitution and ending such degrading customs as sexist advertising and beauty contests. In 1989, the FMC had nearly 3.4 million members (Lutjens 1995). One of the most significant struggles the FMC waged was raising consciousness about the importance of incorporating women into the work force. The motivation for women to work full time was driven not only by the needs of the Revolution, but also encouraged by the Cuban leadership, which pronounced that women's oppression stemmed from their being confined to the home, isolated from broader social life, and economically dependent on their husbands. An important first step toward the integration of women into the work force was the voluntary labor that women carried out throughout the 1960s. By 1968, a new stage of incorporating women into the labor force began with the initiation of a gigantic FMC campaign: to bring 100,000 new women into full-time work each year. Additionally, during these years, advances were made in eliminating stereotypes about the types of jobs women could and could not do. Women became doctors, engineers, lawyers, university professors, and technicians. Women also began to work in the sugar mills, factories, and in other light industries (Jennissen and Lundy 2001; Smith and Padula 1996).

Over time it became clear that the goal of increasing the number of women workers was not being met. In her main report to the Second Congress of the FMC in 1974, Vilma Espín attributed the reasons for women's declining labor force participation to a lack of social services, inadequate safety and hygiene at work sites, and a lack of understanding of women's social and familial roles. Most importantly, the FMC denounced the unequal division of labor in the home and traditional notions of patriarchy that marginalized and overburdened women. As a result, the 1975 Family Code was introduced to replace pre-Revolutionary laws on marriage, divorce, adoption, and alimony. The most controversial aspects of the family code focused on Articles 24 through 28, which stipulated that women

should be equal in marriage and that men should share in housework and raising children. This section of the code also stated that both partners should have an equal right to pursue an education and a job and they should cooperate with each other to make it possible. Although the country's leadership put its authority behind the code, there were many Cuban men who strongly objected. Nonetheless, the Family Code was passed by an overwhelming majority of the population with Articles 24 to 28 included. The code became law on March 8, 1975, International Women's Day (Jennissen and Lundy 2001; Smith and Padula 1996). Despite the elimination of much gender inequity in Cuba, the eradication of patriarchy has been more illusive. While it is true that Cuban families became more egalitarian after the passage of the Family Code, several studies reported to the Fifth Congress in the 1980s demonstrated a persistent imbalance in men's and women's work in the home.

In the 1990s, the objectives and activities of the FMC continue to reflect the overall priorities of the socialist state (Lutjens 1995). According to Lutjens (1995), "The FMC continues to organize women in pursuit of the goals determined by the socialist ideology...it has shared the official view of equality and the causes and consequences of ongoing inequalities and discrimination, actively rejecting 'bourgeois' feminism and the idea of a separate struggle for women" (p.108). Although criticized for its hierarchical structure and lack of organizational autonomy, the FMC vigilantly advocates for women's health care, sexual education, and familial rights. One of the most important challenges currently facing the FMC is protecting the gains women made in a country undergoing dramatic economic transformation. Although the state has been an important advocate for women's rights, it remains to be seen whether Cuba's entrance into the global capitalist economy will completely undermine the gains made by "the revolution within the revolution." In the next section we describe how we became a research team and the methodological strategies we developed to undertake research in Cuba during the Special Period.

Methodology: A Cross-Cultural Feminist Collaboration

Our desire to engage in collaborative work in Cuba emerged while we were attending a Women's Studies Conference at the University of Havana in the fall of 1999. The ramifications of Cuba's transition from a socialist to a market economy fascinated us. While attending the Women's Studies Conference, we met with Cuban academics and began to ask questions that intrigued us about what we observed. At the hotel, we took notes and reflected upon what Cubans were telling us about their lives at the time. As our trip came to an end, we began to discuss the possibility of returning to Cuba to conduct research to further understand the impact of the Special Period on the lives of Cuban women and men.

Upon our return home we each began to review the literature, talk to colleagues, gather contacts, and study the kind of questions that Cubanologists in

Cuba and in the United States were asking (Campbell 1999; Gutiérrez Castillo 2000; Jatar-Hausmann 1999; Lara 1999; Oswald and Henthorne 1999; Parker 1999; Pastor 1996; Pérez Jr. 1999; Pérez Villanueva 2000; Ruiz 1998; Sánchez Egozcue 2000; Triana 2000). We found that although there is a substantial amount of research on the impact of the Revolution on Cuban women (Cole 1986; Díaz Vallina and Pagés 1999; Fleites-Lear 1999; Lutjens 1995), and some on the general conditions of their lives (Catasus Cervera 1996; Vasallo Barrueta 1998), a critical analysis of how gender shapes their daily existence was missing (Safa 1995). These preliminary research strategies allowed us to acquire the necessary background knowledge as well as an understanding of the material, cultural, and interpretive circumstances of Cubans (Holstein and Gubrium 1995; Heyl 2001). We crafted our research questions based on the initial conversations we had with Cubans on our first trip (Reinharz 1992).

In the summer of 2000, we returned to Cuba to conduct our research. Generally, we were concerned with the social and economic repercussions of the emergence of a two-tiered economy. In addition, we were interested in investigating how the newly implemented economic reforms impacted both the workplace and the family. As feminists, we were also intrigued with the current situation of the "woman question" in the Cuban socialist project at the turn of the twenty-first century.

The unique composition of our research team facilitated the interpretation and analysis of data from three different perspectives.[1] As three active interviewers we were able to trace how interviewees responded physically and emotionally to questions. We watched closely for shifts in the conversation, for hesitations and expressions that indicated a struggle to communicate a coherent answer, and to contradictory stories indicative of the various identities and meanings embodied by respondents. Having three people involved in the research process allowed us to witness and discuss these shifting identities and reconcile how seemingly contradictory meanings reflect what Holstein and Gubrium, (1995) refer to as "alternative validities" in which multiple narratives based on a variety of roles and self identities are indeed legitimate (Heyl 2001).

By nature, cross cultural research entails a range of difficulties, among the most critical is access to respondents. In our case we had the advantage that one member of our research team had been doing political work and research in Cuba for over a decade. Through her friendship networks we were able to gain access to a diverse group of respondents who trusted us and felt comfortable sharing their experiences. In any research project gaining access and trust from respondents is often extremely difficult. In a country that is undergoing radical economic and political transformation, gaining trust can be even more challenging. In our case, as a result of one member of our research collective's entrée in the Cuban community, we had the trust of many people who referred us to their friends and family. This connection provided us with our initial contacts, which ultimately became a snowball sample.

We conducted thirty-five interviews with Cuban women and men across a broad range of social locations. Interviews were conducted in Spanish but translated into English throughout the course of the interview. This was necessary because one member of the research team had some knowledge of Spanish, but was not fluent. Subsequently one researcher asked a question in Spanish, another researcher translated it into English, and the third researcher wrote it verbatim in English. In addition, field notes were simultaneously taken in Spanish. A strategy that proved extremely useful was our ability to collectively process data, field notes, and interview transcripts immediately after they were collected. In addition, every night we made a concerted effort to discuss and write about our experiences.

Interviews took place in the homes of respondents and in our temporary residence in Cuba. We purposely stayed with a Cuban family at their guesthouse to gain a first-hand account of Cuban life. Staying with a family allowed us to participate in daily routines, attend parties, and witness neighborhood life unfold, something that would not have been accessible had we stayed at a hotel. As a means to understanding the context of this study, it is first necessary to describe and explain the current economic crisis, known as the Special Period.

THE SPECIAL PERIOD: CURRENT ECONOMIC CRISIS

The Special Period refers to the economic crisis that began in the early 1990s after the collapse of the Soviet Union and the tightening of the U. S. economic blockade. Once the Soviet Union embraced capitalism, Cuba lost a significant trading partner with which to exchange products for food and medicine. Subsequently, in the early 1990s Cuba lost 85 percent of its foreign trade and experienced a 51 percent decline in foreign exchange earnings. In addition to a loss in foreign trade, there was also a decline in Cuba's gross domestic product, nonsugar-related production, and oil importation. Furthermore, sugar, nickel and petroleum exports fell precipitously (Campbell 1999). As a result of the U.S. blockade and the discontinuing trade with the former Soviet Union and other Eastern Block countries, food consumption in Cuba also declined considerably. The lack of food and the loss of petroleum products exacerbated problems of malnutrition. Cubans experienced substantial weight loss and their diet was severely limited. Jose, for example, remembered "one day in 1992, I ate just rice and mustard. I decided I would never eat rice and mustard again. I was a professional dedicated to my work, why should I eat rice and mustard?" Dietary changes led to severe health problems such as those Maria experienced. During the Special Period she became unemployed and had to support the family by sewing.

> During the Special Period I made a lot of money by sewing. Rice and beans were 40 pesos per pound. I made 3,000 pesos during the Special Period, but that was not enough. I was in a relationship with a musician who didn't work. There were five people in my family and I supported the entire family. Then I got sick and

couldn't walk. I had a debilitating disease, a major vitamin and protein deficiency. When you get meat, you feed your kids first, and then eat what's left over.

Cubans could no longer rely on cars and buses for transportation and many were forced to ride bicycles or walk to work. As one informant described it:

> Prior to the Special Period, I was happy with socialism. I felt we were taken care of. There was transportation and it was cheap. I could go outside the city for a picnic for only 5 pesos. You could really live. You had everything you needed. I never aspired to be rich, but I had everything I needed. Maybe other families felt differently. We had everything we needed to live and it wasn't that bad.

As the crisis continued the Cuban peso depreciated significantly and state revenue from production fell drastically. To preserve normative living standards, the Cuban government maintained salaries at precrisis rates. To replace the loss of revenue the state simply printed more pesos. Subsequently, people had large quantities of pesos left over after they purchased whatever goods were available. The lack of consumer goods and the surplus of pesos led to a thriving underground economy, *el mercado negro* (black market). As the black market expanded, the exchange rate of dollars for pesos increased substantially. The black market exchange rate rose from 6-7 percent in 1989 to 12-13 percent in 1990, to a high of 130-135 pesos per dollar in the spring of 1994 (Campbell 1999). Concurrent with the onset of the black market new words describing U.S. dollars arose. *Fula, guano, guaniquiqui, varo, peso, and verde* linguistically reflected the counterrevolutionary act of seeking U.S. dollars in a country where people were previously penalized for possessing them. In order to ease Cuba's financial burden, Fidel Castro legalized the possession of dollars and their free circulation in 1993. The law was intended to increase the government's access to hard currency, to pay for food imports, and to reinvest in other parts of the economy. In addition, the state wanted to curtail the black market and prevent the undermining of the ideals of the Revolution. One unintended consequence of the decriminalization of the possession of dollars has been the development of a two-tiered economy. Cubans with access to dollars can buy food, clothing, health related products, and services, otherwise unavailable to people with who rely solely on pesos.

Gender and Work during the Special Period

Cuban women have made great strides in professional occupations such as a medicine, law, politics, academics, and other typically male-dominated occupations (Smith and Padula 1996; Díaz González 1995). According to Elena Díaz González (1995), the participation of Cuban women in the formal labor force increased from 27.4 percent in 1975 to 40.6 percent in 1993. When looking at occupational categories, women accounted for 58.1 percent of technicians, 90.9 percent of administrative workers, 63 percent of service workers, and 28.8 percent of management personnel. Díaz González (1995) adds that although women have made impressive gains in the formal labor force, their participation in management and other positions of power lags behind men.

In this section, we examine the impact of the changing political economy on women's work experiences in Cuba in the formal and tourist sector. In our research, we found that although the government has successfully incorporated women into the labor force, the Special Period has hit women workers particularly hard. Under the current economic crisis, women have been redirected into occupations in the service sector that are frequently part time, temporary, low paying, and lack opportunities for mobility. Ironically, one area of the service sector that offers women higher wages is tourism, a field for which women are often overeducated. Clearly, the entrance of Cuba into the global economy undermines the successes that women have achieved in the labor market as a result of the Revolution. Although the entrance of Cuba into the global economy has not followed the traditional route of development via export processing zones, remarkably, the end result has been similar to its Caribbean neighbors in which the feminization of the labor market has occurred. Like other Caribbean nations, Cuba has turned to tourism as a quick fix to generate the much-needed capital to reanimate the economy. The Special Period has shaped women's experiences in both the formal and informal economy.

Formal Sector

A consistent theme found in our interviews with women who were employed in diverse occupational categories was a general feeling of job insecurity. For example, Maria, an attorney, captures this instability when she states that:

> My job structure is currently changing. In my sector, I am guaranteed a job. They could transfer me or make me a secretary, but I can secure a job at the same salary. I will not be unemployed. Professional employees in this country are pulling their hair out because there are more qualified people than there are positions (for example, 2 jobs for a lawyer only 1 salary.) We have a shortage of money in Cuba. There is a mandate from the state that dictates that an agency/work unit that is no longer meeting its needs and generating profit must be closed or restructured. However, if there is a restructuring of the job market, many people may lose their jobs ... jobs are scarce. If the number of jobs shrinks, where will people find work?

A problem that exacerbates women's work experiences in the formal labor market is the low salaries. Janet struggled to support her family with her meager wages as a bank employee.

> I work in a bank. I make 211.00 pesos per month. It is very difficult, it is not sufficient for the needs of my family, but my husband's salary does help out.

In fact, low wages sometimes encouraged women to drop out of the labor market, as was the case of Maribel who was able to quit her job because she received child support from her ex-husband in Miami:

> I don't work anymore as a nurse. It is very difficult for health care workers. I earned about 230.00 pesos, which is about $12.00 a month, which is without any days absent to take care of my daughter. It isn't worth it! I worked as a nurse for 10 years, but haven't worked for the last four. It is more work to work than not to. While I was working I didn't make enough to eat. It takes more than 10 pesos to eat breakfast, lunch, and a snack for the week. Even if I didn't eat anything all day long and stayed hungry, it is not enough to purchase other necessary stuff.

One of the ways that the state tries to compensate for low wages is through *jabitas* (work incentives). However, these incentives are not distributed evenly as Janet explains:

> The type of job you do determines salaries. Those who earn more have more responsibility. The banking industry has not kept up with incentives. We don't have the special perks that other workers get. The state prioritizes who is going to get *jabitas*. Work that is directly related to production, like factory workers, gets these incentives. At the end of the year people can also get food and household incentives, chicken, beans, rice, dishwashing soap, oil, etc.

Yet there were other women who, in spite of difficult working conditions and job insecurity, continued to embrace the ideals of the Revolution and were firmly committed to their professions. Mariana spoke with great pride about her career as a microbiologist. She was particularly proud of the fact that the medical research she was conducting resulted in Cuba's developing a meningitis B vaccine unavailable anywhere else in the world. She also spoke frankly about her unwillingness to leave Cuba despite the economic difficulties currently plaguing the country.

> I have to be honest with you, I have traveled all over the world and I have seen everything. Even though I didn't receive job offers, I had the opportunity to stay if I wanted to, but I did not. Another great source of satisfaction for me is my job. I love my work. In my work I have everything I need to do my job efficiently and well. Any of the tools and resources we need to do our work are available.

Another respondent, Isabel, who is a general family practitioner, expressed her pride as a community physician and what she thought of the day-to-day problems and challenges she met in the process of caring for her patients.

> In Cuba, doctors are one of the highest paid workers in pesos, but given the economic crises it is not enough. In fact, I live with my mother and my sister and we

each contribute to the survival of the household. The role of doctors in society is positive especially since health care is free. When you give a doctor money, they aren't really caring about individuals as people, it is an exchange. But here [in Cuba] they have a responsibility to the community. Doctors are well respected and well trained, they are very capable but the country doesn't have resources to help them reach their capabilities.

In discussing the shortage of medicine, Isabel explains how she deals with the limited resources available in her profession.

I use a lot of homeopathic remedies. We can't resolve all the medical problems we have, but if it is a life and death situation, the state will do whatever they can to save the person's life. The state sent seven people out of the country for medicine. There are so many things we don't have anymore that it becomes normal. People are happy they have family practitioners. For example, when there is no Tylenol we get stuff from neighbors. What can I do? It is an unfortunate situation but we find solutions with neighbors and friends to maintain the health of the community. I know a lot of people who have connections and can help get certain medicines.[2]

The economic hardships these professional women encountered, as a result of their low wages, were buffered by family members who received money from abroad or worked in the tourist industry and were paid in U.S. dollars. For example, Mariana's husband works in the South African embassy and drives a *botero* (Cuban taxi). Isabel's brother sends money from Germany and her sister works in a joint venture and is paid in dollars.

In the next section, we discuss the emergence of tourism as an economic development strategy and its impact on Cuban women, men, and their families. Although traditionally conceptualized as a sector of the formal economy, in Cuba tourism encompasses both the formal and informal economy.

Tourism

Tourism has become central to Cuba's economic recovery and is currently an important source of capital. Cuba has reshuffled its state bureaucracy to accomodate this growing industry. For example, in April 1994 the National Tourism Institute (INTUR) was upgraded to the Ministry of Tourism. In addition, Cuba reaffirmed ties with its Caribbean neighbors and actively sought regional economic integration among a variety of Caribbean countries. Cuba renewed its ties to the Caribbean Community and Common Market (CARICOM), was admitted to the Caribbean Tourism Organization (CTO) in 1992 and was inducted into the Caribbean Hotel Association (CHA) in 1994. Cuba hosted a joint meeting of the CTO and Caribbean Hotel Association (CHA) in Havana in June 1994. As a result of these events, Havana joined key Caribbean organizations promoting regional tourism. In order to further attract regional investment and facilitate economic integration, Cuba made 100 percent stock ownership options available to Latin American and Caribbean investors. In addition, the Cuban government pledged to refrain from nationalizing industries developed by outside investors (Cotman 1999).

Renewed trade between Cuba and Caribbean nations developed despite intense pressure from the U.S. government to boycott Cuba. The 37-year-old U.S. trade embargo was tightened by the 1992 Torricelli Bill, which barred U.S. subsidiaries in other countries from doing business with Cuba. In the same year, President George Bush signed the Cuban Democracy Act, which tightened the embargo even further, and in 1993 the Office of Foreign Assets Control of the U.S. Treasury published new regulations that expedited the Cuban Democracy Act. These regulations prohibited other countries and non-U.S. firms from exporting goods to Cuba that contained in excess of 20 percent U.S. inputs and prohibited other economic activities such as trading with, shipping to, or traveling to Cuba. Despite continued pressure from the United States to prevent Caribbean nations from trading with Cuba, Caribbean leaders and members of CARICOM agreed to renew business with Cuba. In fact, in 1993, at the 14th CARICOM summit, participants agreed to the creation of a CARICOM-Cuba Joint Commission to aid economic, scientific, and cultural exchange. In 1993, Robert Torricelli and three other members of Congress wrote a letter to CARICOM urging them to break ties with Cuba. CARICOM remained unshakable in its commitment to trade with Cuba and ignored Torricelli's threat to withdraw aid to the Caribbean Basin. Given the fact that both Mexico and Canada never broke ties with Cuba and the U.S. orchestrated the North American Free Trade Act (NAFTA) with them, members of CARICOM felt justified in stepping up trade with Cuba (Cotman 1999).

Joint ventures in the tourist economy have provided Cuba with the foreign investment not only from the Caribbean but from other regions as well. Concomitant with the rise in international tourism in Cuba has been an increase in global capital. The largest foreign investment in Cuban tourism occurred during the summer of 1996 when Canadian hotel mogul Walter Berukoff and Wilton Properties agreed to split the cost of a $400 million investment in eleven hotels and two golf courses with Cuba's state-run Gran Caribe (Facio 1999). This partnership represents a significant component in the globalization of Cuba's burgeoning tourist economy. Tourist development at the white sand beaches of Varadero (80 miles east of Havana), Santiago de Cuba, and Holguin's Guardalavaca is still up for grabs. By July 1994, Cuba reported 146 joint ventures with foreign capital, with 130 more under negotiation. A dozen of those in operation involve financial capital of Caribbean origin (Cotman 1999). More recent figures indicate that tourism in Cuba is currently a billion dollar-a-year industry, an impressive fivefold increase in less than one decade (Facio 1999). In fact, gross revenues from tourism increased from 4.8 percent to 23.3 percent of total export earnings, and from 4.5 percent to 17.7 percent of total foreign exchange earnings from 1989 to 1992. Revenues from tourism of $500 million in 1992 were second only to sugar exports. Since 1992, gross income from tourism has surpassed sugar exports, though the ratio of net profits is still higher in the sugar industry (Cotman 1999).

The development of the tourism industry in Cuba has been one of the most controversial strategies of their post-Soviet economic recovery plan. Between 1988 and 1991 there has been a dramatic increase in the number of foreign visitors (especially Canadians, Latin Americans, and Europeans) to Cuba. As a result, extensive debates have taken place in Cuba over the relative social costs and benefits of the expanding tourism industry. The renewed emphasis on tourism has created a host of new social problems. For example, some Cubans feel that tourism has subverted the purpose of the revolutionary state, which is to promote equality. As tourist dollars (particularly U.S. dollars) pour into the country, there is increasing stratification between Cubans who have access to these dollars and those who do not. One unfortunate outgrowth of global investments in Cuba and the opening of tourism is that it has created what one person called "an unexpected new class of rich service workers" as a waiter at a beach resort makes more money than a surgeon or a university professor. Similarly, Cubans who work in the tourism industry and obtain dollars can purchase food and goods in the many stores that accept only dollars. Indeed, the inequity between the dollar and peso (the exchange rate is 100-120 pesos to one U.S. dollar) has created an increasingly stratified economy, in which bellhops, waiters/waitresses, taxi drivers, bartenders, and so on make more money in tips than doctors and college professors do in salary. In addition, the tourism economy has led to a severe problem of underemployment in which workers are frequently overqualified for their jobs. For example, one respondent said "when you learn all you learn in school it is frustrating because afterwards there aren't enough jobs and salaries are very low." Nancy who worked for a French tourist agency as a secretary expressed her frustration with her current job.

> I am not happy with my work. I studied for 5 years to be a translator. I studied English literature and language for 5 years and now I work as a secretary. I type letters, organize documents, send faxes and answer the phones, which is not very satisfactory. I'm supposed to work 44 hours per week but I work many more hours. My boss is French and he treats me very badly. We have many arguments. He yells at me and I tell him he doesn't have the right to curse at me. He threatens to fire me, but I don't care. If I lose my job, I could get another job since I speak English, Italian, and French. Soon the boss will leave. I get paid in pesos and dollars. I haven't left my job yet because I can't keep moving around. I wish to be a translator for the government in the conference center, but unfortunately it is not profitable to work for the government.

Other highly educated professionals have left their careers because their wages were insufficient to provide for their families and instead have turned to the new employment opportunities available in tourism. In our sample, a college educated public relations consultant was able to use her skills in her new job as the owner-operator of a guesthouse. Laura explains how and why she became self-employed as the owner of a guesthouse that rents rooms to foreign tourists:

> I entered into this profession because I didn't have a choice! I had to do it. Economic problems are the reasons for my entry into this business. My ex-husband had the idea. I had a job, but the salary was not enough to support my children. My ex-husband had big dreams, but was pretty lazy. He had the dreams and I did the work. He proposed that we look for a bigger house with more space. I agreed thinking I would be able to keep my job in the tourist industry, but I couldn't. I worked in the hotel industry for 2 years. Before that I was a university professor. I worked at a university that trains engineers and architects for the military. I taught computers there from 1986-1996. It was my first job after getting out of college. In the hotel, I worked in information systems and public relations. That's when I had my second child, my daughter. My ex-husband received an offer to work in the tourist sector but he didn't want it and I wanted out of teaching because there were few opportunities for mobility. I felt I was falling behind. I went to apply for his job and was told I was over qualified for it, but they still gave it to me.

Within the small business sector, proprietors used both legitimate and illegitimate methods for sustaining their enterprises. As Laura explains:

> I work as an "arrendataria," a guesthouse owner. I rent rooms to foreigners. In Cuba this type of work requires a lot of capital. There are people who operate this business legally and illegally. I do it legally. It is very hard work. My estimated income is hard to determine. It depends on the number of clients I receive. Monthly I may have guests for 12 days. Depending on the number of clients I have, I can earn as much as $200.00. There are months when I have no clients and still have to pay for operating costs. The license costs $200. Then the state comes to inspect and evaluate the home and determines the number and size of the rooms that you will be renting. This is separate from the monthly fee, which is $100.00 per room whether or not you have clients. If you modify the license, for example adding a room you must pay $100.00 per month for the room plus $50.00 extra to modify the license each time it is changed. Once that change is made you are locked into it and cannot modify the arrangement for 3 months. You must pay the license whether or not you have guests. You can close rooms anytime but you cannot open them for 3 months. At the end of the year you also pay tax on the profit made all year. They take my books, look at all the names, and add all my expenses and income. They give me back 2 percent for a discount for expenses. At the end of the year, you must also pay 10-15 percent tax on the yearly profits. This license is only for rooms, not for food. So, whatever I earn for providing meals is my profit alone. If I declare that I feed people, I have to pay taxes on that also. If I don't declare it, it is illegal. I must find my way around the system because when there are not tourists I have to find a way to pay the bills.

Operating a guesthouse is not only an expensive proposition, but is also labor intensive. Political economists have historically overlooked this type of small business ownership because it is women who have typically done it. In the following discussion, Laura describes a typical workday, reflecting a strict gender division of labor often associated with traditional housework.

> I get up and work and work and work all day. I get up in the morning and prepare breakfast for clients and converse with them. They frequently require a lot of information. I am the cook, the waitress, and the public relations officer. When they leave I am the maid. If I have domestic help then I don't have to do it all, but that is not always the case. There is a woman who comes once a week to wash and another who comes 3 times a week to clean. We pay them in whatever we have, usually *pesos convertibles*, which are pesos that are equivalent to U.S. dollars. My father helps by buying the food. I have to buy the stuff you buy in the dollar stores myself. My mother helps in the kitchen. I set the menu and give her the food and she cooks. I help make the juices and desserts. In Cuba, food doesn't come prepared, you have to do everything from scratch. I also have to take care of all the paperwork and licenses. Then, I have to come back and start cooking dinner. [In the middle of the interview the clothesline fell down and all the freshly washed towels fell in the dirt and got all muddy requiring them to be washed again!] "No es facil!" (It isn't easy!) "La vida es muy dura." (Life is very hard.) After dinner is served and food is eaten I have to wash the dishes and do more public relations. In addition, there is other work to be done, taking care of my children, ironing my clothes and my partner's and my children's clothes. Sometimes clients want to learn about the history of Cuba and I want to learn about their countries so we talk. I go to bed around 11:00 P.M.-12: 00 A.M.

Given her education and previous career experience, we were curious about how satisfied she was with her current job. Laura responded:

> I love the public relations part, but I feel that I have no time for myself, for my children and even less for my partner. I miss the work I set out for my career and the progress I could make in that work. The biggest satisfaction of my job is to know I have made people feel comfortable and they have enjoyed their stay, especially when they write and tell me how much they enjoyed their visit.

Laura's experiences reflect how some workers straddle the legal and illegal elements of a changing economic system and the patriarchal organizational arrangements that are being (re)produced within this newly emerging political economy.

La Búsqueda as a Gendered Process: *Jineterismo*

A strategy Cubans use to deal with the changing political economy is by engaging in what they called *la búsqueda*. Although *la búsqueda* is a survival strategy that encompasses both the formal and informal sectors of the economy, in this section we focus our discussion on one of its most insidious forms, *jineterismo* (prostitution). As we have shown, the Special Period has exacerbated gender inequality and placed women in a more vulnerable position in the formal economy. The Special Period has also driven some Cuban women to sex work. *Jineterismo* was a problem almost entirely eradicated by the Revolution, as prostitutes were reeducated, taught to read and write, and given jobs in the paid labor market. As the Revolution evolved, prostitution was no longer necessary as a means of survival and was universally demonized. Although the state argues that women choose prostitution solely to purchase unnecessary consumer goods, many Cubans told us that it is a means to procure food and essential subsistence products.

Background

The role of Cuba in the global sex market can be traced back to the colonization of the Island by Spain and the United States. At different points in time, images of a tropical paradise lured American and European tourists to the "pleasure Island" (Schwartz 1997). According to Hodge (2001) "Havana before the Revolution was little more than a casino and brothel for wealthy U.S. capitalists in search of exotic pleasures" (p.21). An important part of the colonial establishment in Cuba was its military installations. The U.S. military played an important role in the institutionalization of prostitution in Cuba. This form of prostitution, known as "militarized prostitution" (Bertone 2001), developed around the foreign military bases in Puerto Rico, the Philippines, and Cuba. The sexual exploitation of Cuban, Puerto Rican, and Filipina women as prostitutes made U.S. colonialism in these Islands complete. In other words, U.S. colonialism not only took over the political, economic, and cultural institutions in these countries, but also took over women's bodies.[3]

Aided by patriarchal state policies and by the exigencies of a global economy, sex tourism has become "a booming market in the New World Order" (Kempadoo and Doezema 1998:16). As Kempadoo and Doezema state (1998), "[T]he sexual labor of young brown women in these playgrounds of the West has become increasingly important to the national economies, while prostitution remains condemned as degrading and destructive. In Cuba's case, it is viewed as a counterrevolutionary engagement. Nevertheless, state support or tolerance of this from of tourism is evident" (p.16).

Field Observations

In the 1990s, Cuban women who engage in *jineterismo* range from their late teens to early 30s. Most *jineteras* are highly educated, some are employed full time, and many are of African descent. Men from Canada, Mexico, Spain, and Western Europe seek out black women because they have internalized racist stereotypes of the "exotic dark-skinned overly sexualized woman." And the Cuban state contributes to the commodification of black women as available sexual partners for foreigner travelers. For example, at the reopening of the tourist industry in 1991, travel brochures pictured black women in bathing suits as opposed to the standard beach scene, alluding to the availability of dark-skinned Cuban women.

Jineteras frequent tourist areas such as hotels, beaches, nightclubs, restaurants, and other enterprises where U.S. dollars circulate. However, as a result of state policy in which Cubans are forbidden from entering hotels (unless they are employed there), *jineteras* are no longer able to freely enter such establishments. Despite these policies, *jineterismo* has not been eliminated from public spaces.

During our research we had an opportunity to observe the sex market in Havana. We saw many Cuban women who entered the bar alone, in groups with other women, and accompanied by men. Most of the women went directly to the bar and many of them obviously knew each other, greeted each other, and hung out together. The women were young (18-25), dressed very provocatively and fashionably. The racial-ethnic makeup was surprisingly diverse. The majority of these women were not black as we expected based on past research. We suspect that there is race and class discrimination taking place among Cubans working at tourist nightclubs. Lighter-skin women with access to dollars and consumer goods are more welcome at tourist sites than black women. Subsequently, black *jineteras* are forced to ply their trade in Habana Vieja (Old Havana) and along *El Malecón*, the famous waterfront boulevard.

There appeared to be different strategies in seeking clients. Sometimes individual women approached individual men at the bar, or groups of women approached groups of men. For example, there were three men sitting at a nearby table and three women who were mingling at the bar. They saw the men and immediately went over and sat down without being asked. We observed many women who came accompanied with men. These were striking couples in that the men were older and the women very young and beautiful, hanging on their every word. Initially, we were unsure whether they were prostitutes, but as the night progressed it became clear to us that they were *jineteras*. One indication was that they did not always stay with the man with whom they entered the bar. For example, we observed one woman come in with one man, stay for a short while, and leave with him. Then, she returned several hours later, and left with a different man. Yet another strategy we observed was a man who tried to encourage his friends to come to the table and couple up.

There was a great deal of competition between women for clients. For example, at one table there were three men and three women. Suddenly two more women came over and sat down. When this happened the original three women moved closer to the men and put their arms around them as a way to indicate that they were already taken. These men also showed the two additional women that they were already accompanied. One man slid the woman across his lap and put her on his other side where she could not easily get out of the booth. In addition to this competition, there was also some networking going on where women already hooked up with clients were trying to find clients for their unaccompanied "friends." We observed a woman who was with a client call two friends over from the bar and introduced them to unaccompanied men.

At the nightclub one of the entertainers asked the audience where they were from. We learned that while most of the men were from Spain, and a few were from Latin America and Western Europe. Throughout the evening, the social exchanges between foreign men and Cuban women were varied. Some were very animated with lots of conversation, drinking and sharing while others were not. At a table nearby we observed a Spaniard with two black women who made very little effort to converse or interact with them. He watched the show and ignored the women as they tried to engage him in conversation, invite him to dance, and make eye contact. Eventually, he indicated that he was ready to leave by jerking his head in a cavalier manner. When they left the nightclub, the exploitation of Cuban women's bodies as sites of pleasure for foreign tourists became abundantly clear. As they slipped from our gaze it was as though these women became shadows devoid of dignity. When we left the nightclub around 3:00 a.m., we were overwhelmed by the blatant manifestations of the emerging sex trade that has become an integral part of the tourism industry in Cuba. Foreign men exploit young *jineteras* for their own pleasure. Cuban women become *jineteras* as a means of survival in an economy in which salaries are abysmally low (Facio 1999). Cuban women can no longer go to these dance clubs to have fun because foreigners, who assume that all young Cuban women are prostitutes, sexually harass them. In addition, Cubans who do choose to go to these clubs are forced to witness the sexual exploitation and denigration of Cuban women.

As feminists, the bar and dance scene in Havana became a complicated site where gender, race, and class inequality in Cuba converged. Hodge (2001) captures the predicament facing Cuban men and women as Cuba is drawn more forcefully into the global economy of sex work when he states that "as capital relations become even more standard in El Vedado and elsewhere on the Island, and the culture of capitalism and materialism more pervasively insinuate themselves into the minds and bodies of Cubans, we can expect an increasingly reconfiguration of gender according to the logic of the market" (p.28).

Gender and Family: The Gender Division of Labor

> *Researchers: What happens when a married woman refuses to do housework in Cuba? Ana: "A Revolution."*

Early feminist researchers analyzed the gender division of labor in the home and the workplace as two distinct and separate spheres (Hartmann 1981; Coverman and Sheley 1986). They theorized that the family is characterized by divergent interests and roles and is the locus of conflict over production and reproduction. Accordingly the gender division of labor in the home and in the market place reflects the interrelations between patriarchy and capitalism, and is not a result of one or the other alone (Sokoloff 1980). In addition, they posited that family relations reflect the underlying social forces of patriarchy and capitalism. In her groundbreaking work, Heidi Hartmann (1981) argued that the creation and perpetuation of hierarchical gender relations depends not only on family life, but also on the organization of economic production and the production of material needs.

When this body of work initially emerged, it was embraced as a radical approach that challenged previous functionalist analyses of the family, which defined it as a safe heaven from a harsh world. The underlying assumption of the functionalist perspective constructed the family as an egalitarian unit in which each member's needs were equally meet. Feminist scholars of the family pointed out that men benefit directly and indirectly from the unequal division of household labor. More specifically, Evelyn Nakano Glenn (1985) articulated that men "contribute less labor in the home while enjoying the services that women provide as wives and mothers, and indirectly in that, freed of domestic labor they can concentrate their efforts in paid employment and attain primacy in that area" (p.15). Furthermore, Glenn (1985) also notes that by focusing exclusively on gender as the central variable in the analysis of productive and reproductive labor, early feminist researchers universalized women's experiences and ignored race, class, and national differences.

Feminist development scholars have extended this literature by examining the interdependence of the state, economic structure, and family life in Third World countries. They have critiqued the claims that the state is a monolithic entity and have identified a variety of state approaches that institutionalize gender relations through law and policy (Moghadam 1998). In addition, feminist development scholars examine how gendered law and state policy emerge in the context of a changing geopolitical economy (Chow and Berheide 1994). In her most recent book, *The Myth of the Male Breadwinner: Women and Industrialization in the Caribbean* (1995), Helen Safa illustrates how the state institutionalizes patriarchal familial relations in Cuba, Puerto Rico, and the Dominican Republic. Safa (1995) found that "even in Cuba, where under socialism the state has assumed the most complete responsibility for social reproduction, it is evident that women still focus their demands on the state within a domestic framework, emphasizing practical needs, such as daycare and housing, over gender equality" (p.58). Ironically, in the context of a country in which gender equality in the home was legislated through the Family Code, women are still primarily responsible for housework and child rearing.

Despite the great strides Cuban women made in the aftermath of the Revolution, scholars have documented the persistence of gender inequality both in the home and the workplace (Safa 1995; Smith and Padula 1996). In this section, we contribute to this body of work by focusing on how Cuban women and men continue to negotiate the gender division of labor within the home in the context of the Special Period. We found that the gender division of household labor has been exacerbated by the current economic crisis in Cuba.

In a lively exchange between a woman and a man, we witnessed the tensions in the Cuban family with respect to the gender division of labor. We posed the question: Is there equality in the home? Roberto replied: "Yes, there is equality." In a forceful tone, Ana replied:

> "Como tu eres hombre." (Because you are a man.) He says we are equal, but that is not the way it is. I am the one who carries the weight of the housework. "Lo que te toca a ti, lo que le toca a el, pero yo soy la que llevo el peso. El comparte con los quehaceres, todo menos cocinar. Por ejemplo, el lava los platos 3 veces a la semana cuando esta en casa, pero cuando no esta, yo lo tengo que hacer." (There is my work, there is his work, but I am the one who carries the load. My husband shares some housework. For example, when he is home he washes the dishes three times a week, but when he is not, I am the one who has to do it.) Cuban men are *machistas* and you don't change that overnight. It is going to take a long time.

Maria echoed Ana's sentiments when she succinctly stated, "in Cuban society it is understood that the household is the woman's domain and machismo is very strong. Equality exists in the law, but it doesn't exist in reality." It was often the case that when we interviewed men and women together, men claimed that they shared equally in family labor. During these interviews, women glanced, smiled, and winked at us suggesting that there is another version of the story that is not being told. In the following quote, Ana elaborates about the difficulties and challenges she faces as a working woman:

> My husband is a journalist. I am the one who gets home first. If my son needs to be picked up, I am the one who has to pick him up. If my husband gets home first, he will pick him up and they will watch TV together and look at the clock, waiting for me to arrive. When I arrive, I have to run to the kitchen and cook dinner. He will wash the dishes *if* he is home. Then I have to help my son with his schoolwork, prepare his uniform and get everything ready for the following day. My husband watches TV! I read to my son before going to bed. My husband does it every once in a while, but I'm the one who usually does it. These are my responsibilities. If I do not do them, they will not get done.

Cuban men frequently stated that they shared equally in the household. Jose explained:

> My wife cooks. If it is easy, I do it, but if it is too difficult my mother-in-law does it. I hate cooking because I hate the heat. I clean the rice. My mother-in-law does

the dishes because my wife hates it. I help. My mother-in-law does most of the wash. I help with small things like underwear. Mostly we wash by hand because our Soviet washing machine mangles our clothes. I have some quarrels with my wife because she uses the bookshelf for knickknacks and I hate cleaning all those things. It's too hard, so she does it. I sweep the floor; I help her, if I see it needs to be done. I make the bed if I sleep later than her. I clean the bathroom. The one who dedicates time to our son is me. My wife is drowsy in the morning because of her asthma pills. I prepare breakfast for my son, help get him ready for school, and I help with his homework. I also bathe him at night. I read to him and sing songs in English before he goes to bed. Lately with my new job, I have no time, so he goes to bed alone and my mother-in-law washes dishes.

When we interviewed Jose's wife independently she said, "I do ALL the housework! I am totally responsible for this family. All Jose does is make coffee in the morning and help our son with his homework."

Implicit in Jose's statement are profound contradictions about how Cuban men perceive their participation in the gender division of household labor. Although his wife and mother-in-law do the majority of household work, Jose claims to be sharing equally, even as he calls his labor "help." This illustrates that in Cuba, as in other industrial and developing countries, there has not been a paradigm shift in the way men perceive their household responsibilities in the family. Men continue to see themselves as "helpers" rather than equal partners. Men's ability to avoid contributing equally in the household division of labor is facilitated by the presence of female extended-family members. Safa (1995), who conducted research in Cuba prior to the Special Period, has observed this point: "[T]he high percentage of three-generation households reinforces traditional patterns of authority and domestic labor. Additional women in the extended family may provide working mothers with important assistance in childcare and other household tasks, but they discourage men from taking more responsibility" (p.163). Safa (1995) also found that women relied on the state to provide childcare services rather than requiring more from their husbands, as mandated by the Family Code. Our data suggest that during the Special Period, working women no longer expect the state to provide familial resources, such as childcare, but rather turn to their partners to provide both material and emotional support.

As a result of the severe housing shortages during the Special Period, two- and three-generation households have become even more common. The severe shortages of food, medicine, and other household supplies have made the presence of extended family members even more critical to the survival of the family. As illustrated throughout this paper, it is rare to find a family that does not rely upon the help of older women. Throughout our fieldwork, we observed numerous examples of retired grandmothers, fictive kin, and unemployed neighbors who provided childcare, collected rationed goods, and purchased resources in the dollar stores when they had U.S. dollars. Similar to Safa's (1995) results, we found that during the Special Period, women were overwhelmed by their work and family responsibilities. In our study, however, women spoke forcefully about the need for more involvement from their partners in all aspects of family. Women also expressed anger and frustration at their partners' resistance and refusal to share in the day-to-day activities of the household.

Our data augments the contention made by feminist development scholars that the family must be examined in the context of the state apparatus and the political economy. In Cuba, despite the state's attempt to legislate equality in the home through the Family Code, gender inequity continues to persist in the home. Women told us they felt that this gender inequity was exacerbated during the Special Period because they could no longer rely on the state for help and men often refused to participate in childcare and housework. As we have shown, Cuban women continue to wait for the gender revolution in the household division of labor.

INTERSECTION OF GENDER, WORK, AND FAMILY: CONCLUDING DISCUSSION

The integration of Cuba into the global capitalist economy took place within the context of the fall of the Soviet Union that precipitated a severe economic crisis. As a response to this crisis, the state entered the global market, while simultaneously remaining committed to the goals of the Revolution. Cuba opened its doors to foreign investors to develop joint ventures in an embryonic tourist industry. It also relaxed laws that allowed self-employment and small business ownership. In addition, the decrimininalization of the ownership of dollars allowed for the emergence of state-owned dollar stores that generated much needed capital to help revitalize the economy. These changes have resulted in the development of a two-tiered economy that continuously subverts the goals of the Revolution. For example, despite legislation that criminalizes prostitution and attempts to curtail it, the state has turned a blind eye to the reemergence of prostitution and thus has become complicitous in the sex tourism business. These economic policies have created profound contradictions for the Cuban revolutionary state, which in turn have resulted in material, ideological, and socio-emotional dissonance for Cubans across all social locations.

State development policies and economic exigencies have also caused a redistribution and relocation of workers throughout the labor force. In the formal sector, both men and women have born the brunt of low wages, unstable working conditions, and unemployment. However, we found that women were disproportionately affected by economic restructuring during the Special Period. Women were redirected to low wage, part-time, temporary work in the service sector and found they have been resegregated into female-type occupations. Women and men also experienced a great deal of downward mobility as they moved from professional to higher paid, less skilled jobs in the tourism industry. We interviewed a number of college-educated women who worked as secretaries, waitresses, and hotel domestics in the tourist industry. Paradoxically, Cuba has among the highest rates of literacy in the world, yet unlike its Caribbean neighbors, it has a large overqualified and underemployed work force. We also found that women have left secured professional jobs to join the growing small business sector to operate *paladares* (cafeterias) and guesthouses that cater to tourists, resituating them into highly gendered work. This places women in a vulnerable position because of the unpredictable nature of small business ownership. In addition, there is also the added pressures of exorbitant taxes, licensing fees, and the ebb and flow of tourism. Those women workers, who were unable to enter the formal tourist economy, became part of a growing informal sector organized around *"la búsqueda."* An important manifestation of the gendered nature of *la búsqueda* is *jineterismo*, an insidious form of oppression because it (re)constructs Cuban women's bodies as sites of commodification. In a country that has fought to institutionalize respect for women's bodies, intellect, and worth as workers and as human beings, *jineterismo* undermines these values.

The integration of Cuba into the global capitalist economy has also impacted Cuban families adversely. Despite state attempts to legislate gender equity within the family, patriarchy was never fully eradicated in the home. This failure of the revolutionary project has been exacerbated by the country's current economic crisis. The burden of this crisis has fallen more heavily on women who continue to shoulder the responsibility for household work and childcare. Women also have the added responsibilities of waiting in lines for scarce consumer goods and supporting their families with increasingly meager resources.

Our research contributes to the argument articulated by development feminist scholars that a more comprehensive gendered analysis of the global economy must be attentive to the links between the family, the economy, and the state. Cuba offers an important case study to observe the particularities of a state's approach that once aimed to institutionalize gender equity through law and social policy in the home and workplace, but that has succumbed to the demands of global capitalism. The economic changes implemented to meet the demands of global capital irrevocably altered gender relations in the home and workplace. Our research supports the reciprocity between productive and reproductive spheres of life articulated by feminist scholars. In other words, the stressors that women encounter in the home are intertwined with the demands placed on them as workers in a changing political economy.

Our work raises several important questions. Based on the principles of the Revolution, Cuban women internalized a strong feminist consciousness. Through grassroots organizing, the Federation of Cuban women persuaded the state to pass legislation that aimed to dismantle patriarchal relations in the home. The Cuban state responded by passing the Family Code. As the social services the state provided erode under the demands of global capitalism and men resist changes in the gender division of labor, it remains to be seen whether women will mobilize to eradicate patriarchal familial relations intensified during the Special Period. Alternatively, will Cuban women, like other Third World women, be reduced to negotiating with patriarchy with respect to the gender division of labor? Will Cuban women utilize current legislation that mandates gender equity in the workplace—such as equal pay for equal work and maternity leave—to protect themselves from newly emerging forms of workplace inequality? Finally, Cuba offers feminist development scholars a unique opportunity to study the ramifications of the transition from a socialist to a market economy, rather than the typical movement from an agrarian to an industrial economy characteristic of most Third World countries. Despite the different trajectories used to enter the global economy, there are remarkable similarities between Cuban women and those in other developing nations. Women workers around the world find themselves segregated into low-paying, low-skilled, dead-end jobs and continue to be primarily responsible for the bulk of housework and childcare. Once again, we are confronted with how patriarchy transcends economic systems.

NOTES

1 Our expertise, experience, and training complement each other very well. We are all trained as feminist sociologists and do research on communities of color. All three of us have extensive ethnographic research experience using the tools of feminist methodologies.

2 Jennissen and Lundy (2001) report that from 1996 to 1998 more than three million Cubans were treated with *"medicina verde"* (natural medicine). Interestingly, in an attempt to cope with the shortage of manufactured drugs, Cuba has incorporated a range of homeopathic and organic approaches to illnesses. The combination of natural and conventional medicine has made Cuba a country of choice in the global market for health tourism (Oswald and Henthorne 1999).

3 Although very little is known about this form of prostitution in Cuba, in Asia for example, militarized prostitution has required active negotiation on the part of colonial and military authorities to procure sex for the soldiers, whose sexual needs are an important part of maintaining morale and offering rewards for overseas service (Bertone 2001). In fact, Asian states have historically looked the other way as more girls and women are lured to the cities and abroad for work in the global sex market (Bertone 2001; Lie 1995, 1997). Asian states have actively participated in the ideological and institutional exploitation of women's bodies leading to what Lie (1995, 1997) calls "the state as a pimp." For example, Japan during World War II play the paternal role of protecting Japanese women by forcibly recruiting Korean women to serve the sexual needs of its soldiers. The state not only participated in recruiting women, but also, most importantly, promoted the development of a sex industry in Japan that today continues to draw women from the Asian periphery.

REFERENCES

ACOSTA-BELÉN, Edna and Christine E. Bose.
    1993. *Researching Women in Latin America and the Caribbean.* Boulder, Colorado: Westview Press.

BENERÍA, Lourdes and Martha Roldán.
    1987. *The Crossroads of Class and Gender: Industrial Homework, Subcontracting, and Household Dynamics in Mexico City.* Chicago, Illinois: University of Chicago Press.

BENERÍA, Lourdes and Catharine R. Stimpson.
    1987. *Women, Households, and the Economy.* New Brunswick, New Jersey: Rutgers University Press.

BENGELSDORF, Carollee and Alice Hageman.
    1978. "Emerging from Underdevelopment: Women and Work in Cuba." *Race and Class* XIX(4):361-378.

BERTONE, Andrea M.
    2001. "Sexual Trafficking in Women: International Political Economy and the Politics of Sex." *Gender Issues* 18(1):4-28.

CAMPBELL, Al.
    1999. "The Cuban Economy Has Turned the Corner: The Question Now Is Where Is It Going?" *Global Development Studies* 1(3-4):150-192.

CATASUS CERVERA, Sonia I.
    1996. "The Sociodemographic and Reproductive Characteristics of Cuban Women." *Latin American Perspectives* 88(23):87-98.

CHOW, Esther N. and Catherine White Berheide.
    1994. *Women, the Family, and Policy: A Global Perspective.* Albany: State University of New York Press.

COLE, Johnnetta and Gail A. Reed.
    1986. "Women in Cuba: Old Problems and New Ideas." *Urban Anthropology* 15(3-4):321-353.

CONSTABLE, Nicole.
    1997. *Maid to Order in Hong Kong: Stories of Filipina Workers.* Ithaca, New York: Cornell University Press.

COTMAN, John.
    1999. "Caribbean Convergence: Cuba and CARICOM after the Cold War." *Global Development Studies* 1(3-4):193-217.

COVERMAN, Shelley and Joseph Sheley.
    1986. "Change in Men's Housework and Child-Care Time, 1965–1975." *Journal of Marriage and the Family* 48:413-422.

DÍAZ GONZÁLEZ, Elena.
    1995. "Economic Crisis: Employment and Quality of Life in Cuba." In *Economic Reforms, Women's Employment, and Social Policies: Case Studies of China, Viet Nam, Egypt, and Cuba,* edited by Valentine

Moghadam. World Development Studies (4). Helsinki, Finland: World Institute for Development Economics Research.

DÍAZ-VALLINA, Elvira and Julio César González Pagés.
1999. "The Self-emancipation of Women in Cuba." *Global Development Studies* 1(3-4):12-29.

FACIO, Elisa.
1999. "Jineterismo during the Special Period." *Global Development Studies* 1(3-4):57-78.

FLEITES-LEAR, Marisela.
1999. "Women, Family, and the Cuban Revolution: A Personal and Sociopolitical Analysis." *Global Development Studies* 1(3-4):31-56.

FREEMAN, Carla.
1997. "Reinventing Higglering across Transnational Zones: Barbarian Women Juggle the Triple Shift." In *Daughters of Caliban: Caribbean Women in the Twentieth Century*, edited by Consuelo López. Bloomington: Indiana University Press.

GHORAYSHI, Parvin and Claire Belanger.
1996. *Women, Work, and Gender Relations in Developing Countries: A Global Perspective.* Westport, Connecticut: Greenwood.

GLENN, Evelyn Nakano.
1985. "Racial Ethnic Women's Labor: The Intersection of Race, Gender, and Class Oppression." *Review of Radical Political Economics* 17(3):86-108.

GUTIÉRREZ CASTILLO, Orlando.
2000. "Cuba, Turismo y Desarrollo Económico." In *La Economía Cubana: Coyuntura, Reflexiones, y Oportunidades*. Havana, Cuba: Centro de Estudios de la Economía Cubana (CEEC).

HARTMANN, Heidi.
1981. "The Family as the Locus of Gender, Class, and Political Struggle: The Example of Housework." In *Feminism and Methodology*, edited by Sandra Harding. Bloomington: Indiana University Press.

HEYL, Barbara.
2001. "Ethnographic Interviewing." In *Handbook of Ethnography*, edited by Paul Atkinson, Amanda Coffey, Sara Delamont, John Lofland, and Lynn Lofland. Thousand Oaks, California: Sage Publications, Inc.

HODGE, Derrick G.
2001. "Colonization of the Cuban Body: The Growth of Male Sex Work in Havana." *NACLA Report on the Americas* 34(5):20-23.

HOLSTEIN, James A. and Jaber F. Gubrium.
1995. *The Active Interview*. Thousand Oaks, California: Sage Publications, Inc.

HONDAGNEU-SOTELO, Pierrette and Cynthia Cranford.
1999. "Gender and Migration." In *Handbook of the Sociology of Gender*,

edited by Janter Saltzman Chafetz. New York, New York: Plenum Publishers.

JATAR-HAUSMANN, Ana.
1999. *The Cuban Way: Capitalism, Communism and Confrontation*. West Hartford, Connecticut: Kumarian Press.

JENNISSEN, Therese and Colleen Lundy.
2001. "Women in Cuba and the Move to a Private Market Economy." *Women's Studies International Forum* 24(2):181-198.

KEMPADOO, Kamala and Jo Doezema.
1998. *Global Sex Workers: Rights, Resistance, and Redefinition*. New York: Routledge.

LARA, José Bell, ed.
1999. *Cuba in the 1990s*. Havana, Cuba: Instituto Cuban Del Libro.

LEACOCK, Eleanor and Helen I. Safa.
1986. *Women's Work: Development and the Division of Labor by Gender*. South Hadley, Massachusetts: Bergin and Garvey Publishers.

LIE, John.
1995. "The Transformation of Sexual Work in 20th Century Korea." *Gender & Society* 9(3):310-327.

———. 1997. "The State as Pimp: Prostitution and the Patriarchal State in Japan in the 1940s." *The Sociological Quarterly* 38(2):251-263.

LÓPEZ-SPRINGFIELD, Consuelo.
1997. *Daughters of Caliban: Caribbean Women in the Twentieth Century*. Bloomington: Indiana University Press.

LUTJENS, Sheryl L.
1995. "Reading between the Lines: Women, the State, and Rectification in Cuba." *Latin American Perspectives* 85(22):100-124.

MARCHAND, Marianne H. and Janet L. Parpart.
1995. *Feminism, Postmodernism, and Development*. London, England: Routledge.

MARCHAND, Marianne H. and Anne Sisson Runyan.
2000. *Gender and Global Restructuring: Sightings, Sites, and Resistances*. New York: Routledge.

MOGHADAM, Valentine.
1995. *Economic Reforms, Women's Employment, and Social Policies: Case Studies of China, Viet Nam, Egypt, and Cuba*. World Development Studies (4). Helsinki, Finland: World Institute for Development Economics Research.

——— 1998. "Gender and the Global Economy." In *Revisioning Gender*, edited by Myra Marx Ferree, Judith Lorber, and Beth B. Hess. Thousand Oaks, California: Sage Publications, Inc.

NASH, June and M. P. Fernandez-Kelly.
1983. *Women, Men, and the International Division of Labor*. Albany:

State University of New York Press.
OSWALD, Sharon and Tony L. Henthorne.
   1999. "Health Tourism: A Niching Strategy for Marketplace Survival in Cuba." *Global Development Studies* 1(3-4):220-233.
PARKER, Dick.
   1999. "The Cuban Revolution: Resilience and Uncertainty." *NACLA, Report on the Americas* 32(5):17-20.
PASTOR, Manuel.
   1996. "Cuba and Cuban Studies: Crossing Boundaries during the Special Period." *Latin American Research Review* 31(3):218-234.
PÉREZ, Louis A., Jr.
   1999. *On Becoming Cuban: Identity, Nationality, & Culture*. Chapel Hills: The University of North Carolina Press.
PÉREZ VILLANUEVA, Omar E.
   2000. "Estabilidad Macroeconómica y Finaciamiento Externo: La Inversión Extranjera Directa en Cuba." In *La Economía Cubana: Coyuntura, Reflexiones, y Oportunidades*. Havana, Cuba: Centro de Estudios de la Economía Cubana (CEEC).
REINHARZ, Shulamit.
   1992. *Feminist Methods in Social Research*. New York, New York: Oxford University Press.
ROY, Kartik C., Clement A. Tisdell, and Hans C. Blomqvist.
   1996. *Economic Development and Women in the World Community*. Westport, Connecticut: Praeger.
RUIZ, Evelio Vilariño.
   1998. *Cuba: Socialist Economic Reform and Modernization*. Havana, Cuba: Instituto Cubano Del Libro.
SAFA, Helen I.
   1995. *The Myth of the Male Breadwinner: Women and Industrialization in the Caribbean*. Boulder, Colorado: Westview Press.
SÁNCHEZ EGOZCUE, Jorge Mario.
   2000. *Cuba, Inflation, and Stabilization*. Havana, Cuba: Centro de Estudios de la Economía Cubana (CEEC).
SCHWARTZ, Rosalie.
   1997. *Pleasure Island: Tourism and Temptation in Cuba*. Lincoln: University of Nebraska Press.
SMITH, Lois M. and Alfred Padula.
   1996. *Sex and Revolution: Women in Socialist Cuba*. New York, New York: Oxford University Press.
SOKOLOFF, Natalie J.
   1980. *Between Money and Love: The Dialectics of Women's Home and Market Labor*. New York, New York: Praeger.
STONE, Elizabeth.

1981. *Women and the Cuban Revolution.* New York, New York: Pathfinder Press.

TORO-MORN, Maura.
1999. "Globalization, Gender, and Migration: A Historical Overview of Migratory Movements." Paper presented at the *Women's Employment: Linking the Local and Global Conference.* Normal: Illinois State University.

———. Forthcoming. *A Gendered View of Migration.* Unpublished book manuscript.

TRIANA, Juan C.
2000. "La Economía Cubana en 1999." In *La Economía Cubana: Coyuntura, Reflexiones, y Oportunidades.* Unpublished papers from Centro de Estudios de la Economía Cubana (CEEC). Havana, Cuba: Centro de Estudios de la Economía Cubana (CEEC).

TRUE, Jacqui.
2000. "Gendering Post-socialist Transitions." In *Gender and Global Restructuring: Sightings, Sites, and Resistances,* edited by Marianne H. Marchand and Anne Sisson Runyan. New York: Routledge.

VASALLO BARRUETA, Norma.
1998. "La Mujer Cubana ante los Cambios Económicos Impactos en su Subjectividad." *Hacia una Mutacion de lo Social* 2(2):119-130.

WARD, Kathryn.
1990. *Women Workers and Global Restructuring.* Ithaca, New York: Cornell University Press.

PSYCHIC AND SOMATIC VULNERABILITY AMONG PROFESSIONAL WOMEN IN ARGENTINA AS A RESULT OF THE PRECARIZATION OF LABOR LINKED DURING THE SOCIOECONOMIC CRISIS

Susana Masseroni* and Susana Sauane**

ABSTRACT

This article deals with the effects of the worsening conditions—a deterioration of the economy, the precarization of labor conditions and general social decline—on the subjectivity of middle-class women with high levels of education in the Buenos Aires metropolitan area. Based on data collected through in-depth interviews and focus groups, situations of psychological and somatic vulnerability are discerned through the interpretation of experiences, feelings, and emotions. Transformations in the labor market in Argentina have been a determining factor as well as a consequence of the new economic model, and have caused the precarization of working conditions and of life in general. A degradation in the political apparatus, which causes great uncertainty, has exacerbated this situation. This situation, and the speed at which it has taken place, has generated negative consequences for the women's subjectivity, demonstrated in a decline in self-esteem and an alteration in thought processes.

INTRODUCTION

The purpose of this article is to identify the effects that economic changes of the last few years have produced on the subjectivity of highly educated, middle-class women in urban Buenos Aires.[1] In particular, we attempt to ascertain the role of work in the lives of these women and how they interpret changes in the organization of work in different areas, as well as how they live such transformations. Additionally, we pinpoint situations of psychic or somatic vulnerability among these women as a consequence of the general crisis in which they now live.

Generally, studies that approach the effects of structural changes over the conditions of work, about the quality of life among women, and about how these changes are experienced, have been focused on women from the less-protected sectors, when in fact the deep changes that have resulted from neoliberalism affect the entire population. People with high educational levels are also affected: in spite of having better-ranked positions, their living and working conditions also worsen. In this context, it is relevant to examine the situation of middle-class women, especially those with higher educational levels. Focusing on the middle class allows us "to access a minimal base of social resources" (Sautu 2001:22),

---

*   Gino Germani Research Institute, School of Social Sciences, University of Buenos Aires, Santiago del Estero 478 1° Piso - C.P.1075 Capital Federal, Buenos Aires, Argentina.
** Research Institute, School of Psychology, University of Buenos Aires, Teodoro García 2224 9° Piso -C.P. 1426, Capital Federal, Buenos Aires, Argentina.

and therein considering women with university degrees or other types of higher education allows us to examine the broader effects of structural changes. These women have had and have the possibility of attaining posts which require a certain degree of training and specialization, which are also the best paid jobs in the labor market. We believe that middle-class women, as a social group, share a certain system of values (Sautu 2001). To a large extent, women in this segment also share life experiences and have the possibility of interacting with other people. These points are relevant to understand their way of thinking. And, it is in this field of interaction that they create and interpret their subjective reality. Our interest in this sector of the population is related to the considerable increase of groups with higher education since the 1970s, and even more in the last decade. Also, because in the last few years this increase has taken place mainly among women, this has caused a remarkable increase in the relative weight of women among said working professionals in Argentina.

Historically, those with high educational levels have filled positions requiring higher qualifications and receiving higher salaries. The economic changes implemented since 1991 gave rise to the steady and profound precariousness of the general conditions of the labor force, which greatly affected the professional sectors and especially women. Although the neoliberal model that was implemented in the early 1990s already existed in Argentina since 1976 (started by the military government), it continued to be applied by succeeding democratic governments. The main feature of this process was transforming "the Argentine economy into an economy of financial accumulation, and the permanent transfer of funds abroad" (Lozano 2002:1) through (1) the general opening of the economy and (2) the perennial indebtedness promoted by the state itself. Thus, the predominant characteristic of the period was financial investment and an abrupt decline of productive investment, because it took place within the framework of an economy open to foreign markets—which introduced imported products at very low prices. As a consequence, there was a steady increase in unemployment rates, accompanied by a permanent and significant decline in wages. With the state deeply in debt, a process of economic restructuring was started through the *Plan de Convertibilidad y Reconversión Económica,* which has been firmly in place since 1991,[2] giving rise to a more mature period of capitalism that imposed a set of very strict rules.[3]

The transformation of the labor market was a condition, and also a consequence, of the new economic model because it required new labor patterns, working conditions, and mechanisms of selection, recruitment, and monetary compensation of the work force. It was a generalized process and its most outstanding feature was the replacement of the state by the market in the role of "social manager."[4] Throughout the decade unemployment increased enormously even among the most highly qualified workers.[5] Undoubtedly one of the most relevant consequences, however, was the precariousness of working conditions, with profound effects on life in general. This process deepened in the 1990s. Thus, the

1990s started with an even more indebted state and large transfers of funds abroad through privatized companies and financial institutions. This situation got progressively worse and thus, by the end of the decade, the country was bankrupt. As a result, the government confiscated bank accounts, changed the monetary parity, and devaluated the currency, unleashing an inflationary process of a huge magnitude. This process, within the context of existing high unemployment, generated a crisis that was not only economic, but also one that "nearly collapsed the social situation as well" (Lozano 2002:2). It has augmented and expanded poverty,[6] reaching now the middle-class workers as well. A number of dramatic changes appeared that altered the labor conditions even more, putting at risk the psychophysical health of the people.

Theoretical Approach

We have resorted to approaches from different disciplines and theories (Vasilachis 1992) to build a conceptual perspective that enables us to interpret the testimonies of the women in this study. In order to understand the consequences of the array of socioeconomic transformations in the different areas of everyday life, the sociological framework of symbolic interactionism has been of great value.[7] And as changes have been so rough as to cause consequences in subjectivity, it has been necessary to resort to a psychological perspective to interpret the women's stories about their experiences, feelings, and emotions.

We assume that economic transformations have affected not only employment conditions, but also the composition and the levels of retribution of the demand, as has been demonstrated by several macro-level studies (Cortés 2000; Beccaría and López 1994, 1996; Sautu 1999, 2000). Thus, we have tried to understand how these macro-transformations are experienced and interpreted by the actors themselves.[8] Symbolic interactionism and the psychoanalytic perspective make up an appropriate framework to examine the individual and the social self—its emotions and symbols—interacting with others within conditions around them. In the women's stories and interpretation of their personal experiences there appear intermingled events and situations in which they have participated or that they have witnessed, and emotions and feelings that these have provoked in them.

We try to integrate both approaches in the belief that they are complementary since they allow us to focus on different levels of analysis of the same phenomena. Thus, the framework of interpretation widens and it allows us to examine the evaluations and images underlying the stories and to explore the meanings that reality and social problems (i.e., job opportunities and changes in working and living conditions) have for the women—viewing them through their own interpretations with their categorization of objects and situations, values, and meaning attributed to the facts. For symbolic interactionism, interpretations are made through the reflexive use of our knowledge, shared meanings, and the processing of past experiences and experiences shared during interaction. In addition to interpretations about reality, the women have essential elements to understand their actions and the feelings involved in them, taking into account the assumption that ideas about reality are built through interacting with others, in different fields of experiences conditioned by the person's own biography (Fine, 1993). On the other hand, psychoanalysis gives us the theoretical tools about psychic functioning before traumatic situations, allowing the study of emotions, features of thought processes, and defensive mechanisms subjects use at a particular time.

Aulagnier (1977 and 1984) proposes a way of thinking about self-representation—an activity of the thinking and of the ego (Freud 1923)—where individuals are considered to be the consequences of a story that precedes them. A central aspect in this perspective is the notion of the "identifying project" (*proyecto identificatorio*) or image construction, where personal desires and parental and social values are mixed. The self compares itself to this image over and over again throughout life, resulting in self-appreciation or self-esteem. All "subjects"[9] have an ideal model, in reference to how they want to configure their own self in the future. This model goes on configuring following parental, social, and personal ideals (Freud 1923). This model, or future mirror in which the subjects look at themselves, supposes a gap with their present self. The movement or process through which the present self moves to concrete the future self is called the "identifying project." Thus, what the ego wants to become will be deeply related to the objects that it hopes to attain, objects that entail sense and value from the very history of the individual and the social discourse imposed on it. The self can only "exist" on the basis of the goods that it values, depending on the image reflected by somebody else. That is why anguish arises when achievements are endangered or lost.

In the interaction the individual is exposed to multiple stimuli that have to be processed psychically. When this processing cannot be carried out—either for its characteristics or its magnitude or its mere temporal or structural inability[10]—it can result in psychic as well as somatic symptoms. From this perspective the concept of vulnerability facilitates the study of the predisposing factors, or those giving rise to or exacerbating psychopathologic factors, as well as somatic disorders and also the psychological repercussion of the latter.

We make use of some Freudian concepts linked to the aforementioned considerations that prove useful in interpreting the study women's testimonies. A central concept is that of trauma (Freud 1920) seen as: (1) an event in the individual's life characterized by its intensity and by the inability of the individual to respond to it properly or (2) the long-lasting disorder and pathogenic effects provoked in the psychic organization. In its intent for overcoming this traumatic situation, the individuals are exclusively concerned with the traumatic event (they speak about it, evoke it, dream of it) and it generates true panic attacks or "automatic anguish"; that is, a reaction whenever the individual faces a traumatic situation, when submitted to an affluence of excitement of diverse external or internal origin, and which the individual is unable to control.[11]

When faced with an external danger—which is a real menace (Freud 1920) for the individual—and the anguish is impossible to tolerate, it turns into traumatic anguish and creates reactions that weaken the individual at the psychic, behavioral, and the somatic level. For example, in the experience of a loss (affective trauma) it is necessary to soothe the pain and emptiness through mental elaboration and emotional support (social and family networks). If the individuals do not possess processing tools at the mental level, they are faced with something unthinkable, which disorganizes them, and they then follow an alternative way: to act (on impulse, through an addiction, or avoidance) and to somatize.[12]

In times of crisis, stress, calamities and other dangers, the individual will be anguished and will show hopelessness or depression. While trying to handle these complex situations, the human being is exposed to automatic neurovegetative reactions and tissue lesions. Vulnerability would depend on the traumatic or stressing nature of the problem and the individuals' capacities to elaborate it mentally in relation to their psychic functioning and the social support network on which they can count (Wolfberg 1996).

During a social and economic crisis, such as the one taking place in Argentina today, the degree of trauma is extreme in as much as it breaks down all that is known to the person and increases social and personal uncertainty to extreme levels. The levels of anguish are traumatic because they are unexpected, they are impossible to tolerate given failing legal warranties, and they have serious consequences to continuing the individual's life the way it had been planned. Additionally, they cause great uncertainty about the future as well.

Methodological Design

The general aim of the study is to analyze the effects of the profound socioeconomic transformations on the subjectivity of graduated-professional women in Buenos Aires. The specific objectives are: first, to examine the meaning that professional (work) performance has for these professionals who represent the middle sectors; second, to explore—through their own interpretations—the changes that took place in the last years in the conditions in which they carry on their activities and, third, to detect situations of psychic and somatic vulnerability caused by these changes and by the situation of general crisis. To achieve these objectives the study used a qualitative design oriented to the subjective reconstruction of the actors' experience.[13]

The axis around which the women's experiences were reconstructed is the discourse (story) of a group of women with high levels of education, older than thirty years, who live in the Metropolitan Area of Buenos Aires. Every selected woman is professionally active, and all but one are married or divorced and have children. Information was obtained in two stages: first, thirty semi-structured interviews were conducted in the second half of 2000 and the second half of 2001. The interviews[14] were recorded and transcribed textually for the analysis and they enabled the researchers to reconstruct the professional trajectories and family histories in line with the changes that occurred in the different stages of the life cycle.

Those interviewed provided us with their interpretations of the changes in labor conditions within the framework of economic transformation. Along with the descriptions and interpretations of their own experiences and narration of the aforementioned events, emotions and feelings also emerged.

In the second stage of data collection, women who had been interviewed in the previous stage took part in four different discussion groups.[15] The focus groups were conducted during the months of January and February of 2002 and they were focused on events that occurred beginning in December 2001. The discussion groups were composed of six participants each and a guide was used to lead the discussions, all of which were tape-recorded. The recordings were transcribed textually and the intervention of each participant in the discussion was identified. Group techniques enabled the researchers not only to access rational arguments but also opinions, evaluations, feelings, and emotions that appeared more superficially in the individual interviews (Ibáñez 1979; Morgan 1988; Romero 1990). Group interchange also stimulated individual interventions, enabling the participants to compare their opinions about the present social events, how the current situation is viewed, and what feelings it provokes.[16] The general instructions prepared for the focus groups guided the discussions about the perceptions and impact of the present situation, the changes in working conditions, private, family and labor ties, and somatic disorders. To analyze the collected material, the researchers followed a procedure of reduction and deployment of facts as suggested by Huberman and Miles (1994). The strategy employed, for the interviews as well as for the focus groups, is based on a thematic analysis, and this was developed from the themes proposed in the task guides as well as in the categories emerging from the stories. In the particular case of the group discussions, the researchers developed categories for the different groups, and then added the specific ones that emerged in each of the groups.

From the perspective of symbolic interactionism, descriptions and interpretations are based on personal life experience, memory, and perceptive processes through which significance is given to the events experienced. From the psychoanalytic perspective, personal narration enabled researchers to infer the image that professional women have of themselves, (Romero and Sauane 1995) the extent to which their attainments translate their identification projects—self-esteem—as well as the mental elaboration of their experiences. The testimonies allow researchers, at the same time, to obtain a description of the evolution of the situation, making it possible to analyze the modalities of psychic functions and the defenses used, detecting moments of automatic or massive anguish with its consequences on the psychism and in the soma.

Ideals of the Middle Class: Work as Support of Self-image

Work gives people something more than the possibility to support themselves; it also sets up a framework for time management (habits and routines), provides nonfamily bonds, and is a source of status and social identity. "Work is what positions you, what links you to the world and to everything." That is how Ana R., a fifty-six year old architect, summarizes the place that work has for the middle class. The majority of the women in our study commented that they had chosen their profession through deeply felt vocation. Carolina, a fifty-four year old sociologist, admits that "you love your profession, you love what you do, and you are right that [that's what defines you]. When that moves [changes] everything else moves as well."

From observations the researchers gleaned that for people in this social stratum, their profession is a representation of themselves and affords them self-worth and brings them closer to the identifying project they set for themselves on the basis of—among other aspects—the social mobility ideals inherited from their parents. In the stories the women recounted, their self-images appear closely linked to having been able to graduate from university, which embodies the ideal of social mobility.

Identity is organized around the jobs the women performed. It is evident that in Irene's narration (a forty-nine year old neurosurgery technician) work means:

> Independence. It means being myself. Doing something for me. I mean, I love being a wife, I love being a mother, I love being a daughter, but that is an obligation I have to others. *Work is an obligation one has to oneself,* and this is what dignifies us. I feel that in my work I can be myself fully. I have a responsibility to work with a whole team. So this has to do with the fact that you do what you do because it is your responsibility, because it is what you learned [at the home: parental values and, of course, at the university].

The personal commitment to their work is so great for most of these professional women that it is sometimes equated to good health. "Yes, to me work is also health," says Marian (a 53 year old psychologist).

A job with high social status allows these women to feel successful, although being a university professor is not remunerated as well as it should be (given the responsibility and effort that goes into it). Thus, the search for status is evident when the women make reference to high-ranking academic positions, to the importance of intellectual work, and to their social engagement. Marian recalls: "I had an obligation in my work because I was a director," when she describes her work as a psychologist at a center for low-income people. Likewise, Lidia, a 47 year old with a Ph.D. in Chemistry, points out, "My thing was the intellectual aspect . . . so my best professional moment is now, because [with an academic position] I'm doing all that I like to do and I get recognition for it."

At this moment of profound crisis in Argentina, both in economic and social spheres, there has been a disruption in the meaning that work used to have. At present, fulfilling one's career goals is not attainable as they should be. The general transformation has not only changed the meaning of work itself, but it also has affected the individual. Initial expectations developed out of a socialization that placed great value on one's capabilities and now these expectations are difficult or even impossible to fulfill. In the group studied, for instance, the underemployment of overqualified workers and a general precariousness of working conditions have caused a deep crisis that jeopardizes self-esteem and the self itself due to the wide gap between self perception and ideal image. Ana, a fifty year old chemist, points out that her husband, a surgeon, was made redundant (and subsequently fired) from different positions because the social assistance projects where he used to work were sold to third parties, private entities.

> When we came back from our holidays, when he was supposed to resume working, the receptionist said in amazement "Doctor, what are you doing here? Haven't you received the telegram [informing you that you were let go]?"

In addition to the shock of dismissal, there is a lack of explanation and respect that places the individual into a very traumatic situation.

Permanent Risk as a New Form of Work

As a result of the new economic model implemented a decade ago, there have been important transformations in the organization of work. The best examples of such changes are those that have taken place in all state agencies as a result of their privatization, along with changes in the private sector as well.

In other countries these modifications have been shaped by different approaches to management implementation and changes in work dynamics, which are part and parcel of the current global market. In Argentina these changes were implanted circumstances within a framework of a recessive economic process that has been going on for several years. Thus, they have extracted a heavy toll and brought suffering to the people affected. In this context of growing unemployment, there is an increase in underemployment and a precariousness of the general conditions in which people labor. These situations emerge in the women's stories as traumatic experiences, not only because they do not meet the professional expectations of these women now, but also because the women compare themselves to their parents' experiences. In general, their parents worked in jobs that required lower qualifications, worked relatively shorter shifts, but earned enough to support themselves and did not experience the worsening conditions and downward mobility that these professional women are currently experiencing.

The case of private enterprises is more than appropriate to illustrate the current process of worsening conditions and the emotions it evokes. Ana R. is an architect working for a large transnational communications company, one of the two privatized telephone companies. She has lived all the process and evaluates it as sheer madness, like everything that has happened in Argentina in the last few years. The company was neatly dismantled in order to be given away as a present. Every year I become more and more convinced that the previous telephone [state] company was a solid company in the best possible sense. It had a sound foundation, a very good structure to affront any challenge. The problem was that it was badly managed, it was always managed by the military, unskilled people, you see . . . Thus the company was obviously stripped of its assets, there was no more investment, it stagnated, and it came to a stop. There was even a moment when there was not any more wire to fix a telephone line. The people protested and society as a whole was made to take sides against the company.

Today, several years after the privatization of the company, Ana does not feel comfortable, mainly because of the precariousness of her work. As she explains:

First and foremost because I think that what I said before, that there is a deep degradation at the professional level, at the level of doing a job. Everything is done so quickly, to get away, to fill in holes, nothing is planned; everything is done in a careless way. The human resources department has a terrible policy, awfully bad. During the past ten years the employees have been trembling because of the redundancy telegrams [through which people are informed that they are fired] that arrive twice a year and nobody knows whose turn is next. And nobody gives any explanation, it is as if nobody was interested in what happens to people or what people feel, that is, there is terrible abuse towards the people in the company. On the other hand, they tried to sell us the idea that greater effort will bring us greater appreciation, that good workers would be awarded a prize . . . "nooooo" . . . that's all lies, nothing of the sort happened.

The topic of precariousness emerges in the women's stories in different situations, and they make evident the tension that accompanies it, which has serious consequences for the psychophysical health of the women due to stress. Ana María, a forty-eight year old public accountant, works for a privatized telephone company. When she was interviewed, she stated:

What we are going through is critical. There is a lot of movement in the company, but it's all in the direction of downsizing; they are inviting lots of people to leave . . . because of uncertainty, of instability. We don't know whether tomorrow we'll be here or not. And there is also my age. I know that if they invite me to leave I won't be hired on a regular basis anywhere else . . . Here, in the private sector, every year we undergo restructuring of some sort, and since I joined the company the tendency has always been to downsize, always cutting and cutting . . . and now they are firing people of all ranks. Previously they fired the low ranks, now they are firing directors and deputy directors who are too expensive for the company.

The women in our study felt exposed—and at the risk of being left out of their social networks at any moment—unappreciated, unnecessary and, worse, unable to support themselves through their work.

The characteristic discourse about the world of work used to place great emphasis on the individual's own capabilities, on their responsibilities and dedication, which served to guarantee security in their position. This made the individual put all their efforts into trying to fulfill their obligations as best they could. But this approach has changed now. Companies characterize the new scenario as "dynamic," which allows change itself to acquire a permanent nature. Thus, companies are able to implement conditions and rules that, masquerading in the guise of having workers reinvent themselves as requirements change (Sennett 2000), generate submissiveness on the part of the worker.

Nowadays companies have short-term organization policies and there is an apparent streamlining of targets, which is why the composition of the staff is continually redefined. In fact, many companies have adopted the system of continuously hiring and firing staff. This pattern is evident in every privatized company in Argentina and it is causing a "cumulative" disappointment among the workers. María, a 35 year old with a degree in labor relations, joined one of the privatized telephone companies because her father worked there. She said that she could not stand to work in the department of human resources where she was hired because there it was practically

> [a]ll lay-offs . . . I hadn't studied for that, I mean, you don't study to fire people, you study to do something else . . . So it was sort of a shock, we kept thinking what might happen to ourselves. You needed to have the guts to do that [fire coworkers regularly] then . . . and now.

The women's stories demonstrate that in this environment they cannot continue to keep their compromise with their professional goals, which for them is a pillar in their conception of themselves, and this generates a break down in their self-image and self-esteem.

In Argentina, in addition to the "flexibility" of the new organization of work, the instability of the market—where lay-offs abound—must be added, causing situations of emotional instability and anguish. From the women's stories, the researchers gleaned that they had been socialized to work in a hierarchal environment where promotions required great effort and a sound identity that would allow them to reach gradual benefits and certain stability throughout their economically active years. Today, due to current circumstances and the women's experiences, work in general entails a permanent risk as a consequence of the short-term policies of the companies whose only goal is the immediate maximization of profits. Ana María notes, "We have to downsize, profits aren't good enough."

Such qualities as commitment, loyalty, and achieving targets—"which are naturally long term" (Sennett 2000:29)—have lost value and now seem outdated. In a context of very high unemployment, as in the Argentine case, submissiveness to any requirement of the company ensues and relationships among coworkers deteriorate. In this sense, privatized companies are paradigmatic. Ana G., a fifty-three year old sociologist working at one of the privatized telephone companies, describes the changes brought about by privatization as *"brutal"* because

> [t]here was a marked deskilling of all of us who were working for the old telephone company. All of us were subjected to maltreatments, terrible pressures . . . of all kinds. I was in charge of a group of workers [in a supervisory position], and they [my bosses] would call a meeting on Friday and would tell me: OK, on Monday morning you have to let us know who'll be the next one fired. It was terrible, terrible. Or they would ask you to do something today, and they needed it for tomorrow, which meant that you had to work all night to produce it.

Ana finally resigned from the company due to a permanent situation of stress that made her life intolerable.

In spite of the new policies, privatized companies demand absolute commitment from their employees due to the permanent risk of unemployment and uncertainty, thus narrowing the gap between personal and work life. For instance, Diana, a fifty-three year old librarian, mentioned that the employees' cell phones are always on, so as to always be on call in case the company needs anything, even on weekends or during holidays. Elisabeth, a thirty-nine year old public accountant, states:

> It appears that they shrink more and more and at the same time leave us with the same amount of work and we have to do with fewer personnel. It's as if we live inside the company. Look, I start to work at 9 A.M. . . . but last week I left the office at nine [at night], actually, fifteen past nine. I mean I don't have fixed working hours.

The women's stories also indicate the presence of mechanisms that affect the person's thinking process itself. This is how Ana María describes the situation:

> I don't like to think that I may be made redundant [fired] because if I do, I become a nonperson, I am erased, and if that happens I am a step closer to being thrown out in the street . . . I don't like to think, I don't think.

And for Elisabeth, pressure has become generalized in her life:

> We live under pressure constantly; the private telephone company puts pressure on employees in general and on managers in particular . . . This causes unnecessary strain.

This general situation leads to more submissiveness on the part of the employees because of the latent messages they receive: any divergence or directions that are not strictly followed can easily translate into being fired. Ana María comments:

> I say yes to anything because if I say no, I know what's coming. So if they ask me, "Can you do this?" I say yes. "And how about this?" Again, I say yes, even though I know these are impossible tasks to undertake.

In many of the cases in this study there seemed to be an acceptance on the part of the workers of the message that management is trying to get across, which leads them to take responsibilities beyond their control. For Ana Maria:

> The companies are trying to downsize and reduce expenses otherwise they won't make a profit and they fear that shareholders will withdraw their money and take it elsewhere where it's more profitable. So we have to accept that our benefits are reduced, that our salaries are also reduced, and everyone accepts this during these tough times.

In her assessment, Ana Maria dissociates the company from the shareholders, and ends up identifying with the shareholders. Through this reasoning one can ignore all the labor codes existing in Argentina before 1990, which include workers' rights, and thus neglect the social costs of the current working conditions. The issue is reduced to a conflict of interests between parties with the same bargaining power and current and past labor history (and any gain on the part of labor) is forgotten.

Many instances of twelve-, fourteen-, or sixteen-hour workdays were found because of the companies' needs and, in the case of professional workers; because of the multiple jobs they must work in order to put a living wage together. In this context people end up exhausted, thus, running the risk of making mistakes that affect theirs or the others' health.

From this analysis we can infer that flexibilization, exacerbated by the precariousness of working conditions and supported by a normative system that turns it legal, as well as rising unemployment levels, generate a state of general anesthesia or abandonment to the will of the other, the almighty represented by the company. Freud (1926) theorizes that a social trauma generates "initial stupor, gradual dullness, attachment anesthesia, loss of sensibility, abandonment of any goals, and distancing from others," (p.122) which are feelings amply known among the unemployed, who marginalize themselves and are marginalized by others.

Subjective View of the Present Situation

When the women in this study described the present situation, they focused on their everyday lives, mainly around the work and family spheres. Both are very significant for middle-class women. The situation is perceived as "chaotic," as having "no way out," and as being "unsupportive." This is how Cora, a 52 year old with a degree in fine arts, summarizes it: "In principle the situation is chaotic and, in general, I don't see any silver lining. I see everything very dark and somber, somber."

Current conditions are perceived as having no way out because the economic crisis is generally associated with an institutional breakdown[17] and with a situation of unprecedented general corruption that cannot be reversed. In addition, people assess the situation as "maddening" because basic parameters used to understand daily life occurrences essentially have been turned upside down. For Carolina: "If we analyze it strictly from a political point of view, everything is negative. We are immersed in a chaotic situation, one of corruption and hopelessness." Araceli, a forty-seven year old psychologist, goes even further, adding a certain dramatic quality: "It is like a feeling of death; there is no support whatsoever." This association with death indicates that the feelings of bitterness, insecurity, and desperation provoked by current events turn into hopelessness, with a certainty that there is no way out and, as a consequence, that there is no future.

But not everyone sees the situation as bleak. Some women maintain a certain optimism and contemplate hope. For example, Carolina says:

> I feel something very contradictory. On the one hand I can see a chaotic panorama, of hopelessness as you say, but on the other hand I am participating in the neighborhood organizations and though I don't attend the meetings I'm in touch with people who do, and I can see there is something happening and something is being done with relation to how one can express oneself and that gives me some hope.[18]

When they refer to the socioeconomic situation such as was "unveiled" since the events of December 2001, many women draw parallels with the military's dictatorship, mostly in the uncertainty, fear, danger, and powerlessness and impotence the current situation provokes. The human rights violations, tortures, and clandestine killings reemerge in the minds of the women, causing fear among them. Ana R. explains:

> The fundamental problem for us, our age group, is fear . . . so many years of repression . . . fear to suffer again and that our children may suffer as well. I can't tell them [my children], "Go, participate in a meeting" because I went through much suffering . . . all the disappeared and all that.

Cora also recognizes this issue:

> We, in our generation, we lived through "the process" [the military dictatorship]. [We experience] that feeling of desperation, that something bad is going to happen, but you don't know what it is. Now I feel that something is going to happen . . . maybe even worse . . . at any moment, it'll explode.

This feeling of general discontent and the protest demonstrations lead to a fear of a violent outcome and, of course, repression. Thus, the similarity that the women speak about between the present and the days of state terrorism has to do with the subjective assessment of living in a tense and hostile situation that can end up in violence and can endanger their lives. The tension the women feel is so great that some even draw comparisons to what happened in concentration camps. There, except when you were able to escape, the only certainty about the future was death. Nelly, a fifty-six year old social worker and psychologist, refers to this when she says, "I feel that this is like the Nazi genocide. The only ones that will be saved are those that don't care what they leave behind, those that left the country to save themselves." Zoraida, a fifty-two year old gastroenterologist whose children have left the country, also speaks of emigration as the only alternative:

> It was like telling them, "get away from here." It's as when you feel that something is sinking and you want to save your kids and you throw them away from you. I encouraged them to leave.

Zoraida is a physician working in Greater Buenos Aires, where she sees increasing levels of poverty everyday. She explains that the current situation is like genocide because it leads huge sectors of society to death:

> With the first genocide [the days of the Military Process] a whole intellectual generation was wiped out, . . . a massive death of thinkers. With the present genocide, it is a massive death [she refers to the increase of poverty]. Our mortality rate has gone from twelve per thousand to nineteen per thousand and we already have twenty-four per thousand in some regions of the country. But those little children who die, those adolescent mothers who die on delivery, who suffer malnutrition . . . And those who don't die are going to die all the same in the short term, because as they are poorly fed they will be cheap work force to be oppressed and exploited. They will also die very young or will have serious illnesses. The one who hasn't died in its infancy is going to die very young because he will get tuberculosis or chagas disease. That is why I say that this is genocide.

For the middle class there is another factor that up until now was relatively unknown: in the face of the uncertainty of obtaining a reasonable pension, people thought they might make up for that with savings that could be accumulated throughout their economically active life. Those are the savings that today have been "lost." The confiscation of the money deposited in banks and the state's use of the funds earmarked for private pensions to buy bonds to meet payments on the external debt, give rise to feelings of "having lost the future." Stella, a fifty-six year old mathematician, for example, tells us how she and her husband felt about it:

> When I told him about the AFJPs,[19] I told him "We aren't going to get a pension." He tells me then, "I already told you that some time ago," and I saw him so down. And seeing an elderly man who has toiled his entire life and you can't

say anything to him . . . Because when you are thirty you say, "OK let's go somewhere else," but at this point that's no longer an option.

Undoubtedly, the current crisis has generated a lack of trust in institutions because the state has ceased to protect its own citizens. The state is seen as an accomplice of the international financial agencies that have imposed measures that have created almost feudal-like situations. This is why some women use the metaphor of terror when referring to the current crisis. Cora says:

> There is the feeling of desperation, anguish, the feeling of wanting to be somewhere else, in another country. But the images in my mind are not very clear. Sometimes I feel like this is a movie and I would like to get out of it.

In many cases, informants cannot conceive of a viable way out of this crisis, for as in Freud's (1926) conceptualization, social trauma generates initial stupor followed by gradual dullness. Thus, Araceli comments, "The Argentineans used to believe that we had solutions to everything. I don't know if you remember, but we used to believe that we could fix the country in hours, we all felt that way. Now I ask people around, and they say 'I don't know.'" The fear associated with the possibility of ending up unemployed—either the women or their partners—impinges seriously on working relations. Ana R. explains, "You must guard your job, as a piece of bread during war time. If you have to survive, to eat, and you only have one piece of bread, you can kill a person who's trying to take it away from you." The social trauma that currently affects the group in this study—as well as others in the middle class—brings about negative consequences at the personal and at the primary and social links. Such consequences can be discerned in physical effects and in somatic disorders.

PSYCHIC EFFECTS OF TRAUMA

Self-representation and Self-esteem

The women's stories demonstrate the negative consequences that recent changes in Argentina have had both on the their self-representation and on their self-esteem. Silvia, a forty-nine year old social psychologist, explains what it means to be unable to get a job commensurate with one's experience and efforts:

> Only when I was answering the questionnaire that you gave us, in fact writing my story, I told myself "What am I doing here?" Given my career, all that I have done, all that I have studied, I should be filling another position, shouldn't I?

A frequent feeling that the women experienced is shame and fear of sharing their current experiences. When the meetings for the four focus groups were organized, several women told us that they could not make it because they would feel embarrassed if others saw them in their situation, having no control over their lives, which is very important for everybody to have. They also experience shame when they mention the possibility of needing their children's help to meet the household expenses. Ana, with a degree in chemistry and married to a physician, comments:

> My son works, works and takes care of his expenses. I mean I don't have to give anything to him and . . . well I have tried not to ask anything from him so far because it is sort of annoying, isn't it? But I have been wondering about it. Because suddenly you come to a point where there are things that you cannot pay. Perhaps I'm going to ask him, I don't know, for now.

In the women's discourse there is also guilt for not having been able to prevent the current situation. This feeling can be interpreted as giving the women the illusion that they are still able to do something about the situation *because* the blow they have been dealt to their self-esteem is too great to tolerate. Generally, before similar circumstances, the individual will try to avoid thinking about the situation, and even deny it, or feel responsible for the situation so as to recognize that they are powerless. Guilt, however, paradoxically affords them a way out; if they accept responsibility, then maybe they can change the situation. The exchange in the focus groups provides some examples. Loty, a fifty-six year old sociologist, says, "I don't know . . . the Argentines . . . sincerely I sometimes wonder how we could let things go by . . . go by . . . and go by." Zoraida answers, "Because we were annihilated as a society. There were thirty thousand missing people." Then Zoraida echoed Loty, "Society is to blame, everybody is to blame." The logic of the thinking process breaks down, as the same person states something and denies it later without realizing they are contradicting themselves. We will continue with this discussion in the following section, where we describe the disorders registered in the thinking process as a consequence of social trauma.

Features of Thinking

Sometimes the women stated one thing and then later they denied it. The women's discourse allowed us to unveil such cracks in the logic of their thinking processes. They also returned again and again to the same topics trying to understand what has caused so much suffering. In this situation, the psyche will naturally try to make up a reasonable sequence that can offer a possible way out.

One manifestation of anguish among these women is confusion in their discourse. Many of the women in this study, who generally have a structured discourse, now speak in a disorderly way as soon as they describe situations that cause them intense emotions. For Viviana, a forty year old demographer:

> Everything is messed up here, all of us run great risk, but we also need to protest because we can't perceive freedom . . . we cannot use that freedom, obviously the

possibility to protest was positive to me, but the fact is that we also run certain risks.

What she is saying is that protesting can be dangerous because it can be repressed with violence; it also is dangerous because there may be infiltrated rioters. But in turn she admits that not protesting means not using freedom. These represent breakdowns in the thinking process that tend to occur among severely perturbed patients. This has serious repercussions for the women's mental health, as they become aware of the incongruities in their speech.

The possibility of putting into words what is happening is the only way for the psyche to elaborate or process it. This is why when something dramatic that endangers the possibility of self-preservation occurs the individual repeats it again and again. This is because automatic anguish causes a narcissistic rebound that makes it difficult to speak of anybody else or to pay attention to anything else. This is manifested in the compulsion to speak, which they also recognize in other people. Araceli talks about her patients and says, "A permanent compulsion to speak, speak, speak, speak, to complain, without any search for solutions, this can't be tolerated, you can't do that." Norma, a sixty year old dentist, also states:

> The words that have been buzzing around me all the time is uneasiness, anguish. Besides the people you meet, your friends, always talk about the same subject. The other day I did an exercise of walking ten blocks listening to what people said, and everybody was talking about the dollar, the bank, that is the only subject.

In as much as the codes—including constitutional rights—have been violated, the meaning of some words referring to those codes has been subverted. When logical thought has been disjointed, there are negative consequences for the thinking process. Ana Maria says:

> I don't think that I may be made redundant [fired], because if I am, I will be paralyzed, I will break down . . . and those around me as well. If I break down I become useless and if I am useless I am that much closer to being fired.

Ana Maria resorts to an attack on her ability to think which is usually utilized as a means to get ready so that certain circumstances do not become traumatic. Her story involves a strong contradiction; she needs to deny reality so as to keep her good judgment. In another example of denial but also of "magic and almighty thinking" (*pensamiento mágico y omnipotente*), which is a defense mechanism that is a form of denial but also of defense characteristic of small children, Ana Maria says:

> I have children aged 21, 18, 13, and well I try not to show the situation to them, not to show it in order not to disappoint them, try to be supportive to them as well

with my employees, the people working with me, "come on, everything's all right, we can, we can."

She treats her children and her employees as if they were small children. She convinces herself that if she hides what is going on, they are going to be fine because they will not be aware of the situation.

The majority of the women also mentioned difficulties concentrating, reading, thinking, and even watching a movie. Silvia comments:

> Yes, I have a lot to read. During this time I usually have a lot to read, but I cannot concentrate. I'm anxious, so I don't feel like concentrating on something abstract. Obviously, this is related to the current situation, no?

FEELINGS AND EMOTIONS

The women in this study admit to having experienced anguish, hopelessness, pain, depression, and uneasiness. The loss of jobs implies not only an economic breakdown but also a feeling of failure. Norma says:

> For the last fifteen years we have been pivoting around the same thing, and they are subduing us, and they will succeed in subduing us, and they are going to come here and we are going to have another flag, that is what we see, what we foresee. Well that fills us with anguish, so we are in anguish.

To that anguish about professional and career losses and of future security, one needs to add affective losses as well. The young generations are emigrating, looking for new horizons, which increase the women's sadness and anguish. Zoraida is deeply affected by that:

> I'll tell you this; I would sue the state for family destruction. We were six and now we are three. Three of my children have already left. I invite you to go to the airport some day and watch the farewell among family members. It's heartbreaking.

Another emotion the women mentioned is aggressiveness, which is expressed in several ways and in different environments, such as in the spheres of family and work. Since the recent increases in prices, Ana Maria mentioned that sometimes she goes into a store just to ask for a price, and then argues with the clerk about it. In her words: "I went into Garbarino, into Frávegas [supermarkets], just to ask for the prices and then I would scream about them." She also mentions that all the frustrations she is experiencing have affected her marital life. Cora agrees and comments:

> Today we made peace but last night we almost killed each other. Just like that. I think it's because we're just crazy these days. It had been a long time since we

had a fight this bad.

Ana also admits that the atmosphere in her family has been tense:

> You get ill tempered and take it out on the one next to you, and you argue, you know, for little things, because you changed the place of the saltshaker for instance. Because you feel so bad, bad, bad . . . I mean tension rises.

SOMATIC EFFECTS OF TRAUMATISM

Even though the women in this study demonstrated a certain reluctance to speak of somatic disorders, they nonetheless mentioned insomnia, migraines, allergies, muscle strain, and ulcers. Sometimes they related them to specific circumstances, for example, the loss of one's job or one's spouse's job. When speaking about her husband's lay-off a few months ago Loty says, "I got an ulcer. It was very hard to listen to him saying, 'And tomorrow when I wake up what shall I do?' It demolished me." Other women at first said that they had not suffered any disorder whatsoever but then remembered some dramatic situations. Ana R. said, "Oh, I had forgotten what happened to me when the company was restructured." She goes on to describe how, though she had never suffered from any allergies, the changes at work caused her such a serious allergy that now she takes an injection of cortisone regularly to prevent a possible glottis edema.

The relationship between psychic and somatic disorders is widely known among the women in this study, as many of them are professionals in mental health areas. That is why the researchers think that their forgetfulness can be related to the fear of being exposed to others in the focus groups, of unveiling their fragility, and of shame since these would be signs of just how much current events affect them. Similar to forgetting the physical problems is disguising psychic symptoms, which appeared through examples about third parties or frequently with certain comparative reference. Norma, for example, says, "I feel a little depressed, but I have to get out of bed all the same, because if not my husband breaks down completely, because he really is prone to depression."

SUMMARY AND CONCLUSIONS

The neoliberal model implied reforms that included processes of flexibilization and deregulation of working conditions, which have affected the stability and quality of jobs. As a consequence there has been an increase of unemployment and precariousness in working conditions, which have entailed negative consequences on the individuals' subjectivity. Flexibilization applied in a recessionary environment produces a high level of deterioration in the conditions of life and tension ensues. It affects the psychophysical health of the workers because of the levels of stress it produces. This process is significant among highly educated women who have seen their working conditions and standards of living deteriorate, especially from the general crisis beginning in late 2001. For the group of middle-class professionals in this study, work means much more than simply earning an income. For many of them it is the foundation of self-worth and it brings them closer to their identifying project built upon inherited ideals of social mobility.

The women in this study feel vulnerable in many respects, such as being left out of a social network, feeling unable to support themselves, or of being appreciated and valued. Thus, this situation leads to their subordination to the companies and to a deterioration of their relationships with colleagues. Instability plus the precariousness of labor—sustained by regulations that make them legal— and the growing unemployment produce submissiveness and complete obedience to the companies and, as a consequence, a general state of terror, of impotence, and of being left at the will of their companies.

In addition to this process of general deterioration, social trauma that has deeply affected the middle class and, above all, women should be added. In many instances, women have to stand up to the responsibility of supporting their households; they have to see their colleagues out of work and their families broken up by emigration of some of its members. As a consequence there are negative effects on their self-esteem and self-representation, their thinking processes, as well as their feelings and emotions. Emotional disorders are the result of social trauma that modify in such a dramatic way the life of the individuals that they can produce psychopathological as well as physical symptoms.

NOTES

1. In the higher levels of education we are including women with university, as well as with higher nonuniversity, degrees.

2. The so-called Development Model of the World Bank.

3. The rules are: open economy regulated by capital, commodities, and the work force; free movement of capital and technology; concentration and transnationalization, and a normative system that supports and legalizes such changes.

4. The labor reform implemented since then shows the prevailing role placed by nonnegotiated processes of flexibilization and deregulation of the working conditions which have affected the stability of employment as well as the quality of the logic of the relationships within the labor market (Masseroni 2001).

5. The unemployment rate climbed from between 5 percent to 7 percent to over 20 percent.

6. In 1975, Argentina had 22 million inhabitants with the poor population around 2

million. Today, with 37 million inhabitants, the number of poor people reaches 15 million, many of who live in indigence. These are the ones whose total family income barely amounts to $62 (62 pesos) monthly (current exchange rate of dollar vs. peso: U.S$3.6 = $1).

7. Fine (1993) points out that there are interactionists today who admit that not everything in the world is the product of individual action and that it is necessary that phenomena be understood within the whole scope of social circumstances.

8. We think that social structure is the first matrix for the opportunities and objectives people have. Undoubtedly, there are differential life opportunities depending on the objective attainments related to the patterns of social organization and, though we know that they are not absolutely determined by them, they do limit or condition them.

9. When we say subject, we mean subject for the psychoanalysis, that is, the subject embedded in culture.

10. It refers to the structure of the self, psychic constitution.

11. Anguish must be considered as a consequence of the state of psychic powerlessness of the newborn baby, which is evidently the counterpart of its state of biological powerlessness (Freud 1926).

12. The axis hope/hopelessness has been an especially apt indicator to study somatic vulnerability. In a recent paper coauthored by U.S. and Finnish physicians, 2,438 cases of middle-aged men are described with moderate or high degree of hopelessness and showed several kinds of increased unspecific risk. Also, it was found that the risk of death was three times higher among highly hopeless men than in the sample group. High hopelessness predicts myocardial infarct and moderate hopelessness is associated with cancer.

13. Subjective reconstruction of the experiences implies placing the target of the research at the micro-level of social relationships, such as those that take place in work and family environments.

14. To assure the quality of the information obtained, the interviews were all conducted and transcribed by Susana Masseroni, the researcher in charge of the project.

15. The rsearchers in charge of the project created the guides, were in charge of coordinating the groups, and did the transcriptions.

16. Assuming that—as a context—there are some limitations appearing as a consequence of elements located at the level of social organization, we look into those limitations that are a consequence of the historical situation from the perspective of the interviewed women.

17. This includes those fundamental principles of the capitalist system that are mentioned in the National Constitution: private property and equality before the law.

18. The modification of social patterns that has arisen from the neighbors' meetings, where the people meet to protest but also to think of ways to reverse the situation, is perceived as a challenge and a possibility to find a way out, that "light of hope."

19. AFJPs are the Agencies of Pension Funds, private institutions that were forced to buy bonds of the foreign debt with the money deposited by the people.

REFERENCES

AULAGNIER, Piera.
    1977. *La Violencia de la Interpretación: Del Pictograma al Enunciado.* Buenos Aires, Argentina: Amorrortu Editores.
———. 1984. "Condenado a Investir." *Rev. De Psicoanálisis* XLI.
BECCARIA, Luis and Néstor López.
    1994. "Reconversión Productiva y Empleo en Argentina." *Revista Estudios del Trabajo,* No. 7. Buenos Aires, Argentina.
——— 1996. "Notas sobre el Comportamiento del Trabajo Urbano." In *Sin Trabajo: Las Características del Desempleo y sus Efectos en la Sociedad Argentina,* compiled by Luis Beccaría and Néstor López. Buenos Aires, Argentina: Editorial Biblos.
CORTÉS, Rosalía.
    2000. "Arreglos Institucionales y Trabajo Femenino." In H. (Comp.) *Ley, mercado y discriminación. El Género del trabajo,* compiled by Haydée Birgin. Buenos Aires, Argentina: Editorial Biblos.
FINE, Gary Alan.
    1993. "The Sad Demise, Mysterious Disappearance and Glorious Triumph of Symbolic Interactionism." *Annual Review of Sociology* (19):61-87.
FREUD, Sigmund.
    1920. *Más Allá del Principio de Placer.* Buenos Aires, Argentina: Amorrortu Editores.
———. 1923. *El Yo y el Ello.* Buenos Aires, Argentina: Amorrortu Editores.
———. 1926. *El Malestar en la Cultura,* Vol. XXI. Buenos Aires, Argentina: Amorrortu Editores.
HUBERMAN, A. Michael and Matthew B. Miles.
    1994. "Data Management and Analysis Methods." In *Handbook of Qualitative*

Research, edited by Norman K. Denzin and Yvonna S. Lincoln. Thousand Oaks, California: Sage Publications.

IBÁÑEZ, Jesús.
    1979. *Más Allá de la Sociología: El Grupo de Discusión Técnica y Práctica.* Madrid, Spain: Siglo XXI.

LOZANO, Claudio.
    2002. Speech made at the Members' General Meeting, Frente Nacional Contra la Pobreza (FRENAPO), Buenos Aires, Argentina, 23 February.

MASSERONI, Susana.
    2001. "Ocupación y Género: Las Consecuencias del Ajuste Económico sobre los Sectores Medios del Área Metropolitana de Buenos Aires." Paper presented at the XXIII Congress of the Asociación de Estudios Latinoamericanos, Washington, D.C., 6-8 September.

MORGAN, David L.
    1988. *Focus Groups as Qualitative Research,* vol. 16. London, England: Sage Publications, Qualitative Research Methods Series.

ROMERO, Roberto R.
    1990 *Grupo: Objeto y Teoría,* vol. I. Buenos Aires, Argentina: Lugar Editorial.

ROMERO, Roberto R. and Susana Sauane.
    1995. *Grupo: Objeto y Teoría,* vol. III. Buenos Aires, Argentina: Lugar Editorial.

SAUTU, Ruth.
    1999. "Modelos de Desarrollo, Profesionaliación y Feminización de la Mano de Obra." In *Papeles de Población*, Año 5, No. 20. México D.F.: Centro de Investigación y Estudios Avanzados de la Población.

—— 2000. "'Marketización' y Feminización del Mercado de Trabajo en Buenos Aires: Perspectivas Macro y Microsociales." In *Estudios Demográficos y Urbanos,* Vol. 15, No. 1, México, El Colegio de México.

—— 2001. *La Gente Sabe: Interpretaciones de la Clase Media Acerca de la Libertad, la Igualdad, el Éxito y la Justicia.* Buenos Aires, Argentina: Ediciones Lumiere.

SENNETT, Richard.
    2000. *The Corrosion of Character: The Personal Consequences of Work in the New Capitalism.* New York, New York; London, England: W. W. Norton & Company, Incorporated.

VASILACHIS DE GIALDINO, Irene.
    1992. *Métodos Cualitativos: I. Los Problemas Teórico Epistemológicos.* Buenos Aires, Argentina: Centro Editor de América Latina.

WOLFBERG, E.
    1996. "Psiconeuroinmunoendocrinologia y Campo Psicosomático." *Revista Argentina de Psiquiatría* VII (26): 245-249.

WOMEN AND SURVIVAL STRATEGIES IN POOR URBAN CONTEXTS: A CASE STUDY FROM GUADALAJARA, MEXICO

Rocío Enríquez Rosas[*]

ABSTRACT

Urban poverty in countries like Mexico nowadays shows a new dynamism that calls for an interdisciplinary approach to allow us to sort out the underlying mechanisms that keep many Mexican households in poverty. Based on current theoretical debates about survival strategies and relying on an anthropological approach, this paper analyzes how urban poor households confront their condition. The analysis starts out from a case study, the world of meanings that underlie poverty and the alternatives that the urban poor currently develop, especially urban poor women, who are mothers (whether they be heads of household or not), in order to survive daily.

INTRODUCTION

Urban poverty in countries like Mexico nowadays shows a new dynamism that calls for an interdisciplinary approach to allow us to sort out the underlying mechanisms that keep many Mexican households in poverty. Based on current theoretical debates about survival strategies and relying on an anthropological approach, this paper analyzes how urban poor households confront their condition. The analysis starts out from a case study, the world of meanings that underlie poverty and the alternatives that the urban poor currently develop, especially urban poor women, who are mothers (whether they be heads of household or not), in order to survive daily. This study is situated within the legacy of the economic crisis of 1994 in Mexico. This crisis was the culmination of an increasing deficit in the balance of payments and it is also linked to the devaluation of the peso, so as to arrest inflation and the accompanying massive transfer of capital abroad. Between December 1994 and August 1995 the unemployment rate tripled in Mexico, the GDP declined by 6.2 percent, and the inflation surpassed 53.3 percent (Román, 1998).

The conceptual frame that organizes this study grows out of current discussions about the survival strategies of the urban poor and the approach in regard to the asset-vulnerabilities developed by Moser (1996). To explore the underlying meanings of poverty, the mechanisms behind subsistence means that the urban poor utilize, necessarily implies the study of subjectivity. A central aim of this paper is to examine poor urban households as contradictory spaces where the relationships of support and conflict coexist, and where gender and age play a central role in the distribution of resources and in participation in decision-making (González de la Rocha, 1986; García and de Oliveira, 1994 among others).

---

[*] Instituto Tecnológico y de Estudios Superiores de Occidente (ITESO), Guadalajara, Jalisco, Mexico.

THEORETICAL CONTEXT

The Home: Social Field of Meetings and Nonmeetings

The analysis of the roots of poverty has been a task tackled by various authors and from different theoretical and methodological approaches. The literature on this topic reflects a movement from an understanding of poverty centered on individual shortcomings of the poor, to a perspective that pays attention primarily to the resources and the responses developed by the poor in order to face their condition. The analysis of poor households has resulted in their conceptualization as social arenas where the struggle for individual and collective interests and the relationships of inequality and subordination by gender and age, play a decisive role when making decisions and in the creation of alternatives that promote a greater well being for each of the members of the household. The analysis of survival strategies in poverty environments has resulted in important debates and questions that have led to new theoretical frameworks to understand an extremely complex phenomenon.

In order to understand the behavior of the urban poor, it is necessary to deepen our knowledge of the social spaces where the primary relationships among individuals are created and recreated. I am talking about the domestic spaces and the central role that they play in the struggle for daily survival. Most scholars of the topic have put the romantic and idealized vision of the home as "the shelter" par excellence vis-à-vis life's adversities aside. The family is the privileged social stage to cultivate the deepest and longest lasting affections and hatreds throughout life. Family relationships reflect in their complexity the coexistence of emotions such as hatred and love, guilt and forgiveness, separation and reconciliation, solidarity and competition, and trust and doubt.

To live in a family necessarily involves the daily confrontation with inequality and the open or covert conflict among the different members. It is in this social space where opposed interests converge and, in most cases, where they lead to gains for some and loses for others. The possibilities for negotiation are greatly determined by the hierarchical position and the gender of each of the household members. The decisions about the ways and forms of living in a family cannot be seen then as the product of an equitable and unconditional participation; in the family, each member risks daily emotional or physical inclusion. To study poor households requires uncovering power relations and the subordination that dwell within them and that the dominant ideology legitimizes. The paths that are built and traveled by those households that struggle daily for existence must be analyzed in the light of the inherent contradictions of family life, the economic and social structural changes to which they are exposed throughout their existence.

Various authors have emphasized the need to analytically scrutinize the household. González de la Rocha (1994) argues for the importance of understanding the household as a heterogeneous and diverse unit where access to resources is differentiated and where power relations create situations of conflict and confrontation when making decisions. Selby et al. (1994) point out the importance of adequately differentiating concepts such as family, household, and domestic unit. For these authors, the family is a cultural category, whereas the domestic unit is an analytical category. The domestic unit is then understood as a group of individuals who dwell together and share consumption and guarantee their material reproduction from a common financial pool to which all must contribute. In this sense, the domestic unit is normally based on a family but does not make it up as such (1994:95). Roberts (1995), as well as Selby et al. (1994), also comments on the importance of differentiating terms such as household and family. The household is then the basic dwelling-together unit, whereas the term family refers to a complex network of normative relationships.

For González de la Rocha (1999a), the analysis of survival strategies in poverty and exclusion contexts implies that households need to be seen as mediating between the individual and the greater social and economic structures. The household is the stage where decisions are made and actions are implemented according to changes in the labor market and the general social conditions. Wolf (1994) identifies the complexity of the analytical category "home" and notices the importance of understanding it as a stage where consensus does not necessarily exist behind each decision made and where the altruistic participation of each of the members is not guaranteed either. Power dynamics, coercion, and rebellion are intimately involved in each of the decisions made inside the household. For this author, the domestic space is the obvious arena to begin the analysis of the effects of broader economic changes; however, this analysis must go beyond the domestic sphere and point out the ways in which these domestic transformations affect greater social and economic structures.

Survival Strategies and Vulnerability of Poor Households: Conceptual Scopes and Limits

For authors like Moser (1996), González de la Rocha (1994, 1999a), Kaztman and Filgueira (1999), Zaffaroni (1999), and Wolf (1994), among others, the individuals, the households, and the communities are not passive in the way they face economic crises. They develop a series of strategies and tactics that are intended to attenuate the effects of the economic crises and accompanying deterioration in living conditions. The concept of survival strategies tries to put aside structuralist approaches that ignore human agency and the rationality of the individual. Current views are centered on the analysis of resources and the potential that the poor have for accessing the structure of opportunities. From this vintage point, an attempt is also made to pay attention to the diverse structural elements that determine and restrict the possibilities of poor households to confront adversity. In this sense, the conflict of interests and the relationships of inequality and subordination that are produced within the households are also emphasized.

Selby et al. (1994) criticize the concept of survival strategies and their use in the analysis of poor Mexican households, and underline the importance of being able to distinguish between the colloquial use of the concept of strategic survival and its analytical approach. Morgan (in González de la Rocha 1994) suggests three basic conditions for the analysis of survival strategies in poor urban households: the existence of resources, the material as well as immaterial nature of these resources and the power relationships involved in the management of these resources. Kaztman and Filgueira (1999) differentiate between survival strategies, social mobility, and integration strategies. The former refer to short-term responses that urban poor households develop to deal with poverty, where social capital plays a fundamental role. The latter reflects the presence of long-term plans that are intended to invest in human capital assets that allow access to the structure of opportunities in society. Finally, for González de la Rocha (1994), the concept of survival strategies has made it possible to build alternative explanations to social change putting aside the structuralist paradigm. In this sense, in spite of the forces that restrict and limit the making of decisions inside the households, individuals have the capacity to act. The author points out that it is precisely in poor contexts where individuals look for survival and this is achieved in part through networks of mutual help and reciprocal exchange of the poor.

The cumulative and progressive deterioration of the living conditions of many groups around the world and the criticisms of the benefits and limitations of the concept of *survival strategies* have resulted in the emergence of new approaches to the understanding the structures that underlie poverty. Once again, the emphasis is oriented towards the analysis of resources and existing assets in the households and the way in which they interact in order to generate alternatives to combat poverty. Moser (1996) includes the concept of vulnerability in her analysis about poverty and inequality in four communities located in different places of the world that have faced significant changes in their economy and standard of living in recent years. Vulnerability is understood as the insecurity in the levels of well being of the individuals, the households or the communities vis-à-vis the changes in the environment. The concept of vulnerability implies the understanding of poverty as a process instead of a static condition. Like González de la Rocha (1994), Moser emphasizes the importance of analyzing the household according to their stage in the domestic cycle and the conditions of inequality and subordination with regard to gender and age among the members that compose the domestic group. Moser also notices the fundamental role that social support and reciprocal exchange networks play when facing economic crisis and change.

Kaztman and Filgueira (1999) include the central concepts of Moser (1996) in a study that links the structures of opportunities in Uruguayan society and the ability of households to develop and mobilize assets in order to take advantage of those opportunities. The authors start from two premises that strengthen Moser's explanation (1996) and clarify, for its part, the existing relationship between the structure of opportunities and the consequent behavior of the households. The authors also note the need to link the specific conditions in the households and the macro characteristics that determine the access possibilities to the opportunity structures. They define three factors that shape the structure of opportunities: the role the market plays, the weakening of institutions (like the family and the community), and the state (which in recent years has decreased its protection and social security functions). Various authors, such as Bazán (1998), González de la Rocha (1999b), and Estrada (1999) have observed the lessening of the family and neighborhood networks in the pursuit of social integration and survival. An attempt has been made to delegate to the market, and to society in general, the improvement of living conditions and well being. Social policies have lost, in many cases, their universal scope and have been reduced to the design of focused policies that have not been able to respond to the phenomenon of downward social mobility that prevails in various regions of the world.

The approaches described reflect the authors' concerns with finding a conceptual framework that has enough analytical capacity to critically support the methodologies used in the evaluation, characterization, and measurement of poverty. The contributions show a convergent conclusion instead of a divergent one. In this sense, the approach of survival strategies is enhanced and enriched by new proposals that take, as a point of departure, the analysis of the factors that affect a greater or lesser vulnerability of the households. There are, however, significant differences that show the importance of recognizing those strategies that respond to the daily struggle of living in poverty and those strategies that stem from major economic, social, and political changes that involve greater emphasis in the survival mechanisms previously used or the development of new ways of acting.

In sum, the most important findings of Moser (1996), Roberts (1995), González de la Rocha (1999a), Kaztman and Filgueira (1999), Zaffaroni (1999), and Selby et al. (1994); among others, point out the responses to poverty that prevail in poor households:

- For Moser (1996), work is the most important response that poor households use to confront their situation, which involves the participation of new members of the domestic unit in the labor market, mostly women and, secondly, children. González de la Rocha (1999a) emphasizes that in the current manifestation of poverty, work is not just another resource the poor count on but also the most important "resource" to survival. The wages obtained in the labor market cannot be replaced by the strategies of self-supply and subsistence production. With regard to the increase in female work as a survival strategy used by the majority of poor households, Chant (1996)—like González de la Rocha (1994), Roberts (1995), and Moser (1996)—warns of the implications that this activity has for the living conditions of many women. Double or triple workdays have intensified and women's contributions are not matched in many cases by a greater economic participation by the men. Far from that, many women currently live in situations of domestic violence as a consequence of their economic participation for the survival of the domestic group.

- Esteinou (1994), as well as Moser (1996) and Kaztman and Filgueira (1999), observes the weakening of the welfare state and the decrease in economic and social supports experienced in recent years and points out that it is precisely when women significantly increase their economic participation vis-à-vis the decay of living conditions, that the welfare state reduces its functions and supports for the households, affecting mostly those who are socially and economically disadvantaged. Chiarello (1994) and Mingione (1994) focus on women's participation in the informal economy as a survival strategy in the poor sectors of society. However, while the first author sheds a positive light on the benefits of the informal economy, the second author warns about the implications, the social costs, and the disadvantages of the "irregular" work in poverty contexts.

- Lodging, in its many variations, is one of the strategies that the poor use more intensely when the economic situation becomes more critical and uncertain. Moser (1996) and Chant (1996) analyze in detail the various ways in which housing is used. Most transactions related to housing, whether leased, borrowed, granted, shared, enhanced, redistributed, or partially sold imply informal negotiations established by the poor in their immediate environments—whether it be with family or with neighbors. It allows them resources to maintain and improve their living conditions. The authors also point out the importance of designing a legal framework to simplify and back this kind of survival mechanism that the poor use.

- Changes in the family structure are another strategy used by the impoverished households. Moser (1996) points out that the changes in the structure of the households, in order to strengthen the support networks, are the result of the existing conditions of vulnerability and also are a strategy to reduce such vulnerability. The author emphasizes the response of the households in their composition and function vis-à-vis greater economic changes to which they are exposed. She questions, in a way similar to González de la Rocha (1999c) and Chant (1988, 1997), the causal relationship between households headed by females and poverty. Moser (1996), in contrast to Selby et al. (1994), points out that at present large units are facing conditions of greater vulnerability due to the increase in the number of dependents and the low total income that the domestic group obtains. Various authors like González de la Rocha (1994), Roberts (1995), Zaffaroni (1999), and Kaztman and Filgueira (1999) point out the importance of analyzing the role of the domestic cycle in the kind of responses households develop to confront poverty.

- Finally, various authors like Zaffaroni (1999), González de la Rocha (1999b), Moser (1996), Kaztman and Filgueira (1999), and Roberts (1995) question the capacity and efficacy of social networks to face adversity. The low salaries, unemployment, and unsteady employment erode the possibilities that the poor can maintain their membership and activity in reciprocal exchanges and mutual-help networks. In the same way, the erosion of social relationships due to insecurity, corruption, and mistrust—which large sectors of the population experience daily—have significantly lessened the possibilities for reciprocity among individuals and households.

To understand the poor as social actors who actively construct various strategies to face adversity is, without doubt, an important step to combat poverty. The inclusion of subjectivity analysis in the complex poverty phenomenon is a key factor that can get us closer to the social-cultural dimension of what it means, at present, to be poor. In the same way, to understand the household as a contradiction-filled stage where conflict, inequality, and solidarity coexist, is an important step that allows us to demonstrate the influence that family relations have in the expansion or reduction of poverty.

METHODS AND DATA

With the aim of learning the meaning the urban poor give to poverty and how they face it, sixty mothers who reside in an irregular neighborhood in the outskirts of the Guadalajara metropolitan area, Mexico were interviewed using a semi-structured interview schedule.[1] In-depth interviews were also carried out to understand the ways in which their families develop alternatives to guarantee their survival. A third source of data for this study was the field diary. In order to process the information from the interviews, categories were inductively developed; in other words, each of the responses given to the questions were separated as minimal units of analysis and later categorized according to the methodological guidelines that González (1998) proposed for qualitative data analysis. The material, from the in-depth interviews and the field diary, was codified and analyzed by using ethnography.

Ten of the women were between 19 and 25 years; 33, between 26 and 45 years; 13, between 46 and 65 years; and four women were over 65 years of age. With regard to formal education, 18.33 percent of the women reported not having had any education (mainly those found in the most advanced stages of the life cycle); 45 percent had completed some grade of elementary school (27 cases), and 33 percent had completed some grade of middle school (20 cases). Finally, there were 2 women (3.3 percent) who had completed some secondary grade. Forty three percent of the women were "housewives" and the rest, 57 percent, perform mostly irregular jobs that were classified as primary or secondary. A primary job means all activity is performed during working days for close to 8 hours per day, with some regularity of schedules and income (for instance: domestic employees, traders, unskilled laborers, workers, children's nurses, and so on). The average monthly income in these jobs was 1,100.00 pesos (110 dollars). Secondary work refers to those activities that generate an income but that are performed in an independent way, during shorter times and more irregularly, and generally performed in one's home. These activities are perceived by the women as "financial help" for the household and usually consist of activities such as selling used clothing, washing and ironing someone else's clothes, selling at a corner store, or working as a seamstress at home. The average monthly income for these types of activities was 300.00 (30 dollars) per month. It is noteworthy that a significant number of women perform not only work considered as primary but also one or several secondary activities.

CONTEXT OF THE STUDY

The research was carried out in the irregular urban development of Las Margaritas[2] in the state of Jalisco, with a population of 5,991,176 (the fourth largest of Mexican states). Thirty-six percent of the population lives in rural areas with less than 5,000 inhabitants while 55 percent of the economically active population (EAP) receives salaries below the poverty line[3] with an economic dependency factor of 2.3. The underemployment currently reaches 16.1 percent of the EAP of the state while unemployment is calculated at 2.7 percent. Regarding education, 13.5 percent of the children and adolescents do not know how to read or write, a population that in a near future will have serious difficulties fitting into the productive sector. With regard to health, 54 percent of the population does not have social security and most of the medical units with third-level services are concentrated in the Guadalajara metropolitan area. The percentage of school age children who are undernourished reaches 12.3 percent. The state of Jalisco currently has 548 social organizations (nongovernmental organizations) that represent an important human and social potential for developing alternatives and proposals to promote better living conditions for the population with greater needs (Pozos and Barba 1999).

The central urban region of Jalisco includes the municipalities of Guadalajara, Tlaquepaque, Tonala, and Zapopan. Fifty-four percent of the state's population is concentrated within this territorial space, yet this region has fewer levels of extreme poverty than the state as a whole (13.4 percent and 17.9 percent respectively). The percentage of EAP in poverty, however, is greater than in the state as a whole (41.2 percent and 37.1 percent respectively). These data reflect an important contrast: while the intensity of poverty is greater in rural areas, the concentration of the poor is greater in the central urban region (Pozos and Barba 1999).

The urban development under study is the neighborhood "Las Margaritas," located in the municipality of Tlatepaque and populated mostly during the year 1995. Currently it has no public services and residents have built their own houses. The neighborhood is located on the outskirts of the Guadalajara metropolitan region and has a population of 600 families. To get to know the characteristics of the households in this neighborhood, a formal sample of 60 households was selected, which corresponds to 10 percent of the total households of this population. The results show that the total average of members per households is 5.45. Seventy percent of the households are nuclear units and the remaining 30 percent are extended units. With regard to the stage in the domestic cycle (González de la Rocha 1986), 40 percent of the households are in expansion, 27 percent in consolidation, and 33 percent in the stage of dispersion. In this sample there were eleven households headed by women, which represents 18.33 percent of the households (a percentage slightly above the one reported for the nation) leaving a total of 41 households headed by men (81.67 percent). However, analysis of female-headed households showed 14 cases, or 23.3 percent, where the partner was present but the woman financially supported the family.

WOMEN EXPLAIN POVERTY

Of the sixty women interviewed, 90 percent stated that there is currently an economic crisis in Mexico. The strategies used by the women and their families to face this crisis are presented in Table 1. The data indicate that at least 50 percent of the responses mention reducing expenses "to adjust to what is available" in order to survive daily. The evidence shows an important tendency to look for the last resources inside the household to deal with poverty. Therefore, it is not about the search for strategies oriented to alternatives outside of the household but to adjustments inside the domestic group that allow them to survive with the "minimum required" through alternatives like: "eat once a day" or "eat what is cheaper." This situation of hunger and multiple shortages results in important consequences inside the domestic groups: the relationships of power and inequality between the genders and generations are made worse; the conflict regarding the distribution of food daily affects the lives of many of these households; and the possibilities to continue attending school are limited for many women and men as they are forced to abandon their formal instruction because the domestic group is

Table 1.
Strategies to Face the Crisis

What have you and your family done to face the crisis?	Number of responses	Percentage
1. The expenses have been reduced, tightened	49	51.04
2. The woman started working	21	21.87
3. One (or more) of the children started working	9	9.37
4. The man gives more for the expenses	8	8.33
5. The man took an extra job	5	5.20
6. Request "charity" (alms)	3	3.12
7. Grow a large family	1	1.04
Total responses	96	100.00

unable to cover the necessary minimal expenses.

The second most-used strategy by households facing poverty is that the woman starts working and later the sons follow. The greater contributions of the men (family heads) as well as their extra employment, received lower percentages in the surveys. The evidence shows that mostly the women, through adjustments they make in the households' resources and their participation in the labor market, are the ones who face the current crisis in a decisive manner. This situation has produced extreme conditions in the lives of many households and many women: they face work overload, stress due to the lack of food for their children, the need to look for income outside the home, the concern about the children when they (mothers) go to work, fatigue and stress accumulated day after day, and tensions with the partner when the woman earns income.

After asking about the general crisis in Mexico and the strategies used to face this situation, each woman was asked whether she thought she lived in poverty. We found that 58.33 percent (35 women) consider that they live in poverty. This response reflects an interesting psychological phenomenon. When an individual is asked about his or her living situation, they generally compare themselves with those who surround them daily and use this contrast to evaluate their own situation. Many women commented that they do not live in poverty because they find themselves in better conditions than other families who live in the same area. Some made an important difference between "misery" and "poverty"; misery being an extreme condition in which one does not have access "even to a grain of salt." Poverty, in contrast, involves living with many shortages but with access to food, even when the diet is based on beans and tortillas. Behind this rationality there is a key reasoning: "hunger." It is not a matter of having adequate housing or clothes and shoes, much less the necessary resources to take care of health; rather, it is a question of obtaining food to be able to survive.

To better understand this point, we examined the way in which women define and give meaning to poverty. The question posed was: "*Tell me what is*

Table 2.
Meanings of Poverty

Main Categories	Frequency of responses
1. Hunger	40
2. To be in financial straits	35
3. Housing and urban development deficiencies	33

poverty for you?" A total of 157 responses were obtained and they were grouped in nine categories. The three more common categories that convey current perceptions of poverty in the group studied are presented in Table 2.

The category *hunger* includes the greatest number of responses (forty). Some examples are: "not to have something to eat," "we eat only once a day," "not have money to purchase tortillas nor beans," "not to be certain about what the children will eat." These responses convey the idea of poverty in terms of the "hunger" that is suffered daily in the households. The way in which the women compose their phrases shows the concern for food in the daily events. It is not a concern about what will be consumed beyond today, instead it is worrying about the "here and now" to ensure food, mainly for the children. It is also important to notice the positions from which the women speak with regard to their conception of poverty. Many of them do so in first person and give examples of specific situations: "to see that my children are hungry and not to have something to give them." Other women explain it in the second person and distance themselves from what they state: "one who has her small children and one does not have what is necessary to give them to eat." Still other women, in fewer proportions, provide their explanations in function of an "exclusive I" that separates and differentiates them from the concept of poverty that they describe: "the people who don't have not even a kilo of beans to eat." These constructions allow us to understand the women's point of view with regard to their ideas about poverty. They also confirm that the women visualize the problem of poverty mostly as a problem of hunger, of dissatisfaction with the most important basic need. This issue demonstrates the type of poverty that currently threatens the lives of many Mexican households in urban areas.

The problem of hunger is experienced in different ways inside the poor domestic groups. Gender and age play a central role in the ways that resources are distributed. Questions—such as who eats what, who does not eat what, what portion is for each one, how many times per day will someone eat—elicit answers that untangle domestic behaviors and show them in the light of their contradictions, differences, and power relations. Thus, it is not enough to understand what the consumption pattern of a domestic unit is; it is necessary to figure out the reasoning that creates the differentiated distribution of resources. This point can only be examined using an ethnographic perspective that centers on social-cultural structures based on gender, age, and hierarchy that then sheds light on unfair distribution of food.

Various authors like Wolf (1994), González de la Rocha (1999a), and Selby et al. (1994)—among others—have pointed out the importance of understanding the household as a heterogeneous social stage in which, day in and day out, each of its members occupies a position of greater or lesser privilege in the distribution of the resources. The ethnographic work and analysis of the interviews in this study, unveil the small transformations that are developed in poor domestic groups to lessen the unfair distribution of the resources. The narratives of the women show small differences in how they manage their resources and a clear concern for the children to be fed with the resources that the household is able to get.

Juana, a fifty-eight year old study participant who did not finish elementary school, commented on the way in which the food was distributed in her parents' household when she was small. She was the oldest daughter and that placed her in a position of lesser access to food:

> [M]y mother cooked beans with broth and everything, then there was just enough to give to all the children and to my dad; and she and I would stay . . . because there was not enough for us . . . then what my mother would do was to grind a red pepper and she would cook it with onions and that is what she and I would eat with tortilla, when there was, when there wasn't, well it is not shameful to say it, I would go to the houses to ask for tortillas.

Maricela, who is 38 years old and also did not finish elementary school, remembered a Sunday from her childhood. In that scene, she sketched the interplay between the tortilla and a portion of meat as well as her mother's strategies to balance the greater power of the father to access food:

> [I]t was classic, on Sundays they used to purchase for us a small piece of meat and hot tortillas, there you'd see us all passing the small piece of meat to the other tortilla, our breakfast on Sundays was delicious...[B]ut my dad was that kind of man who, when it was time to eat, used to buy his soft drink but not for others. Then I remember that my mother would purchase a Pepsi, one of those small ones that there used to be, and would give to all of us, well, how much would she give us? From one Pepsi for all, well then all of us had a party, no?

Celina, a twenty-five year old with a middle school education, married, and in a household in the expansion stage, showed the changes that took place in her original family as a result of her parents' separation. Later she (C) pointed out to the interviewer (E) the strategies that she developed to distribute food in her own household:

> E: In the past the father received food and cahir before the other members of the family, now, how is it in your own household?
>
> C: Well now, already here it is for all, now my mother...well it is already equal, she says: "here I set aside for all, I store the food for the one who has not arrived yet," previously for instance, my mom used to set aside food for his [her dad] arrival, as they say "the best," and if my sister arrived or whoever, what remained, but not now, now since she starts serving, at once she sets aside for all, she does not discriminate against anyone.
> And now that I am married, I don't think "oh, for Jose!" [her partner], no! If I am going to do something, I try to buy something for all, so that we receive the same, the same with my sister who sometimes comes to stay with us. I don't like to discriminate against her, not even because they are visiting I say: "oh, this is for Jose!" not. As if this is normal.

In the young households, the mothers have an explicit desire to feed their children adequately. However, to gain more ground here also involves important negotiations with the partner and with those family members of the household who become income earners. Having access to income implies a position of power within the domestic group. Micaela's story illustrates this point: Micaela and her family arrived in the "Las Margaritas" neighborhood seven years ago. They came from the northern part of the country and have gone through difficult financial situations. Micaela and her husband currently have eight children living at home, four more have already settled independently. Some of her children are adolescents and others are kids. For Micaela the most serious and worrisome problem is that oftentimes she does not have food to give to her children. Her husband is a mason helper and earns very little, about 200 (20 dollars) per week, two of her daughters work as assistants to a street food vendor and sometimes they give her money and sometimes they do not contribute. When they do, one of them gives 50 (5 dollars) per week and the other gives 100 (10 dollars) per week. Micaela explains:

> If they [the daughters who work] want to give me money, well that's fine, I don't ask them to, only if they want to. And then one of the daughters who gives me money becomes too demanding, she tells me: "Mom, I already gave you money, cook well for me, show through the food that I am contributing ... no more beans only." And I tell her that I don't have enough, that we are many and that how can she expect to eat well for a whole week with 50, that that would not be enough, not even for one person, the way she wants it.

Determining the paths food travels in reaching the households, the hands that touch it, and the mouths that eat it, as well as the eyes that only look at it, is a topic that deserves more attention. Through the paths that food travels and the hollow tracks it leaves, we can glean the power relationships inside the domestic unit.

The next most frequently mentioned category was *to be in financial straits*. This category had a total of thirty-five responses; most of them refering to the lack of resources in general: "to want things and not to be able to have them," "not to have what is necessary to live," "if we buy something, we don't buy something else." This category shows a group of responses based on a comparison with those who have more, with those who have enough money, with those who have access to goods. It is a discourse that starts out from exclusion and from the voices of those who are excluded. It is also the discourse of the mothers worried once again about the impossibility of satisfying the basic needs of their children as well as the demands that the latter make as a result of what other children have and do not have.

The third category, *housing deficiencies and urban development*, obtained a total of thirty-three responses, which were subdivided in four groups: (a) those that define poverty around the lack of a place to live (e.g., "that one does not have a roof over one's head"), (b) those that emphasize the situation of partially built dwellings (such as, "to have a house that has not been completed"), (c) those that refer to the house's furnishings (like, "poverty in the things that are basic needs like the bathroom"), and (d) those that refer to the absence of public services (such as, "we don't have electricity and the water has to be purchased from the water suppliers—*pipas de agua*").

Understanding poverty involves the study of subjectivities, of the meanings that the social actors attach to their living conditions. Frameworks to try to understand survival strategies of the poor (Moser 1996; Selby et al. 1994; Kaztman and Filgueira 1999) also require exploring the world of meanings that the poor develop regarding their living conditions. After all, it is the poor who write the script of their survival every day.

Poverty is a diverse and complex phenomenon, as Maricela points out in her narratives of the meaning of being poor in a context of exclusion, where the importance accorded to the image and the access to material resources make a difference and often are valued more than human beings. In a society where "money is what makes the world go around," dignity and respect seem to be prohibited. Relations of solidarity are threatened even among those who have achieved some upward social mobility. In this sense, as Kaztman and Filgueira (1999) propose, it is not enough that the poor be able to fit more or less successfully in the structure of opportunities. It is also a matter of understanding the world of meanings that washes over the social relationships and that produce differences in the perception of others according to what they posses or the power that they are capable of exercising in the society. Mariluz, who is 39 years old, studied to become a teacher but now works cleaning offices. She commented:

> [W]hen I was a child, I did not have the idea that I now have, truly, because when one is a child one does not care at all about having, doing, no, just to live and be comfortable and my mother cooked a pot of beans with broth and with a peso of cheese "that was delicious," wasn't it? And even now when I am an adult and I remember that, I say: "Gee . . . how poor we were, a pot of tea, always a pot of tea, always, always . . . not milk." That is why I now try to feed my children with more than just beans . . . and the way they see me, that is how they treat me, they no longer treat you considering what one feels or for the values that one might have, if you go looking elegant to a bar, with good clothes and all that, immediately people run to greet you: "Oh yes, how are you? Who invited you? Come in, have a seat." Immediately they offer you a chair . . . and if they see you like this with clothes, with poor clothes, with old shoes . . . "What did you want, what, what, what do you want lady?" No, it is not the same treatment that they give to a person who is educated and fine, it is not the same treatment anywhere. I have experienced that also and I have gone through that in my children's school. When my son was going to graduate from high school, he told me, "You know what mom, buy good clothes and good shoes and color your hair, because when they see you coming in, they are going to say 'Look, his mom did not attend, there comes Efren's grandmother,'" I felt very much hurt but I did it, I colored my hair, dressed myself in the best way that I could, I bought shoes, I

bought a new dress and I showed up with a mask to his party, like what I was not because I did not feel comfortable that way, because I am not that way. That is why, then, immediately, "It is my mom, it is my mom, it is my mom" like one, like one jewel that is being shown off, "Look, she is my mother, she is my mother." "Oh, Mrs., I am so pleased to meet you" even when they do not feel that way.

With regard to the question about the causes of poverty, the 121 responses received were grouped into seven categories. Table 3 contains the responses that appeared with the highest frequencies.

Table 3.
Causes of Poverty

Main Categories	Frequency of responses
1. Problems related to work	33
2. Attitudes related to poverty	30
3. To be in financial straits	26
4. Lack of help from friends and relatives	16

Work had the highest frequency of responses. The main cause of poverty, from the point of view of the study participants, is centered around the difficulties that they and their families face daily to contribute to the support of the household. In their responses we can observe the obstacles that women need to overcome in order to get a job. Many of them have to do with the disjunctive involved in working and caring for the children, which is aggravated by the rigidity of working hours of the jobs that they try to get. The words of the women also point to the situation which various households face, where the man or the woman is disabled and cannot get a job. Finally, the women emphasized how few job opportunities were available to them and the members of their domestic groups. This confirms the importance of having a job in the struggle to survive (Moser 1996; González de la Rocha 1999b; Chant 1996). In this sense, it is impossible to continue to ask that reciprocal exchange networks perform a survival function that can only be guaranteed through employment and a salary (González de la Rocha 1999c). Some women commented: "I can't start working because I don't have someone to leave my children with, my mom lives very far," "I can't find a job," "Without a job one is poor."

The second largest category of responses referred to *attitudes regarding poverty*. In this category there was a series of attributes that the women listed, where the cause of poverty is internal. Here they indicate a "place of inner control" that implies attributing to oneself the causes of poverty that is experienced or that others, in poverty conditions, are living. This information is relevant because it allows us to examine subjective readings that configure and determine the behavior of the individuals with regard to the shortages they face. Moreover, this type of interpretation about poverty—such as, "the poor are lazy and they do not try to improve"—reflects an ideology that is present in many sectors of society.

The analysis of the attitudes about poverty deserves special attention. The attitudes are built from three basic elements: the cognitive (the beliefs), the affective (the emotions), and the behavioral (the consequent manner of proceeding). When an individual expresses or backs an attitude that is far from liberating, she limits her agency and her possibilities for transformation are weakened. Thus, even though the locus of control is internal (meaning the causes of the conditions faced lie within oneself), the possibilities for change are few because the perception is based on a negative reading that limits the individual. We know that poverty is a phenomenon embedded in the history of broader structural conditions in society and that it is multidimensional—that is, greater than the individual or the abilities and limitations of the family. However, the analysis of the subjective perception of the phenomenon plays a transcendental role in the construction of transforming solutions. Some women commented: "Poverty is pure laziness," "We don't know how to fight for what we want," "We have been poor all life long."

To be in financial straits comes next. In this category the women describe poverty as a lack of resources to satisfy basic daily needs. Poverty is perceived as a changing phenomenon that gets worse as time passes. The resources that were previously available are no longer enough and several women described the high cost of basic items. Moreover, some of the women's words allow us to examine, up close, the emotional face of what is involved when someone is living in poverty. The shame of having to accept, before others, that one does not have resources and the sadness of having to ask for help, reflect an important emotional uneasiness. It is interesting to observe how both emotions are built from a reading of reality that involves the social actor and her or his relationship with others. In this sense, the shame and the sadness are socially built emotions that acquire a specific meaning and sense in the social group under study. In the words of some of the women: "Money does not stretch," "The shame of admitting that one does not have...," "I feel very sad about not having and having to get."

Lack of help from relatives and friends shows the role played by the absence or the weakening of the social and mutual-support networks in the deterioration of living conditions. The women speak of the importance of the lack of help from their partners for supporting the household. The explicit reference that several women made about their partners' alcohol or drug consumption related to the lack of help in supporting the household. The lack of help among neighbors is also linked to the lack of resources that prevails in most of the families of the area. Lastly, they refer to the current difficulty of counting on their own families to face the problems inherent to poverty: "I don't count on help from my husband as it should be," "one has to be a father and a mother," "to have vices," "one's family can't help out."

Several authors have discussed how networks of social exchange and mutual help have weakened. Zaffaroni (1999), Kaztman and Filgueira (1999),

González de la Rocha (1999a), Moser (1996), and Roberts (1995), among others, warn about deteriorating networks of support and the impact that this has on the possibilities for survival. In the specific case of the urban poor, the very conditions of the settlements where they live significantly hinder the possibilities of tapping their informal networks. The cost of urban transportation, the distance of the places of residence, the absence of a pattern of urban mobility, the lack of facilities for telephone communications as well as their high cost, all produce situations of social isolation.

With regard to the question about the consequences of poverty, a total of 140 responses were received and the main categories are listed in Table 4.

Table 4.
Consequences of Poverty

Main Categories	Frequency of responses
1. Undernourishment	26
2. The lack of resources in general	24
3. Emotional uneasiness	20
4. Family disintegration	16

Deficient nutrition is the consequence of poverty that worries women the most, especially in regard to the children: "Every time, there is less to eat...the children grow very thin, weak, anemic and they get sick." "If I work, I leave them alone, if I don't work...what will my children eat?" Once again, hunger appears to be the first face of poverty. The lack of public services, health care services, and a dignified dwelling, are consequences of poverty that are relegated to the background when hunger is experienced daily. This point emphasizes an important qualitative difference in regard to studies about urban poverty conducted in settlements similar to "Las Margaritas" at the beginning of the 1990s in the Guadalajara metropolitan area. In a study conducted by Enríquez, Urzúa, Romero, and Torres (1992), the main need that arose among the urban poor was to have public services for the neighborhood as well as green areas and more social security coverage. Eight years later, the discourse of poverty shows an abrupt descent of the living standards and, above all, makes clear that hunger is the main need.

The consequences due to *a lack of resources in general* concentrated an important number of responses. Women emphasized the implications of the lack of resources on their children's well being: "that every day things are more expensive and we don't have enough," "feel unsatisfied because one does not give to the children what they want." Sadness, despair, anger, discouragement, and "to feel thrown to the trash can" are some of the emotions (*emotional uneasiness*) with which the women point out the effects that the daily situation of poverty produces in themselves and their families. This hidden face of poverty shows the suffering experienced day after day by many families that do not have the necessary minimum to meet their needs. To understand poverty necessarily implies having a deep dialogue between that inner world, where the emotions are re-created, and that external world where the material conditions of life become evident. Poverty deeply damages the self-esteem of the human being and promotes hopeless and discouragement: "one feels thrown to the trash can," "when there isn't, . . . I feel depressed and I feel sad and desperate."

Several women mentioned *the disintegration of the family* as an important consequence of poor living conditions. This point seems central because it reflects once more the effects that neediness in multiple areas have on family relationships. Women talk first about addiction and alcohol consumption problems. They also mention the existing friction within the families and the possible breakdown of relationships. In their words: "the disintegration of the family because then the man leaves due to so many problems," and "a separation decision."

Later we inquired about *what people can do to get out of their situation*

Table 5.
Alternatives to Get Out of Poverty

Main Categories	Frequency of responses
1. Work	39
2. Attitudes to overcome poverty	20
3. Give and receive help to/from others	19
4. Money and resource administration	14

of poverty. A total of 107 responses were received and classified into six groups. The central categories by frequency of responses are listed in Table 5.

Work, in agreement with what Moser (1996) found, rises as the fundamental strategy to combat poverty. It is the main alternative for fighting against the lack of resources. The women talked first about the need to continue working and even increase their workloads: "to work as much as one can." In a subcategory, the women explained the need to look for work: "to look for one's job, even as a *gata* (maid)." Finally, the women emphasized the possibility of looking for a job that can be performed at their home or at least nearby. They commented, "for example, that they would bring me candy to prepare at home."

The attitudes to get out of poverty were the second topic the women approached. In their narrative we see two conflicting positions: on the one hand are those women who think that "no matter what they do" there is no possibility of getting out of poverty and, on the other hand, there are those women who show optimism and willingness to find solutions. In the first group, we find the discourse of hopelessness and accumulated impotence through the years and multiple efforts that yield no results. This group, according to Kaztman and Filgueira (1999), is vulnerable to marginality. It refers to families that have experienced a sharp and continuous deterioration in their material and social conditions as a result of poverty. Their discourse rises from the daily deficiencies and from a feeling of loss of control over the demands and requirements of daily life: "I can not do anything, even if I work day and night, one does not get out of the same."

In the second group, responses concentrate around a category that

Kaztman and Filgueira (1999) denominated as vulnerable to poverty. This refers to families who have bet their chances of survival in keeping employment "at all costs" and in the opportunity of investing in human capital for the better well being of future generations. Some of the women commented: "to work as much as one can," "to prepare the children so that they can have a better life than us."

With regard to *giving and receiving help from others,* the women approached three levels of support and exchange: the community, the family, and the relationship with the partner: "to help each other (solidarity in the community)," "help from the children," "that the woman helps her partner to earn money." Another alternative that they mentioned was the adequate *administration of the money and the resources in the household,* "to try to stretch the money."

The story of Mariluz shows the multiple strategies that poor urban households carry out to obtain the necessary resources for their daily subsistence as well as the emotional and physical costs that these decisions imply. The accurate administration of the household income, the financial participation of Mariluz (as a worker and by washing and ironing for others), the possibility of purchasing on credit at the (neighborhood) store with the certainty of being able to pay every week, the participation in raffles at her husband's work, among other strategies, have allowed this domestic unit to keep the children in school. However, the costs have been high and Mariluz lives stressful situations daily with her partner, who suggests she change the family diet to the basic consumption of beans. "To go out trotting," as Mariluz explains the daily search for her family's well being, has exhausted her. In this sense, the increase in female work as a survival strategy of the urban poor has had high costs (Chant 1996; Roberts 1995; Moser 1996; among others) that do not necessarily guarantee better living conditions. In Mariluz's words:

> [W]e manage the money. Look, he gives me two hundred pesos per week, I am earning one hundred ninety per week also, for four days that I go [cleaning offices], then well that's it, in the store they keep track of what I use, if I lack something because the money is not enough for me, what my husband gives me is not enough for me, then, ah, because I have to give him food to take for lunch and then, ah, well the milk that . . . a heap of, a heap of expenses and then the market, one hundred pesos go away in the market and I still have one hundred and there for the whole week to be stretching, then there in the store they take note and I, later, when they pay me I pay, I pay with my own, with my own I pay and then once again, another week . . . and he has a raffle and is contributing and when they pay him, he brings the mason and thus we have, ah, . . . well each person, to go out for the money, so that it be stretched well more than everything indeed . . . and then sometimes he [her partner] tells me: "Well no it has to be enough, make ends meet with what I give you" and I tell him: "Well yes, if it were you and me but it is a world of people" and then he says: "Well cook beans and give that to your children, it is because you are unwilling to give them just beans"

and I don't do that, I am not that way, I don't want them to be undernourished or something and even then we are almost improvising, indeed, it is not enough.

Finally, we asked the women what recommendations they could offer to deal with the current situation of poverty (to the government, to institutions, to neighbors, and to citizens in general). We obtained 102 responses and grouped them in two categories (see Table 6).

Table 6.
Recommendations

Main Categories	Frequency of responses
1. Government	68
2. Help among relatives, neighbors and friends	34
Total	102

Government received sixty-eight responses that were divided into subcategories according to the type of recommendation stated. In the first place, the women requested help from the government (thirty) in general, and emphasized above all their desire to be taken into account and to be treated in a humane way. Their words are a call to the government to "put itself in the shoes" of those who live daily in poverty. In the second subcategory, the women talked about work and requested that government create employment (twenty-three responses). The women's words unveil a series of alternatives that they formulate around employment, especially those that promote joint projects in which the government helps with money and credit. They also request more work flexibility as well as better wages. The women talked about children's work and justified it as a preventive measure to keep the children from using drugs or breaking the law. In this same subcategory, the women talked specifically about their situation and the conditions that they need in order to be able to work. They stated the importance of creating jobs with flexible hours and, above all, receiving support through work in their homes. The women know very well what they need and to what degree the government should be able to respond to these requests. It would be possible, then, to progress in a coordinated and efficient way. In the third subcategory, the responses are grouped around the need for the government to not increase the price of basic items (nine responses). Some of the women's words include: "government, do not rise anymore the price of things so much, they do not think on the hunger that one goes through." One last subcategory concerns requests of help from the institutions of health care and education (six responses): "that the institutions support and that we give something in return," "that the schools don't charge so much through the so-called voluntary fees and the school items."

With regard to the category *help among neighbors, relatives, and friends* (thirty-four responses), the women greatly emphasized that neighbors need to participate in a united and harmonious way. The women creatively propose various strategies of mutual help and exchange. They also recommended giving to those who have least and to care for the neighborhood relationships, avoiding fights and envy. They also promoted the neighbors' participation when looking for services like water, light, and drainage. In their words: "we could be united and go the town hall or I don't know where and ask for drainage, because that is a type of poverty."

The networks of support and mutual help are part of the social imaginary that the women build in their search for survival. However, these possibilities of association and solidarity do not seem to be present as real assets in their struggle for survival. Authors like Zaffaroni (1999), González de la Rocha (1999b), Moser (1996), Kaztman and Filgueira (1999), and Roberts (1995) have questioned the current capacity of social support networks as resources to face financial instability. Which are the factors behind this impossibility of actively maintaining the social capital that aids survival? Low salaries, unemployment, and unsteady employment have eroded the possibilities of maintaining effective membership in this social fabric that cushions the decay of living conditions (González de la Rocha 1999b). However, there are other factors also which have a decisive influence, such as the social phenomenon called "urban mistrust." The social development of trust in the city has suffered strong blows in recent years, a psychological togetherness that allows empathy for others and the material as well as symbolic exchange has been broken from different directions. The fight with others in order to get some land, the weakening of meaningful social links due to the constant changes of residence within the urban setting, the lack of resources to maintain the existing links, the uncontrollable waves of urban violence that find a fertile ground among those who are least protected, and the overwhelming appearance of consumption and sale of drugs have generated an atmosphere of daily suspicion about the true intentions of others.

FINAL COMMENTS

The current picture of the irregular settlements in the urban areas of Mexico, particularly in the city of Guadalajara, is qualitatively different to what was found in previous decades. After the economic crisis of the 1980s, with its consequent fall in the standard of living, followed by the crisis of 1994 and the reduction in social spending, the outlook for many urban poor is worrisome. The purpose of this article was to contribute to the understanding of poverty from a subjective point of view (Schteingart 1997; Mogrovejo 1997; Palomar 2001).

The withdrawal of the state and its support of housing institutions produced serious consequences in the living conditions of the urban poor. The government has significantly reduced housing credit for built or in-progress dwellings. Instead, it has focused its support on programs that attempt to combat extreme poverty in rural areas. Since such programs have not been available to the needy people in large cities, there is no affordable housing supply for the urban poor. Current housing policies have left many urban poor without the possibility of finding a "legal roof." They then develop a strategy for shelter and survival by settling in irregular land lots.

The current state of irregular settlements does not reflect anymore those massive invasions, or, those small groups that in a gradual way would become owners of common land (Ramírez Sáiz 1995). During the 1990s, and even more so after the crisis of 1994, what we find in settlements like Las Margaritas, are strategies of "ant-like squatting," which are basically individuals moving towards irregular spaces with the main purpose of getting a piece of land and thus stop paying ever-increasing rents. This kind of progressive and individual squatting greatly obstructs the possibilities of association among the settlers. The collective initiatives for the social management of the services and the regularization of land become impossible objectives, which exceed the possibilities of an incipient social fabric that has been broken many times during continuous urban movements.

The economic crises in Mexico have had serious consequences on the well being of poor urban households. Irregular employment and the lack of resources have forced many families to send more than two wage earners, mostly women, to the job market (García and de Oliveira 1994, among others). When someone lives in a context of unmet basic needs, the "time" factor acquires a particular meaning. Currently the urban poor use each hour of the day to search for survival. There is little or no time left for socializing or for the social administration of the environment in which they live.

The experience of *hunger* is part of the daily life of the families of Las Margaritas and of those households located in newly created irregular settlements in large cities of Mexico. I used Scheper-Hughes's (1992) definition of hunger as: "the hunger of those who eat everyday but in insufficient amounts or with a lower quality or with almost no variation, which leaves them unsatisfied and hungry" (p.139). Thus, I refer to constant and chronic hunger as opposed to hunger that happens in certain regions of the world, which is characterized by its cyclical, acute, and explosive manifestation. It is about hunger reflected in the consumption of rough, basic, heavy foods that enlarge the "belly" and keep the body undernourished. It is about the consumption of foods in attempts to stave off or stay hungry instead of meeting the necessary nutritional requirements of the body (Scheper-Hughes 1992).

Urban hunger is deceptive and paradoxical. In spite of the uncontrollable flow of flavors, forms, sizes, tones, and textures that are combined in many ways for producing very diverse foods—which are generously shown and sold in the commercial spaces of the urban context—there are hundreds of thousands of urban families that are poorly fed. The city polarizes and shows us its daily dance between hunger and excess, poverty and wealth. Urban hunger is deceitful because it is chronic, meaning it does not involve the shock of famine or the impact of epidemics and massive deaths. Urban hunger takes place "in a natural way" everyday and in every extremely poor household located in the big city. Urban hunger then becomes just another element that merges with the urban landscape.

The information presented in this article demonstrates that for women, *poverty* equals hunger; the *causes of poverty* lie in not having a job or having unsteady jobs; the *consequences of poverty* are equal to hunger; *alternatives to poverty* are equal to work. Work, as stated by Moser (1996) is the central resource for survival. The participants in this study did not point to kinship or neighborhood social networks, nor to the urban participation processes, or to developing solidarity links as the central strategies to face poverty. For them, having access to a job and a salary that is enough for the family's survival are the main solutions for poverty in the city. These conversations show the important place that a job has to guarantee survival. To understand the objective and material conditions in the lives of the urban poor is not enough. To include the subjective perspective in the analysis of poverty is necessary to design social policies for the well being of poor urban men and women.

In Mexico, the transition from a social-policy system, inspired in the universalistic tradition, to specific schemes has resulted in designing programs directed toward the poorest and the gradual disappearance of subsidies so that the presence of the state is reduced to a minimum (Gendreau 2000). This approach has been mostly directed to rural areas through a program called PROGRESA (education, health, and nourishment), which provides basic assistance and targets the families as recipients, in contrast to community-oriented programs. The urban areas were left unattended. It is only at the beginning of 2002 that the federal government has expanded the PROGRESA program into urban areas. Based on the discussion presented in this paper, I develop the following reflections to combat urban poverty.

The design of social policies oriented to family and community development (as stated by González de la Rocha 1986; Moser 1996; among others) must consider the great diversity of family arrangements that currently exist in Mexico. We cannot talk about the family as a homogenous and static reality. It is necessary to approach it in its complexity and heterogeneity; in this sense, taking into account dimensions such as type of family structure, stage in the domestic cycle, and head of household being essential elements to understand their problems. Multidisciplinary teams must be involved in designing programs so that they generate comprehensive proposals. The development of specific actions involves continuous dialogue among governmental authorities, social organizations, community representatives, and researchers. There needs to be a continuous evaluation of the effect of programs, where the social and cultural dimension of the assisted populations is taken into account.

With regard to women's economic participation, and taking into account the conditions of poor urban families, it is necessary to generate employment for women, so that they can count on social security for themselves and their families, as well as have choices of jobs that offer greater flexibility in schedules and possibilities to work at home. Health, nutrition, and housing are important priorities in the poor urban settlements as well, for the benefit of the women and of their families. The economic crisis unleashed in 1994 in Mexico has affected a wide range of sectors of the population. In the case of families who live in extreme conditions of poverty and who live in the country's metropolitan areas, particularly in the adjacent areas of Guadalajara, this study has shown the sharp deterioration in their living conditions, the over-saturation of the women's burden facing the precarious situations of their lives, and the urgency of integrated responses on the part of all the social actors involved so that poverty can be eradicated.

NOTES

1. The survey design was based on that used in "Los Pobres Explican la Pobreza: El Caso de Guatemala" [The Poor Explain Poverty: The Guatemalan Case] carried out by the Rafael Landivar University and the Instituto de Investigaciones Económicas y Sociales de Guatemala [Economic and Social Research Institute of Guatemala] in 1995. It is also based on the instrument of González de la Rocha (n.d.) "Organización de los grupos domésticos" (Domestic Groups Organization).

2. The name of the place has been changed.

3. According to CEPAL, extreme poverty includes the percentage of EAP that earns less than the minimum salary while poverty includes the EAP percentage that earns up to two minimum salaries.

REFERENCES

BAZÁN, Lucía.
    1998. "El Último Recurso: Las Relaciones Familiares Como Alternativas Frente a la Crisis" [The Last Resource: The Family Relationships as Alternatives to Facing the Crisis]. Paper presented at Latin American Studies Association (LASA) conference, Chicago, Illinois.

CHANT, Sylvia.
    1988. *Mitos y Realidades de la Formación de las Familias Encabezadas por Mujeres: El Caso de Querétaro, México. Mujeres y Sociedad* [Myths and Realities in the Creation of Families Headed by Women: The Case of Querétaro, México. Women and Society]. Zapopan, Jalisco, México, C.P.: El Colegio de Jalisco, Centro de Investigaciones y Estudios Superiores en Antropologia Social (CIESAS) Occidente.

    ———. 1996. *Gender, Urban Development and Housing.* New York, New York: United Nations Publications, United Nations Development Programme (UNDP).

———. 1997. *Women-headed Households. Diversity and Dynamics in the Developing World*. Houndmills, Basingstoke Hampshire, England: Macmillan Press Ltd.

CHIARELLO, Franco.

    1994. "Economía Informal, Familia y Redes Sociales." In *Solidaridad y Producción Informal de Recursos* ["Irregular Economy, Family and Social Networks." In *Solidarity and Irregular Production of Resources*], compiled by René Millán. Coyoacán, México D.F.: Ciudad Universitaria, Instituto de Investigaciones Sociales, Universidad Nacional Autónoma de México (UNAM).

ENRÍQUEZ, Rocío, Constanza Urzúa, Sonia Romero, and Magdalena Torres.

    1992. "Aproximación Psicosocial a Familias de Escasos Recursos de una Zona de Guadalajara" [Psychosocial Approach to Families That Have Few Resources in the Guadalajara Area]. Master's thesis. Unpublished thesis, Universidad del Valle de Atemajac, Guadalajara, México.

ESTEINOU, Rosario.

    1994. "Fuentes de Solidaridad: Familia y Estado Benefactor." In *Solidaridad y Producción Informal de Recursos* ["Sources of Solidarity: Family and the Beneficial State." In *Solidarity and Irregular Production of Resources*], compiled by René Millán. Coyoacán, México, D.F.: Ciudad Universitaria, Instituto de Investigaciones Sociales, Universidad Nacional Autónoma de México (UNAM).

ESTRADA, Margarita.

    1999. *1995: Familias en la crisis* [1995: Families in the crisis]. Colección Antropologías. México: Centro de Investigaciones y Estudios Superiores en Antropología Social (CIESAS).

GARCÍA, Brígida and Orlandina de Oliveira.

    1994. *Trabajo Femenino y Vida Familiar en México* [Female Labor and Family Life in Mexico]. México D.F.: El Colegio de México.

GENDREAU, Mónica.

    2000. "El PROGRESA en el Debate Actual en Torno a la Política Social. Reflexiones Finales." In *Los Dilemas de la Política Social: Cómo combatir la pobreza?* ["The PROGRESA in the Current Debate Regarding the Social Policy. Final Reflections." In *The Dilemmas of the Social Policy. How Do We Combat Poverty?*], edited by Enrique Valencia, Mónica Gendreau, and Ana María Tepichín. Zapopan, Jalisco, México: Universidad de Guadalajara (UdeG), Instituto Tecnologico y de Estudios Superiores de Occidente (ITESO), Universidad Iberoamericana (IBERO- México, D.F.).

GONZÁLEZ, Luis.

    1998. "La Sistematización y el Análisis de los Datos Cualitativos." In *Tras las Vetas de la Investigación Cualitativa: Perspectivas y Acercamientos desde la Práctica* ["The Systematization and Analysis of Qualitative Data." In *Searching for the Layers of Qualitative Research: Perspectives and Approaches from the Practice*], edited by Rebeca Mejía and Sergio Sandoval. Zapopan, Jalisco, México: Universidad Jesuita en Guadalajara, Instituto Tecnologico y de Estudios Superiores de Occidente (ITESO).

GONZÁLEZ DE LA ROCHA, Mercedes.
    1986. *Los Recursos de la Pobreza: Familias de Bajos Ingresos en Guadalajara.* [*The Resources of Poverty: Low-income Families in Guadalajara*]. Guadalajara, Jalisco, México: Colegio de Jalisco, Centro de Investigaciones y Estudios Superiores en Antropologia Social (CIESAS).
    ———. 1994. *The Resources of Poverty: Women and Survival in a Mexican City.* Oxford, United Kingdom and Cambridge, Massachusetts: Blackwell.
    ———. 1999a. "Assets and Vulnerability: Approaching Coping Strategies in the Context of Transition and Structural Adjustment." Unpublished manuscript.
    ———. 1999b. "La Reciprocidad Amenazada: Un Costo Más de la Pobreza Urbana." In *Hogar, Pobreza y Bienestar en México.* ["The Threatened Reciprocity: One More Cost of Urban Poverty." In *Household, Poverty and Well-being in Mexico*], edited by Rocío Enríquez. Zapopan. Jalisco, México: Universidad Jesuita en Guadalajara, Instituto Tecnologico y de Estudios Superiores de Occidente (ITESO).
    ———. 1999c. "Hogares de Jefatura Femenina en México: Patrones y Formas de Vida." In *Divergencias del Modelo Tradicional: Hogares de Jefatura Femenina en América Latina* ["Households Headed by Women in Mexico: Patterns and Ways of Life." In *Divergence from the Traditional Model: Households Headed by Women in Latin America*], edited by Mercedes González de la Rocha. Col. Tlalpan México D.F.: Centro de Investigaciones y Estudios Superiores en Antropologia Social (CIESAS).
KAZTMAN, Rubén and Carlos Filgueira.
    1999. "Notas sobre el Marco Conceptual." In *Activos y Estructuras de Oportunidades. Estudios sobre las Raíces de la Vulnerabilidad Social en Uruguay* ["Notes about the Conceptual Framework." In *Assets and Opportunity Structures: Studies of the Roots of Social Vulnerability in Uruguay*], edited by Rubén Kaztman. Montevideo, Uruguay: Programme des Nations Unies pour le Développement (PNUD)-Uruguay y Comisión Económica para América Latina y el Caribe (CEPAL).
MINGIONE, Enzo.
    1994. "Sector Informal y Estrategias de Sobrevivencia: Hipótesis para el Desarrollo de un Campo de Indagación." In *Solidaridad y Producción Informal de Recursos* ["Irregular Sector and Survival Strategies: Hypothesis for the Development of an Inquiry Field." In *Solidarity and Irregular Production of Resources*], compiled by René Millán. Coyoacán, México D.F.: Ciudad Universitaria, Instituto de Investigaciones Sociales, Universidad Nacional Autónoma de México (UNAM).
MOGROVEJO, Norma.
    1997. "Relatos de Vida de las Mujeres de las Colonias Populares: La Otra Cara de la Ciudad." In *Pobreza, Condiciones de Vida y Salud en la Ciudad de México* ["Life Stories of the Women from Low-income Neighborhoods: The Other Face of the City." In *Poverty, Living and Health Conditions in Mexico City*], edited by

Martha Schteingart. México D.F.: Colegio de México.

MOSER, Caroline.
    1996. *Confronting Crisis. A Comparative Study of Household Responses to Poverty and Vulnerability in Four Poor Urban Communities*. Environmentally Sustainable Development Studies and Monographs Series No. 8. Washington, D.C.: The World Bank.

PALOMAR, Joaquina.
    2001. "La Pobreza y el Bienestar Subjetivo." In *Los Rostros de la Pobreza: El Debate* ["Poverty and Subjective Well Being." In *The Faces of Poverty: The Debate*], edited by Rigoberto Gallardo and Joaquín Osorio, 2nd ed. Sistema Educativo, Universidad Ibero Americana-Instituto Tecnologico y de Estudios Superiores de Occidente (SEUIA-ITESO). México D.F.: Limusa Noriega Editores.

POZOS, Fernando and Carlos Barba.
    1999. "Atlas Social de Jalisco y sus Regiones." In *Pobreza y Desarrollo Social. Una Estrategia para el Combate a la Pobreza en Jalisco* ["Social Atlas of Jalisco and Its Regions." In *Poverty and Social Development: A Strategy to Combat Poverty in Jalisco*]. Jalisco, México: Gobierno del Estado de Jalisco. Disco com pacto.

RAMIREZ SAIZ, Juan Manuel.
    1995. *Los Movimientos Sociales y la Política* [*The Social Movements and Politics*] Guadalajara, México: Universidad de Guadalajara, El Comité Popular del Sur de Guadalajara.

ROBERTS, Bryan.
    1995. *The Making of Citizens: Cities of Peasants Revisited*. London, England: Arnold.

ROMÁN, Ignacio.
    1998. *La Microeconomía Va Bien y la Macroeconomía Va Mal?*. Avances no. 8. Cuadernos de Investigación y Análisis. Guadalajara, México: Instituto Tecnologico y de Estudios Superiores de Occidente (ITESO), Editorial.

SCHEPER-HUGHES, Nancy.
    1992. *Death Without Weeping: The Violence of Everyday Life in Brazil*. Berkeley: University of California Press.

SCHTEINGART, Martha, ed.
    1997. *Pobreza, Condiciones de Vida y Salud en la Ciudad de México* [*Poverty, Living and Health Condition in Mexico City*]. México D.F.: Colegio de Mexico.

SELBY, Henry, Arthur Murphy et al.
    1994. *La Familia en el México Urbano. Mecanismos de Defensa Frente a la Crisis (1978–1992)* [*The Family in Urban Mexico: Defense Mechanisms vis-à-vis the Crisis (1978–1992)*] Col. Centro, C.P., México, D.F.: Consejo Nacional para la Cultura y las Artes (CONACULTA).

WOLF, Diane L.
    1994. *Factory Daughters: Gender, Household Dynamics, and Rural*

Industrialization in Java. Berkeley: University of California Press.

ZAFFARONI, Cecilia.
1999. "Los Recursos de las Familias Urbanas de Bajos Ingresos para Enfrentar Situaciones Críticas." In *Activos y Estructuras de Oportunidades. Estudios sobre las Raíces de la Vulnerabilidad Social en Uruguay.* ["The Resources of Low-income Urban Families to Face Critical Situations." In *Assets and Opportunity Structures. Studies of the Roots of Social Vulnerability in Uruguay*], edited by Rubén Kaztman. Montevideo, Uruguay: Programme des Nations Unies pour le Développement (PNUD)-Uruguay y Comisión Económica para América Latina y el Caribe (CEPAL).

FAMILIES ON THE VERGE OF BREAKDOWN? VIEWS ON CONTEMPORARY TRENDS IN FAMILY LIFE IN GUANACASTE, COSTA RICA

Sylvia Chant*

ABSTRACT

As in many other countries, family life in Costa Rica has changed in recent decades. Marriage is declining, divorce and separation are on the rise, out-of-wedlock births are increasing, and women head a growing number and proportion of households. Nationally and internationally, statements issued by the media, government bodies and the religious establishment indicate that these trends have provoked anxiety about "family breakdown." Yet it is less well known if similar concerns are felt at the grassroots.

The present paper explores reactions to family change among 176 low- and middle-income women and men from different age groups in Guanacaste province, northwest Costa Rica. A key finding is that although some trajectories in family life are perceived as encompassing possibilities for new, more flexible and egalitarian domestic arrangements, others are regarded as weakening family unity. Moreover, concerns about "family breakdown" are more common among adult males than their female counterparts or younger people. The reasons behind these disparate views relate to social, legal, and economic processes that have destabilized "traditional" gendered divisions of labor, power, and rights within Costa Rican households.

INTRODUCTION

Costa Rica has experienced a number of significant changes in family life in the last few decades. Prominent trends include a growing incidence of lone motherhood and female-headed households. These are linked, *inter alia,* with falling levels of legal marriage, rising numbers of out-of-wedlock births, greater rates of divorce and separation, and mounting involvement of women in the historically male preserve of family breadwinning. Similar processes have been noted in many other parts of Latin America, not to mention elsewhere in the world, and have been variously attributed to globalization, neoliberal economic restructuring, the changing nature of work, increased access to population control, and post-1960s feminist movements (see for example Arriagada 1998; Benería 1991; Castells 1997; Cerrutti and Zenteno 1999; Chant with Craske 2003; Comisión Económica para América Latina [CEPAL] 2001; Datta and McIlwaine 2000; Folbre 1991; Geldstein 1997; González de la Rocha 1995; Jelin 1991; Kaztman 1992; Safa 1995; United Nations 2000).

In a number of quarters, nationally and internationally, these trajectories

---

* Department of Geography and Environment, London School of Economics, Houghton St., London, WC2A 2AE, U.K.

have been regarded as indicative of a "breakdown in the family," and have frequently provoked anxiety, especially in relation to the potential impacts on children (see Moore 1994). While the media, official reports, and statements from the religious establishment have often documented concerns about family breakdown, it is less well known, however, how they reflect sentiment at the grassroots. Do people themselves perceive that major shifts are taking place in family and household organization? If so, to what do they attribute these changes? Are the changes identified deemed to be precipitating family breakdown, and to what extent does this hold across gender, age, and socioeconomic boundaries? This paper addresses these questions on the basis of interviews and focus group discussions with 176 low- and middle-income men and women of various ages in Guanacaste province, northwest Costa Rica.[1]

The first section of the paper details major changes in family patterns in Costa Rica in recent decades and considers key structural factors that have impacted upon household form and organization. This discussion also includes a brief account of the manner in which current trends have been viewed by public bodies (such as government and religious organizations). With reference to the survey population in Guanacaste, section two examines perceptions of family change at the grassroots and the main factors to which shifts are attributed. Section three explores reactions to change among different groups within the sample, including the factors singled out by some as constitutive of family breakdown. The fourth and final section critically evaluates the relevance of the term "breakdown" in the wake of family transitions in Guanacaste. It also suggests ways in which the public sector might better assist families to adapt to some of the problems that are perceived as deriving from them.

CHANGES IN COSTA RICAN FAMILY LIFE IN THE LATE TWENTIETH CENTURY

Although the "traditional" nuclear-family unit—comprising a male breadwinner, female housewife, and their biological children—has arguably not been as long-lived nor as numerically dominant in Costa Rica as it possibly has been in other parts of the world,[2] the proportion of households conforming with this model fell from around one-half to one-third of households between the 1970s and the 1990s (Centro Nacional Para el Desarrollo de la Mujer y la Familia [CMF] 1996:20). The decline is mainly attributable to an increase in people living alone, a rise in complex or extended households, and mounting numbers of one-parent units, nearly all of which are headed by women (Fauné 1997:92; Pereira García 1998:187). Although lone-mother and female-headed households are not synonymous (Chant 1997), the proportion of female-headed households climbed from 16 percent 1973 to 22 percent in 1997 (Budowski and Guzmán 1998). According to the 2000 Census, this figure has now increased slightly to 22.2 percent (Instituto Nacional de Estadísticas y Censos [INEC] 2001, table 31).

As part and parcel of the fall-off in male-headed family units, marriage rates dropped from 30.8 to 23.5 per 100 between 1980 and 1994 (Ministerio de Planificación Nacional y Política Económica [MIDEPLAN] 1995:5-6), and between 1980 and 1996, divorce rates rose from 9.9 to 21.2 per 100 (Proyecto Estado de la Nación [PEN] 1998:210). Official figures also indicate that the proportion of births outside marriage in Costa Rica increased from 23 percent in 1960, to 38 percent in 1985, to 51.5 percent in 1999 (Budowski and Rosero Bixby forthcoming; Instituto Nacional de las Mujeres [INAMU] 2001:8).[3] In addition, the proportion of children without fathers registered on their birth certificates rose from 21.1 percent in 1990, to 30.3 percent in 1999 (INAMU 2001:9). The fact that nearly one in three children born in Costa Rica now has a *"padre desconocido"* ("unknown father") is significant insofar as traditionally only formally acknowledged children have received their father's surname and entitlement to paternal support (Budowski and Rosero Bixby forthcoming). Two-thirds of births from unreported fathers occur to women under 19 years of age (INAMU 2001:8), which conceivably helps to explain why as many as 16 percent of single parents in the country are under 18 years of age (see also note 3).

Divisions of Labor in Households and Workforce Participation

In addition to shifts in the legal and demographic contours of family life, there have also been important changes in intrahousehold divisions of labor, especially in respect of the rising labor force participation of women in their childbearing years (CMF 1996:20). While there was only one female worker for every three men in the 20 to 39 years of age cohort in 1980, the gap had narrowed to one in two by 1990 (Dierckxsens 1992:22). Between 1980 and 1995, the share of the workforce made up by women in Costa Rica rose from 24.3 percent to 30.5 percent (Fauné 1997:58), and in 2000, this figure had reached 32.1 percent (INEC 2001, cuadro 2). Despite the fact that women's average wages are lower than men's, and that women in general are more likely to be unemployed, increases in male unemployment have been noted in the 15 to 25 year and 45 to 70 year age cohorts, with periods of unemployment also becoming longer (Arias 2000:26, table 1). Some of these changes have been driven by sectoral shifts in the Costa Rican economy. Agriculture, for example, a predominantly male domain, recruited only 20 percent of the national workforce in 2000, compared with 51 percent in 1960.

Moreover, mounting emphasis on agroexports over time has been associated with increased casualization, seasonal unemployment, and temporary migration of men in search of work. These trends have been juxtaposed with significant growth in the share of the labor force in services (from 30 percent to 53 percent between 1960 and 2000), which has tended to favor women. Women are currently half of the workers in this sector, which occupies as many as 84 percent of the economically active female population in the country (INEC 2001, cuadro 13).

The expansion of light manufacturing in free-trade zones, mainly around the San José Metropolitan Area, has also opened up opportunities for female workers (see Sandoval García 1997). Additional impetuses to rising female employment have emanated from declining birth rates associated with increased access to birth control, the growth in female education, and, more recently, mounting pressures on households to expand and diversify their sources of earnings in the wake of neoliberal economic restructuring. As elsewhere in Latin America, the progressive "feminization of employment" also seems to be linked with a "feminization of household headship" (see Bradshaw 1995a,b; Chant 1997; Chant with Craske 2003:181; Safa 1995, 1999).

Legislation, Social Policy, and Family Change

While economic and demographic trends have clearly played some part in household transitions, another important set of influences undoubtedly derives from gender-aware legislation and social programs. From the 1970s onwards, particularly during the presidency of Rodrigo Carazo (1978-1982), pressure from women's advocacy organizations contributed to an unprecedented recruitment of women into national political life. Then, in 1986, following the conclusion of the United Nations Decade for Women, Costa Rica established its National Centre for Women and the Family (*Centro Nacional para el Desarrollo de la Mujer y de la Familia* [CMF]). This organization, which in 1998 became the National Institute for Women (*Instituto Nacional de las Mujeres* [INAMU]) and is now headed by a Minister for Women, has played a major role in initiatives that have strengthened women's position and rights within and beyond the family. This is especially so since the passing of the far-reaching *Law of Social Equality for Women* (Law no. 7142) in 1990, which aimed not only to promote, but to guarantee, women's equality with men (see Chant 1997:136-137).

In addition to introducing clauses on the compulsory joint registration of property in marriage (or in non-formalized unions, registration in the woman's name), prohibition of dismissal from jobs on grounds of pregnancy, and greater rights for victims of domestic violence to evict the perpetrators from their homes (see Badilla and Blanco 1996; Investigaciones Jurídicas S.A. [IJSA] 1990), the *Social Equality Law* paved the way for several new legislative initiatives with important implications both for women's personal rights and entitlements, and for the material and social viability of "nonstandard" households. Prominent developments in this regard have included: the *Law Against Domestic Violence* (Law no. 7586 [1996]), the *Law for the Protection of Adolescent Mothers* (Law no. 7739 [1998]), the *Law for Women in Conditions of Poverty* (Law no. 7769 [1998]), the *Law for Responsible Paternity* (Law no. 8101 [2001]), reforms to articles 84, 85, and 89 of the *Family Code*, recognizing children born outside marriage (Law no. 7538 [1995]), the addition of articles 242-246 to the *Family Code* acknowledging the legal validity of consensual unions, and reform of article 5 from the same eliminating the equivalence of women and minors (see CMF 1996:22; Colaboración Area Legal 1997; Instituto Mixto de Ayuda Social [IMAS] 1998; INAMU 2001).

Much of this legislation has been accompanied by the introduction of significant new gender policies and programs, particularly during the National Liberation Party regime of President José María Figueres (1994-1998). Not only was this administration responsible for establishing a National Equal Opportunities Plan (*Plan Nacional para la Igualdad de Oportunidades entre Mujeres y Hombres* [PIOMH]), and a National Plan for the Attention and Prevention of Intrafamily Violence (*Plan Nacional para la Atención y Prevención de la Violencia Intrafamiliar* [PLANOVI]), but the first dedicated program for female-headed households in the country: the Comprehensive Training Program for Female Household Heads in Conditions of Poverty (*Programa de Formación Integral para Mujeres Jefas de Hogar en Condiciones de Pobreza*) (IMAS, 1999a). Launched in 1997, this latter intervention was spurred, in part, by a rise in poverty among women-headed households from the mid-1980s[4] and the fact that following ratification of the Universal Declaration of the Rights of the Child in 1989, the Costa Rican state has made concerted moves to increase guarantees of children's well being (see United Nations Children's Fund [UNICEF] 1998).[5]

The main thrust of the Female Household Heads program was to award a stipend to beneficiaries for up to six months during which they would take training courses in personal development, self esteem, and employment and income-generating skills (see Marenco et al. 1998). In the present Social Christian Unity regime of President Miguel Angel Rodríguez, this initiative has been continued in a revised form as "*Creciendo Juntas*" ("Growing Together"), which forms part of the *Plan Nacional de Solidaridad* (National Solidarity Plan). Although *Creciendo Juntas* has been extended to all women in poverty, around half the 15,000 or so beneficiaries reached between 1999 and 2001 were heads of households.[6] Two ancillary programs, aimed at the young, also accompanied this scheme. The first of these, *Amor Jóven* (Young Love), launched in 1999, is concerned with heightening sexual awareness and preventing pregnancy among adolescents; the second, *Construyendo Oportunidades* (Building Opportunities), seeks to (re)integrate teenage mothers into education, and to equip them with personal and vocational skills to enhance their own lives and those of their children (see Chant 1999a, 2000; IMAS 2001; Primera Dama de la República 2001). Aside from these initiatives for women and lone mothers, the National Solidarity Plan encompasses a program geared to strengthening family cohesion (*Programa de Fortalecimiento Familiar*), which assigns basic income supplements to families in extreme poverty, and another (*Programa Infancia y Juventud*) which provides assistance for children and youth from low-income families, mainly in the form of care, after-school activities and youth development (see IMAS 1999b,c).

Public Concerns about "Family Breakdown?"

While the Costa Rican state is clearly concerned about protecting and promoting the rights of vulnerable groups and, thanks largely to the efforts of CMF/INAMU, has shown itself willing to work with more flexible definitions of "family" than are often found elsewhere (see Chant 1999a, 2002b), this is far from being an open endorsement of family plurality. For example, many official (and academic) publications continue to use the term *"familia completa"* ("complete family") to denote units comprising two parents and their children, whereas one-parent households are consigned to the category of *"familia incompleta"* ("incomplete family") (see Sagot 1999:101). Moreover, although CEPAL (2001:V16) notes that for Latin America more generally the term *"desintegración familiar"* ("family breakdown") is seldom defined explicitly and/or is used to describe factors as disparate as rising divorce rates, new family functions, and lack of intrafamily communication, one of the principal evocations in the Costa Rican case relates to the absence or irresponsibility of one or both parents, normally fathers, as encapsulated in another increasingly common term: *"paternidad irresponsable"* ("irresponsible fatherhood"). This again tends to reinforce the idea that "family" is synonymous with the "in-tact" male-headed unit and is the standard from which other configurations deviate.

In turn, links are sometimes drawn between decline of "the family" and other social ills. As one author writing in the prominent Social Science journal *Ciencias Sociales* put it: "Disorganization and disintegration of the family are the cause of declining moral values, economic pressures and social problems such as prostitution, alcoholism, drug addiction and violence" (Loaíciga Guillén 1994:10; *author's translation*). These latter issues, in turn, are of major significance to Costa Rican society more generally, with nearly one-quarter of the population ranking delinquency (including violence) and/or drugs as Costa Rica's biggest contemporary problem.[7] Although perceptions of rising violence could in part be due to increased denouncements of intrafamily abuse (facilitated by the new support mechanisms for women and children itemized above), it is also the case that violent muggings and murders are on an upward trend, possibly relating to mounting levels of arms ownership in the country (see PEN 1998:44). As far as the Catholic establishment and its *"Movimiento Familiar Cristiano"* ("Christian Family Movement")[8] are concerned, the erosion of social values within the country also owes to increased sexual freedom (Schifter and Madrigal 1996:62).[9] Falling rates of marriage, increased illegitimacy, prostitution, and the rising visibility of homosexuality are targeted as primary concerns here, and have provoked numerous Church appeals for adults to set good examples for young people by eschewing the evils of libertinism and modern consumerism, and conserving "family traditions." Similar messages are promulgated among Costa Rica's growing Protestant community.[10]

Although there are clearly assumptions embedded in these discourses about the ideal form that households should take, it is also true to say that many public discussions of "family breakdown," at least on the part of secular bodies, emphasize the importance of *intrafamily relationships,* particularly those between parents and children, and link problems in this domain not so much with factors internal to families (such as "breakdown" in their membership or "deviant" social behavior), but with wider structural processes. For example, a number of press and academic articles in recent years have expressed concern about declining parental involvement in the daily care and socialization of children. This is attributed not only to rising economic pressures and growing work burdens on parents, but to the spread of new technology and exposure to media. A study conducted on adolescent depression in 1999 by a consortium of national and international agencies, for example, concluded that one of the main reasons for rising rates of depression among the young was that "parents have abandoned their role through overwork; the television and computer have taken the place of parents" (see also CEPAL 2001 on Latin America more generally; *author's translation*).[11] This is endorsed by other recent research that has asserted that the hierarchy and hegemony of the family are being displaced by modern communications, especially television, thereby weakening traditional support systems for children and adolescents (see Tiffer 1998:116; Moreno 1997). Indeed, Costa Rica has one of the highest rates of access to television and personal computers in Latin America, at 387 television sets per 1,000 people in 1998, and 39.1 personal computers (the regional averages for Latin America and the Caribbean in the same year were 225 and 33.9, respectively) (World Bank 2000:310-311, table 19). The number of Internet hosts per 1,000 people in the year 2000 was 4.1, which placed Costa Rica in sixth place in the region after Uruguay (19.6), Mexico (9.1), Argentina (8.7), Brazil (7.2), and Chile (6.2) (United Nations Development Program [UNDP] 2001:48-50, table A2.1).

In summarizing the views of public bodies on family change, a range of apparently contradictory tendencies can be identified. Although, on one hand, a decline in "traditional" patriarchal households may owe partly to the efforts of the state to secure basic human rights and welfare for vulnerable groups, the male-headed nuclear unit still seems to be something of a normative ideal in public (and especially in religious) circles. Concern also remains about the potential effects of its demise on social stability, cohesion, and reproduction. By the same token, there is recognition that the quality of family life and intrafamily relationships are not governed simply by the configuration of households, but by wider structural factors over which individuals have little control. This, as I have argued elsewhere, has led to a situation in which public discourses of changing patterns of family life in Costa Rica are perhaps more strongly marked by notions of a "crisis *for*" rather than a "crisis *in*" the family (Chant 2002b:376). In other words, if families are "breaking down," then this is not just because of the "new" ways that people are organizing their lives, but because social structures and values have been undermined by development and globalization. To what extent to these kinds of interpretations mirror those at the grassroots?

GRASSROOTS VIEWS ON FAMILY CHANGE IN GUANACASTE

As stated earlier in the paper, in examining popular views on family change, I draw from a 1999 survey of 176 low- and middle-income men and women from three broad age bands (see Table 1).[12] The survey consisted mainly of focus group discussions, organized as *"talleres"* or "workshops," in which participants were invited to reflect on gender and the family in Guanacaste at the end of the twentieth century, and how things had changed (or not) in their own lifetimes (see Chant 1999b for fuller details). My assistant and I gave our informants substantially free rein to talk about issues that mattered to them, and, in the interests of "respondent autonomy," attempted to keep our own interventions to a minimum.

Table 1.
Interview Sample by Age, Gender, and Socioeconomic Status

	Parents/adults		Adolescents/ young adults		Children/young adolescents	
	(>25 years)		(14–24 years)		(10–13 years)	
	Male	Female	Male	Female	Male	Female
Middle-income	8	20	8	38	4	7
Low-income	14	21	20	15	6	15
TOTAL	**22**	**41**	**28**	**53**	**10**	**22**

Aside from "setting the ball rolling" up on key topics, such as what the concept of "family" summoned up for people, and if people felt that family life was changing, we tended only to intervene (a) where we felt that assertions needed substantiation and/or corroboration (for example, where there seemed to be an over-idealization of the past), and (b) to ensure that people who wanted to speak got a chance to do so. In line with this methodology, the present and following sections consist mainly of basic reportage using transcripts from individual interviews and group sessions. Most of the critical analysis of this material is left until the concluding part of the paper.

The Context of the Survey

The setting of the survey was the province of Guanacaste in the northwest of the country. This area is distinguished from other parts of Costa Rica on a number of counts, particularly in respect of its high levels of poverty and un- and underemployment. In 1998, for example, unemployment in Guanacaste was 7.2 percent and underemployment was 19.8 percent, compared with national levels of 5.6 percent and 13.1 percent, respectively (Ministerio de Economía, Industria y Comercio [MEIC] 1998; Aguilar et al. 1998). This is mainly due to the fact that until the 1990s, when international tourism began to take off along Costa Rica's north Pacific coast, the province was reliant on a small number of agricultural activities (primarily cattle ranching, rice and sugar production), with limited or only seasonal demand for labor. This, coupled with the fact that earnings are considerably lower in Guanacaste than in other parts of the country (male wages are on average 13 percent less in Guanacaste than in San José for example—Arias 2000:21), has given rise to high levels of permanent migration[13] as well as short-term outmigration, particularly on the part of low-income men. Moreover, the shrinking of agriculture's role in the provincial economy in recent years has given rise to a situation where, in contrast to the rest of the country, rates of underemployment and open unemployment among men have exceeded those of women. In 2000, for example, male and female levels of unemployment in the "Chorotega" planning region (which comprises mainly of Guanacaste) were 5.9 percent and 5.4 percent, respectively, and the figure for male underemployment was as high as 18.2 percent compared with 16.5 percent for women (INEC 2001, cuadro 9).

Male underemployment and periodic outmigration have, in turn, been associated with considerable instability in household composition and livelihoods in the province (see Chant 1992, 2000; Moreno 1997). Long-standing tendencies for men to desert their spouses and children, and/or to engage in heavy drinking and multiple sexual relations, are widely attributed to the economic and physical hardships of migration combined with the psychological and emotional stresses on couples engendered by frequent and/or prolonged periods of separation. Formal marriage has traditionally been less common here than in other parts of Costa Rica, with only 30.9 percent of women with coresident partners being legally married in low-income settlements in Guanacaste in the 1980s, compared with 73.3 percent at a national level (Chant 1997:170). Similarly, whereas in Costa Rica as a whole in 1996, 52.8 percent of births occurred to married women, in Guanacaste this was only 34.7 percent (Dirección General de Estadísticas y Censos [DGEC] 1997:25). According to the 2000 census, the proportion of female-headed households in the Chorotega Region was 23.4 percent as against a national average of 22.2 percent (INEC 2001, cuadro 31). By the same token, links with extended family members, especially among women, have often helped to compensate for the weakness of conjugal unions and/or the precarious nature of male support. The fact that patterns of conjugal informality and extended family support networks seem to be an ongoing reality in Guanacaste, especially among the poor, conceivably constitute major reasons why the erosion of the "traditional" male-headed household model now occurring at a national level did not elicit undue interest or commentary in our group discussions.

People's Perceptions of Family Change and Its Causes

Leading on from the above, discussions of family change across the groups as a whole were dominated by two main themes: first, the decline of "family values" such as "respect," "morality," "integrity," "responsibility," and "decency"; second, the mounting difficulties of intergenerational communication and parental control over children. While people often found it hard to pinpoint precise reasons for these trends, four main sets of processes emerged as significant in their discourses.

Development and International Tourism in Guanacaste

Among older people, and especially those whose recollections dated prior to the 1980s when the bulk of Guanacasteco livelihoods were still in farming, a common reason given for the decline in "family values" was Guanacaste's conversion to a "modern" economy reliant on "science," external capital and international tourism. Consumerism, together with the influx of foreign visitors, residents and entrepreneurs, widely deemed to have "loose morals" and "antisocial" habits on account of their dress, sexual practices, and use of drink and recreational drugs, were singled out as having seriously undermined "traditional" patterns of behavior. This arose not only from social interaction (especially among the young), but also from the pernicious effects of "demonstration." As expressed by Doña Imelda, a fifty-two year old retired primary school teacher from the village of 27 de Abril:

> Lo que pienso es que nos gusta imitar, y en la zona de Villareal, que es la que yo conozco bastante, que está más afectada. Ellos andan a como comenzó a venir, sin que ofenda la palabra "gringos," pero desde que comenzó a venir, la gente se ha influenciada, que comenzó a andar en shorts, o casi desnudos, presentarse en una oficina donde se debe tener cierto respeto a una institución, se meten en sandalias. En el tiempo de "los hippis," andan con pelo largo. Todo el mundo dice que todo el mundo andan con pelo largo y es la única excusa que hacen, pero eso de que no nos han llevado en realidad a resolver los problemas económicos, no que nos haya servido. Que sí tienen trabajo por el momento, pero esto se está perdiendo un montón de valores que nuestra gente sencilla y humilde, que es la que llega ahí a trabajar, está adquiriendo por el hecho de vivir ahí. Ese contacto que tienen, es completamente otro mundo, y si hablamos de Flamingo todavía peor, porque eschucho que hay lugares donde se bañan desnudos y todas esas cosas. Para nuestra gente, que tenía un poquito de principios—nuestra gente se asombra. Hemos estado unas veces a la playa y se ve una pareja ahí, una sola maleta de arena, y nuestros pequeños! Y uno hace aspavientos porque uno no está acostumbrado a ver esas cosas. Si hablamos de lo moderno, pues así tendrá que ser, pero quién sabe que otras cosas peores tendremos que ver?
> [What I think is that we like to copy, and it's the area around Villareal, which I know best, which has been most affected. The people there go about—and while I don't wish to offend by using the word "gringos"—since they started coming, people have gone around in shorts, or half-naked, and wearing sandals into offices where one should have a bit of respect. And in the era of "the hippy," they

have long hair. Everyone says that it's because everyone has long hair these days and its the only excuse they give, but that hasn't actually done anything to solve our economic problems. It hasn't helped us at all. People may well have work at the moment, but at the same time, there's a massive loss of values among our simple and humble folk who go there to work, that comes about from just living there. What they come into contact with is another world entirely, and if we speak of Flamingo [a deluxe beach resort a few kilometers from Villareal], it's even worse, because I hear that there are places where they swim in the nude and all that kind of thing. We have been to the beach sometimes and there's a couple there, making out in the sand, and there are our little ones! And we make a fuss because we're not used to seeing that type of thing. If we talk about the modern age, then that's how it has to be, but who knows what else we'll have to see?]

Some younger participants attributed the loss of values and decline in intrafamily communication not only to economic modernization, but also to the fact that parents set bad examples to their children. As commented by Luis Emilio, a sixteen year old schoolboy who formed part of a mixed group of low-income adolescents in the village of Bernabela:

Yo creo que eso se debe a que los tiempos cambian, y la sociedad se va corrompiendo cada día más . . . así entonces, los valores como la comunicación entre los padres se van perdiendo. También se puede mencionar la infidelidad entre los padres, y eso provoca la desunión entre la pareja y en algunos casos provoca que el hijo tome el mundo de drogas y algo así.
[I think that it (the decline of the family) owes to changing times, and that society is getting more corrupt by the day . . . this explains why values such as communication between parents is declining. It can also be said that infidelity between parents provokes breakdown in their relationships and in some cases pushes the child into the world of drugs or something else like that.]

Technology and Mass Media

Echoing public concerns discussed earlier, another set of factors identified as significant not only in the erosion of family values, but in the decline in intergenerational communication, was the increased influence of television and other forms of mass media such as the Internet. These were regarded by respondents as having exposed children and youth to "undesirable influences" such as violence, individualism, materialism, consumerism, sexual licentiousness and "global culture."[14] *Telenovelas*" (TV soap operas), for example, were held responsible for setting bad examples of "libertine behavior" and "offensive language." Growing access to technology and mass media was deemed to have presented children with more stimuli than in the past that detracted from a formerly narrow range of activities and fixed reference points.[15] These processes were noted not only by older age groups in the survey, but by young people as well, such as Andrey, a sixteen year old schoolboy from the Bernabela group:

> Bueno yo creo que las familias se han ido rompiendo, o sea se han desintegrado. O sea, la gente de antes era más culta. Pero con los cambios de la tecnología, la televisión, la prostitución, la pornografía . . . todo eso fue influyendo para que muchos hombres o mujeres . . . ya o sea, quisieran experimentar en otros rumbos. Y se van perdiendo las familias . . . Hay mucha gente que dice para qué voy a estar en mi casa si puedo estar...no sé . . . viendo una película o algo así? O sea otras alternativas que puede tomar el jóven no precisamente de familia, porque ven la familia como aburrido.
> [Well, I think that families have been breaking down, that they have disintegrated. People in the past were more cultured. But with changes in technology, television, prostitution, pornography . . . all this has made a lot of men and women . . . want to experiment in other areas. And families are getting lost in the process . . . There are many people who say why am I going to stay home if I can be . . . I don't know . . . watching a film or something? In other words, young people have other alternatives that haven't got much to do with the family, because they see the family as boring.]

Similar sentiments were expressed by young middle-class adults taking university degrees in psychology in Liberia, the provincial capital, with Fiorella (21 years) observing that she had hardly sat down to a family meal in ten years. In her household everyone had either a television or computer in their room, and usually retired there to eat alone. Another student, Angie (23 years) described technology as an *"arma de doble filo"* ("double-edged sword"): it might be good for economic progress, but it also tended to alienate people and to impede the need for human contact.

Perceptions of a widening technology-related chasm between parents and children seem to be greatest among low-income groups where many parents have not had more than primary schooling. Much as though parents might be proud of, and respect, their children's greater education and technological capabilities, they also find the situation threatening. Today's adults not only feel ill equipped to teach their children in the way their own parents did, but unable to exert authority. This compounds a more general tendency, noted particularly by older respondents such as Don Bertirio, a sixty-six year old casual farm laborer from Liberia, that the youth of today *"quieren mandar a sus padres"* ("want to order their parents around"). Notwithstanding that more knowledge on the part of children could contain seeds for greater democratization in family life, from the perspective of a number of adults it seems that a widening intergenerational "digital divide" has contributed to a situation whereby instead of children fearing their parents, parents are tending to fear their children (see also Chant 2002b; Moser and McIlwaine 2000a,b on Colombia and Guatemala).

Lack of Time and New Work Patterns

Leading on from this, a third major factor held responsible for problems of communication between parents and children was lack of time. This was not only a result of orientation to an ever-widening range of extra-domestic activities, but the increasingly hectic pace of life, economic pressure and the need for both parents to generate income. Don Efraín, a fifty-nine year old farm worker who formed part of a small male-only focus group in Santa Cruz commented that *"desarrollo"* ("development") in the province had brought a *"presión bárbara"* ("fierce pressure") into people's lives that had robbed them of the time they once devoted to their families. Moreover, older people often attributed the increased rarity of family members eating together to the fact that mothers were no longer a "constant presence" in the home. As stated by Sonia, a forty-six year old chemistry lecturer from Liberia:

> Claro que sí ha variado! En el sentido de que ya cuesta un poco más esa unión de familia. Cuesta un poco más el sentarse a comer juntos, por diferencia de horas, porque ahora la mujer trabaja también, al igual que hombre . . . Normalmente, en mi época, mi mamá siempre estaba metida en la casa. Era ama de casa. Había una persona fija, que llevaba como ese rol . . . de hogar, casi constante.
> [Of course it (family life) has changed! In the sense that it now takes a little more effort to maintain family unity. It takes a little more effort to sit down and eat together, because of differences in hours, because women work the same as men . . . Normally, in my era, my mother was always in the house. She was a housewife. There was a fixed person who took on this role . . . in the home, almost always.]

As echoed by a fellow Liberiana, Doña María Cecilia, a fifty-one year old landlady:

> Hoy en día, exigen que la mujer tiene que trabajar, entonces el TV se convierte en la niñera de los hijos.
> [Nowadays, it's necessary for women to work, so the television becomes the nanny of the children.]

Interestingly, women tended to emphasize that even if they did make an effort to organize family meals, it was harder to entice children to eat at home given their growing tastes for foreign and/or junk food (*"comida chatarra"*) such as chips and hamburgers. By the same token, many women felt guilty at the thought they might be neglecting children (see Dobles Oropeza 1998). Low-income mothers in particular consoled themselves with the fact that at least they only worked part-time or from home, or left their children in the hands of relatives. Middle-class children, on the other hand, were perceived as spending most of their time with domestic servants and nannies. Notwithstanding that better-off people have always had assistance with child care, from the perspective of the poor, middle-class lives had become so dominated by money that parents were substituting cash for time with children. While low-income respondents felt that this was a means by which parents assuaged their guilt, the process exacerbated the evils of modern consumerism, as well as contributing to a new generation of undisciplined youth. As observed by Don Carlos Luis, a 62-year-old farmer from the village of 27 de Abril:

> Hay varios ejemplos que tenemos que los hijos de los educadores o las parejas que trabajan como profesionales, son los hijos más desordenados. Por qué? Porque en la unión de familia no están nunca los padres para saber que están haciendo. Se les puede dar lo económico y todo pero no es lo suficiente.
> [There are many cases where the sons and daughters of teachers or professional couples are the most unruly. Why? Because the parents are never in the family home to see what they are doing. They can give them financial support and everything, but this isn't enough.]

While middle-class parents themselves tended to rationalize having to work harder in order to oblige their children's financial *needs* (rather than demands), whether for education, computer equipment, clothes and so on, they also recognized that this impinged on the amount of time they had available for children, and they were worried about it.

State Intervention in Family Relationships

The increased influence of the state in child protection (such as the abolition of corporal punishment and the extension of children's rights) was the fourth, and final factor, widely identified as having diminished parental control over children. The role played by organizations such as the National Child Protection Agency (*Patronato Nacional de la Infancia* [PANI]) in enforcing bans on the use of physical discipline at home and at school received particular attention. For many parents, especially fathers, curtailment of their freedoms to use physical force were perceived as having diluted their power to exert authority. Although this situation could potentially favor more egalitarian family relationships based on mutual respect and friendship rather than fear, men tended to emphasize the negative aspects, claiming instead an association with a loss of values and disturbing new social phenomena. Somewhat contradictorily perhaps, increased checks on male violence were often linked in respondent discourses with a rise in female prostitution. As noted by Don Benito, a fifty-six year old casual farm laborer:

> [S]e ha venido desarrollando la prostitución porque el padre de familia no tiene

la autoridad que debería tener como antes. Por qué digo yo esto? Porque si un padre de familia castiga a un hijo y el vecino o cualquier otra persona lo ve, lo denuncia inmediatamente, y va a preso.

[(P)rostitution has been on the increase because the head of the family does not have the authority that he ought to, like before. Why do I say this? Because if a family head punishes a child, and a neighbor or other person sees it, they denounce him immediately and he ends up in prison.]

Hostilities to state intervention were also found in a national study on lifestyles and public opinion of nearly 1,300 urban households carried out in 1996 by a team of Costa Rican psychologists and the then Centre for Women and the Family. A total of 46 percent of the sample declared that the state ought not to intervene in family problems, and another 42.6 percent stressed that it was men's role to exert authority within the family (Dobles Oropeza 1998:36).

It should also be noted that men fear PANI not only because it limits the scope for corporal correction, but also because it can force them to provide child support (through docking wages, blocking applications for exit visas, and so on). Coupled with more recent initiatives such as the *Law for Responsible Fatherhood,* it is unlikely that men's antipathy towards state "interference" will go away. Indeed, for some men in the Guanacaste survey, attempts by the state to step up protection for women in the home were regarded as decidedly overzealous, as revealed in the following section.

GRASSROOTS REACTIONS TO FAMILY CHANGE IN GUANACASTE

It is clear that many people in Guanacaste are uneasy about some of the changes they perceive to be occurring in family life in their own locality, and in the country at large. Even if a tendency to berate the present and romanticize the past may well repeat itself across time, and the problem of a "generation gap" is not unique to these cohorts, this does not diminish the fact that concerns about the loss of control over children and youth, the lack of time for parent-child communication, and declining family values, are deeply felt. While changes in these aspects of family life were almost universally viewed in a negative light, however, views on other aspects of change were more divided, particularly those relating to gender. Among older age groups in particular, changing gender divisions of labor, and the growing power of women within and beyond the family, were the subject of divergent opinion. For the most part, divided views on gender corresponded with the gender of the informants themselves.

Changing Patterns of Gender: The Views of Male Adults

Many men in our survey, particularly those who were middle aged or older, expressed disquiet about changing patterns of gender, and identified mounting rates of conflict between husbands and wives (whether legal or common-law) as having played a major role in weakening family cohesion. One of the main reasons given by male respondents for this state of affairs was that new legislation and social programs had increased women's rights in their homes and in wider society. Many felt that these interventions had gone "too far" and that women were "abusing" their new privileges.[16] As Edgar, a 46-year-old instructor in educational orientation from 27 de Abril, expressed it:

> (E)l problema con la liberación femenina es que la mujer no se ha podido liberar y mal interpreta su papel de liberación. Piensa que la liberación es parársele al hombre y pegarle o qué sé yo.
> [(T)he problem with female liberation is that women have not been able to liberate themselves and misinterpret their freedom. They think that liberation is about challenging men, and hitting them, or whatever.]

Another middle-aged male respondent in the same (mixed) group declared that:

> La igualdad de las leyes, la igualdad del hombre y la mujer han venido a tener un montón de problemas en la familia. Por qué? Porque cuando hay muchas parejas ahí en pleito, hasta que la mujer mata a su marido. Antes quién veía que una mujer le pegaba a su marido? Quién oía decir que un esposo mataba a su señora? Antés no sucedía eso ... Le pegaba el esposo a la señora. Sí, le pegaba, pero no, no ... no digamos ... a un extremo de que hubiera tanta agresión ... Diós guarda! Si un esposo toca a una señora hasta a la carcel puede ir a dar!
> [Equality in the law, equality between men and women, has brought with it a whole host of problems for the family. Why? Because where you have couples in conflict, the woman can even kill her husband. Whoever used to see a woman hitting her husband in the past? Whoever heard of a husband killing his wife? This didn't happen before ... Husbands beat their wives. Sure, they beat them, but not ... shall we say ... to the point of such aggression ... God forbid! If a man (now) so much as touches his wife he can go to prison for it!]

The other major factor held responsible by men for women's declining submission was their growing labor force participation. In line with national trends, women's employment opportunities have increased as services have become a more important part of the regional economy. Although women's share of the labor force in the Chorotega region, at 27.7 percent, is less than the countrywide average (see previous discussion), 63 percent of women workers have full-time regular employment, compared with only 53.3 percent of men. This represents a bigger differential than for Costa Rica as a whole, where the figures are 70.9 percent versus 66.1 percent, respectively (INEC 2001, cuadro 9). The fact that open unemployment in the region is presently higher among men than women (see previous discussion) is also significant, especially given that as recently as 1994, the situation was the reverse, with 8.5 percent of women being unemployed compared with 7.2 percent of men (Chant 2000:210). On top of this, the gap between male and female average earnings is now negligible: women in the Chorotega region (excluding nonremunerated workers) earn 97.6 percent of the male average, compared with 82.5 percent nationally (INEC 2001, cuadro 16). For many men these labor market trends have eroded their own sense of self-worth, given women too much power, and acted to undermine the "normal" order of family life (see also Salas 1998:66).[17] As noted by Don Solón, the forty-seven year old director of a village primary school:

> Uno no sabe ni siquiera quién es él que manda . . . Bueno, pero, sí, sí, sí, el jefe de la familia, el eje de la familia es el varón, ese es el jefe, pero lo que pasa es que hay varones que no juegan ese rol, que el jefe de la familia es la mujer verdad?
> [One doesn't even know who's running the home . . . Well, but, yes, yes, yes . . . the head of the family, the axis of the family is the man, he is the head, but what is happening is that there are men who are not playing this role, and the head of the household is the woman, right?]

Rafael, a forty-five year old assistant prosecutor interviewed in Liberia, expressed similar sentiments:

> Cuando el padre deja el rol de proveedor, o no puede proveer para satisfacer las necesidades de sus hijos, le cuesta que le respetan los hijos como figura de autoridad.
> [When a father abandons his role of breadwinner, or when he cannot provide enough to fulfill his children's needs, it becomes difficult for him to be respected by his children as a figure of authority.]

Women's growing economic autonomy was also deemed to be associated with two other processes which fed into what men perceived to be a general trend towards "family breakdown." More women were having children on their own was one process. As articulated by Albert, a thirty-three year old statistics lecturer from Liberia:

> Yo creo que la familia, como la concebimos ahora, va a desaparecer, porque ahora cerca de la mitad de los niños que nacen son de madres solteras. Entonces, como concibo la familia del futuro va a ser el matriarcado—las madres, los hijos, y el hombre, no sé haciendo que. En Costa Rica, la cantidad de madres solteras está aumentando, no disminuyendo. Ahora tengo varias primas que son madres solteras, y muchos chiquillos que conozco . . . Y si seguimos así, la familia va a desaparecer.
> [I think that the family, as we conceive of it at the moment, is going to disappear,

because now around half of the children who are born are to single mothers. So, as I see it, the family of the future will be a matriarchy—women, children, and the man doing what, I do not know. In Costa Rica, the number of single mothers is increasing, not decreasing. At the moment I have several cousins who are single mothers, and many children I know . . . If we go on like this, the family will disappear.]

A second reason why women's economic autonomy was felt to be undermining the "traditional" family, was that it had made women who were already in relationships more likely to break up with their spouses, especially where men found it difficult to get regular employment. As stated by Don José, a sixty year old farmer from Santa Cruz:

Estoy de acuerdo en una parte, pero hay una división, tal como ahora, si la mujer no halla trabajo entonces se va de ama de casa. En cambio, si el hombre no encuentra trabajo tendría que irse de la casa porque no está aportando nada . . . y ese es el problema grande porque hay mujeres que quieren sentirse bién, casarse bién, disfrutar su vida y el hombre se quedó ahí!
[I agree to some extent (with women working), but there is a division now, such that if the woman doesn't find work she can be a housewife. In contrast, if the man doesn't find work, he has to leave home because he's not contributing anything . . . and this is the big problem, because there are women who like to have a good time, to marry well, to enjoy their lives, but men have been left behind!]

The perception that men were losing ground in the labor market as women's share rose was regarded as particularly threatening by low-income adult male respondents and bears out the findings from a more dedicated study I had carried out with eighty low-income men in 1997.[18] Several participants in this survey had talked about feeling less needed and appreciated by their wives and children, and having less say and authority in the home. Martín, a thirty year old bricklayer, for example, had declared that: "La mujer que tiene su propia plata pierde el cariño para el esposo. Muchos matrimonios han fracasado por eso" ["A woman who has her own money loses affection for her husband. Many marriages have been ruined because of this."] In turn, Luis, a thirty-three year old waiter, stressed that when a man cannot provide for his wife and children, his self-image and his image in the eyes of others "ya no vale nada" ["isn't worth anything"] (see Chant 2000:211).

While many men thus attributed "family breakdown" to changes in women's situations and behavior, and lamented this trend as negative, in light of men's historically tenuous attachments to spouses and children in the province, I would suggest that "family breakdown" *per se* was not their principal problem. Instead, as I have argued elsewhere, a more important factor as far as men are concerned is probably that decisions within and about their families are perceived to be increasingly out of their own hands as a result of growth in women's employment, rights and legal protection. In short, the key issue at stake is men's perceived loss of power in domestic units, not the dissolution of domestic units *per se* (see Chant 2000, 2002b; Dobles Oropeza 1998; McCallum 1999 on Brazil; Safa 1999 on the Dominican Republic).[19]

Changing Patterns of Gender: The Views of Female Adults

This reading of the situation would seem to be borne out by the views of adult women in the survey. While they themselves reflected on their increased civil and economic rights with pride and enthusiasm, they were only too aware that men were finding it difficult to adjust to the new scenario. As Marta, a thirty-four year old social worker from 27 de Abril, stated:

> Las leyes que protegen a la mujer hoy en día . . . se le ha permitido a la mujer quererse superar y salir de ese círculo en que ella ha estado. Entonces, el hombre no le gusta que ellas se superen. Ha habido un gran choque, digamos, del hombre y la mujer como una lucha de poder, pienso yo, o sea, "yo mando aquí" y ya la mujer al quererse superar entonces él piensa que va a estar por debajo. Es como una lucha de poder dentro de la familia verdad? Que eso ha perdido los valores que la familia antes tenía entonces. Yo pienso no es que las mujeres estemos peor ahora que antes sino que la mujer ya tiene otra visión diferente. Se ha valorado más. Ella ha medido realmente la capacidad que ella tiene hoy en día de llegar a ser hasta Presidente. Ustedes ven que a las mujeres antes no se les daba la oportunidad de llegar a un puesto político, a ser Diputada. Hoy en día a la mujer se le ha reconocido esa capacidad que ella tiene. Entonces, yo pienso que por ahí ha dado ese cambio.
>
> [The laws that protect women in this day and age . . . have permitted women to want to get ahead and escape from the trap they've been in. But men have not taken kindly to the fact that women get ahead. There's been a big clash, shall we say, between men and women, like a power struggle I think. Like "I'm in charge here," and because the woman wants to get ahead, the man thinks that he'll go under. It's like a power struggle within the family isn't it? It has caused a loss of family values that we had previously. But I think that it's not that we women are worse now than we were before, but that we have a different vision. Women value themselves more. It's dawned on them that they have the capacity nowadays to become President if they want. We know that women in the past were never given the chance to occupy a political position, to be a Deputy. But nowadays women have recognized their capacity. For this reason, the change has come about.]

As echoed by Ana Isabel, a forty-three year old primary school teacher, from the same group:

> Las mujeres de antes eran sometidas por el hombre. Era lo que el hombre decía y se acabó, porque yo me acuerdo este. Mi abuelita nos decía este a mi mamá: "Mirá . . . la mujer está en la casa, por qué tiene que andar bailando, por qué tiene que andar aquí, por qué tiene que andar allá?" . . . Suerteramente, o desgraciadamente, llegó la liberación de las mujeres y entonces cogimos alas, cogimos fuerzas, y ahora Usted ve muy poco que la mujer se deje pegar del hombre.
> [Men in the past subordinated women. What men said went, and that was that. I remember this. My grandmother would say to my mother: "Look . . . women should be in the home, so why go out dancing, or be going here and there?" Fortunately, or unfortunately, women's liberation came along, and we grew wings, we gained strength, and now it's very rare that you see a woman letting a man hit her.]

For many women, work is also viewed as a necessity, as evident in another interjection by Ana Isabel:

> Vea, ahora las mujeres nos hemos dado el rol de que . . . pucha! Si nosotras las mujeres nos quedamos ahí en la casa, vamos a seguir siendo cucarachas, y yo creo . . . bueno al menos yo personal, yo digo yo no nací para ser cucaracha. Yo nací para volar. Porque vea, mi marido, dos años tenía yo de trabajar cuando él me dice, no, "Deja de trabajar porque tenés que estar en la casa." Yo le digo: "Un momento papacito. Yo estuve cinco años en el colegio quemándome las pestañas para yo irme a quemarme los ojos en la cocina. Estás muy equivocado." Y vean que si yo lo hubiera hecho me estuviera llevando San Quintín[20] ahorita, porque él se fue con otra y yo me hice cargo de mis hijos sola. Y si yo no hubiera tenido mi trabajo, hubiera tenido que irme para Los Laureles [21] a la prostitución. Eso es lo que toca a las mujeres: irse a la prostitución para sacar adelante a sus hijos.
> [Look, nowadays, women have been given the role of . . . for heaven's sake! If we women stay at home, we're going to continue being underdogs, and I think—well personally at least—that I wasn't born to be an underdog (literally, "cockroach"). I was born to fly. Look, I had two years of work behind me when my husband said: "Stop working, because you've got to be at home." I said to him: "Just a minute little papa. I wasn't five years in high school burning my eyelashes just so I could burn my eyes in the kitchen. You're mistaken." And, look, if I'd done what he said, it would have been a disaster now, because my husband left me for another woman and I was left with the children. And if I hadn't had my work, I'd have had to go to The Laurels and become a prostitute. This is how it is for women—to go into prostitution in order to give their children a life.]

Unlike men, women did not feel that their widening vista of personal, civil and professional possibilities was a cause of "family breakdown." While recognizing that there were more practical problems to address now that so many women were working outside the home, for example, they did not feel this had undermined the family in any fundamental way, since most women rationalized paid work as a means of providing a decent home for their children and helping them get ahead (see also García and de Oliveira 1997 on Mexico). Indeed, if anything, women saw the family as strengthened by their increased opportunities in this domain, as well as through their enhanced entitlement to property following conjugal dissolution. The fact that women in the region have rarely been able to count on men as stable figures in their lives is extremely significant here. Women have often had to fend for their children without substantial male help. Accordingly, having greater scope to leave men who do not put much into family life is regarded positively rather than negatively. Moreover, despite men's claims that women nowadays are much more likely to leave them if they cannot bring money into the household, in fifteen years of my own research experience in this region, I have rarely witnessed women abandoning their relationships unless forced to do so on account of extreme behavior, such as their spouses giving up searching for work altogether, or being violent towards them, or engaging in repeated infidelities (see Chant 1997).

To all intents and purposes, therefore, from women's point of view, changes in their own lives did not mean that family breakdown was more likely. The continuity of family life from women's perspectives was also marked by their ongoing contact and interaction with extended networks of kin centered on their natal families (see earlier). Despite observations about people in general having less time to invest in family ties, links among blood relatives seem to be as strong, active, and valued as ever. In particular, the use of kin for child minding—whether within or beyond the household—seems to be playing a vital role in facilitating the labor force participation of mothers (see Chant 1997).

**Changing Patterns of Gender and Family Organization:
The Views of Young People**

As with adult women, some of the changes taking place in gender and family life were also welcomed by adolescents and young adults in the survey (see Table 1). While this applies more to the female members of these cohorts, an appreciable proportion of young men seemed to accept the idea that women should have their own jobs or careers, and that in an ideal world, childcare and housework would be a joint parental venture. When one male participant in a mixed group of low-income secondary school students aged between fifteen and twenty years in the village of Villareal joked that women really belonged in the home looking after children, he was cried down with retorts of *"machista, machista!"* by other male and female members. In turn, both male and female participants in a middle-class focus group drawn from psychology undergraduates at the University of Costa Rica in Liberia expressed approval for a decline in familial authoritarianism. As articulated by René, a nineteen year old male member of this group:

> Yo pienso que muchas de las causas que están alterando la familia podría ser el machismo porque se ha ... diversificado. O se puede decir que el concepto de lo que es una familia ... y muchas personas, no digo siempre los hombres porque hay mujeres que lo hacen, toman la posesión a esa familia. Entonces, es ahí donde viene naciendo la agresión. Empiezan a decir "bueno, yo me casé con esta mujer, es mía, entonces yo le puedo pegar y la puedo mantener debajo de la cocina."
>
> [I think that among many of the things that are altering the family is that machismo has ... changed. Or one could say that the concept of what a family is ... and this doesn't only apply to men, because some women also do it, (namely) take charge of the family. And it's here where the aggression starts. They begin to say, "Well, I married this woman, she's mine, and so I can beat her, and I can keep her chained to the kitchen sink."]

While young people envisaged that their own families, and those of the next generation, would probably continue to consist of a core of parents and children, there also appeared to be considerable openness about the form that household arrangements might take, even if the functions might remain more or less the same. As Cintia, a twenty year old student from the Liberia psychology group, noted:

> El concepto de la familia ha evolucionado considerablemente, y es por tal motivo que considero que, dentro de 20 años, conceptualmente hablando, la familia ya no será la misma. Se podría hablar incluso de un núcleo familiar constituido solo por hermanos, o simplemente individuos con una convivencia mutua para de esta manera, hacerle frente a una sociedad cada vez más dominada por los intereses económicos. Si bien el concepto tiende a cambiar, la funcionabilidad puede no verse afectada de manera considerable. La familia seguirá siendo el ente de socialización primario, por medio del cual los individuos obtendrán los conocimientos básicos para insertarse en un ambiente social específico.
>
> [The concept of family has evolved substantially, and for that reason I think that, 20 years from now, conceptually speaking, the family won't be the same. One could even talk about a family nucleus consisting only of siblings, or simply individuals who come together to cope with a society increasingly dominated by economic interests. Even if the concept is tending to change, the functions themselves are unlikely to alter dramatically. The family will continue being the primary agent of socialization, through which individuals will obtain the basic skills to insert themselves in a specific social environment.]

As noted by another member of this focus group, twenty year old Sonia:

> A mi me parece que este concepto de familia es una cuestión que cada una de las personas construye, alrededor de su propia vivencia dentro de una familia,

cualquiera que sea, y que pueden existir tantas definiciones de familia como per sonas y carácteristicas tenga, digamos.
[As far as I'm concerned, this concept of "family" is a something that each person constructs for him/herself, around their own experience within a family, whatever that might be. Let's say that there are likely to be as many definitions of family as there are persons and characteristics.]

Another dimension of this perspective was the idea that relationships born of affection rather than biology had more value for children. Some firsthand experience of being abandoned by fathers and/or growing up in stepfamilies was relevant here.[22] As José, a sixteen year old member of the low-income focus group in Villareal reported:

Bueno, en el caso mío . . . yo vivía con mi padastro y yo siempre me llevé muy bien con él, y desde los ocho años que mi mamá se casó con él, siempre me he llevado muy bien. Y más bien yo pienso a veces que yo le quiero más que a mi verdadero papá, porque él me dió el amor que nunca tuvé de él.
[Well, in my case . . . I lived with my stepfather and I always got along very well with him, and in the last eight years since my mother married him, I've always got along with him fine. In fact, at times I think I love him more than my real father, because he gave me the love that I never got from him (my father).]

Another sixteen year old male, Mauricio, in a mixed group of low-income adolescents in Bernabela, expressed the opinion that having a violent man around, even if he was the biological father, was in no one's interests:

Mejor que se vaya . . . tan sólo que le pegue a mi mamá, hasta ahí ya!
[Better that he goes . . . He just needs to hit my mother, and he's gone too far!]

Accompanying a general openness to diverse family forms, and recognizing the need for flexibility in a situation where conjugal relationships have been historically unstable, several young people also favored consensual unions (*uniones libres*) over marriage. Among low-income youth, many of whom had come from families where biological parents had not been formally married and/or had been involved with other partners, marriage was regarded as overly restrictive and potentially harmful to children insofar as poor relations between spouses who stayed together only because there *were* married could impact negatively on the young (Chant 1997, chap. 8). An additional reason offered against marriage by this group was that divorce was expensive. Although in practice marriage is more common among the middle classes, and adults still tend to uphold this as a normative ideal, most youth from this sector profess that there is little difference between formal and informal partnerships, and are open to the notion of flexible, plural forms of family organization. Moreover, although these respondents agreed that some changes in family arrangements were unsettling, there was also broad agreement that the aftermath of this "transition phase" could be positive. As Adriana, a twenty-one year old student from the Liberia psychology group, suggested:

> Los cambios son buenos, siempre y cuando no caigamos en los extremos . . . Creo que las transformaciones actuales serán para el buen funcionamiento posterior de la familia.
> [Changes are good, as long as we don't fall into extremes . . . I think that current transformations will actually benefit the family in the long term.]

As fellow student, twenty-one year old Yadira, echoed:

> Lo que yo veo es que aquí se ha tratado el concepto de crisis como muy negativo, y yo pienso que a mí me parece, que OK, hay transición, hay crisis que es necesaria para hacer cambios, pero que tal vez esa crisis no es que está empeorando la familia, no les está haciendo daño . . . La familia era mejor tal vez, eso de que los hijos se rebelan y está empeorándose, pero hay otras en que mejoran la familia. Se está sacando, esa gente que fue, que ha sido por mucho tiempo agredida, y que ahora tiene la posibilidad de hablar . . . Que tal vez no se va a liberar completamente de la agresión, no vamos a tener la familia perfecta, pero que por lo menos quizás se mejore y a partir de esa crisis, que sería una crisis con una consecuencia positiva.
> [As far as I see it here, the concept of crisis has been treated as something extremely negative, and as far as I can see, OK, there's a transition, there's a crisis that's necessary in order to effect change, but perhaps this crisis isn't making the family worse, or destroying it . . . The family was better in the past maybe, and children rebelling nowadays are making things worse, but there are other things that are making the family better. It's coming out now, those people who were abused for a long time and who never had the possibility of speaking about it . . . Perhaps we're never going to be completely liberated from aggression, or have a "perfect family," but perhaps things will get better as a result of this crisis. Maybe it will be a crisis with a positive outcome.]

In many respects therefore, there is evidence of optimism about various tendencies in family change among the younger generation (particularly on the part of women), that seems to imply not so much that "family breakdown" is on the cards, but "family breakthrough" or "betterment." The possibilities for renegotiating family life thrown up by recent transitions have offered scope for greater openness, more tolerance, more equality and democracy, and less abuse. As articulated by Karina, a twenty-one year old psychology student from Liberia:

> Siempre, siempre ha estado la violencia, y siempre han existido niveles de tolerancia y los niveles de desunión familiar, solamente que tal vez hay hoy una mayor

apertura, porque todo el mundo habla del tema. Yo creo que una familia del siglo pasado no era más completa, ni más unida, ni mejor de lo que son ahora nuestras familias, simplemente que el contexto no dejaba apuntar ciertas cosas. Por ejemplo a una hija la casaban y la hija no tenía derecho decir con quién quería casarse, y ninguna hija podría revelarse, y la señora tampoco podría a denunciar el marido, porque le pegaba. Eso no le hacía una familia mejor. Tal vez estaban en un contexto diferente y ciertas cosas no eran valorizadas como "violencia intrafamiliar," ni "irrespeto," ni "atropello de los hijos," ni nada verdad? Tal vez ahora que haya una mayor apertura, y no digo que la situación ahora sea más crítica, a nivel de violencia, a nivel de problemas sociales también, verdad? Pero tampoco siento que la familia haya sido así como siempre perfecta y que ahora es cuando el caos, y ahora es que . . . bueno y que ahora pongámonos a discutir de familia porque la familia es culpable de todo.

[There's always, always been violence, and there's always been degrees of tolerance and degrees of family disunity, it's only that perhaps nowadays there's more openness, because everyone is talking about the subject. I don't think that the family of the past century was more complete, or more united, nor better than our families today, it's just that you couldn't raise certain issues then. For example, they married off their daughters, and the daughters had no right to say whom they'd marry, and no daughter could reveal anything, and she couldn't denounce her husband because he was beating her. This didn't make the family better. Perhaps they were in a different context, and certain things weren't interpreted as "family violence," or "disrespect," or "child abuse," or whatever right? Perhaps now, there's more openness, even if the situation now is no more critical, in respect of violence, of social problems and so on, right? But neither do I feel that the family was always perfect, and that only now are we in chaos . . . yet we go on about how the family is to blame for everything.]

Despite the generally positive views described above, it is important to remember that on account of various of the processes described earlier (development, financial pressure, the explosion of information technology and media and so on), one big concern among young people was the idea that there was increasingly less time to invest in domestic life and family relationships. As one boy in the mixed group of low-income adolescents in Villareal commented rather poignantly, the family of the future "va a faltar más comunicación, porque ambos padres van a trabajar tal vez en trabajos diferentes, donde salen cansados y tal vez los hijos salen con la empleada" ["the family of the future will lack communication, because both parents will work, and perhaps in different jobs, where they will come out exhausted, and perhaps the children will go out with the maid."]

DISCUSSION

Having presented views on various aspects of family change among different groups in Guanacaste, it becomes clear that it is difficult to establish whether families in the province are "on the verge of breakdown" in any generalized sense. While there are obviously some worries about family change which are common to all groups in the survey population (particularly the growing difficulties of intergenerational communication and the perceived loss of positive "family values"), there are also lines of divergence, with much contingent on the age and gender of respondents, and their different experiences and interests. For older men, for example, a strong sense of "breakdown" prevails, largely on account of changes in gender that are making men's own roles in families less assured than in the past. Yet among women and younger age groups (especially female members), many contemporary transitions—towards greater flexibility, equality, openness, permissiveness, and sharing—are seen as embodying prospects not only for enabling continuity in family life, but enriching it too. These observations highlight the profoundly subjective nature of the concept of "family breakdown," and underscore the need to use it selectively, that is, to make clear who is concerned about it and what their particular concerns are.

While attention to subjectivities is critical in the interpretation of family change, two other factors emerging from this and previous work I have done in Guanacaste suggest that family life is, actually, and prospectively, in a state of relative health. One is that even if couples are more likely to split up now than in the past, the extended family remains strong, and is a vital support mechanism not only for women, but also for men, who following conjugal dissolution often return to their natal families (see Chant 2000). Second, the will seems to be there to retain "the family," broadly defined. This is evidenced in the many positive (if idealized) images of family life that were offered by respondents. Most maintained that, in principle, some form of "family" (whether grounded in kinship or friendship), was an essential part of people's development and well being, and should ideally offer a secure, supportive and loving base for interacting with wider society.

If these positive visions of family life are to translate into lived experiences in the future, then it is important for policymakers to do what they can to assist the process, preferably by devising interventions based on in-depth surveys and consultative exercises with people at the grassroots. On the basis of the present project it would appear that salient needs include help with managing the dual responsibilities of parenting and paid work, and improving communication between adults and youth. Although amenities for child and after-school care already exist, along with various sources of family guidance such as the state-run *"Escuelas de Padres"* ("Parents' Schools") and the Catholic Church's *Movimiento Familiar Cristiano,* many participants in the survey expressed a desire to receive more publicly provided help in these domains, even if they could not necessarily elaborate on what this might entail.

Among various possibilities that might be considered here, a critical starting point is for public bodies to explore ways to maximize the use of parental resources without overloading any one group of individuals. As far as I can see, a good deal of the responsibility for spending time with children tends to devolve upon women, and not enough interest has been paid to examining how fathers, whether resident in the household or not, could be encouraged to take on a more equal share of this vital function. Although a nationwide survey on masculinity and "responsible fatherhood" was carried out by the then Centre for Women and the Family in 1996 (see CMF 1996; Gomáriz 1997), and men are nominally included in the current programs "Young Love" and "Building Opportunities" (Primera Dama de la República 2001), both the latter remain overwhelmingly oriented to women, bearing out a more general pattern in Latin America for women to be the primary constituency in both family policies and gender policies (see CEPAL 2001:V20). Moreover, the recent *Law for Responsible Paternity* in Costa Rica may get men thinking about preventing pregnancy, but not actually lead to their greater commitment to fathering, or a broadening of the role to encompass care and emotional attention alongside financial provision.[23] Strategies to do this might include those suggested by UNICEF such as promoting "culturally acceptable and positive images of men and women that can potentially demonstrate a balance of roles and responsibilities" (UNICEF 1997:33). If more could be done in this regard, then it might help increase the overall time for contact between children and parents. Additional benefits could include relaxing pressures on mothers, and reducing gender-typed socialization (UNICEF 1997:27). Moving ahead with initiatives to redefine men's roles within a renegotiated family may also help to allay men's current fears about being marginalized from family life, and thereby diminish male alienation and hostility to current transitions in women's positions.[24] Ideally, emphasis should be also be given to sensitizing young men and women about the virtues of more equitable undertaking of parental obligations such that they start out by coparenting on this basis.

Recognizing the importance of facilitating better intra-, as well as intergenerational relationships though making parenting more male inclusive does not mean that reconciling the "work-life" balance can or should be resolved through this route alone, especially given increasing economic pressures on the majority of households in Costa Rica. While middle-class groups can solve the dilemma to some extent by hiring nannies and domestic helpers, for low-income people, an important mechanism would be to increase publicly sponsored facilities for day care and after-school activities, and preferably in a way that these become seen as part of an extended family life, rather than separate from it. To some extent, this could be done by expanding Costa Rica's existing "community-home" model whereby children are cared for by known individuals such as neighbors and relatives in their local environments.[25] Indeed, given the fact that many children already spend time with relatives or with nonbiological kin such as stepparents, and recognizing that the quality of relationships they have with others often counts more than *who* those others actually are in kinship terms, then it is possibly a small step to promoting the notion that cultivating intimacy and trust with caring "outsiders" is an important adjunct to parental contact. An expanded range of functions might also be taken on under the auspices of paid "community care," such as shopping or preparing meals for parents who are particularly time deficient. In emphasizing that it is not just the *quantity* of time parents, or other caregivers, spend with children, but *quality* of time, more attention might also be given to training adults in new technology. This could help not only to diminish the part perceived to be played by the "digital divide" in reducing intergenerational communication, but also have the additional benefit of diversifying employment possibilities for older age groups.

Employers too could play a part in helping their employees to manage their home and working lives better by recognizing the value that workers who have families bring to the workplace. As Diane Elson (1999:612) has argued, employers tend to conceive of the unpaid caring of their employees as "costs" rather than as "benefits," when the latter can accrue from the fact that workers bring skills to the workplace that derive from their roles as parents and as household managers. In short: "[T]he reproductive economy produces benefits for the productive economy which are externalities, not reflected in market prices or wages." One way to reduce the "costs" to employers, of maternity or paternity leave and so on, might also be to finance these out of general taxation rather than on a firm-by-firm basis (Elson 1999:622).

Last but not least, many of the previous suggestions for policy would arguably work better if conceptualizations of the family were to embrace a more inclusive range of options. On one hand, Costa Rica's *de facto* support to "alternative households" constitutes an important step towards working with the diversity that currently exists in the country. By the same token, this also comes across as a pragmatic response to alleviating poverty rather than a positive endorsement of family plurality, especially given that both the current and previous administrations have expressly identified that they have no wish to provide "perverse incentives" for the formation of female-headed households. As Vega (1987, cited in Moreno 1994) observes, although there is lip service in Costa Rica to family diversity, the daily-used term "family" conjures up an impression of a uniform institution comprising of a married, monogamous couple with distinctive gendered duties (see Güendel and González 1998:19-20; *author's translation*).[26] Yet as echoed by CEPAL (2001:V11) for Latin America more generally, a major hiatus exists between traditional discourses and new practices of family life. As long as adherence to outmoded ideas remains, then this will conceivably act to depress the legitimacy of other types of household arrangement and present barriers to more generalized strategies to help people manage the increasingly complex nature of their domestic and working lives.

More explicit acknowledgement should, therefore, be given to the arguments advanced by feminist groups in Costa Rica that patriarchal household arrangements can increase rather than diminish the vulnerability of women and children (see Grupo Agenda Política de Mujeres Costarricenses [GAPMC] 1997;

Chant 1997, chap. 8 for a more general discussion). This should be accompanied by a fuller realization that families are not synonymous with households, and that where family ties remain strong, these can help to overcome the fragility of individual household units, as evidenced by the continuity of extended family support networks in Guanacaste. In addition, the role of *de facto* kin such as step-relations, friends and neighbors should be recognized In short, an appreciation of, and concern for, the quality of intimate social relationships needs to override any atavistic attachment to a normative family form. If the Costa Rican state wishes to consolidate its record on securing and upholding the rights and welfare of children, then it needs to think about finding ways to improve the quality of interpersonal relationships, which would arguably best be achieved by reducing inequality between families, and inequality between people more generally.

ACKNOWLEDGEMENTS

I would like to thank Maria Leiton and Eugenia Rodríguez for information, and Diane Perrons and three anonymous referees for their encouraging and insightful comments. The revision process also benefited from a presentation of this paper at the Institute of Latin American Studies, University of London in December 2001.

NOTES

1. Interviews and focus group discussions were conducted during the summer of 1999 under the auspices of a project entitled "Youth, Gender and Family Crisis in Costa Rica." The research was funded by the Nuffield Foundation (Award no. SGS/LB/0223) to which thanks are duly registered. I am also indebted to Wagner Moreno, Faculty of Social Psychology at the University of Costa Rica in Guanacaste for his valuable collaboration in interviewing and analysis, and to the members of our field team—Sonia Alvarado, Emma Hernández, Juan José Morales and Lisette Ondoy—for their painstaking work on transcription. This paper also utilizes some survey work conducted for two other projects: "Institutional Perspectives on Family Change in Costa Rica," carried out during Easter 1999, and funded by the Central Research Fund and London School of Economics, and "Men, Households and Poverty in Costa Rica" carried out in the summer of 1997, co-funded by the Nuffield Foundation (Award no: SOC/100 [1554]), and ESRC (Award no. R000222205).

2. The historian Eugenia Rodríguez (1999) claims that the nuclear household only became a powerful normative concept with the rise of liberalism in Costa Rica in the nineteenth and twentieth centuries, although Catholic marriage was first introduced in the mid-eighteenth and early nineteenth centuries in the Valle Central (see also Budowski 2000a:61; Rodríguez 2000 forthcoming). As it is,

diversity in family forms seems to have been common throughout history not only in Costa Rica (see Gudmundson 1986), but in other parts of Central and South America as well (see Cicerchia 1997; Dore 1997; Kuznesof 1980).

3   Out-of-wedlock births are mainly concentrated among younger age groups, with 74.8 percent of the total in 1996 occurring to women who were 29 years or younger (DGEC 1997:25). This, coupled with other evidence given in the paper, supports the observation of a progressive weakening of marriage-based parenting over time.

4   While female-headed households were only 20.1 percent of poor households in 1986, they represented 27 percent by 1995 (Trejos and Montiel 1999:10). As of 2000, they were 30 percent of households in poverty (INEC 2001, cuadro 31).

5   In some respects, the family support programs of the 1990s were a reinvention under different social and economic conditions of social democratic reforms implemented during the 1970s. The latter included the establishment of the Social Assistance Institute (*Instituto Mixto de Ayuda Social* [IMAS]) in 1970 under the presidency of José Figueres Ferrer, which had the remit of combating poverty and extending health care to all (see Lara, Barry, and Simonson 1995:61). With the introduction of new taxes on sales and wages, finance was also made available for a self-sustaining Fund for Family Allowances and Social Development (*Fondo de Desarrollo Social y Asignaciones Familiares* [FODASEF]). Related initiatives during the 1970s included the creation of the CEN-CENAI (*Centros de Nutrición-Centros de Atención Infantil* [Centers for Nutrition-Centers for Child Attention]).

6   María Leiton from the coordinating body, IMAS, kindly provided this information.

7   These figures derive from an opinion poll conducted by the firm Borge y Asociados in 1999 to ascertain levels of satisfaction with the incumbent government, and prospective voting preferences for the 2002 election. Results published in the national newspaper *Al Día* on 2 September 1999, revealed that 25 percent of respondents rated the cost of living as Costa Rica's major contemporary problem; 19 percent, the country's economic situation; 16.4 percent, delinquency; 10.2 percent, corruption, 7.2 percent, unemployment, 6.8 percent, drugs, 6.6 percent, poverty, and 2.4 percent, government.

8   The Latin American *Movimiento Familiar Cristiano* (MFC), which originated in Argentina in 1948, started in Costa Rica with a small group in 1958 and became a full-fledged regional movement in the 1960s (Rodríguez Cháves 1999). The objectives of the movement are to promote "human and Christian values in the

family and in the community," and to provide assistance to families (MFC 1997). These services include a range of programs designed to strengthen marriage and to help people lead "Christian family lives," such as prenuptial courses, support groups, matrimonial retreats, "family integration" weeks, and a marriage advisory service (see Napolitano 1998 for a discussion of the MFC in Mexico).

9 In the context of research on lone motherhood in Costa Rica and the rise in births unacknowledged by fathers, Budowski (2000b) observes that the Catholic Church has been more outspoken about these trends than any other single group in the country, regarding them as the outcome of "sinful" behavior, and as highly threatening to the moral and social order. Indeed, the Church has recently withdrawn its support for "Young Love," the government program promoting sexual awareness and the prevention of adolescent pregnancy (see earlier), because the educational materials were deemed to be too explicit (*La Nación*, 24 December 2000, p. 5A).

10 Protestant churches in the evangelical tradition have been increasing in numbers and followers in Costa Rica in recent years, with Guanacaste province alone being host to nine denominations and several individual churches, including the Emmanuel Bible Church, Assembly of God, Church of God and the World Missionary Movement. Attempts to safeguard family cohesion and welfare on the part of these sects have included income-generating activities for women, and efforts to reduce alcoholism among men (Interview with José Blas Diáz Castillo, Emmanuel Bible Church, Liberia, 14 September 1999).

11 The University of Costa Rica, the Pan American Health Organization, the Ministry of Health and the Costa Rican Social Security Institute carried out this study, "*Depresión en Jóvenes.*" It was reviewed on publication in *La Nación*, 22 September 1999, p. 8a.

12 See note 1.

13 According to the 2000 census, a total of 28.23 percent of persons born in Guanacaste were resident in other provinces of Costa Rica in this year, which is higher than any other of its seven provinces except Heredia (INEC 2001:12, cuadro 10).

14 Klak (1999:111) notes for Middle America in general that media flows from the North have increased since the onset of neoliberal economic restructuring.

15 A similar argument is made a textbook in common use in Costa Rican primary and secondary schools: *Orientación Educativa* (Educational Orientation). In not-

ing that family structure in the past was more stable, often linked to a particular geographical location in which all the elements existed for subsistence, the author, Pereira García (1998:45), writes that the family, the school, community, and church served as a mark of reference and gave security to members. Nowadays, however, Pereira García argues that conditions of life are changing constantly, especially in urban environments where people face a bewildering array of socioeconomic interactions, market forces, environmental pollution, personal insecurity and an accelerated pace of life which threatens physical and mental well being (see also UNICEF 1997:23; *author's translation*).

16   In the nationwide study carried out by the Psychology Institute of the University of Costa Rica cited in the penultimate section, 54.1 percent of the sample felt there was equality of opportunity between men and women in Costa Rica, with this view being held much more strongly by men than women (Dobles Oropeza 1998:36).

17   This is also noted for Peru by Fuller (2000) although she argues that: "among popular sector men, this crisis affects their self-esteem and may lead them to have doubts concerning their capacity to fulfill expectations as men, but does not lead them to question the hegemonic definition of masculinity as this is one of the few ways for them to accumulate social prestige" (p.109).

18   See note 1.

19   In relation to her research on Salvador da Bahia, Brazil, McCallum (1999:275) notes that: "In local talk, about sexual morés and parenting, the dominant theme is the 'liberal' and 'decadent' character of the modern age. Modernity is equated with a loss of control over female sexuality and reproduction." McCallum further argues that discussion about "women's loss of restraint and respectability functions as a brake upon pressure for change" (p.275).

20   The reference to San Quintín (San Quentin) symbolizes "disaster," and probably derives from a prison with a particularly notorious reputation by this name in the United States (personal communication, Eugenia Rodríguez).

21   "Los Laureles" ("The Laurels") is an old and well-known brothel about a mile out of the town of Santa Cruz, which is the canton to which the village of 27 de Abril belongs.

22   See CEPAL (2001) and Chant (2002a) for discussion of the growth of "blended" or "reconstituted" households in Costa Rica and elsewhere in Latin America.

23   The *Law for Responsible Paternity* passed in 2001 requires men who do not vol-

untarily register themselves as fathers to undergo a compulsory DNA test at the Social Security Institute. If the result is positive, they not only have to pay alimony and child support, but are also liable to contribute to the costs of the pregnancy and birth, and to pay their child's food bills for the first twelve months of life (see INAMU 2001).

24 As noted by Salas (1998:66) in the context of a research project on masculinity and domestic violence with 200 men, the fact that so many men have been ousted from their position as breadwinners by "criminal programs of economic and structural adjustment," is a major factor in perpetuating male displacement and the consequences that this entails, such as domestic violence (*author's translation*).

25 The "Community Home" ("*Hogares Comunitarios*") scheme dates back to the presidency of Rafael Calderón (1990-1994), but only took off in a major way during the regime of President José María Figueres (1994-1998). Administered by the Social Welfare Institute (*Instituto Mixto de Ayuda Social* [IMAS]), and concentrated primarily in low-income settlements, women running "community homes" are given training in childcare and paid a small state subvention for looking after other people's children in the neighborhood. Individuals using this service pay what they can as a token gesture and lone mothers are technically given priority for places (see Sancho Montero 1995).

26 This is borne out by a variety of fairly recent surveys and opinion polls. For example, a survey carried out by the Centre for Women and the Family in 1997 revealed that 73 percent of men and 75 percent of women felt that men should provide for the household, and 75.4 percent and 78.2 percent of men and women, respectively, stressed that women's main responsibilities should be home and family (see PEN 1998:44). This echoes a poll conducted earlier in the 1990s that indicated the marriage-based nuclear family, comprising male breadwinner and female homemaker was favored by three out of four people in the country as most desirable arrangement for raising children (Fernández 1992; see also Budowski 2000a; Muñoz 1997).

REFERENCES

AGUILAR, Gretel, Dagoberto Arias, Juan Carlos Burgos, Sonia Cervantes, and Jaime Echeverría.
    1998. *Diagnóstico Funcional: Plan de Acción para la Cuenca del Río Tempisque, vol. IV: Socioecónomica*. San José, Costa Rica: Liberia, Asociación para el Manejo de la Cuenca del Río Tempisque/Ministerio de Ambiente y Energía.

ARIAS, Omar.
    2000. *Are All Men Benefiting from the New Economy? Male Economic*

Marginalization in Argentina, Brazil and Costa Rica. Washington, D.C.: World Bank, Poverty Reduction and Economic Management Sector Management Unit, Latin America and the Caribbean Region (LCSPR).

ARRIAGADA, Irma.
    1998. "Latin American Families: Convergences and Divergences in Models and Policies." *CEPAL Review* 65:85-102.

BADILLA, Ana Elena and Lara Blanco.
    1996. *Código de la Mujer* San José, Costa Rica: Editorial Porvenir S.A./Centro de Capacitación para el Desarrollo (CECADE).

BENERÍA, Lourdes.
    1991. "Structural Adjustment, the Labour Market and the Household: The Case of Mexico." In *Towards Social Adjustment: Labor Market Issues in Structural Adjustment,* edited by Guy Standing and Victor Tokman. Geneva, Switzerland: International Labor Organization.

BRADSHAW, Sarah.
    1995a. "Women's Access to Employment and the Formation of Women-headed Households in Rural and Urban Honduras." *Bulletin of Latin American Research* 14(2):143-158.
    ———. 1995b. "Female-headed Households in Honduras: Perspectives on Rural-Urban Differences." *Third World Planning Review* 17(2):117-131.

BUDOWSKI, Monica.
    2000a. "'Yo Valgo': The Significance of Daily Practice: The Case of Lone Mothers in Costa Rica." End of Award report, Grant no. 82-04-27891. Berne, Switzerland: Swiss National Science Foundation.
    ———. 2000b. "Lone Motherhood in Costa Rica: A Threat for Society or a Chance for Change?" Revised draft of paper delivered for publication of the Proceedings of the symposium "Order, Risk and Catastrophe," Berne, Switzerland, October 11-13, 1999.

BUDOWSKI, Monica and Laura Guzmán.
    1998. "Strategic Gender Interests in Social Policy: Empowerment Training for Female Heads of Household in Costa Rica." Paper prepared for the International Sociological Association XIV World Congress of Sociology, Montreal, July 26-August 1.

BUDOWSKI, Monica and Luis Rosero Bixby.
    Forthcoming. "Fatherless Costa Rica? Child Acknowledgement and Support among Lone Mothers." *Journal of Comparative Family Studies*.

CASTELLS, Manuel.
    1997. *The Power of Identity*. Oxford, England: Blackwell.

CENTRO NACIONAL PARA EL DESARROLLO DE LA MUJER Y LA FAMILIA (CMF).
    1996. *Plan Para la Igualdad de Oportunidades entre Mujeres y Hombres (PIOMH) 1996-1998*. San José, Costa Rica: CMF.

CERRUTTI, Marcela and René M. Zenteno.
    1999. "Cambios en el Papel Económico de las Mujeres entre las Parejas

Méxicanas." *Estudios Demográficos y Urbanos* 15(1):65-95.

CHANT, Sylvia.

　　1992. "Migration at the Margins: Gender, Poverty and Population Movement on the Costa Rican Periphery." In *Gender and Migration in Developing Countries,* edited by Sylvia Chant. London, England: Belhaven.

———. 1997. *Women-headed Households: Diversity and Dynamics in the Developing World.* Houndmills, Basingstoke, England: Macmillan Press Ltd.

———. 1999a. "Women-headed Households: Global Orthodoxies and Grassroots Realities." In *Women, Globalization and Fragmentation in the Developing World,* edited by Haleh Afshar and Stephanie Barrientos. New York, New York: St. Martin's Press Ltd.

——— 1999b. "Youth, Gender and 'Family Crisis' in Costa Rica." Report to the Nuffield Foundation, London, October.

———. 2000. "Men in Crisis? Reflections on Masculinities, Work and Family in Northwest Costa Rica." *European Journal of Development Research* 12(2):199-218.

———. 2002a. "Women, Men and Household Diversity." In *Challenges and Change in Middle America: Perspectives on Development in Mexico, Central America and the Caribbean,* edited by Cathy McIlwaine and Katie Willis. Harlow, England: Pearson Education.

———. 2002b. "Whose Crisis? Public and Popular Reactions to Family Change in Costa Rica." In *Exclusion and Engagement: Social Policy in Latin America,* edited by Christopher Abel and Colin Lewis. London, England: University of London, Institute of Latin American Studies.

CHANT, Sylvia with Nikki Craske.

　　2003. *Gender in Latin America.* London, England: Latin America Bureau/New Brunswick, New Jersey: Rutgers University Press.

CICERCHIA, Ricardo.

　　1997. "The Charm of Family Patterns: Historical and Contemporary Patterns in Latin America." In *Gender Politics in Latin America: Debates in Theory and Practice,* edited by Elizabeth Dore. New York, New York: Monthly Review Press.

COLABORACIÓN AREA LEGAL.

　　1997. "Pulso Legislativo: Nuevos Proyectos de Ley." *Otra Mirada* 1(2):51.

COMISIÓN ECONÓMICA PARA AMÉRICA LATINA (CEPAL).

　　2001. *Panorama Social de América Latina 2000-2001.* Santiago, Chile: CEPAL.

DATTA, Kavita and Cathy McIlwaine.

　　2000. "'Empowered Leaders'? Perspectives on Women Heading Households in Latin America and Southern Africa." *Gender and Development* 8(3):40-49.

DIERCKXSENS, Wim.

　　1992. "Impacto del Ajuste Estructural Sobre la Mujer Trabajadora en Costa Rica." In *Cuadernos de Política Económica,* edited by Marvin Acuña-Ortega. Heredia: Universidad Nacional de Costa Rica.

DIRECCIÓN GENERAL DE ESTADÍSTICAS Y CENSOS (DGEC).
   1996. *Encuesta de Hogares.* San José, Costa Rica: DGEC.
   ———. 1997. *Estadística Vital 1996.* San José, Costa Rica: DGEC.
DOBLES OROPEZA, Ignacio.
   1998. "Algunos Elementos Sobre la Violencia en la Familia en Costa Rica: Un Estudio Nacional en Sectores Urbanos." In *Violencia Doméstica en Costa Rica: Mas Allá de los Mitos,* edited by Eugenia Rodríguez. San José, Costa Rica: Facultad Latinoamericano de Ciencias Sociales (FLACSO) Sede Costa Rica, Cuaderno de Ciencias Sociales, No. 105.
DORE, Elizabeth.
   1997. "The Holy Family: Imagined Households in Latin American History." In *Gender Politics in Latin America: Debates in Theory and Practice,* edited by Elizabeth Dore. New York, New York: Monthly Review Press.
ELSON, Diane.
   1999. "Labor Markets as Gendered Institutions: Equality, Efficiency and Empowerment Issues." *World Development* 27(3):611-627.
FAUNÉ, María Angélica.
   1997. "Costa Rica: Las Inequidades de Género en el Marco de la Apertura Comercial y la Reestructuración Productiva. Análisis a Nivel Macro, Meso, Micro." In *Crecer con la Mujer: Oportunidades para el Desarrollo Económico Centro Americano,* edited by Diane Elson, María Angélica Fauné, Jasmine Gideon, Maribel Gutiérrez, Armida López de Mazier, and Eduardo Sacayon. San José, Costa Rica: Embajada Real de los Países Bajos.
FERNÁNDEZ, Oscar.
   1992. "Qué Valores Valen Hoy en Costa Rica?" In *El Nuevo Rostro de Costa Rica,* edited by Juan Manuel Villasuso. Heredia, Costa Rica: Centro de Estudios Democráticos de América Latina.
FOLBRE, Nancy.
   1991. "Women on their Own: Global Patterns of Female Headship." In *The Women and International Development Annual,* vol. 2, edited by Rita S. Gallin and Ann Ferguson. Boulder, Colorado: Westview.
FULLER, Norma.
   2000. "Work and Masculinity among Peruvian Men." *European Journal of Development Research* 12(2):93-114.
GARCÍA, Brígida and Orlandina de Oliveira.
   1997. "Motherhood and Extradomestic Work in Urban Mexico." *Bulletin of Latin American Research* 16(3):367-384.
GELDSTEIN, Rosa.
   1997. *Mujeres Jefas de Hogar: Familia, Pobreza y Género.* Buenos Aires, Argentina: UNICEF-Argentina.
GOMÁRIZ, Enrique.
   1997. *Introducción a los Estudios Sobre la Masculinidad.* San José, Costa Rica: Centro Nacional para el Desarrollo de la Mujer y Familia.

GONZÁLEZ DE LA ROCHA, Mercedes.
    1995. "Social Restructuring in Two Mexican Cities: An Analysis of Domestic Groups in Guadalajara and Monterrey." *European Journal of Development Research* 7(2):389-406.

GRUPO AGENDA POLÍTICA DE MUJERES COSTARRICENSES (GAPMC).
    1997. *Agenda Política de Mujeres Costarricenses*. San José, Costa Rica: GAPMC.

GUDMUNDSON, Lowell.
    1986. *Costa Rica Before Coffee: Society and Economy on the Eve of the Export Boom*. Baton Rouge: Louisiana State University Press.

GÜENDEL, Ludwig and Mauricio González.
    1998. "Integration, Human Rights and Social Policy in the Context of Human Poverty." In *Adolescence, Child Rights and Urban Poverty in Costa Rica,* edited by Nited Nations Children's Fund (UNICEF). San José, Costa Rica: UNICEF/United Nations Centre for Human Settlements (HABITAT).

INSTITUTO MIXTO DE AYUDA SOCIAL (IMAS).
    1998. *Ley No. 7769 Atención a las Mujeres en Condiciones de Pobreza*. San José, Costa Rica: IMAS.
———. 1999a. *Programa: Atención a las Mujeres en Condiciones de Pobreza*. San José, Costa Rica: IMAS.
———. 1999b. *Programa Construyendo Oportunidades*. San José, Costa Rica: IMAS.
———. 1999c. *Plan Anual Operativo 1999*. San José, Costa Rica: IMAS.
———. 2001. *Area Atención Integral para el Desarrollo de las Mujeres. Programas: Creciendo Juntas, Construyendo Oportunidades*. San José, Costa Rica: IMAS.

INSTITUTO NACIONAL DE ESTADÍSTICAS Y CENSOS (INEC).
    2001. *IX Censo Nacional de Población y V de Vivienda del 2000: Resultados Generales*. San José, Costa Rica: INEC. Available on-line at http://www.inec.go.cr/.

INSTITUTO NACIONAL DE LAS MUJERES (INAMU).
    2001. *Responsible Paternity Law*. San José, Costa Rica: INAMU.

INVESTIGACIONES JURÍDICAS S.A. (IJSA).
    1990. *Ley de Promoción de la Igualdad de la Mujer.* San José, Costa Rica: IJSA.

JELIN, Elizabeth.
    1991. "Introduction: Everyday Practices, Family Structures, Social Processes." In *Family, Household and Gender Relations in Latin America,* edited by Elizabeth Jelin. London, England/Paris, France: Kegan Paul International, UNESCO.

KAZTMAN, Rubén.
    1992. "Por Qué Los Hombres son Tan Irresponsables?" *Revista de la CEPAL* 46 (Abril):1-9.

KLAK, Thomas.
    1999. "Globalization, Neoliberalism and Economic Change in Central America and the Caribbean." In *Latin America Transformed: Globalisation and Modernity,* edited by Robert Gwynne and Cristóbal Kay. London, England:

Edward Arnold.
KUZNESOF, Elizabeth Anne.
    1980. "Household Composition and Headship as Related to Changes in Modes of Production: São Paulo 1765–1836." *Comparative Studies in Society and History* 22(1):78-108.
LARA, Silvia, with Tom Barry and Peter Simonson.
    1995. *Inside Costa Rica*. Albuquerque, New Mexico: Interhemispheric Resource Center.
LOÁICIGA GUILLÉN and María Elena.
    1994. "Acerca de la Educación Superior Pública en Guanacaste." *Ciencias Sociales* 66:7-20.
MARENCO, Leda, Ana María Trejos, Juan Diego Trejos, and Marienela Vargas.
    1998. *Del Silencio a la Palabra: Un Modelo de Trabajo con las Mujeres Jefas del Hogar*. San José, Costa Rica: Segunda Vicepresidencia.
MCCALLUM, Cecilia.
    1999. "Restraining Women: Gender, Sexuality and Modernity in Salvador da Bahia." *Bulletin of Latin American Research* 18(3):275-293.
MINISTERIO DE ECONOMÍA, INDUSTRIA Y COMERCIO (MEIC).
    1998. *Encuesta de Hogares de Propósitos Multiples*. San José, Costa Rica: Area de Estadísticas y Censos.
MINISTERIO DE PLANIFICACIÓN NACIONAL Y POLÍTICA ECONÓMICA (MIDEPLAN).
    1995. *Estadísticas Sociodemográficas y Económicas Desagregadas por Sexo, Costa Rica, 1980-1994*. San José, Costa Rica: MIDEPLAN.
MOORE, Henrietta.
    1994. *Is There a Crisis in the Family?* Geneva, Switzerland: United Nations Research Institute for Social Development (UNRISD), Occasional Paper 3, World Summit for Social Development.
MORENO, Wagner.
    1994. "Condiciones de Vida y su Incidencia en la Identidad Personal-Social de Adolescentes Nicoyanos." *Ciencias Sociales* 66(4):37-44.
———. 1997. "Cambios Sociales y Rol del Adolescente en la Estructura Familiar." *Ciencias Sociales* 75(9):95-101.
MOSER, Caroline and Cathy McIlwaine.
    2000a. *Urban Poor: Perceptions of Violence in Colombia*. Washington, D.C.: World Bank.
———. 2000b. *Violence in a Post-conflict Context: Urban Poor Perceptions from Guatemala*. Washington, D.C.: World Bank.
MOVIMIENTO FAMILIAR CRISTIANO (MFC).
    1997. *Reseña Histórica del MFC en Costa Rica*. San José, Costa Rica: MFC.
MUÑOZ, Eduardo.
    1997. "Madres Adolescentes: Una Realidad Negada." *Otra Mirada* 1(3):43-45.
NAPOLITANO, Valentina.

1998. "Between 'Traditional' and 'New' Catholic Church Religious Discourses in Urban, Western Mexico." *Bulletin of Latin American Research* 17(3):323-339.

PEREIRA GARCÍA and María Teresa.
    1998. *Orientación Educativa*. San José, Costa Rica: Editorial Universidad Estatal a Distancia.

PRIMERA DAMA DE LA REPÚBLICA.
    2001. *Programas: Amor Joven y Construyendo Oportunidades* San José, Costa Rica: Oficina de la Primera Dama.

PROYECTO ESTADO DE LA NACIÓN (PEN).
    1998. *Estado de la Nación en Desarrollo Humano Sostenible*. San José, Costa Rica:PEN.

RODRÍGUEZ, Eugenia.
    1999. "La Redefinición de los Discursos sobre la Familia y el Género en Costa Rica (1890-1930)." *Populaçao e Familia* (July-December):147-182.

———. 2000. *Hijas, Novias y Esposas: Familia, Matrimonio y Violencia Doméstica en el Valle Central de Costa Rica (1750-1850)*. Heredia, Costa Rica: Editorial Universidad Nacional.

———. Forthcoming. "Construyendo la Identidad Nacional y Redefiniendo el Sistema de Género: Políticas Socialies, Familia, Maternidad y Movimiento Femenino en Costa Rica (1850-1950)." *Revista de Historia de América*.

RODRÍGUEZ CHÁVES and Bach Guiselle.
    1999. *Diocésis de Tilarán: Análsis del Quehacer Pastoral con Enfasis en la Diocésis de Tilarán*. Tilarán, Costa Rica: Diocésis de Tilarán.

SAFA, Helen I.
    1995. *The Myth of the Male Breadwinner: Women and Industrialization in the Caribbean*. Boulder, Colorado: Westview Press.

———. 1999. *Women Coping with Crisis: Social Consequences of Export-led Industrialization in the Dominican Republic*. Miami, Florida: University of Miami, North-South Center, North-South Agenda Paper No 36.

SAGOT, Monsterrat, ed.
    1999. *Analysis Situacional de los Derechos de las Ninas y las Adolescentes en Costa Rica*. San José: United Nations Children's Fund (UNICEF)/Universidad de Costa Rica, Maestría Regional en Estudios de la Mujer.

SALAS, José Manuel.
    1998. "Algunos Apuntes Sobre la Violencia Doméstica desde la Perspectiva de los Hombres." In *Violencia Doméstica en Costa Rica: Mas Allá de los Mitos*, edited by Eugenia Rodríguez. San José: Facultad Latinoamericano de Ciencias Sociales (FLACSO) Sede Costa Rica, Cuaderno de Ciencias Sociales No. 105.

SANCHO MONTERO and Silvia María.
    1995. *El Programa Hogares Comunitarios en Costa Rica, Sus Primeros Pasos: Primera Parte*. San José, Costa Rica: Institute Mixto de Ayuda Social, Dirección Hogares Comunitarios.

SANDOVAL GARCÍA, Carlos.
    1997. *Sueños y Sudores en la Vida Cotidiana: Trabajadores y Trabajadoras de la Maquila y la Construcción en Costa Rica*. San José: Universidad de Costa Rica, Colección Instituto de Investigaciones Sociales.

SCHIFTER, Jacobo and Johnny Madrigal.
    1996. *Las Gavetas Sexuales del Costarricense*. San José, Costa Rica: Editorial IMEDIEX.

TIFFER, Carlos.
    1998. "Status of Adolescents in Conflict with the Criminal Law: The New Model for Juvenile Criminal Justice in Costa Rica." In *Adolescence, Child Rights and Urban Poverty in Costa Rica,* edited by United Nations Children's Fund (UNICEF). San José, Costa Rica: UNICEF/United Nations Centre for Human Settlements (HABITAT).

TREJOS, Juan Diego, and Nancy Montiel.
    1999. *El Capital de los Pobres en Costa Rica: Acceso, Utilización y Rendimiento*. Washington, D.C.: Inter American Development Bank.

UNITED NATIONS (UN).
    2000. *The World's Women 2000: Trends and Statistics*. New York, New York: UN.

UNITED NATIONS CHILDREN'S FUND (UNICEF).
    1997. *Role of Men in the Lives of Children*. New York, New York: UNICEF.

———. ed. 1998 *Adolescence, Child Rights and Urban Poverty in Costa Rica*. San José, Costa Rica: UNICEF/United Nations Centre for Human Settlements (HABITAT).

UNITED NATIONS DEVELOPMENT PROGRAM (UNDP).
    2001. *Human Development Report 2001: Making New Technologies Work for Human Development*. New York, New York: Oxford University Press.

VEGA, Isabel.
    1987. "Aportes Teóricos de la Actualidad en el Estudio de la Familia." *Revista Costarricense de Psicología* 10-11:15-23.

WORLD BANK.
    2000. *World Development Report 2000/2001: Attacking Poverty*. New York, New York: Oxford University Press.

HOUSEHOLDS AND INCOME: AGEING AND GENDER INEQUALITIES IN URBAN BRAZIL AND COLOMBIA

Maria Cristina Gomes da Conceição[*]

ABSTRACT

This paper discusses the ageing process in Brazil and Colombia according to gender and socioeconomic inequalities. The ageing process is related to reforms in social policies in each country. Reforms in the pension systems show contrasting results for the family structure and income. In Brazil, the extension of pensions to rural and informal workers leads to empowering poorer elderly women and men in economic and domestic relationships. Universalizing pensions allows the elderly to chose to live alone or to support adult children. On the other hand, in Colombia the reform created the individual saving system, reinforcing social exclusion and inequalities at the end of the life course. At the same time, the structural adjustments of the economy have generated new social contracts and economic order, but in different ways. The universal or individual character of the new pension system redefines in each country the profile of gender, generations, and socioeconomic inequalities. The universal reform can mitigate the economic and domestic exclusion of poorer and rural elderly, as in Brazil; and the individual reform can reinforce inequalities and, as a result, reproduce gender roles of domestic submission and dependence for poorer women in advanced ages.

INTRODUCTION

The Brazilian and Colombian populations are becoming older and the relative proportion of infants is diminishing, while the adult and elderly proportions are increasing. In this demographic transition, the higher life expectancy of women accentuates gender inequalities in advanced ages. Both trends affect the economy and policies in both countries, but in different ways, due to the complexity and cross-cultural differences in these societies. Ageing and gender differences interplay with existing income inequalities within and between countries. This complex interaction is at the center of the discussion about the reforms in social policies. New social policies suggest that community and family have to support the economic and affective demands of different generations. However, in this article some indicators show the limits of the family to assume all the needs of informal care and supports demanded by the elderly and adult generations at the same time. To analyze these limits, we underscore the impact of social and gender inequalities in both societies.

Macroeconomic trends in Latin America have been felt in both Brazil and Colombia. Brazil is in the upper-medium income group and holds the eighth posi-

---

[*] Facultad Latinoamericana de Ciencias Sociales (FLACSO), Carretera Al Ajusco n.377, Colonia Heroes de Padierna, Mexico.

tion in gross national product (GNP) in the World. Columbia is a lower-income country and ranks thirty-seventh in GNP in the world (World Bank 1997). The Colombian GNP is ten times lower than the Brazilian and, historically, while the annual rate of exports has varied, it has grown more in Colombia from 1981 to 1995 than in Brazil (Thorp 1998). Additionally, the Colombian external debt is seven times higher than the Brazilian debt in absolute terms. Housing is financed and built mainly by the private sector and it is mostly poorly built. Taxes and transfers are more progressive in Colombia (with more benefits and subsidies) and Brazil shows a more regressive economy.[1] Income inequality persists in both countries and poverty is still increasing even after the decrease in fertility rates from 6 to 2.5 in the two last decades.[2]

There also are inequalities in educational levels and income distribution by sex, social groups, and regions in each country (World Bank 2000). Nevertheless, a comparison of these countries according to different sources[3] indicates that inequality is larger in Brazil. For instance, in 1998 the Gini Index (which is used in a mathematical formula to determine the measure of dispersion in a concentration) of inequality was sixty in Brazil and fifty-seven in Colombia. During the last five decades, the level of education has increased more in Colombia[4] than in Brazil, while adult illiteracy rates for both sexes were 16 percent in Brazil and 9 percent in Colombia (Gomes 2002).

On the other hand, in 1999 Brazil's total population was 168 million inhabitants, while Colombia's was 42 million (DANE 2000). Both countries show similar demographic dynamics; however, in Brazil the life expectancy and total fertility rates are lower while the proportion of urban population is higher than in Colombia.[5] In both countries the formal labor market has never employed the entire economically active population, but citizenship rights depend on having formal employment and social benefits are restricted to specific groups of the population. Nevertheless, formal work is much more frequent in Brazil than in Colombia. The female labor-force participation rates are substantially low in the two countries, where close to 35 percent of the women participate in the labor force in both countries. This percentage differs according to some household characteristics, with higher proportions of female heads working in Colombia than in Brazil.[6] Spouses, however, work in higher proportions in Brazil than in Colombia (Gomes 2002).

In these countries, the social security systems have been created from the corporative insurance system and saving cooperatives, which have been centralized by the government at different times. In Colombia this centralization occurred in 1946 through a National Congress decision while in Brazil the military dictatorship centralized them in 1967. Employers (80 percent in Brazil, 74 percent in Colombia) and workers (20 percent in Brazil, 26 percent in Colombia) pay taxes in different proportions. Additionally, the government contributes in different ways to the Brazilian and Colombian Social Security Systems with human and administrative resources.[7] The main social security benefits are pensions (in cash) and health resources and services.

Between the 1950s and 1970s, the number of taxpayers and tax values[8] increased. Between the 1980s and 1990s, however, tax collection was reduced due to decreases in formal employment, in the number of taxpayers, in wages, and in tax revenue. Expenses tripled due to the general Latin American economic crisis, reinforced by inflation and increases in the number of those pensioned (as a result of the increase in life expectancy). Currently, most of the taxpayers have survived beyond 60 years of age and retired (Jaramillo 1994; Ruezga Barba 1994; Beltrão, Passinato, and Oliveira 1996). Criteria to get a pension are different: in Brazil retirement results from a period of time worked (30 years for women and 35 years for men). In Colombia retirement is set by age: 55 for women and 60 for men. The amount of pensions are set around the minimum wage: 70 percent of retired people in Brazil, and 40 percent in Colombia receive a pension equivalent to the minimum wage.[9] The reforms were limited to solve gaps in the Social Security Systems, and these led to contradictory solutions. In Brazil, the reforms extended benefits, and today pensions also cover informal and rural workers. Beltrão, Pinheiro, and Oliveira (2001) note the social impact of these low pensions in rural areas, where this type of income has empowered elderly individuals in economic and domestic relationships. In contrast, Colombia did not universalize pensions and health benefits. Instead, reforms divided the pensions into two simultaneous systems, both of which are managed by the government. One is defined as the "benefits regime" and the other as an "individual-saving regimen" and clients (beneficiaries) can change between systems (Congress of the Colombian Republic 1993). These programs permit different social groups to affiliate and contribute according their social and economic characteristics, and to their own interest and capabilities to save. As a result, poorer and richer workers are divided in two pensions systems, cutting out the redistributive characteristic of the previous system and reinforcing social inequalities among retired people.

The reforms in these social programs took place at the same time that structural adjustments of the economy were implemented. These included flexibilization of work and cutbacks in employment, wages, and social programs. Transformations in implicit and explicit social contracts modified the outlines of the previous economic, social, and institutional order in both countries. At a micro-level, these changes have affected families and individuals. They have experienced informal employment and poverty more frequently, with decreases in welfare and life quality. As a result, professional, family, and individual trajectories are breaking up; and the social security programs are not enough to support all their social demands for health and pensions benefits (Goldani 2001).

Economic and demographic trends, especially the ageing process, will force institutions and families to reorient calculations of intergenerational transfers. Today, the populations of Brazil and Colombia are ageing rapidly and in the next two decades they will have, with Mexico, the largest elderly populations in Latin America and the world (United Nations 1999). In these countries, the social security systems will experience problems in their economic equilibrium: elderly generations will have higher proportions of beneficiaries, while adult generations will contain a smaller proportion of taxpayers. Thus, support assistance and existing resources for the elderly will be even less sufficient to solve the economic and social problems related to the impact of this accelerated ageing process.

In the domestic sphere, men and women have to reorganize families and to redistribute resources to support elderly individuals. In the phases of formation and expansion of families, large generations of adult men and women have married, worked, and had children. In the next two decades, these large generations will reach the end of their lives, their adult children will form their own families and, probably, another household. This phase is considered the beginning of a household's dissolution. In Western countries, the main trend in this phase is a high proportion of the elderly living on their own, as a couple without children (the "empty nest"). After this phase, most women experience widowhood at advanced ages and live in one-person households—the last phase of elderly household dissolution. Several authors have observed that in some developing countries, during this phase the elderly are used to living in extended families, with children or other relatives (Knodel, Chayovan, and Siriboon 1996; Uhlenberg 1996; Morioka 1996). However, in Latin-American countries, the phase of household dissolution and the availability of resources to support the elderly are not well documented. This article seeks to call attention to the limits and needs of elderly[10] men and women's households in Brazil and Colombia, taking into account their normative living arrangements, their domestic resources, and the gender and socioeconomic status of the elderly. Due to data restrictions,[11] we compare only individuals and families in urban areas.

To bring gender and generation into focus, this article examines household structure to unveil some trends in gender inequalities across generations (Young 1986; Kuijsten 1996). Thus, here I consider gender roles in the household, the number of members, the structure of the households, co-residence among generations, and gender differences in the household structure and in types of income.

Family and Gender Perspectives

Family and kin relations are an important academic topic. Frederick Le Play considers that the norm in the past and preindustrial societies was the stem household—where children married and the new couple resided with their parents and grandparents (a three-generation household). According to this author, in developing countries, today and in the past, the extended family is supposed to be the norm (Goody 1969, 1972). In developed countries, however, industrialization promoted a nuclearization of the households. Laslett and Wall (1972) argue that preindustrial European households were small and nuclear because children left their parent's home to marry and form their own separate households (Guinnane

1996). Today extended households are more frequent than in the past, due to the higher life expectancy of parents and children, who are surviving jointly. However, they are living separated, in nuclear households (Laslett and Wall 1972; Goody 1972; Tuirán 1993). In fact, the analysis of census data in Brazil shows that families have been mainly small and nuclear since previous centuries.[12]

In this article I examine family structure in both countries, with an emphasis on households with elderly men and women. Moreover, I search to discern prevalent trends during the accelerated aging process in Brazil and Colombia, and to access the effects of structural changes on these dynamics, especially the impact of reforms in social policies on the welfare of the elderly.

Examining these population's dynamics from a gender perspective would lead us to focus on differences in family and intergenerational relationships. From this angle the focus will be on adult women—female heads—in active ages having a labor life history related to the process of empowerment by women (Chant 1991; Flores 1990). However, adult women are also seen as the main providers of support to spouses, children, grandchildren, ageing parents, and women and men friends. Consequently, as caregivers, adult women experience increased levels of distress when family members need support and become emotionally and/or physically demanding.

Furthermore, studies about ageing and gender are centered on the quantity and dynamics of the support exchanged among generations and the male and female roles in these dynamics (Höhn 1994; Kono 1994; Concepción 1994; Knodel 1996). The link between gender and generations is meant to make elderly women and spouses more visible (Varley and Blasco 2001). In Latin American countries, most women of older generations were not in the labor market and, therefore, today they are not included in social security systems. In Brazil, elderly women can get a pension, but in Colombia, they have scarce resources and are at a disadvantage in their exchanges with adult generations.

Kin Composition, Age, and Sex of Household Members

The roles the elderly assume in the household are related to power relations and the available resources to establish a separate and independent household, as well as to the need for support and co-residence between adult children and the elderly. Being the head of the household is sometimes used as an indicator of the empowerment for women in economically active ages. However, in older ages the concept of "head" is biased by types of household that characterize this phase of the life course, and by life styles, values, and preferences of generations surviving jointly.

Obviously, to be the head of a one-person household does not indicate having power in intergenerational relationships. On the one hand, the elderly can choose to live in one-person households if they have resources to support themselves and, thus, they prefer to live in a separate household. On the other hand, some elderly live alone as a result of a lack of resources or abandonment. Therefore, adult children perceive the elderly without resources as a disadvantage (Varley and Blasco 2001).

In both countries, to be a head of the household is supposed to be a male role. Official statistics show that in Brazil men are heads for 65 percent of the households while only 35 percent of women are heads. In Colombia, 76 percent of the households are male-headed and in 24 percent women assume this role. Moreover, to be a head of a household[13] varies according to gender and age. In Brazil and Colombia men are heads in economically active ages, when they are working and supporting a nuclear family with children. However, women show higher proportions as heads of households in both countries at just over fifty years of age. Divorced and widowed women survive longer and assume an important position as the responsible individual of the household, especially at the end of their life-course.

Kin relationships and the household composition indicate that women assume different roles in the household, according to the phases of their life-course. In the adult phase women are mainly spouses between twenty and fifty-nine years of age in both countries, while men are mainly heads of the households. Very few young women are heads in the household and, in Colombia, there are female heads but an important group of women are other relatives of the heads.[14] At the end of the life-course changes emerge in the pattern of gender roles and in the cross-cultural comparison. On the one hand, in Brazil, elderly women over sixty can be heads or spouses, while in Colombia they are mainly other relatives. On the other hand, elderly men keep being the heads of their households in both countries. In fact, of all the female heads in Brazil, one-third are elderly, whereas in Colombia elderly women represent only one-quarter of female heads. These proportions indicate that the frequency and status of female heads are strongly related to the surviving and ageing process.

DATA AND METHODS

This article relies on data collected through national surveys in Brazil and Colombia. The Brazilian data were collected through the National Survey of Households (PNAD) undertaken in 1995 by the IBGE (National Institute of Geography and Statistics). The main goal of the PNAD (which has been taken annually since 1967) is to collect data on the socioeconomic characteristics of the population—such as sex, age, education, labor force participation, income, and housing. In 1995 the PNAD included also variables such as migration, fertility, and marital status. The PNAD uses a broad criterion to define workers: individuals who received monetary or nonmonetary payment; individuals who produced foods or built their own household, and individuals who worked without payment to help another worker in domestic entrepreneurship, in a religious institution, in cooperatives, or in training. The reference period is to work one hour in the previous week. The PNAD-95 asks about income according to types: wage/salary, pension, rent, and interest (investment in a bank or other institutions).

The DANE (National Department of Administrative Statistics) collected Colombian data through the National Survey of Households (ENH) in 1995. The main goal of ENH, which has been conducted annually since 1976, is to generate basic statistics related to the demographic, social, and economic profile of the population—such as sex, age, education, work, income, and housing. In 1995 the ENH covered only the ten main cities in the country. The ENH-95 considers workers as individuals over twelve years old who worked for pay during eight hours in the previous month or two weeks in the previous year. Workers without wages are excluded. The ENH-95 asks about the following categories of income: wage/salary, pension, rent, donations (money interchanged directly among individuals as support or as a gift), and government subsidies.

In Colombia the household survey covers only ten capital cities in the country. Thus, to make the two cases comparable, I selected only data from the largest eleven cities in the national Brazilian survey. In both countries the household is defined as a group of individuals that shares a budget and food. In the Brazilian survey there are two variables to define the household. In this case I used the variable more similar to that used in the Colombian survey. The head of the household in Brazil is the "reference person" in the household and in Colombia the head is the person who brings the higher income to the household. To make household comparisons possible between the two countries, I used the classification that Rodolfo Tuirán (1993) proposed to aggregate households, instead of using the criteria classification from each country. The variable "relatives" was created according to Tuirán criteria to represent groups of households in both countries.

Demographic Dynamics, Household Size, and Structure

In this section the analysis is based on household structure. Life expectancy is higher in Colombia; therefore, I expect to find more households with elderly in Colombia than in Brazil. Nevertheless, the percentage of households with individuals over sixty years of age is 23 percent in Brazil and only 13 percent in Colombia. This result leads us to take a closer look at the characteristics of the households with individuals over sixty in each country, as elderly individuals can live jointly. Moreover, men and women of different generations of the elderly can have different characteristics. Therefore, the next analysis considers three subgroups of households, according to their generational composition:

1. Households with at least one individual sixty to seventy-nine years old;
2. Households with at least one individual seventy to seventy-nine years, and
3. Households with at least one individual eighty years old or over (see Table 1).

Table 1.
Types of Urban Households by Different Elderly Generations

Type of Household	Survey	%	Population	%
Brazil	27,045	78.10	9,694,311	76.90
Households with individuals below 60				
Households with individuals 60/79	6,620	19.10	2,542,450	20.20
Households with individuals over 80	957	2.80	367,790	3.00
Total	**28,022**	**100.00**	**12,604,551**	**100.00**
Colombia	24,404	87.01	3,122,225	86.60
Households with individuals below 60				
Households with individuals 60/79	2,385	12.50	330,711	12.40
Households with individuals over 80	288	0.90	3,6171	1.00
Total	**28,022**	**100.00**	**3,604,875**	**100.00**

Source: Calculations based on the PNAD (1995) and ENH (1995).

This typology helps us to study domestic trends in different phases of the end of the life-course. For the total elderly population, to live jointly (co-residing household) with an adult child is a type of intergenerational support, while to live alone (one-person household) can mean independence or abandonment. According to this typology, we can use the size and type of households as indicators of whether the elderly are co-residing with adults or not. Figure 1 shows the distribution of different generations of the elderly in both countries, according to the size of the households. In Colombian society, co-residence among generations is more normative than in Brazil, as shown by the larger size of elderly households in Colombia. In Brazil the elderly live mainly in two-member households (25 percent), while three-member households (17 percent) and one-member households (16 percent) are less common. In Colombia there is no typical household size; the elderly live in households of two, three, or four members (18 percent each type).

Figure 1.
Percent Household Distribution by Size and Elderly Generations

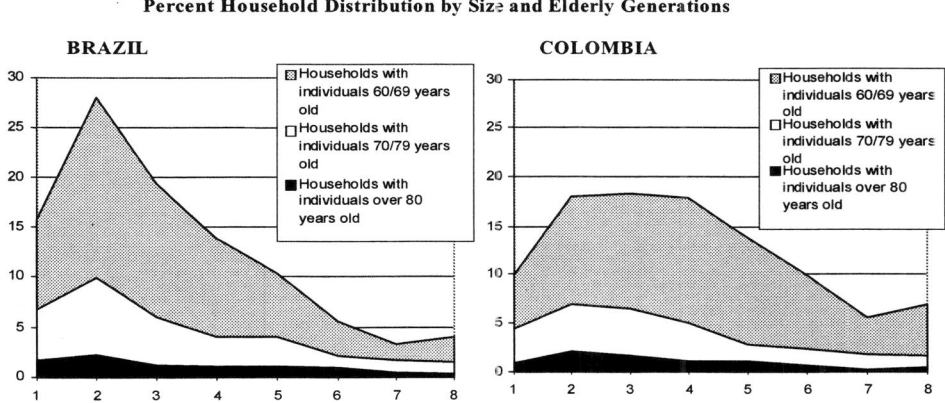

Source: Calculations based in the PNAD-1995 and ENH-1995

An analysis of how these patterns vary—according to gender—shows that in both countries elderly women live mainly alone, in one-person households. In Brazil, the female two-person households are clearly predominant (27 percent) compared to one- or three-member households (15 percent and 17 percent, respectively). The Colombian female-household structure shows similar proportions for one-, two-, and three-member households (23 percent, 22 percent, and 20 percent, respectively), and higher proportions of households with over four members, compared to Brazil. Taking into account oldest generations in Colombia, women between seventy through seventy-nine and over eighty years of age more frequently live in larger households in Colombia.

Very few elderly men live alone (only about 5 percent in each country). In Brazil, 29 percent of elderly men live in two-member, 20 percent in three-member, and 15 percent in four-member households. In Colombia, elderly men live in larger households: 20 percent in four, 18 percent in three, and 17 percent in five-member households, indicating that in Colombia co-residence is an important pattern among elderly men and women.

Prior trends in size and composition of the households have led us to study the household structure, and to investigate the way in which households with individuals over sixty are composed and structured by gender. We classified households with a criterion that would make it comparable between countries.[15] In Brazil and Colombia, one may distinguish elderly generations living alone as well as in two-member households, with only a male elderly and his spouse. These last groups are of particular interest, as they indicate how co-residence became a norm in Colombia, but not so in Brazil.

In Brazil, the complete nuclear household is a norm among elderly men. A couple with children is the arrangement more common among elderly ages sixty to sixty-nine. When adult children leave the parents' household, their parents are older—over seventy years old—and live alone as a couple. In Brazil, this alone couple, or the "empty nest," is the most common domestic arrangement among men and women over seventy. The final life course households vary temporally, according to the ageing process: male elderly sixty to sixty-nine live as a couple with children, but between seventy to seventy-nine years of age they live as a couple alone, while those over eighty are mainly incorporated as other relatives in extended households. In the arrangement "head with children and other relatives," the head can be men or women, but in general is an elder. Until advanced ages, men live mainly married, with only a small proportion not married, and co-reside with adults. In contrast, elderly women frequently live alone in one-person households (one-third of them). One-quarter of them are heads without a partner and live with their children. Lower proportions of elderly women live in extended households without children, as a head or a couple with other relatives. Compared to elderly men, extended and one-person households are more common among elderly women and their proportions increase in more advanced ages.

The distribution of households in Colombia shows that nearly 40 percent of elderly men live as a couple with children and 26 percent live in an extended household—a head with children and other relatives. The "empty nest" is not as frequent as in Brazil. Other types of households, such as heads with children, a couple with other relatives, composed and co-resident households represent 10 percent each. In contrast with Brazil, in Colombia there are no important changes in living arrangements by generations among elderly, all of them live mainly with adult children.

Sources of Income and Household Structure among Individuals Over Sixty Years of Age

In households where individuals over sixty years of age have some type of income, there are important cross-cultural and institutional differences. In Brazil the elderly income comes from their pensions—76 percent of elderly women and 62 percent of elderly men have a pension. The second type of income among the elderly is the salary, with 31 percent of the elderly men receiving a salary while only 13 percent of elderly women do so. Few elderly receive interests[16] or rent (11 percent of men and 8 percent of women) and only 5 percent of elderly women receive donations from other individuals. In Colombia it is not common for the elderly to have any kind of income. The proportions of the elderly with each type of income have never gone up to 10 percent in both sexes. Nearly 5 percent of elderly men receive salaries, pensions, or subsidies,[17] while among elderly women, 8 percent receive pensions, 8 percent receive donations (remittances, monetary contributions, or gifts) from other individuals, and only 4 percent have salaries.

In both countries increasing longevity is related to intergenerational resources and socioeconomic conditions, but the way in which this relation works is country-specific. In Brazil, the survival of several generations jointly and exchanges among generations are mediated by the social security system. Much intergenerational dependency has been resolved by pensions, although some families remain the main caregivers, but only for a minority of the elderly generations. In contrast, in Colombia there is not an institutional support to establish intergenerational relations. As a result, extended families support the elderly, and kin relationships organize a network through which generations exchange resources. However, it cannot cover the majority of elderly people. As a result, support in advanced ages is not based on monetary resources, but on co-residence and family.

These patterns of unequal institutional settings by country reproduce different types of elderly living arrangements by gender in Brazil and Colombia. Households where the elderly have some type of income show differences by gender. Elderly men with monetary income live more frequently as a couple with children or as a couple alone. But elderly women with income live mainly in one-person or single-parent households.

Gender and Monetary Resources at the End of the Life Course

This section discusses the distribution of types of elderly income by gender. In Brazil, most elderly women (near 80 percent) receive pensions in all types of households. Elderly women head one-person or single-parent households and contribute to the domestic economy mainly with a pension. In extended households, elderly women receive a pension also. In contrast, elderly men are heads and live with a partner. However, the pension is their more frequent contribution only when they head a couple alone or a couple with children, in the later phase of the older life-course. Elderly men in the sixty to sixty-nine age group live with a spouse and children, and they can still be working in high proportions (50 percent). After adult children leave the home, parents are older, live as a couple alone, retire, and get a pension. As a result, a salary is less frequent among elderly men ages seventy to seventy-nine (30 percent). The majority of elderly men who live in extended households do not receive a pension as frequently (Couple and Children and Other—20 percent) as the majority who live in their own nuclear household. In the extended households it is more common for elderly to receive a pension only if the elderly men live as a couple with other relatives (70 percent).

Figure 2 shows differences by gender in Brazil, and indicates that pensions are a norm among the elderly of both sexes. But among elderly women this happens independently of the type of household where they live.

Figure 2.
Percent Distribution of Types of Income by Gender and Household (Brazil)

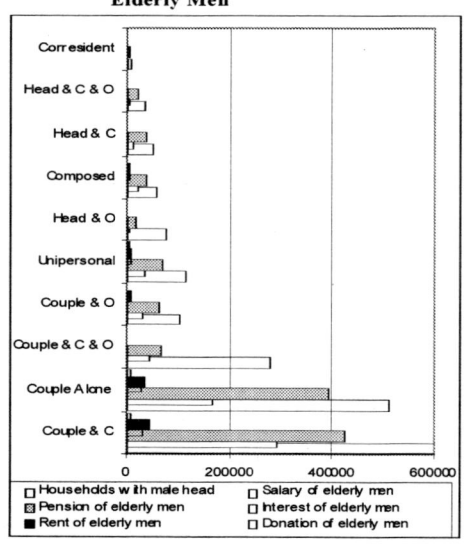
Elderly Men

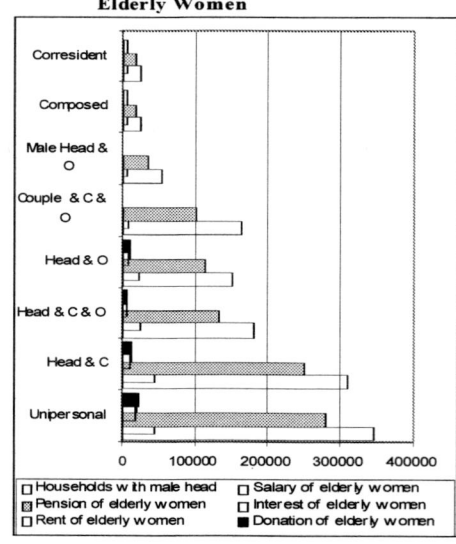
Elderly Women

Source: Calculations based in the PNAD (1995) and ENH (1995).

In contrast, for elderly men with a partner and children, pensions are an important source of support, but elderly men who co-reside with other relatives do not receive a pension. Therefore, it is possible that these elderly men co-reside because they do not have enough monetary resources to support their own household. In absolute numbers, there are close to 1 million elderly men and 1 million elderly women with pensions in Brazil, and coverage by type of household is a little more frequent among women than it is among men.

In Colombia pension is a scarce resource for elderly men and women. Most of them do not have any type of income, and among the few resources they receive, the more frequent are donations among individuals, especially for elderly women (8%). Salary is a scarce resource also, with rents and interests (Figure 3). Coresidence is the main support for elderly of both sexes and intergenerational relations depend mainly on family support, and to live jointly is fundamental for elderly welfare. First, donations and pensions are relatively more frequent among elderly women, and absolute the numbers of pensions is three times higher among elderly women (165,000 pensioned women) than among elderly men (46,000 pensioned men).

Figure 3.
Percent Distribution of Types of Income by Gender and Household (COLOMBIA)

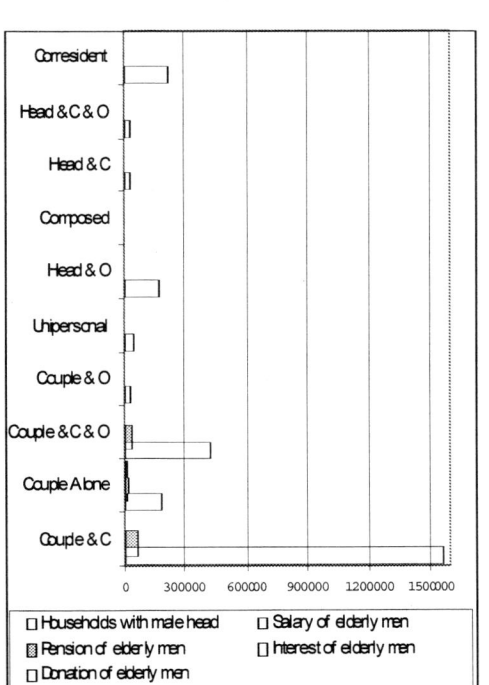
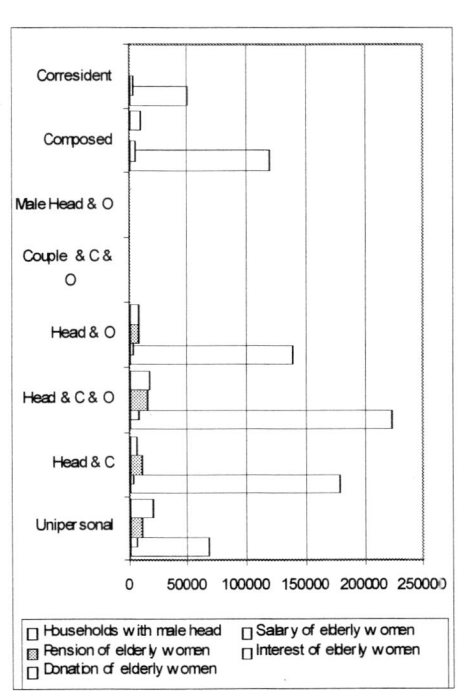

CONCLUSIONS

In spite of the lower life expectancy in Brazil, parents who see all their children leave the home experience living alone at the end of their life course, and mainly elderly women live in single-person households. In Brazil, generations have a lower probability of living jointly and do not co-reside as frequently as they do in Colombia. However, the survival of several generations living jointly and kin relationships are not the only factors that affect the household structure. Formal work and the universal pensions system permit the elderly to support their separate household.

In Colombia, where life expectancy is higher, generations have a higher probability of living jointly, but monetary resources to support the elderly are rare, and co-residence of adults and elderly emerges as the main form of support at the end of their life course.

The different patterns in each country imply that co-residence does not by itself entail monetary support, just as lack of co-residence does not mean that children do not exchange monetary resources with elderly parents. In Brazil, intergenerational resources are exchanged between adult and older generations mainly through the social security system. Moreover, rent and interest are types of resources less frequent among elderly, but they exist in some of their one-person or couple households. In Colombia, generational exchange occurs in the household itself (in co-resident households), but monetary resources (institutionalized or not) are scarce. Very few co-resident elderly receive pensions or donations, and rent and interests are practically inexistent.

In Brazil, the universal coverage of the pension system guarantees homogeneity in domestic income structure, while in Colombia a very diversified income structure emerges among heads and other members of the household, showing important differences by gender and in domestic roles in the household. Differences in gender can indicate advantages or disadvantages for women. In Brazil, elderly women are beneficiaries of the universal social security system, and pensions can permit them to live in separate households, or to be more attractive for intergenerational relationships. In Colombia, co-residence coincides with a lack of monetary resources for the elderly, especially for women. It is difficult to state that co-residence is a preferred living arrangement in Colombia. The lower proportions of elderly who receive donations or pensions co-reside more, but this trend can be linked to the disadvantageous position of the elderly who live in other living arrangements.

These trends indicate that the family depends on economic resources to exchange among different generations. In Colombia, where there are important deficiencies in formal resources to support ageing, families do have limits to substitute or to complement the collective needs of their members. In this context, policies aimed at decreasing social inequalities and at supporting the elderly target the family as a unit to promote social programs. But these policies can accentuate the difficulties families face during economic crisis and can generate conflicts among generations. Adult members of the household are mainly in the informal labor market, while the majority of elderly members do not have pensions. Thus, the ability of adult generations to support their ageing relatives with donations depends on fluctuations in the informal labor market. However, the elderly who depend on adult generations for their resources, and who do not have enough resources with which to reciprocate, do so by contributing domestic work. Elderly women are at the center of this intra-domestic exchange: they can offer services—like cleaning, washing, and taking care of grandchildren—and receive economic donations from their adult children.

Therefore, these family-oriented policies reproduce the role of women as main caregivers for different generations, including the elderly who need to co-reside or receive support from adult women. This accumulation of economic, physical, and affective support on the family falls mainly on the women, who reproduce their role of main caregivers for all the present generations in the household as well as until the final phase of their life-course. Therefore, co-residence does not seem to be only a cultural preference of different generations to live jointly. In Colombia, for example, it can also be a need to cover the lack in monetary and institutional support. In Brazil, however, the universal pension system diminishes the domestic pressure on adult generations to take care of the elderly. Here pensioned elderly can support adult children in economic crisis, such as when adult children are unemployed.

Gender and generational inequalities show important country and institutional differences, with implications for the household structure, according to the ability of elderly men and women to give and receive monetary support and also their ability to choose their preferred living arrangements. Monetary and institutional resources determine the possibility for exchanging resources within the household, as well as domestic, physical, and affective support. Co-residence and extended households have been an important way for families to support the needs of their members. However, several studies (Cortés 1996; Enríquez 2000; Varley and Blasco 2001) observe that the capacity of extended families to use their members to complement income and to supply support is decreasing in Latin American countries. In the new scenarios of economic crisis and unemployment, elderly without resources, in a situation of extreme poverty, are at a disadvantage to receive family and adult support (Enríquez 2000). Family members who have nothing to contribute to an impoverished domestic group can be excluded from the household. The absence of institutional resources reinforces this vicious reproduction of poverty among generations and increases the risk of abandonment for the poorest elderly.

Moreover, according to Goldani (2001), family-oriented policies looking to decrease social inequalities assume that the family is the main provider of all these kinds of support. This implies several risks. It may affect the relationship between the women and their families, may encourage the women to work with out remuneration, and may transfer to women full responsibility for supplying all the needs of the different generations within the household.

NOTES

1. Subsidies as an income distributive mechanism represented 6.1 percent of the GNP in Brazil (Maddison 1993).

2. In the 1960s, a predominate idea was that declining fertility could be an important factor for fostering development in developing countries. However, in the 1980s most Latin American countries had decreased their fertility rates from six to fewer than three children per woman, yet at the same time these countries experienced economic crises that characterized these years as the "lost decades." For further information about fertility trends in Brazil and Colombia, see Martine (1996) and Rodríguez and Hobcraft (1990), respectively. Additionally, Carvalho and Wood (1988) and McHenry (1991) have examined the relationship between declines in fertility and poverty in Latin America.

3. See World Bank (1997 and 2000) and United Nations (1999).

4. There were important improvements in literacy levels in Colombia, mainly between 1950 and 1974 (Cataño 1989); in Brazil, literacy kept on increasing since 1950 until 1990, but today is lower than in Colombia (Thorp 1998).

5. In Brazil, 81 percent of the population lives in urban areas, while in Colombia, 73 percent do.

6. In Brazil, the proportion of female-headed households is 54 percent, 34 percent and 3 percent for the age groups twenty to thirty-nine, forty to fifty-nine, and over sixty, respectively (Gomes 2002). In Colombia, 51 percent of the total female-household heads work.

7. For further information on Brazil see Beltrão et al. (1994, 1996, 2001) and Lewis (2000). In Colombia, government participation depends on the type of system—Solidarity or Individual Saving System (Congress of the Columbian Republic 1993).

8. The tax, based on the salary (to save and pay pensions in the future), is a proportion of the salary and, therefore, their values vary according to the value of the salary.

9. For further information about Brazil, see Beltrão, Passinato, and Oliveira (1996) and Beltrão, Pinheiro, and Oliveira (2001); for Colombia, the data come from ENH (1995).

10. In this article the elderly are defined as individuals over sixty years old and adults are individuals between twenty and fifty-nine years of age.

11. In Colombia the household survey covers only ten capital cities in the country. To make the data comparative between countries, only data from the largest eleven cities in the national Brazilian survey was used. In both countries data are from 1995.

12. In Brazil, "The analysis of censuses of XVIII and XIX centuries reveals that in the past the nuclear family predominated, and few extended families appear in these censuses" (Marcilio 1973; see also Kuznesof 1986, cited by Metcalf 1996).

13. In both countries the household is defined as a group of individuals who share a budget and food. In the Brazilian survey, there are two variables to define the household. In this case we used the variable more similar to the Colombian survey. The household head in Brazil is the "reference person" in the household and in Colombia the head is the person who brings the higher income to the household.

14. Other relatives can be grandchildren, grandmother, grandfather of the head, and so on.

15. Living arrangements are classified as: (1) One-person, (2) a couple (Couple Alone), (3) a couple with children (Couple & C), (4) a couple with children and other relatives (Couple & C & O), (5) a couple with other relatives (Couple & O), (6) a head with children (Head & C), (7) a head with children and other relatives (Head & C & O), (8) a head with other relatives (Head & O), (9) more than one head (Co-resident), and (10) living arrangements with individuals who are not relatives of the head (Composed). Moreover, households can be classified according to their nuclei: complete or dual parental nuclei (types 2 to 5—the nuclei is a couple); incomplete or single-parent nuclei (types 6 to 8—the nuclei is a head without a spouse) (Tuirán 1993).

16. Interests are returns on investments in a bank or other institutions.

17. In Colombia, the survey asks about government subsidies as a source of income. The Brazilian survey did not include this question about monetary subsidies, and I take into account this source of income only in Colombia.

REFERENCES

BELTRÃO, Kaizô I., Francisco E.B. Barreto, and Andre C. Médici.
    1994. "El Sistema de Seguridad Social Brasileño: Problemas y Soluciones Alternativas." In *Sistemas de Seguridad Social en La Región: Problemas y Alternativas de Solución,* edited by Francisco E.B. de Oliveira. Rio de Janeiro, Brazil: Banco Interamericano de Desenvolvimento (BID) and Instituto Brasileiro de Pesquisas Economicas Aplicadas.

BELTRÃO, Kaizô I., M. Tereza, M. Passinato, and Francisco E.B. Oliveira.
    1996. *Projeções da Situação Econômico-financeira da Previdência Social 1995-2030 e Impactos de Políticas Institucionais Alternativas.* Rio de Janeiro,

Brazil: Instituto de Pesquisas Economicas Aplicadas.

BELTRÃO, Kaizô I., Sonoê Pinheiro, and Francisco E.B. Oliveira.
2001. "La Familia Rural y la Seguridad Social en Brasil: Un Análisis con Énfasis en los Cambios Constitucionales." In *Procesos Sociales, Población y Familia*, edited by Cristina Gomes. México D.F.: Facultad Latinoamericano de Ciencias Sociales (FLACSO) and Porrúa.

CARVALHO, José A. M. and Charles H. Wood.
1988. *The Demography of Inequality in Brazil*. Cambridge, England: Cambridge University Press.

CATAÑO, Gonzalo.
1989. *Educación y Estructura Social: Ensayos de Sociología de la Educación*. Bogotá, Colombia: Plaza y Janés and Asociación Colegio de Sociología.

CHANT, Sylvia.
1991. *Women and Survival in Mexican Cities: Perspectives on Gender, Labour Markets and Low-income Households*. Manchester, England: Manchester University Press.

CONCEPCIÓN, Mercedes B.
1994. "Implications of Increasing Roles of Women for the Provision of Elderly Care." In *Ageing and the Family: Proceedings of the United Nations International Conference on Ageing Populations in the Context of the Family, Kitakyushu (Japan)*, October 15-19, 1990, edited by United Nations, UN ST/ESA/SER.R/124 New York, New York: United Nations.

CONGRESS OF THE COLOMBIAN REPUBLIC.
1993. *Ley Numero 100*. Bogotá, Colombia: Columbian Government.

CORTÉS, Fernando.
1996. Los Avatares del Ingreso en los Ochenta—La Respuesta de los Hogares. Mimeograph, Centro de Estudios Sociológicos (CES). México D.F.: El Colegio de México.

DANE
2000. "Departamento Administrativo Nacional de Estadistica" [online]. Bogotá, Columbia: Departamento Administrativo Nacional de Estadistica. Retrieved July 12, 2002 (www.dane.gov.co).

ENH (Encuesta Nacional de Hogares).
1995. DANE (National Department of Administrative Statistics). Bogotá, Colombia: Columbian Government.

ENRÍQUEZ, Rocío.
2000. "Redes Sociales y Envejecimiento en Contextos de Pobreza Urbana." Paper presented at the VI Reunión Nacional de Investigación Demográfica, Sociedad Mexicana de Demografía y El Colegio de México, México D.F.

FLORES, Carmen Elisa.
1990. *The Demographic Transition and Women's Life-course in Colombia*. New York, New York: United Nations University Publications.

GOLDANI, Ana Maria.
2001. "Las Familias Brasileñas y sus Desafíos como Factor de Protección al Final del Siglo XX." In *Procesos Sociales, Población y Familia*, edited by Cristina Gomes. México D.F.: Facultad Latinoamericano de Ciencias Sociales (FLACSO) and Porrúa.

GOMES DA CONCEIÇÃO, Cristina.
    2002. "Intergenerational Transfers in Income, Health and Social Security: The Experiences of Brazil, Mexico and Colombia." In *Exclusion and Engagement, Social Policy in Latin America,* edited by Christopher Abel and Colin M. Lewis. London, England: University of London, Institute of Latin American Studies.

GOODY, Jack.
    1969. *Comparative Studies in Kinship.* Stanford, California: Stanford University Press.

―――. 1972. "Evolution of the Family." In *Household and Family in the Past Time: Comparative Studies in the Size and Structure of the Domestic Group over the Last Three Centuries in England, France, Serbia, Japan and Colonial North America, with Further Materials from Western Europe,* edited by Peter Laslett and Richard Wall. Cambridge, England: University Press.

GUINNANE, Timothy W.
    1996. "The Family, State Support and Generational Relations in Rural Ireland at the Turn of the Twentieth Century." In *Aging and Generational Relations over the Life Course: A Historical and Cross-cultural Perspective,* edited by Tamara Hareven. New York, New York: Walter de Gruyter.

HÖHN, Charlotte.
    1994. "Ageing and the Family in the Context of Western-type Developed Countries." In *Ageing and the Family: Proceedings of the United Nations International Conference on Ageing Populations in the Context of the Family, Kitakyushu (Japan),* October 15-19, 1990, edited by United Nations, UN ST/ESA/SER.R/124. New York, New York: United Nations.

JARAMILLO, Hernán.
    1994. "Reseña de las Reformas de Políticas Sociales en Colombia." In CEPAL, *Proyecto Regional sobre Reformas de Política para Aumentar la Efectividad del Estado en América Latina y el Caribe,* HOL/90/S45 (Serie Reformas de Política Pública, n. 27). New York, New York: United Nations.

KNODEL, John, Napaporn Chayovan, and Siriwan Siriboon.
    1996. "Familial Support and the Life Course of Thai Elderly and Their Children." In *Aging and Generational Relations over the Life Course: A Historical and Cross-cultural Perspective,* edited by Tamara Hareven. New York, New York: Walter de Gruyter.

KONO, Shigemi
    1994. "Ageing and the Family in the Developed Countries and Areas of Asia: Continuities and Transitions." In *Ageing and the Family: Proceedings of the United Nations International Conference on Ageing Populations in the Context of the Family, Kitakyushu (Japan),* October 15-19, 1990, edited by United Nations, UN ST/ESA/SER.R/124. New York, New York: United Nations.

KUIJSTEN, Anton C.
    1996. "Changing Family Patterns in Europe: A Case of Divergence?" *European Journal of Population* 12(2):115-143.

KUZNESOF, Elizabeth Anne.
    1986. *Household Economy and Urban Development: São Paulo, 1765 to 1836.* Boulder, Colorado: Westview Press.

LASLETT, Peter and Richard Wall.
>1972. *Household and Family in the Past Time. Comparative Studies in the Size and Structure of the Domestic Group over the Last Three Centuries in England, France, Serbia, Japan and Colonial North America, with Further Materials from Western Europe.* Cambridge, England: University Press.

LEWIS, Colin M.
>2000. "Social Insurance in Brazil and the Argentine: 'Reform' and Some Lessons from History." Paper presented at Facultad Latinoamericano de Ciencias Sociales (FLACSO), México.

MADDISON, Angus.
>1993. *La Economía Política de la Pobreza y el Crecimiento: Brasil y México.* México City, México D.F.: Fondo de Cultura Eonómica.

MARCILIO, Maria Luiza.
>1973. *A Cidade de São Paulo: Povoamento e População*, 1750/1850. São Paulo, Brazil: Pioneira.

MARTINE, George.
>1996. "Brazil's Fertility Decline, 1965-95." *Population and Development Review* 22(1):47-76.

MCHENRY, John P.
>1991. *Socio-economic Development and Fertility Decline: An Application on the Easterlin Synthesis Approach to Data from Fertility Survey: Colombia, Costa Rica, Sri Lanka, Tunisia.* ST/ESA/SER.R/101, Pub. Order No. E.91.XIII.14. ISBN 92-1-151235-2. New York, New York: U.N. Department of International Economic and Social Affairs.

METCALF, Alida C.
>1996. "El Matrimonio en Brasil durante la Colonia: Estaba Configurado por la Clase o por el Color?" In *Familia y Vida Privada en la Historia de Iberoamerica,* edited by Cecilia Rabell and Pilar Gonzalbo. México. D.F.: El Colegio de México and Instituto de Investigaciones Sociales (IIS)-Universidad Nacional Autónoma de México (UNAM).

MORIOKA, Kiyomi.
>1996. "Generational Relations and Their Changes as They Affect the Status of Older People in Japan." In *Aging and Generational Relations over the Life Course: A Historical and Cross-cultural Perspective,* edited by Tamara Hareven. New York, New York: Walter de Gruyter.

PNAD (Pesquisa Nacional de Amostragem por Domicilios)
>1995. "Survey." Rio de Janeiro, Brazil: IBGE (National Institute of Geography and Statistics).

RODRÍGUEZ G. German and John Hobcraft.
>1990. *Análisis Ilustrativo: Análisis de los Intervalos entre Nacimientos con Tablas de Vida para Colombia* . México D.F.: El Colegio de México.

RUEZGA BARBA, Antonio.
>1994. *Estado, Seguridad Social y Marginalidad.* Conferencia Interamericana de Seguridad Social (CIESS), Serie Estudios, 4, México.

THORP, Rosemary.
>1998. *Progreso, Pobreza y Exclusión. Una Historia Económica de América Latina en el Siglo XX.* New York, New York: Banco Interamericano de

Desenvolvimento (BID) and Unión Europea.
TUIRÁN, Rodolfo.
    1993. "Vivir en Familia: Hogares y Estructura Familiar en México, 1976-1987." *Revista de Comercio Exterior* 43(7):662-676.
UHLENBERG, Peter.
    1996. "Intergenerational Support in Sri Lanka: The Elderly and Their Children." In *Aging and Generational Relations over the Life Course: A Historical and Cross-cultural Perspective,* edited by Tamara Hareven. New York, New York: Walter de Gruyter.
UNITED NATIONS.
    1999. *World Population Prospects.* ST/ESA/SER.A/120. New York, New York: U.N. Department of International Economic and Social Affairs.
VARLEY, Ann and Maribel Blasco.
    2001. "'Cosechan lo que Siembran?' Mujeres Ancianas, Vivienda y Relaciones Familiares en el México Urbano." In *Procesos Sociales, Población y Familia,* edited by Cristina Gomes. México D.F.: Facultad Latinoamericano de Ciencias Sociales (FLACSO) and Porrúa.
WORLD BANK.
    1997. *Policy Research Bulletins,* vol. 8, nos. 1-4. Washington, D.C.: Author.
―――. 2000. *Economic Bulletin.* New York, New York: United Nations Publications.
YOUNG, Christabel M.
    1986. "El Ciclo de la Vida Residencial: Efectos de la Mortalidad y la Morbilidad sobre la Organizacion de la Vida." In *Consecuencias de las Tendencias y Diferenciales de la Mortalidad,* edited by Robert S. Northrup. ST/ESA/SER.A/95. New York, New York: U.N. Department of International Economic and Social Affairs.

WORK, GENDER, AND SPACE: WOMEN'S HOME-BASED WORK IN TIJUANA, MEXICO[1]

Silvia López Estrada*

ABSTRACT

This article reveals the array of time-space arrangements that a group of women home-based workers deploy to accommodate paid work in their homes. Based on in-depth interviews with the workers in Tijuana, Mexico, the article emphasizes the consequences of working at home for gender relations within the family. The main argument of this article holds that the variety of women's time-space strategies may result in a variety of situations of integration or conflict. The diversity of ways in which women organize productive and reproductive activities within the household and their consequences are crosscut by their social class, occupation, educational level, and life course, as well as the larger context of their lives. Although working at home, as a strategy of income generation, gives women a new economic role and helps them to negotiate their gender roles and relations, it also may reinforce women's traditional roles.

INTRODUCTION

As a response to economic crises and industrial restructuring, women in less industrialized countries are engaging in home-based occupations, while carrying out reproductive activities in their everyday lives. This requires them to adjust their daily schedules creatively and recreate their home as a workplace. However, being tied-down to the home has consequences for the social ecology of family life, gender relations, and the women's condition. How do women manage to accommodate paid work in the micro geography of the home? Is working at home an effective strategy for integrating occupational and family responsibilities, or does it create problems and tensions?

    This article examines the time-space household arrangements that women home workers make in trying to accommodate productive work within the home, and it emphasizes its consequences for gender roles and gendered spatial relations. Because home-based work is associated with specific cultural contexts, I argue that the diversity of women's spatial strategies and their myriad outcomes—harmonious or conflictive integration—are crosscut by home workers' social class, occupation, educational level, stage in the life course, and the broader circumstances of their individual lives. The data for this research comes from in-depth interviews with women home workers in Tijuana, Mexico.[2]

---

* Department of Population Studies, El Colegio de la Frontera Norte, Tijuana, B.C., Mexico.

Section 1 introduces conceptual considerations about home-based work, and it examines the household as an economic and social site. It also introduces the discussion about integration and conflict in households that are also workplaces. Section 2 presents some features of Tijuana's labor market, particularly in relation to home-based work. Section 3 outlines the methodology and data. Section 4 stresses the diversity of schedules for home-based work and the uses of domestic space that women devise in order to work at home. The article concludes with examples of successful attempts at integrating paid work into domestic life, conflicts that a home-based occupation causes for the women and their families, and the challenging ways in which the women face these problems.

THEORETICAL CONSIDERATIONS

Many scholars consider home-based work to be part of the so-called informal economy in Third World countries. Structural adjustment policies implemented during recent decades affected female employment, and the economic crises resulted in a proliferation of income-generating survival strategies in popular sectors of countries like Mexico (Benería 1992; Roberts 1994). In general, women concentrated in small-scale commerce (Menjívar Larín and Pérez Sáinz 1993; Escobar 1988). These occupations are precarious, poorly paid, and lack benefits. Women who participate in these occupations earn less than those who have formal jobs do. In addition, they frequently engage in subsistence activities requiring intensive workdays. Moreover, women home workers hold jobs that are more precarious when compared to those which men hold (Oliveira and García 1998). However, women who are independent home workers frequently have better labor conditions than do women industrial subcontractors who work in their homes. Noting the conceptual differences between these two home-worker categories, analysts recommend separating them statistically and analytically (Standing 1989).

Some studies in Europe and the United States define home-based work as the production in the worker's household of goods and services for monetary exchange or barter (Oberhauser 1995; García Ramón et al. 1995). The nature of home-based work is diverse, ranging from commerce and service occupations—such as the processing of foodstuffs, the production of handicrafts, the marketing of groceries or catalogue merchandise (Tupperware, cosmetics, clothes), child care, hairstyling, and sewing—to professional services—such as dentistry, accounting, and cosmetology. In this study, "home-based work" refers to self-employment and small businesses established in the homes of women. The use of space within the home and household resources characterizes this type of work. Thus, location is the common factor distinguishing home-based work from other types of activities. Nevertheless, the conceptualization, definition, and consequences of home-based work vary widely. For instance, the greater independence of self-employed women has led some scholars to suggest that this work strategy translates into autonomy for women. This view, however, has been widely debated (Boris and Prugl 1996).

All these productive activities can occur at the employer's or employee's home where work is performed according to unfixed, flexible schedules and income is irregular. In addition, home-based work can be informal or formal, depending on whether the business is taxed or not, and as a result, workers may not enjoy regular salaries and work benefits. Thus, home-based work is heterogeneous in terms of the kinds of occupations it encompasses, the material resources used, the labor conditions, the individual's and family's situation, and women workers' motivations and experiences.

Work, Gender, and Household Strategies

Home-based work is not only a strategy to cope with unemployment in contexts of industrial restructuring and urban poverty resulting from economic recession and structural adjustment policies in third-world countries. In both first- and third-world countries, home-based work enables women—particularly those with small children—to generate income for their families while also fulfilling their domestic roles.

In both developed and less developed countries, the study of the family household and household strategies of social reproduction emerged as a feminist critique in response to gender-biased theories that emphasized the theoretical separation between work and home while ignoring the household as the locus of social reproduction. In general, feminist scholars consider the household as a mediating link between individuals and major social processes (García, Muñoz, and Oliveira 1982, Pratt and Hanson 1991). In trying to overcome the gender-biased definition of the home as a domestic and private space, feminist geographers emphasize the household as a dynamic space where reproduction and production occur and the distinction between private and public is blurred (McDowell 1989). In this view, the household is a significant productive and social environment for women (Oberhauser 1993).

Scholars use the concept of household strategies to study family survival within deprived urban economies (Schmink 1984; Oliveira and Roberts 1993; Roberts 1994), and as a response to economic restructuring in more developed countries (Pratt and Hanson 1991). The concept defines the individual and collective strategies and social networks of household members in terms of their maintenance and social reproduction in a family context of conflict and solidarity (González de la Rocha 1986; Benería and Roldán 1987; García, Muñoz, and Oliveira 1982; Mackenzie 1986; Oberhauser 1993). Studies on the family-household in less developed economies emphasize the sociodemographic characteristics, internal dynamics, and power relationships within the household to explain the responses of working-class groups to socioeconomic structural change

(González de la Rocha 1986; García, Muñoz, and Oliveira 1982; Chant 1996).

In these studies, time constitutes an important variable (Jelin et al. 1986). Examples include the measurement of time spent in domestic work or the increase in the time spent working when a family member has to engage in more than one job (Barbieri 1984). In addition, the life course influences the division of labor within the household. However, much of this research accepts space and spatial relations only implicitly. The ways in which space is shaped and, in turn, affected by production-reproduction processes have not yet been considered. In particular, we need to address how the physical environment of the home influences, and is affected by women's productive and reproductive practices within the home.

Thus, feminist geographers address the spatial dimension of women's work and their strategies of social reproduction at the scale of the household. They emphasize the gendered and changing nature of the relation between production and reproduction as a part of a single process that varies in time and space (McDowell 1989:59; Pratt and Hanson 1991; Mackenzie 1986). This type of analysis addresses gender relations and the use and construction of space at the household level, focusing on women's social practices of everyday life.

Various viewpoints explain differently the intersection between production and reproduction as a part of a single process. This debate informs home-based work in particular. Some authors (Beach 1989; Lindon 1999) suggest that integration between home and work is an ideal strategy that promotes harmony; others emphasize that working at home may lead to opposition and conflict (Christensen 1993). Moreover, as Salmi (1996) argues, these different experiences do not constitute opposing poles but rather form a continuum.

Because home-based work is associated with specific cultural contexts and family-gender systems, I argue that sociodemographic factors such as social class, occupation, educational level, life course, and the broader circumstances of a woman's life influence the myriad outcomes of women's spatial household arrangements—harmonious or conflictive integration. Thus, situations vary widely in how home-based work is carried out and the consequences and different meanings for the women involved. As Salmi points out (1996:150), the strategy of turning to home-based work is not a clear-cut choice, but has complex motivations that may change across time.

I also argue that working at home is a process that takes place across the course of a woman's life. Thus, a woman may encounter situations of conflict and integration at different points in her trajectory as a home-based worker. As I will show, although certain conditions entail opposition and conflict, the pursuit of ideal integration requires other conditions. Thus, certain factors—such as control over the work process, flexible schedules, family responsiveness, and which family members to allow into the workspace—might facilitate a balance between work and family life (Beach 1989:92). Conversely, mutual interruptions between family and work, longer working days, the intrusion of children into the work space, and weakened responsiveness to family and work might exacerbate tensions between domestic life and paid work performed within the home (see Tables 1 and 2).

Economic Crisis and Productive Restructuring in Mexico

In the past 20 years, debt and economic crises have beset Mexico and have led to the implementation of a set of structural adjustment policies that influenced economic restructuring, income distribution, and living standards (Benería 1992; Chant 1996). Structural adjustment measures have included the implementation of massive cuts in government spending, especially in the social sector (Cordera and González Tiburcio 1991; Chant 1996), which has affected a large part of the

Table 1.
Determinants of Integration or Conflict for Women Home-based Workers

Conditions	Integration	Conflict
Type of occupations	Domestic oriented	Nondomestic oriented
Education	Noneducated	Professional, semiprofessional
Position in the Life Course	Middle and advanced	Earlier stages
Number of years working at home	More than 10 years	Less than 5 years
Duration of home-based work	Permanent	Temporary, permanent, seasonal

Mexican population.

The restructuring of the economy affected both low and middle-income groups during the past two decades, leading to an increase in the number of people living in extreme poverty and an intensification of inequity in the areas of health, nutrition, and education. In the opinion of Benería (1992), the economic crisis was privatized in as much as families paid its burden in the absence of a welfare state and in the face of decreasing governmental services and subsidies. Thus, the family became the only source of support and an alternative for survival.

Table 2.
Conditions for Use of Space that Influence Integration or Conflict

Integration	Conflict
Control over the work process	Mutual interruptions between family and work
Flexible schedules	Longer working days
Family members allowed in work space	Children not allowed in work space
Family responsiveness	Weaken responsiveness to family and work

Among the main effects of economic restructuring in Mexico were adjustments in labor markets, which propitiated the growth of informality and self-employment in modalities in which women, in particular, participated, including home-based, income-generating activities. In particular, less-educated women with small children have played a major role in household strategies for income generation (García and Oliveira 1994). Many women entered the informal sector, either permanently or temporarily, and under the poor working conditions associated with this sector. Analysts apparently agree that economic restructuring also has affected middle-class women (Chant 1996, Parrado and Zenteno 2001:474). For example, in Tijuana, the high immigration to this city has attracted not only working-class migrants from central Mexico but also of middle-class families seeking jobs and better living conditions. In these situations, male unemployment or insecure employment has led many middle-class women to engage in independent work within their homes.

In Mexican cities, women's participation in home based-work arose from the scarcity of secure employment, the lack of alternatives for childcare and domestic work (Benería 1992:92), and from the advantage of this strategy to better integrate productive and reproductive activities within the home (Pacheco and Blanco 1998). However, although for many women, flexible schedules and family responsiveness are some of the basic reasons to locate waged work in their homes, in practice, working conditions are far from the ideal of a harmonious integration of domestic and income-generating tasks. As I show here, women face multiple conflicts in trying to balance both.

Home-Based Work in Tijuana

The literature on home-based work often describes its existence as a feature of depressed economies, particularly because of job loss in the industrial sector (Oberhauser 1993). However, some dynamic economies, such as that of Tijuana, promote the emergence of a diversity of forms of home-based work. Border interaction with the United States strongly determines the character of Tijuana's economy. This city's labor market is characterized by high rates of female participation in the manufacturing sector, following the establishment and development of maquiladora enterprises. However, self-employment in the commerce and service sectors has been a traditional source of employment for women in Tijuana. In the 1996 Encuesta Nacional de Empleo Urbano, ENEU (National Survey of Urban Employment), the percentages of female participation in these sectors (66.1 percent) were higher than in manufacturing (30.7 percent).

Oliveira (1990) showed that the national trend toward an expansion of female employment in the informal sector, in occupations that include home-based work, was also true for Tijuana during the years of economic crisis. Some authors argue that the increased numbers of self-employed women might be related to the growing percentage of female heads of household and the strong participation of women with small children (Oliveira 1990). Tijuana has one of Mexico's lowest unemployment rates. While the city's industrial base has facilitated women's participation in the formal labor market, its geographical location, which promotes transborder traffic and tourism, has increased self-employment, including home-based work. The process of productive restructuring and successive economic crises in 1986 and 1994, together with an existing tradition of self-employment, promoted the proliferation of women's home-based work. Thus, Tijuana features a dynamic economy in which diverse types of work coexist, among them, working at home.

Generally, during the 1990s labor markets along Mexico's northern border registered an increase in self-employment. For instance, in the mid-1980s, Tijuana's self-employment rate was 16 percent (Méndez Main 1990), and according to the Encuesta Nacional de Empleo Urbano (ENEU) in 1996, 20 percent of Tijuana's economically active population was self-employed. In particular, the 1994 Encuesta Nacional de Micronegocios (National Survey of Micro-Enterprises, ENAMIN) reported that 15 percent of the population working in micro-enterprise was self-employed and working at home. Out of this population, 73 percent of the men and 27 percent of the women work at home, with or without adequate equipment and furnishings. However, women's participation in home-based work presumably is greater than the data reflects. This underestimation might be due to the use of categories that hide this type of work and because many women home workers are reported as unwaged family workers.

In sum, the available statistical data show that home-based work results from a combination of factors, which may vary from individual to individual. For example, independence and the absence of jobs promote self-employment, in addition to economic need and the attractiveness of flexibility in combining domestic and income-generating work. However, as we shall see, home-based work can often be problematic, and women during their life course must implement new and different time-space strategies to face the conflict between family and paid work at home.

RESEARCH BACKGROUND

As a part of a broader project on home-based work, from February to September 1996, I interviewed fifteen women from diverse occupations, both formal and informal: sewing, dentistry, baking, hairstyling, packing diapers, sales, and childcare. I used the snowball sampling technique to contact women in working-class and middle-class neighborhoods of Tijuana. I selected the participants primarily based on their age (ages ranged from 33 to 67 years) and their marital and motherhood status (most were married or lived with a partner, three were separated from their husbands, and two were widows) (see Table 3). I defined middle-class women as those who were nonmanual workers with more than a high-school education.[3] Although professional women had undergraduate and graduate degrees, most working-class women had only an elementary or a high-school education. An additional criterion to determine class position was residential location.

All respondents lived in the city of Tijuana at the time of the interview. Working-class women lived mostly in small houses, sometimes made of second-hand materials, located in peripheral and densely populated urban neighborhoods. These neighborhoods frequently lacked public services, such as paved streets, sewers, piped-in water, and transportation. Conversely, middle-class women lived in single-family dwellings in well-developed, urbanized neighborhoods with available public services. Most of the interviewees had had formal jobs before they began working out of their homes; only two were full-time housewives before they began to work at home for pay; and only two women had had a long trajectory as home workers.

Table 3.
Sociodemographic Characteristics of Women Home-Based Workers

Name	Age	Marital status	Children	Education	Occupation
Elodia	48	Consensual Union	5	Elementary School	Foodstuffs Production
Rosa	43	Married	2	Medical school	Dentist
Elsa	33	Married	3	Bachelor's degree 1 (one year)	Marketing Diapers
Laura	35	Married	3	M.D.	Cosmetology
Carmen	63	Separated	4	Elementary School	Hair styling
Tony	54	Married	3	Accounting	Marketing medicine
Mariana	42	Married	2	Elementary School/Sewing	Sewing
Juanita	66	Separated	7	Elementary School	Childcare
Elisa	39	Married	3	Elementary School	Foodstuffs Production
Sagrario	44	Married	2	Preschool teacher/Psychology	Tarot-Card Reader/Teacher
Teresa	63	Widow	6	Accounting	Handicrafts and Childcare
Lucía	36	Consensual Union	2	Bilingual Secretary	Handicrafts
Matilde	67	Widow	6	Junior High School	Foodstuffs Production
Lucha	49	Separated	2	Junior High School	Restaurant
Delfina	51	Married	4	Elementary School	Grocery Store

Source: In-depth interviews, February through September 1996.

The Space and Time of Home-Based Work

Women home-based workers display a diversity of schedules and work routines. One advantage of working at home is flexibility in scheduling time for various activities. For instance, women can pace their own work and combine productive and domestic responsibilities. Women may also feel liberated when they no longer have to follow a fixed job schedule and this freedom may give them more control over their lives (Salmi 1993). It allows them to reschedule, increase, or decrease work in order to accommodate particular family needs.

The women workers in this study had heterogeneous work routines, which ranged from a couple of hours up to 50 hours per week. Some worked on weekends, others at night, and others in the morning when children were at school, depending on their reproductive and productive activities. Some women working at home had to set schedules according to the needs of their customers. An example of this practice was the case of a pediatric dentist, who worked only during the afternoons when children were available for appointments.

In other cases, women worked only on weekends. For example, a worker who prepared food preferred to work on the weekend because she felt less pressure to care for her children and husband in terms of preparing their meals and doing their laundry. For some workers, another important reason for working weekends was that the product they sold was in greater demand at that time. This was particularly true for a woman who baked cakes for birthdays, weddings, and other events, since these usually take place on the weekend. Many women worked by appointment because that gave them flexibility. If the client could not keep an appointment, she or he could call to postpone or cancel and, being at home, the woman home worker could continue doing domestic chores, something that would not have been possible if she was working outside the home.

Although this flexibility in organizing time seems to work well for some women, others find that it leads to working longer, harder days than if they had been employed in a formal occupation. For example, Mariana, a seamstress, worked while her husband and children were sleeping, and Tony, a distributor of pharmaceutical products, had clients who came to her home at all hours.

Research has shown that women often engage simultaneously in productive and reproductive activities in a single area of the house (Mackenzie 1986; Christensen 1993; Oberhauser 1993). In my own observations, a seamstress sews while doing her family's laundry, and a distributor of disposable diapers interrupts her work to tend to her own small children.

Nevertheless, domestic and occupational activities are not always carried out simultaneously in the same domestic space (López Estrada 2001). Certain productive activities demand concentration, and under those circumstances, a woman cannot do two things at once. The domestic or nondomestic character of paid activities seems to influence work routines. Women working for pay in domestic activities, such as baking and childcare, can carry out their own reproductive tasks at the same time. However, this is not true for most professional activities. For example, given the higher concentration required, a dentist cannot simultaneously treat a patient and cook.

Women home workers look for alternative ways of organizing their paid activities in the micro geography of their homes. They create new uses of space by remodeling and using them as temporary or permanent workplaces (Mackenzie 1986:89). Spatial arrangements are linked to the kind of activities women perform, available home space, and other domestic resources. In this study, I found two patterns of spatial use. On one hand, those women who had to share space used in areas of the house—such as the living room, dining room, kitchen, and bedrooms–for work activities in addition to their traditional uses. In these spaces, women performed activities such as packing products, sewing, handcrafting, food production, and haircutting. During the day, women using domestic equipment and appliances transformed these areas into a temporary workplace. Sometimes women used these spaces simultaneously for multiple productive and reproductive activities. At other times, they had to shift back and forth between using these rooms for family and work demands (López Estrada 2001a:113).

On the other hand, other women had a separate workplace within the home. In these cases, particularly middle-class women, had the opportunity to remodel certain rooms to house their productive activities permanently. Sometimes only furniture modified these places. For example, while a seamstress turned the TV room into a workshop, the dentist housed her consulting room in a remodeled laundry room. At other times, women built a special workplace. That was the case of a distributor of disposable diapers, who built a roof over the patio of her house, under which she could pack factory seconds of the product (López Estrada 2001a:115).

It is worth noting that women often work in restricted spaces and under inadequate environmental conditions. Some home workers complained about the lack of light and workspace. Poor women, in particular, had more difficulty in finding an appropriate and comfortable area in which to locate their home-based income-generating activities (Watson 1990). Having a specific place within the home to do productive work might help women to balance the relationship between family and work and redefine the content and meaning of gender roles and relations.

Integration and Conflict within the Household

The women workers' demographics, such as their occupations, social class, and life course, influence the balance between work and family. In addition, there are temporal and spatial conditions that influence the various patterns of integration and conflict. In what follows, I present in the words of the women the details of different situations of home-based work integration and conflict in their lives.[4]

Taking into consideration social class and age differences, I found situations of harmonious integration of home and work in the cases of women workers devoted to domestic-related activities, such as sewing, cooking, or selling groceries. Although these activities seem to better suit the features of integration, there are other occupations, such as those performed at a desk, that also allow a balance between productive activities and domestic tasks.

Mariana was a forty-two year old, middle-class seamstress who had worked at home for twenty-nine years. She had contributed to the income of both her family of origin and her own family. When she was a child, her family migrated from the state of Michoacán to Tijuana. Because her father prevented his daughters from going to school, Mariana studied fashion design by mail, and she started sewing at her home when she was a teenager.

After she got married, the family first lived in an apartment and Mariana used to sew in the kitchen. Later, the couple and their two children moved into a three-bedroom house that Mariana's husband built. Here, a counter separated Mariana's workshop, in the TV room, from the kitchen. This spatial organization allowed her to juggle domestic and productive work. While Mariana was sewing, she could cook or check the washing machine, which was in a closet in the kitchen. In her words:

> Well, the laundry room is just right there. So, I stop sewing and I load the washing machine. I do one thing, and then the other. I also stop to check what I'm cooking.

For Mariana, home-based work also had the advantage of allowing her to control her schedule.

> I have noticed that my work is not routine . . . my time is very flexible. I distribute my time in a way that lets me break the routine. Sometimes I'm struggling with my work. It takes me more time than usual because I'm tired and things start going wrong. Then I stop sewing and do something else, and the next day, I can start to take up my work again, and so on.

The workplace's location and the domestic character of sewing facilitated the integration of family and work. In addition, the workplace also located strategically, allowed her to monitor the rest of the house and the activities of the family members.

The function of the kitchen was the one area of the home that was most often modified due to woman's paid work. This was the case, for example, of Elisa, a woman who made pastries in her kitchen while cooking meals for her family. She had been baking goods for sale for many years, and her husband and children had gotten used to it. Moreover, the house was large and the family used the kitchen only for cooking, so its function as workplace intruded very little in family life.

Elisa was born in Tijuana after her parents had migrated there from northern states in Mexico. As a member of a large family, she only went to elementary school. Her father was a baker, and he taught Elisa to bake cakes and bread. Elisa married a butcher. After her husband lost an arm in a work-related accident, he went to work in a supermarket. Elisa knew that she could bake and due to the increased economic needs of her family, she starting baking cakes for neighbors and friends. She usually did this work on weekends when most parties take place.

Elisa worked at home for 10 years, and she had organized her work in such a way that it did not interfere with her family life, although sometimes she juggled multiple tasks, both productive and reproductive, in her kitchen. Her sons were familiar with Elisa's home bakery business, and she allowed them to be in the kitchen while she was working. Sometimes they helped her with tasks such as decorating cakes, and her youngest son even learned how to bake and make candy. For Elisa, the temporal and spatial organization of both paid work and domestic tasks was the key to accommodate her work requirements, avoiding their mutual interference.

> I organize my time so that I can bake cakes and also take care of my family. At the beginning, it seemed difficult to me, but I learned to plan ahead. When they arrive at home, I have the cakes ready, and then I can take care of my family.

Preparing food for pay usually is portrayed as a typical occupation for older women who cannot find work in the labor market. The kitchen is used to cook for both the family and customers and, sometimes, the dining room becomes a cafeteria. Such was the case of Doña Lucha, a working-class woman separated from her husband. She had worked at a food stand located in her neighborhood. However, she was laid-off when the owner could no longer pay her wages. Doña Lucha began to perform home-based work because some of her neighbors and former customers encouraged her to open her own business; they even lent her money to do it.

> I was very excited when I saw my dining room converted into a restaurant. Here, until now, only a family had been living, but suddenly this group came into my home [to take their meals here]. That was why I was so excited. I also feel quite comfortable because I'm in my own home, and I can take care of my daughter, who is the most important thing for me.

She arranged her kitchen as a restaurant, where neighbors and friends could eat their daily meals. For a mature woman who might face difficulties in getting a formal job, working at home had more than just an economic advantage. Because she had spent most of her productive life working outside the home, this strategy also implied a reappropriation of the domestic space. In the past, Doña Lucha's house was empty most of the day, and it had never been a center of social activity, but working at home allowed her to redefine its use, converting it into a very social site in which she and her customers interacted. The ready access that family members had to the kitchen and customers to other areas of the home (such as the bathroom, patio, and living room), facilitated the interaction.

Although Doña Lucha worked more than before, for her, working at home was much better in comparison to her previous job. Even though her income was now irregular, she felt secure because her income depended on herself, not on someone else. Moreover, she could spend more time with her eleven year old daughter, who helped her after school to serve the customers.

The cases of Mariana and Elisa, women representing different social classes but with the same family structure, reflect the practice of similar strategies that led to a balance between work and family. In these cases, at some point in the past, women experienced conflict due to the lack of space and the presence of small children. As the family budget increased and children grew up, however, they gained in space and the levels of domestic chores diminished, contributing to the success of reorganizing activities within the household.[5] Importantly, some of the women have been working at home, sporadically or permanently, for approximately 10 years.

Elisa and Doña Lucha had previous work experience outside the home, but Doña Lucha's story is distinct because of her marital status and stage in the life course. As head of the household, home-based work gave her a level of economic independence,[6] in addition to a flexible schedule and the chance to reappropriate the use of her house by reorganizing the domestic space materially and socially. Other studies (Salmi 1993; Christensen 1993) have found that women working out of their own homes more freely decide their working hours and pace of work. Indeed, this is one of the most valuable advantages of working at home. However, these advantages do not always offset the disadvantages of home-based work, and many women face the conflict of balancing the production-reproduction equation within the home.

Activities that occur simultaneously in the same space may create conflict for women. Some find it difficult to separate work and family in the home. Below I introduce the cases that illustrate how and under what conditions women experience conflict over the use of the home as a workplace, as well as the time-space arrangements they adopted in order to respond to those conflicts, sometimes privileging work, other times privileging home.

For women with professional careers, working at home may benefit family demands but not work demands. Some interviewees had worked outside the home, but they quit their jobs and decided to work at home to dedicate more time to their children. This was the case of Rosa, a forty-three year old dentist and mother of two, who converted the laundry room into a dental clinic so that she could be close to her children. After several months of working as a dentist at her home, this activity started to intrude in her family life because she had more patients than she had expected. In addition, Rosa's husband complained that she did not take good care of the children, and she felt she was losing control over domestic life, as she explained:

> When the number of clients increased, I did not look after my children. I'm a dentist and children come to see me in the afternoons because during mornings they are at school. I stopped supervising [my] children's homework, and my kids changed radically. They watched TV all the time because there was nobody to take care of them, and they did not eat well.

She decided to try another strategy that might enable her to care better for her children while keeping her dental practice:

> A mother cannot divide herself into two. I analyzed the situation, and I had to adopt new strategies, set fixed hours, and raise my prices. This reduced the number of clients. Since then, I have time to see Ale, now I know what he is reading, and what he is doing for school. I did lose three months of the life of my kid, and I did not like it because we [mothers] are the ones who encourage them [children] very much [to do their work].

However, after trying to balance family and work, the tension continued, and she considered closing the dental office. However, she had second thoughts and instead decided to hire a maid (who also worked as the office assistant) to clean the house and look after the children while she was practicing dentistry. Through this new arrangement, domestic work and childcare were better organized, and she could see her patients without worrying about her children. Rosa was able to implement this strategy because her husband supported her decision and because she had the money to hire a maid. In general, while middle-class women may partially resolve the conflicts over work and family by hiring another woman to help them with domestic chores; poor women delegate this work to daughters.

Women's ability to work at home changes across the life course. Home-based work is more difficult for women with small children, but when they leave home or become adults, their mothers are supposed to have more opportunities to use the home as a workplace. This was the case of Tony, who worked at home distributing pharmaceutical products. She lived in a three-bedroom house with her husband and three grown daughters.

Tony and her husband used to work for a pharmaceutical company. In 1992, the company closed the warehouse and asked them to administer the business on their own because this was more convenient for the company. Thus, they set up the distribution office in their home, next to the living room. This was also convenient for Tony. Because they were in their twenties, Tony's daughters did not demand much from her, but she recognized that her home-based work arrangement allowed her more time to be at home and care for her family. For example, although the business seemed to be her priority, the kitchen was right there, and she could supervise what she was cooking while attending to her clients.

However, Tony noted that the workplace, which materially and socially blurred with the domestic space, and the intrusion of work into home life, required a careful negotiation among the members of her family. To resolve this conflict, she agreed with her husband and daughters that they would discuss work issues only in the office, and family issues only in the living room or other parts of the house. This mental separation of spaces is a strategy that helps women to reorganize social relations within the home. Despite this arrangement, Tony's work at home has been problematic for her because the family did not stick to a set work schedule, and clients called on them as early as 7:00 a.m. and as late as 10:00 p.m. Although she told clients that she and her husband were available only during business hours, her husband continued to answer the telephone and receive people in the office at any hour of the day or night.

Additional conflicts can arise from home-based work because women have to share the domestic space with other family members, creating disputes over areas such as the bedroom, living room, and kitchen. For instance, Elsa, a middle-class, thirty-three year old mother of three, packed and distributed factory seconds of disposable diapers. The family moved from central Mexico to Tijuana in 1990 because Elsa's husband, a salesman, was promoted. However, with the economic crisis that affected Mexico in 1994, her husband was afraid of being laid-off and he decided to open the disposable-diaper distribution business. He asked Elsa to manage the business, but initially she hesitated because she had no business experience and she was afraid she would not be able to manage the business well. She started packing the diapers in the living room but, as demand increased, the product spread all over the house, and it soon became an issue for her children and herself.

> I was packing the diapers in the living room, but my home was messy all the time, and my kids could not watch TV. I also felt that I was losing my home. Then, we decided to build a roof over the patio [so that I would have a place] to pack the diapers.

Elsa had to negotiate the use of the domestic space with her three children. It was important to maintain the living room as an area for relaxing and family use. However, once she moved out to the patio, the new work location did not allow to her to supervise her children. Another socio-spatial conflict emerged when she realized that she could not do all the packing herself. Elsa and her husband decided to hire his brother and his brother's wife, but this couple spent the entire day at her home, even on weekends, and Elsa resented the invasion of her space and privacy.

Although Elsa's sons helped by doing some of the cleaning, her husband and children also demanded hot meals and clean clothes. Thus, because of her double role, Elsa's workload was a burden for her:

> The demand for disposable diapers increased, and I had to pack them all the time, so I did not make the beds or cook. When my husband arrived home, he complained about it. My children also missed the cookies and pastries I used to bake for them.

Elsa could not resolve this conflict. Trying to do domestic chores and home-based work was burdensome. She worked all day long, juggling the cleaning and cooking for the family with the packing of the diapers. Finally, Elsa decided to close the business, although she said she would like to reopen it outside the home in a place with better lighting and sufficient storage space. In this way, she could better separate work from family issues.

The dispute over domestic space is even greater for those women who have small houses or large families. Lucia owned a tiny two-bedroom condominium, which she shared with her partner and two children. She had worked for several years in real estate, and after some time, she decided to try her hand as a designer and artisan, making clothes, such as hand painted vests and dresses. She wanted to establish her own business and become independent while being at home with their children. However, she lacked space, so she usually worked in her bedroom, which had the best lighting of any spot in her tiny dwelling:

> I have a place in front of the window, but I also work on the bed with artificial light, depending on what I am doing. It's not the most appropriate place, it's certainly more tiring to cut and do those things . . . but I have adapted myself to what I have.

The nature of her job required Lucia to work long and intense workdays.

> Several weeks ago, we had a request. I got it on Thursday morning, and they asked me to deliver it by Friday morning. My two associates and I worked from 10 a.m. until 4 A.M. the following day. I would like to do this like a normal job: you finish and you leave at the end of the workday.

The needs of their children, particularly the youngest one, often meant interruptions:

> We don't have a separate place for doing work. Domestic work and this work are mixed. And it is an inconvenience that you are working in the same place, because children come and ask you things. They disturb you, you lose rhythm . . . I would like to have a place exclusively for work, where I could leave my things out. Otherwise, if you are working at home, you have to put away everything. I can't leave the materials out . . . because the children can reach them.

Although some women, such as Rosa and Elsa, had more space in their homes for their paid work, in interviews with other women it became apparent that certain rooms in the house were often used for multiple purposes. Situations of shared space are difficult because of the lack of domestic resources. This was the case for Elodia, who had always been a housewife, but who decided to make bread and tamales in her kitchen in order to contribute to the family's meager income. A native of Sinaloa, Elodia came to Tijuana after her partner migrated here looking for a job. In Tijuana, she and her family lived in a squatter community and in a tiny house made of second-hand materials. The family had a serious space shortage and the kitchen served multiple functions (dining room, family room, workplace). In addition, Elodia had inadequate working conditions because her kitchen did not have a sink and faucet, making cleaning difficult. She also complained that her second-hand oven did not work well, so baking bread and tamales took longer than it should have. Because the family members had to share that tiny space, Elodia had to work on the weekends. This allowed her to accommodate her productive and reproductive tasks so that she could avoid the interference of family members while she was baking.

Both Rosa and Elsa, who have small children, found that they experienced constraints and conflicts between their paid work in the home and their role as mothers. Rosa reorganized the work in her home-based dental office so that she could avoid closing it altogether. She also managed to balance her professional expectations with the demands of her family. In contrast, Elsa closed her business because it became a burden for her, and she missed the privacy of her domestic life. She felt trapped between work demands and her family's complaints about her having abandoned them. For her, it was more rewarding to be a mother and wife. Tony partially resolved the conflict between family and work through the mental separation of space but, because of her husband, she could not keep a regular work schedule.

As did Rosa and Elsa, Lucia faced the problem of the children's interference in her paid work and for Lucia and Elodia, the blurring between work and domestic life was more stressful. The limited size of their dwellings forced them to work under inadequate environmental conditions. In this respect, Elodia's situation was extreme because her scantly equipped kitchen served multiple and shifting functions throughout the day. In addition, living in poor neighborhoods these women lacked basic services, such as water and sewers. Consequently, they had to invest more time trying to meet the demands of their productive and reproductive roles.

Overall, the diversity of these women's time-space strategies shows that working at home is a process that changes in temporal and spatial character according to the socio-spatial conflicts that may result from its practice depending on women's occupations, social class (as expressed in available domestic space and resources), and the stage in the course of a woman's life.

Home-Based Work, Gender Relations, and Women's Perceptions of Their Work

The structuring of practices of social reproduction within the home has consequences for how women socially and symbolically envision home and work, and it has implications for gender roles and relations. Regarding the implications of home-based work for women, this type of occupation is portrayed as a strategy that is either exploitative or liberating (Beach 1989). In this study, which addresses only self-employed workers, it would be a mistake to think in dichotomies: "conflict and integration" and "exploitation and liberation." I use these terms only for the purposes of analysis because reality is much more complex. Case studies about socio-spatial conflict and home-based work integration expressed a variety of forms and shades with respect to gender roles and relations (López Estrada 2000).

In Mexico, cultural ideas about gender roles link domestic work to women, with men having primacy as breadwinners. Although by working at home women are performing an economic role, they often consider this role as complementary. The interconnection of domestic and wage work reinforces this idea and contributes to the devaluation of women's economic contribution. Despite the fact that some interviewees valued the wage work they performed, the devaluation arising from its location within the household contributed to the impression that they were not making a significant contribution to the family economy. However, the income from the work of these women contributed not only to the purchase of household necessities but also to buying homes and consumer goods and helping to pay for the children's education (López Estrada 2000). In certain cases, women worked to save money for a particular goal, such as a daughter's fifteenth birthday celebration, a major rite of passage in Mexico. The literature widely recognizes that women contribute a greater share of their income to the family budget (González de la Rocha 1986; García and Oliveira 1994). For women heads of household, their home-based work represented the main source of income for their families.

Although in their discourse women do not identify themselves as providers, in general, I observed that by assuming part of the responsibility of being a breadwinner, women, particularly middle-class women, had more opportunities for negotiating conjugal relations and the terms of childcare with their partners. This was particularly true of women who had previous work experience outside the home. However, women's bargaining power might be affected if they performed poorly paid or unstable jobs that did not provide ongoing or significant contributions to the family income.

Unlike the argument that home-based work promotes gender-role equality (Lindon 1999), the findings of this study support Beach's argument that role integration is a female endeavor. In other words, integration occurs only for female work roles, both productive and reproductive. These double roles, taking place as they do at home, add to women's already burdened workload because the family's domestic demands do not decrease. Changes in the division of labor within the home continue to be the purview of women. While some middle-class women were able to hire domestic servants, poor women delegated domestic chores to other women in the family.

According to the data I collected, husbands and male children did not cooperate much in household work. In general, although home-based work has forced some men to participate in domestic chores and childcare, women still had the primary responsibility for these tasks. These findings are similar to Christensen's (1993) study carried out in the United States.[7] Sometimes the women did not demand their husbands' cooperation with domestic tasks because they considered them to be the family's primary providers. Some women from both social classes, however, were trying to change the traditional division of labor by involving their male children in making beds, cleaning bathrooms, and other domestic chores. In certain cases, the husband and children participated in the women's productive activities. Most families used unpaid family work and this situation was particularly true of women heads of households, who delegated productive and reproductive work to other women of the family, a common strategy in Latin American households. In these cases, this mechanism was fundamental in achieving harmonious home-based work integration.

Scholars agree that women place an ambiguous value on family and work.

While in discourse they privilege family issues over work, in practice, they seem to enjoy their extra-domestic occupations (Velasco 1996; García and Oliveira 1994). Feminist geographers have shown that women's appropriation of the home has resulted in new appreciation for their domestic roles (Dyck 1989). The women in this study had been socialized to think that a good mother was one who stays at home and spends a lot of time with her children, therefore, their priority was their children and home (Christensen 1993:58). However, the interviewees also expressed ambivalence about both the devaluation of mothering and homemaking activities and the homemaker role (Saegert and Winkel 1980:43).

As a social construction, class, gender, and race—among other factors—influence women's meaning of work (Watson 1990). In general, the women interviewed in this study expressed their satisfaction with their work. The working-class women said that their work was necessary for the survival of their families, and, perhaps because of the domestic nature of their occupations, the meaning they attached to their paid work appeared to be less conflictive for them. This aspect needs further investigation.

Middle-class professional women experienced contradictory feelings about family and work. Intrusion of home-based work into family life caused them to perceive that they were not adequately performing their maternal roles. In their narratives, they gave priority to being a mother, but, in practice, this was a source of conflict for them because they wanted to continue doing their paid work. Because being a home worker was also an important part of their identity, these women could not ignore those occupations and the meanings attached to them. Rosa, the forty-five year old dentist with two children, expressed her ambivalence about home and occupational roles:

> I feel a sense of satisfaction from being a mother but it is not the same with my professional work. My occupation is being a mother; the other is an extra. However, I cannot erase myself, and disappear. The most important thing for me is the home, but at least I have the dental office (in the home). If it disappears, I would cry out of sadness. I love it.

While middle-class educated women were more concerned with developing their professional careers, middle-class women with manual occupations were more concerned with being good mothers and housewives. These women seemed to be conscious of their position as a housewife, arising from the status it could bring. Consequently, they fought to preserve this status, and decided to stay at home because their domestic roles were much more valuable for their children and husband—and to them personally—than their roles as workers. This was the case of Elsa, who said to her husband:

> You made me to do this [job] against my will. I was happy at home, and you were not so demanding [about domestic issues]. I knew very well what my duties were,

and there were no problems. So I better quit this [job] and get back to my home, to do my domestic work early, and then to read a book or do whatever I like, instead of killing myself [with this job].

Despite the ambiguity they experienced about their roles, which was greater among middle-class women, in the process of working at home, some of these women realized that this activity did not make them into bad wives and mothers. Instead, they came to feel that they were responsible women, who expected a more egalitarian relationship (Christensen 1989:168; Benería and Roldán 1987). In addition, by working at home, some women gave new meaning to traditional roles, such as being a neighbor. As Rosa argues:

> Ah yes, it has affected my life. It has given me more maturity. By being here, I have learned to be a woman, because I only knew how to be a doctor, a researcher. And now I am more a mom, a wife, a neighbor, who runs to bring soup to the lady next door. I step down to a more common and quotidian reality, what is expected of a woman. I was living in a man's world and [doing] what is expected of him.

The women in my sample define themselves as paid workers. Nevertheless, they believe that working at home is less valued than working outside of the home. In general, extra-domestic work produces ambivalence in women with regard to their gender roles (López Estrada 2001). In the case of home-based work, women suffer even greater ambivalence given the devaluation of this type of work, which is associated to its location. This was particularly true for those women with professional careers. Home-based work may also be devalued in the eyes of clients and customers, who may mislabel the activity, which can be disturbing for working women (Ahrentzen 1997:82). In the words of Rosa:

> Working at one's own home is not the same as working outside the home. When you leave home, you cross the doorway and go to a clinic where you are Dr. Martinez. There, you have the same salary as others in your category. You have respect and a schedule. But when you are working at home, you are the "Mrs." who is a dentist. But you are, first, the "Mrs." I feel as if [dentistry] were a second-hand job.

People's perceptions about home-based work seem to be attached to conventional definitions and the meaning of the home as a nonworkplace. As Rosa said:

> People's perceptions are based on appearance. When we go to a doctor, we look in the waiting room, and at the physical appearance of the secretary. But, here [in my home], there is a baseball bat in the middle of the yard, and the seeds to feed the birds. This is not ideal for a doctor's office. It would never be [this way if I worked outside the home]. That is why I only treat my friends and relatives.

Despite the widespread devaluation of home-based work, some husbands and children recognized the value of their spouse or mother's home-based occupation. They did this not only because of the economic benefits but also because they respected the woman's skills and knowledge. This is particularly significant for children's socialization, since they may learn that home-based work is as respected as work done outside of the home. As Mariana, a seamstress with two children, noted:

> My daughter did not recognize my work until she saw that the only thing her friends' mothers did in the afternoons was to watch TV. Now she thinks that "my mom is very creative," and she is proud of me.

FINAL CONSIDERATIONS

This article discusses women's home-based work as one of the diverse modalities of self-employment that are taking place in the city of Tijuana, as a response to economic crises and productive restructuring that results in the proliferation of informal activities. Married women with children mainly engage in wage work at home to contribute to the family income. While middle-class women work at home to realize their professional aspirations or attempt to maintain their class status, working-class women need this type of work for their families' survival. In addition, many women engage in self-employment because of the insecurity of men's jobs, or because they cannot find a formal job due to their age.

At the micro level, this article focused on women home workers as social actors who, in daily life, have to face the contradictions of their dual roles, which are often manifested spatially and temporally in the reorganization of their households to accommodate paid work. In analyzing some of the socio-spatial productive and reproductive practices of women home workers, this research reveals interrelationships between gender and spatial dimensions.

Home-based work as an integrative strategy is a reality in as much as it involves the daily dynamics of both productive and reproductive activities within the space of the household. Considered as a process, home-based work is related to the larger conditions that affect women's lives, as well as the specific circumstances under which women work at home. The cases presented here show the diversity of ways women experience paid work at home, depending on their social class, occupation, educational level, and stage in the life course. Family structures also play a role in determining how wage work takes place within the home, particularly in the case of women who are heads of households.

Engaging in home-based work can be a harmonious strategy that allows some women to combine productive and reproductive activities within the domestic space. Case studies suggest that these dynamics seem to work well for those women whose income-generating activities are domestic in character. But working at home may also create contradictions in women's daily lives, particularly for those with small children who are trying to pursue a professional career, or for those working women whose homes lack basic services, such as water and electricity, and who live in communities without public infrastructure such as paved streets. As frequently assumed, this diversity of experiences shows that sometimes home-based work is far from being an ideal strategy to combine family and work.

The consequences of working at home for women are related to different social and cultural realities. On the one hand, this type of work offers women advantages such as flexible schedules and more control over their lives. On the other hand, although the spatial reorganization of activities within the home sometimes results in men's incipient participation in childcare, women nevertheless continue to be in charge of domestic responsibilities. As an income-generating activity, home-based work might represent an avenue to increase women's well being, and a tool for negotiating gender relations within the family.

Self-employed women workers also expressed the ambivalence they feel about performing their double roles that, in this case, domestic confinement obscures. I found that although restricted home places and inadequate environmental conditions might be oppressive for some women workers, women's management of the household as a workplace helps them and their families to reevaluate home-based work as well as domestic roles, thus, opening up possibilities for an improvement in women's social condition. Case studies show that the home is a place that continuously is renegotiated—sometimes as a private space, other times, as a public and dynamic socioeconomic site. In the home, then, women experience a diversity of relationships whose nature can range from conflict to solidarity.

Research on labor markets along Mexico's northern border has primarily studied formal employment. Now, however, because of the increasing participation of self-employed women, it is important to document different modalities of home-based work, both self-employment in commerce and service, and piecework. This is particularly true in the case of industrial home-based work, a trend that seems to be emerging in Tijuana because of restructuring processes. This examination would help us to understand the extent of this phenomenon and to identify its articulations with the regional economy, as well as the impact it has on the household's economy, and the implications for the labor, health, and environmental conditions under which women work at home.

This study attempts to contribute to discussions of female home-based work, as a socio-spatial and economic response to major changes in society, to explain the ways in which home environments are pervasively gendered, and to demonstrate how women may change the use of that space depending on their living and working conditions in historical and cultural contexts. The constant interaction between women and their living space may help them to redefine gender roles and relations, as well as the social ascription and meaning of home and work. Consequently, the spatial consideration of productive practices at the scale of the home can help us to better understand the specific modes of work, and its implications for women and family life as well as for the economy more generally.

NOTES

1. I would like to thank the anonymous reviewers of this article for their critical comments and suggestions, which helped me to elaborate my ideas further. However, I take full responsibility for the text.

2. This document is part of a larger study I submitted as doctoral dissertation at the Department of Sociology, CUNY, Graduate Center. I presented an earlier version of this article at a conference, "Women and Families: The Evolution of the Status of Women as a Factor in and a Consequence for Changes in Family Dynamics," organized by the Committee for International Cooperation in National Research in Demography (CICRED), and UNESCO, Paris, February, 1997. In 2000, CICRED published that paper in the conference proceedings.

3. However, my qualitative sample included some exceptions because of the nature of home-based work. Sometimes, income levels are higher in this type of work than in formal employment and the living conditions of workers reflect it. An example was a seamstress who had only a grade-school education, but who lived in a well-urbanized residential area in Tijuana.

4. The quotes come directly from the interviews with these women and their names have been changed to protect their identities.

5. Miraftab (1996), in her study on industrial home workers in central Mexico, reports similar findings. She defines different phases in the spatial modification of dwellings to make room for wage work across time.

6. This situation is consistent with the argument that the economic crisis had some positive effects for women's social condition (Chant 1996; Miraftab 1996).

7. Significantly, the results of sociological studies about family and work in Mexico agree that a primary change in the division of labor within the family is men's involvement in childcare (García and Oliveira 1994).

REFERENCES

AHRENTZEN, Sherry.
    1997. "The Meaning of Home Workplaces for Women." In *Thresholds in Feminist Geography: Difference, Methodology, Representation*, edited by John P. Jones, Heidi J. Nast, and Susan M. Roberts. Lanham, Maryland: Rowman and

Littlefield.
BARBIERI, Teresita de
    1984. *Mujeres y Vida Cotidiana*. México: SEP-80, Fondo de Cultura Económica.
BEACH, Betty.
    1989. *Integrating Work and Family Life: The Home-working Family*. Albany: State University of New York Press.
BENERÍA, Lourdes.
    1992. "The Mexican Debt Crisis: Restructuring the Economy and the Household." In *Unequal Burden: Economic Crisis, Persistent Poverty, and Women's Work*, edited by Lourdes Benería and Shelley Feldman. Boulder, Colorado: Westview Press.
BENERÍA, Lourdes and Martha Roldán.
    1987. *The Crossroads of Class and Gender: Industrial Homework, Subcontracting, and Household Dynamics in Mexico City*. Chicago, Illinois: Chicago University Press.
BORIS, Eileen and Elizabeth Prugl.
    1996. *Home Workers in Global Perspective: Invisible No More*. London, England: Routledge.
CHANT, Sylvia.
    1996. "Women's Roles in Recession and Economic Restructuring in Mexico and the Philippines." *Geoforum* 27(3):297-327.
CHRISTENSEN, Kathleen.
    1989. *Women and Home-based Work: The Unspoken Contract*. New York, New York: Henry Holt and Company.
———. 1993. "Eliminating the Journey to Work: Home-based Work across the Life Course of Women in the United States." In *Full Circles: Geographies of Women over the Life Course*, edited by Cindi Katz and Janice Monk. London, England and New York, New York: Routledge.
CORDERA, Rolando and Enrique González Tiburcio.
    1991. "Crisis and Transition in the Mexican Economy." In *Social Responses to Mexico's Economic Crisis of the 1980s*, edited by Mercedes González de la Rocha and Agustín González Latapí. San Diego: University of California.
DYCK, Isabel.
    1989. "Integrating Home and Wage Workplace: Women's Daily Lives in a Canadian Suburb." *The Canadian Geographer* 33(4):329-341.
ENCUESTA NACIONAL DE EMPLEO URBANO, ENEU (National Survey of Urban Employment) 1996, Mexico.
ENCUESTA NACIONAL DE MICRONEGOCIOS, ENAMIN, (National Survey of Mirco-Enterprises), 1994. Mexico.
ESCOBAR, Silvia.
    1988. "El Comercio en Pequeña Escala en la Ciudad de La Paz, Bolivia." In *La Mujer en el Sector Informal: Trabajo Femenino y Microempresa en América Latina*, edited by Marguerite Berger and Mayra Buvinic. Quito, Ecuador: Instituto Latino-Americano de Desarrollo y de Investigación Social-Quito (ILDIS-Quito), Editorial Nueva Sociedad.
GARCÍA, Brígida, Humberto Muñoz, and Orlandina de Oliveira.
    1982. *Hogares y Trabajadores en la Ciudad de Mexico*. México D.F.: El Colegio

de México, Ciudad Universitaria, México, Instituto de Investigaciones Sociales, Universidad Nacional Autónoma de México (UNAM).

GARCÍA, Brígida and Orlandina de Oliveira.
    1994. *Trabajo y Vida Familiar en Mexico*. México D.F.: El Colegio de México.

GARCÍA RAMÓN, Dolores, Mireia Baylina, Josefina Cruz, Concha Domingo, Montserrat Villarino, and Rafael Viruela.
    1995. El Trabajo Industrial a Domicilio en al España Rural: Un Análisis desde la Perspectiva de Género. Departamento de Geografía, Universidad Autonóma de Barcelona, Spain. Unpublished manuscript.

GONZÁLEZ DE LA ROCHA, Mercedes.
    1986. *Los Recursos de la Pobreza. Familias de Bajos Ingresos en Guadalajara*. Guadalajara, Jalisco, México City, México: Colegio de Jalisco, Centro de Investigaciones y Estudios Superiores en Antropologia Social (CIESAS).

JELIN, Elizabeth et al.
    1986. "Un Estilo de Trabajo: La Investigación Microsocial." In *Problemas Metodológicos en la Investigación Sociodemográfica,* edited by Rodolfo Corona et al. México D.F.: El Colegio de México.

LINDON, Alicia.
    1999. De la Trama de la Cotidianidad a los Modos de Vida Urbanos. El Valle de Chalco. México City, México D.F.: El Colegio de México, El Colegio Mexiquense.

LÓPEZ ESTRADA, Silvia.
    2000. "Making the Home Work: Women's Home-based Work in Tijuana." Ph.D. dissertation. City University of New York, CUNY Graduate Center.

———. 2001. "Uso y Significado de la Casa como Lugar de Trabajo." In *Esto Es Cosa de Hombres. Trabajo, Género y Cambio Social,* edited by Jennifer A. Cooper. México City, México: Programa Universitario de Estudios de Género, Universidad Nacional Autónoma de México.

———. 2001a. "Estrategias Tempo-espaciales de Trabajo Femenino en el Hogar." *Papeles de Población* 29:105-126.

MACKENZIE, Susan.
    1986. "Women's Responses to Economic Restructuring: Changing Gender, Changing Space." In *The Politics of Diversity,* edited by Roberta Hamilton and Michèle Barrett. London, England: Verso.

MCDOWELL, Linda.
    1989. "Toward an Understanding of the Gender Division of Urban Space." *Environment and Planning D: Society and Space* 1:59-72.

MÉNDEZ MAIN, Silvia.
    1990. "El Sector Informal en dos Ciudades de la Frontera Norte: Tijuana y Ciudad Juárez." In *Crisis, Conflicto y Sobrevivencia. Estudios Sobre la Sociedad Urbana en México,* edited by Guillermo de la Peña, Juan Manuel Durán et al. Guadalajara, México: Universidad de Guadalajara/Centro de Investigaciones y Estudios Superiores en Antropología Social (CIESAS).

MENJÍVAR LARÍN, Rafael and Juan Pablo Pérez Sáinz.
>   1993. *Ni Héroes ni Villanas. Género e Informalidad Urbana en Centroamérica.* San José, Costa Rica: Facultad Latinoamericano de Ciencias Sociales (FLACSO).

MIRAFTAB, Faranak.
>   1996. "Space, Gender and Work: Home-based Workers in Mexico." In *Home Workers in Global Perspective: Invisible No More,* edited by Eileen Boris and Elisabeth Prugl. New York, New York: Routledge.

OBERHAUSER, Ann M.
>   1993. "Industrial Restructuring and Women's Homework in Appalachia: Lessons from West Virginia." *Southeastern Geographer* 33(1):23-43.
>   ———. 1995. "Gender and Household Economic Strategies in Rural Appalachia." *Gender, Place and Culture* 2(1):51-70.

OLIVEIRA, Orlandina de.
>   1990. "Empleo Femenino en México en Tiempos de Recesión Económica: Tendencias Recientes." In *Mujer y Crisis: Respuestas ante la Recesión,* edited by Neuma Aguiar. Caracas, Venezuela: DAWN/MUDAR and Editorial Nueva Sociedad.

OLIVEIRA, Orlandina de and Brígida García.
>   1998. "Crisis, Reestructuración Económica y Mercados de Trabajo en México." *Papeles de Población* 15:39-72.

OLIVEIRA, Orlandina de and Bryan Roberts.
>   1993. "La Informalidad Urbana en Años de Expansión, Crisis y Restructuración Económica." *Estudios Sociológicos* 9(3):33-58.

PACHECO, Edith and Mercedes Blanco.
>   1998. "La Perspectiva de Género en los Estudios Sociodemográficos Sobre el Trabajo Urbano en México." *Papeles de Población* 15:73-94.

PARRADO, Emilio A. and René M. Zenteno.
>   2001. "Economic Restructuring, Financial Crisis, and Women's Work in México." *Social Problems* 48(4):456-477.

PRATT, Geraldine and Susan Hanson.
>   1991. "On the Links between Home and Work: Family-household Strategies in a Buoyant Labor Market." *International Journal of Urban Regional Research* 15(1):55-74.
>   ———. 1993. "Women and Work across the Life Course: Moving beyond Essentialism." In *Full Circles: Geographies of Women over the Life Course,* edited by Cindi Katz and Janice Monk. London, England and New York, New York: Routledge.

ROBERTS, Bryan.
>   1994. "Informal Economy and Family Strategies." *International Journal of Urban and Regional Research* 18(1):6-23.

SAEGERT, Susan and Gary Winkel.
>   1980. "The Home: A Critical Problem for Changing Sex Roles." In *New Space for Women,* edited by Gerda R. Wekerle, Rebecca Peterson, and David Morley.

Boulder, Colorado: Westview Press.

SALMI, Minna.
1993. "The Everyday Time Structure and Home-based Work: Time-use and Flexibility in the Everyday Lives of Finnish Home Workers." Paper presented at the 5th International and Interdisciplinary Congress on Women, San José, Costa Rica.
———. 1996. "Finland Is Another World: The Gendered Time of Homework." In *Home Workers in Global Perspective: Invisible No More,* edited by Eileen Boris and Elisabeth Prugl. New York, New York: Routledge.

SCHMINK, Marianne.
1984. "Household Economic Strategies: Review and Research Agenda." *Latin American Research Review* 19(3):87-101.

STANDING, Guy.
1989. "Global Feminization through Flexible Labor." *World Development* 17(7):1077-1095.

VELASCO, Laura.
1996. *La Conquista de la Frontera Norte: Vendedoras Ambulantes Indígenas en Tijuana.* México City, México D.F.: Desarrollo Integral de la Familia.

WATSON, Sophie.
1990. "The Restructuring of Work and Home: Productive and Reproductive Relations." In *Housing and Labor Markets,* edited by John Allen and Chris Hamnett. London, England: Unwin Hyman.

ORGANIZING A SPACE OF THEIR OWN? GLOBAL/LOCAL PROCESSES IN A NICARAGUAN WOMEN'S ORGANIZATION[1]

Jennifer Bickham Mendez*

ABSTRACT

This article analyzes the internal, organizational processes within a Nicaraguan women worker's organization, the Working and Unemployed Women's Movement, "María Elena Cuadra" (MEC) to explore the ways in which place-centered, locally constituted political identities articulate with transnational flows of ideas and discourses to shape actors' collective practices. MEC's changing organizational practices reflect the influence of strategies and practices employed in the mass organizations of the FSLN and transnational flows of discourses and ideas about issues such as feminism, personal and political autonomy, and the relationship between individuals and a collective. I explore the impact of members' experiences within the Sandinista mass organizations on MEC's organizational practices and analyze MEC's uneasy relationship with feminist organizations and Northern-based NGOs. While transnational linkages have opened new opportunities for groups like MEC, certain relations of inequality, such as those based on neocolonialism, persist. The case of MEC sheds light on the complex ways in which power operates through and within transnational organizational relations.

INTRODUCTION

In May 1994, the Working and Unemployed Women's Movement, "María Elena Cuadra" (MEC) emerged from a deep-seated, gender-based crisis within the Sandinista Workers' Central (CST), the largest trade union confederation in Nicaragua. In response to the hierarchical decision-making and *machismo* of the CST leadership, a group of organizers from the Women's Secretariat left[2] the confederation to form their own separate and autonomous organization "by and for women" with the goal of "making visible the role of women at all levels of society" (MEC 1997). MEC's efforts have focused on improving conditions for women workers in the country's Free Trade Zone (FTZ),[3] providing income-generating opportunities, job training, and micro-credit to unemployed women, and educating women about gender issues, such as domestic violence and reproductive health, and their rights at home and in the workplace.

This article analyzes the internal, organizational processes within MEC to explore the ways in which place-centered, locally constituted political identities articulate with transnational flows of ideas, organizational practices and discourses to shape actors' collective practices (see Alvarez, Dagnino, Escobar 1998). MEC's changing organizational practices reflect the influence of strategies

* Department of Sociology, College of William and Mary, P.O. Box 8795, Williamsburg, VA 23187, U.S.A.

and practices employed in the mass organizations of the FSLN and transnational flows of discourses and ideas about issues such as feminism, personal and political autonomy, and the relationship between individuals and a collective. Specifically, participation in both the Nicaraguan autonomous women's movement[4] and the wider transnational feminist movement as well as linkages with international, nongovernmental organizations (NGOs) have played a role in the constitution of MEC's organizational practices and have had an impact on the formation of shifting, experientially based identities of MEC organizers.

The constitution of the MEC organization has involved the localization of transnationally flowing ideas and discourses. Although the influence of a globalized feminist discourse is discernable in MEC's organizational practices, as Thayer reminds us, "practices inspired by a given discourse are not inextricably bound up with it in a seamless package; the two are semi-autonomous with respect to one another, change at different rhythms, and are capable of mutual influence" (2000:208). MEC actors have not only adopted certain elements of a feminist conceptual framework, but have also reformulated feminist notions to coincide with their vision of how an autonomous women's organization should be organized as well as the specific ways in which they have viewed themselves as political actors. Furthermore, depending upon their own particular experiences, different MEC participants have actively adapted and drawn upon feminist discourses in largely diverging ways. Thus, the case of MEC supports the contention that feminist ideas, strategies, and practices do not move in a purely unidirectional manner from North to South. Rather, they "are dispersed into varied local sites where they are picked up and refashioned as they resonate in contextualized ways" (Desai 2002:15).

The observations that I make in this article are based on ethnographic research in Nicaragua undertaken during the summers of 1994 and 1995 and a ten-month period between 1996 and 1997. During this time I worked on a daily basis as an international *cooperante* (volunteer) in MEC's office in Managua and less frequently in the regional office of Granada. Since 1997, I have maintained contact with this group through email communication and participants' visits to the United States. As part of this ethnographic research I conducted intensive interviews with MEC founders and organizers, MEC program participants, workers in the FTZ, and international *cooperantes*.[5]

I set the context for the analysis of MEC's organizational practices by providing a brief overview of the globalization of feminist discourses and practices and the global proliferation of NGOs. Next, I outline some of the forces in post-Sandinista Nicaragua that gave rise to MEC's emergence. Specifically, in order to understand MEC's formation it is necessary to consider three gendered phenomena: the particular impact that neoliberal political and economic policies in Nicaragua have had for women, the gender dynamics within the mass organizations of the FSLN, and the Sandinista labor movement's failure to respond to the needs of women workers and unemployed women. Finally, I explore the ways in which MEC's organizational practices have emerged as part of a complex inter-articulation between transnational flows of discourses and ideas and locally formed identities and organizational practices emerging from experiences within the Sandinista mass organizations.

In order to elucidate these processes, I analyze MEC's uneasy relationship with feminist organizations and discourses and international and Northern NGOs. While transnational linkages have opened new opportunities for groups like MEC, certain relations of inequality, such as those based on neocolonialism, persist. The case of MEC sheds light on the complex ways in which power operates through and within transnational organizational relations.

Globalization, Feminism, and NGOs

The global proliferation of NGOs is a defining characteristic of the international political arena of the last decade. For the purposes of this analysis, I shall use the term "NGO" to indicate organizations from the North or South, which are not affiliated with state institutions or political parties. Such organizations have formed as a response to the spread of neoliberal political and economic policies and the global decline of the welfare state. In addition, international development agencies have placed new emphasis on supporting grassroots initiatives. The complex web of connections among local and international NGOs, social movements, government agencies and transnational networks of grassroots organizations is an important conduit for the movement of ideas, funding, knowledge, and people through various local, national, and international sites (Alvarez 1998; Appadurai 1991; Fisher 1997; Lebon 1996; Safa 1996).

Some have cautioned against generalizing NGOs' functions (i.e., sustainable development and social justice), organizational forms (i.e., professionalized and bureaucratic), and orientations (i.e., progressive) (see Fisher 1997). Indeed, there is little consensus regarding exactly what an NGO really is. The diversity of NGOs calls out for more in-depth analysis of the micropolitics of these organizations and investigation of the specific impact of these supralocal organizations in a given locale.

The rise of internationally funded NGOs adds to the organizational diversity within women's movements in Latin America. Though some scholars view NGOs as embodying a potential for the creation of alternative development discourses and practices (see Fisher 1997; Patkar 1995; Fisher 1993; Wignaraja 1993), feminists have heralded the "NGOization" and professionalization of the Latin American women's movement with differing degrees of optimism (Alvarez 1994:49; see also Lebon 1996; Safa 1996). Whereas one could perceive this process as an expansion of spaces for feminist action, many feminists view the reliance on external funding by increasingly professionalized women's organizations as posing a danger of stimulating clientelism, shifting energy away from attention to grassroots constituencies and towards accountability to international donors, and sacrificing feminist principles for organizational efficiency (Alvarez 2000; Lebon 1996; Safa 1996). International donor agencies and foundations often favor more professionalized NGOs, causing some to fear that this tendency may lead to "difference in power...that threatens to undermine proposed autonomy, to lessen the visibility of feminist organizations without financing, to heighten competition for access to increased funding, and to weaken feminine solidarity as a result" (Vargas and Olea Mauleon 1998:56). Thus, the transnational flow of financial resources represents not only a set of opportunities for local organizations, like MEC, but also a very real set of constraints constituted by imbalances of power and resources.

Alvarez (1998) has observed that Latin American feminisms have "gone global" through the "transnationalization" of feminist discourses and practices or:

> local movement actors' deployment of discursive frames and organizational and political practices that are inspired, (re)affirmed, or reinforced—though not necessarily caused—by their engagement with other actors beyond national borders through a wide range of transnational contacts, discussions, transactions, and networks, both virtual and "real." (Alvarez 2000:30)

The preparatory processes for international conferences, like UN summits, have reinforced global coalition building among feminist NGOs and women's organizations (Desai 2002; Basu 1995, 2000; Stienstra 2000). National, regional, and transnational networks have intensified and linked women's organizations working on a wide range of issues, facilitating the transnational circulation of feminist demands, practices, and discourses (Alvarez 1998).

In this article I seek to shed light on the inner-workings of the globalization of feminism by exploring how one local group of women has actively engaged with, interpreted and responded to the diverse feminist discourses, strategies and ideas that they have encountered in constructing local organizational practices. Such political engagement is mediated through locally constituted identities and experiences, reflecting how global processes are inextricable from place-based, local ones. Thus, by interrogating the relationship between political practice, (often globally circulating) discourse, and identity formation, this study has implications for the conceptualization and study of a "transnational feminist movement."

Post-Sandinista Nicaragua and MEC's Formation

In 1979, the Marxist-Leninist oriented National Sandinista Liberation Front (FSLN) spearheaded the revolutionary insurrection that resulted in the ouster of Anastasio Somoza Debayle, whose family had held dictatorial control over the country for over forty years. In 1979, a Junta made up of representatives of the broad forces that overthrew Somoza (including the oppositional bourgeoisie) took control of the country with the Sandinista party eventually dominating the process of establishing a new government. The stated objective of the revolutionary project of the Sandinistas was to transform Nicaraguan society into a socialist society (Luciak 1995:21-23). Notwithstanding, revolutionary Nicaragua was not entirely capitalist, statist or socialist, but had a mixed economy with state support of the capitalist sector. Participation of "the people" within the Sandinista revolutionary project was to be represented by mass organizations[6] that served to promote and defend the particular interests of each sector of society (e.g., workers, women, students, and grassroots communities). These organizations were to serve as the primary mechanism of popular empowerment as well as a direct communication link between the Sandinista party and its social and political base (Vanden and Prevost 1993:51). Representatives from these organizations were appointed to the Council of State, a national assembly that exercised legislative and policy-making power within the evolving governmental structure. Despite the participative democratic aspects of the mass organizations, a Leninist vanguardism was also reflected in their relationship with the Sandinista party. Thus, when disagreements between the Sandinista party and popular sectors broke out, the vanguard, represented in the FSLN's National Directorate had the final word.[7]

Women were involved in nearly every aspect of the insurrection, and as an important Sandinista mass organization, the Association of Nicaraguan Women, Luisa Amanda Espinoza (AMNLAE), played a crucial role in contributing to the national agenda, which included weathering the Reagan-imposed trade embargo and the U. S.-backed contra war. Gradually, however, AMNLAE began to move beyond adherence to party directives (made by the male-dominated leadership of the FSLN) and to formulate its own agenda based on the needs and interests of grassroots women. Among these were discrimination in the workplace, women's unpaid labor, and domestic violence (Criquillón 1995:218; Randall 1992:47).

By the late 1980s, AMNLAE turned its efforts to establishing mechanisms within the other mass organizations of the FSLN to address "women's issues" and articulate "gender claims" based on the specificities of women's gender experience (Criquillón 1995; cf. Alvarez 1990). These efforts began to bear fruit with the formation of Women's Secretariats within labor organizations, like the Association of Rural Workers (ATC) and the Sandinista Workers' Central (CST). It was out of the CST's Women's Secretariat that MEC was born. Founders were members of the CST's National Women's Secretariat as well as from the Secretariats of various regional federations. Most founders had served in various capacities within the mass organizations of the FSLN party and were considered cadres. In many cases individual MEC leaders were combatants in the armed insurrection. Sara Rodriguez, MEC's coordinator, described the processes leading up to the formation of Women's Secretariats within the mass organizations like the CST:

I see the period up to 1990 as a process of accumulation of forces, the creation of the awakening of the consciousness of women, looking for our own instruments, how to do this work in a traditional mixed sector, conservative and with traditional structures . . . It is difficult to break down our traditional structures. The establishment of the Women's Secretariat has contributed, perhaps not to their breakdown, but to their transformation.

In 1990, the mass organizations along with the entire Sandinista Party entered into a crisis. The FSLN's loss at the polls and the electoral victory of Violeta Chamorro's opposition coalition, UNO, threw the party and affiliated organizations into upheaval. Upon entering office, the Chamorro regime moved quickly to implement economic reforms and structural adjustment policies aimed at creating a favorable climate for foreign investment and fully reinserting the country into the international economy (Metoyer 2000; Evans 1995; Renzi and Agurto 1993). The new government sought to receive International Monetary Fund (IMF) loans under the Enhanced Structural Adjustment Facility (ESAF), a special structural adjustment package (SAP), available to low-income countries. In order to meet SAP conditions,[8] the regime eliminated remaining consumer subsidies and privatized 80 percent of state-owned enterprises (Renzi and Agurto 1993:38; Babb 1996). In 1991, the government launched its first stabilization program, drastically cutting public services, including health and education. Public spending dropped 37 percent from an average of $70 per person in the last half of the 1980s to $44 in 1992 (Renzi and Agurto 1993:34). In addition, the government laid off thousands of workers from the public sector. Between March of 1991 and March of 1992, a total of 22,561 workers had left public employment (including positions in state-owned enterprises), entering the government's Plan of Occupational Conversion, funded by Agency for International Development (USAID). For those remaining in state employment positions salaries were incrementally reduced. By 1993, the average salary of those employed by the state was 60 percent of its value in 1980 (Evans 1995:221).

As in many developing countries, Nicaraguan women have borne the brunt of structural adjustment (Metoyer 2000; Babb 1996; Pérez-Alemán 1992). Given the traditional, and indeed, cross-cultural, role assigned to women as primary caregivers of the family and as having primary responsibility for the maintenance of the household, the reduction of social spending included within SAPs has meant that the burden for household survival shifts to women.

In response to the privatization of state-owned enterprises and the health system that the neoliberal Chamorro regime set into motion, the Women's Secretariat of the CST established women's clinics that were open to women who could not afford the services at private clinics and hospitals. Privatization also involved the systematic dismantling of subsidized, public childcare centers or CDI's (Children's Development Centers) established during the Sandinista years. These government cutbacks profoundly affected women workers, the primary caretakers of children and the elderly. The Women's Secretariat used NGO funds to launch programs designed to assist poor women in facing the specific problems that structural adjustment presents for them—free clinics, subsidized childcare centers and micro-credit programs, among others. The Women's Secretariat also directed efforts at organizing and supporting women workers within the Free Trade Zone. Organizers would continue these efforts later under the auspices of the autonomous organization of MEC.

As the 1990s wore on, the leaders of the Women's Secretariat became more and more convinced that the appropriate organizational space for effectively working for women's strategic and practical gender interests[9] was an autonomous women's organization (Molyneux 1986). As we shall see, events within the CST were the direct catalysts for the formation of MEC, but the exodus (and ouster) of the leadership of the CST's Women's Secretariat along with a great number of active affiliates must also be seen within a context of other events occurring in Nicaragua in the early 1990s.

In 1988, AMNLAE announced a plan to initiate an internal political process to democratically elect a new national assembly and leadership committee. This process marked a sharp contrast with the organization's history in which the FSLN had always appointed the national leadership. Women from the various sectors belonging to AMNLAE came together in a heated discussion about their needs and how they should be reflected in the organization's agenda. To the surprise of many of AMNLAE's members, the FSLN abruptly put an end to this democratic process and removed the organization's national leadership, replacing leaders with party appointees. Occurring just before the electoral defeat of the Sandinistas in 1990, this coup on the part of the FSLN leadership was a major force in setting the stage for the emergence of an independent women's movement in Nicaragua (Criquillón 1995:224; Randall 1992:52).

The year 1991 marked the birth of the vibrant and diverse autonomous women's movement. On March 8, International Women's Day, women's collectives and centers, NGO's, theater and arts groups, and independent feminists gathered together to hold a "Festival of 52 Percent." The festival was scheduled to coincide with AMNLAE's national congress and was organized as an alternative event. The groups in attendance, many of which identified as feminist, asserted their independence from all political parties and other "mixed" organizations. In this manner, participants in the emerging autonomous women's movement "clearly staked their ground and claimed a new social space in which to build a movement" (Babb 1997:59), insisting that "internal democracy and autonomy vis-à-vis the FSLN were essential" (Criquillón 1995:228).

Meanwhile, within the CST as in other mass organizations, too often the gender-based needs of women were being pushed aside in the name of organizational unity. MEC's formation and separation from the CST was the result of a long history of conflicts between the Secretariat's leadership and the male hierarchy of the CST. Divisions and disagreements primarily stemmed from three interrelated issues:

1. Hierarchical decision-making on the part of the CST's leaders and the consistent relegation of "women's issues" (e.g., services for women such as day-care, job training in nontraditional fields, and health clinics) to secondary importance, including the appropriation of funds donated by international NGOs for the purpose of launching gender projects and their redirection into "mixed" programs, which largely benefited male workers.
2. What many saw as corruption within the CST leadership, as leaders negotiated conditions of privatization under the Chamorro government according to their own, often individual, interests.
3. General sexism including the refusal to appoint women to positions of power within the confederation.

These long simmering tensions culminated in the CST's 1994 National Congress. At the congress in what amounted to a dramatic coup, none of the candidates elected at the women's national congress (held a month earlier) were appointed to the National Executive Council, nor was the women's elected choice for the next director of the Women's Secretariat appointed to that office. In addition, the National Executive Council put in place measures to severely compromise the financial autonomy of the Secretariat, making all its projects subject to approval and administration by the CST (male) leadership.

The leaders of the national and certain regional Women's Secretariats responded by forming their own autonomous organization. In May of 1994, leaders of the former Women's Secretariat held a congress attended by approximately 450 working and unemployed women, and MEC was born. Organizers viewed autonomy as an organizational principle upon which MEC was founded. María Luisa, the coordinator of MEC's office in Granada explains:

> Our movement [MEC] was born out of women's very own necessity . . . a women's movement with its own identity . . . The principles with which it was born...were, organic unity, autonomy, pluralism, without political or religious distinction—that it suffice that a woman be willing to be in the Movement [MEC] to open the doors to her without having to say: 'Well, since you are with such and such a party, you can't come.' These are the principles: unity, solidarity among us—gender solidarity among other things.

At the 1994 founding congress Sara Rodriguez was elected as MEC's national coordinator. Subsequently, MEC's founders met to devise an organizational structure and appoint women to various leadership positions. The resulting structure was strikingly similar to that of the former Women's Secretariat of the CST: Sara and a core group that had formed the national leadership of the

Secretariat would now run the *national* office located in Managua which in turn would coordinate the various *regional* offices in the departments of Granada, Matagalpa, Juigalpa, Estelí, Chinandega, and León. Decision-making, then, surrounding program and project implementation tended to be centralized in the national office, just as it had been within the Women's Secretariat of the CST with the national office distributing and administrating funds for the entire organization.

It is not surprising that the women adopted this centralized organizational structure. Though their separation from the CST was in part to flee the hierarchy of the traditional labor movement, the women of MEC remained strongly influenced by over a decade of political "up-bringing" in the FSLN. As Chinchilla (1994) observes:

> [T]he political movement that served as the framework for Nicaraguan women's political coming of age was heavily influenced by the tradition of clandestine armed struggle, which emphasized military hierarchy and discipline, centralization of leadership, compartmentalization of information, the subordination of individual needs to the collective, and the public (productive) sphere as the force behind all change. (P. 193)

Soon, however, it became apparent (especially to the women of the Managua office) that this top-heavy and centralized organizational form was neither viable nor appropriate. In purely pragmatic terms, the old model of the CST hierarchy in which a national coordinating office distributed funding for projects and other support to regional subsidiaries, presupposed a larger institutional support base and human resources that MEC simply did not possess. Meanwhile, Sara and the other founders were exhausted, working superhuman hours with little or no income. As the national coordinator, Sara was simply unable to single-handedly secure funding for individual projects for each region of a national organization.

Regional organizers were angered by the lack of support offered to them by the Managua office—support that many felt they were due for having loyally followed the leaders of the National Women's Secretariat in leaving the CST. On the other hand, Sara and the other organizers of the national office felt that claims of entitlement to project funds based on loyalty was "charging for solidarity" (*cobrando la solidaridad*). They were overwhelmed by the expectations of the regional offices as well as their own funding demands. Sara would often complain, "I'm tired of being the mother hen with the little chicks...In this Movement [MEC] there are no mothers, or aunts, or godmothers, and this Movement is going to need qualified women. Whoever doesn't want to work should get out of the way to make room for those interested in doing so!"

In addition, this centralized organizational structure was reminiscent of the verticalism and centralized decision-making for which the women of MEC criticized the CST. At a deeper level, then, some of MEC's members did not see this structure as coinciding with the overall political vision and the founding principles of the organization. The challenge before the women as they continued in the process of constituting MEC was to balance practical funding demands with MEC's founding principles of personal and organizational autonomy and to devise an organizational form that would reflect "unity in diversity."

As part of this process, MEC organizers secured funding from a Canadian NGO to gather their constituency together for a national meeting and commemoration of MEC's first anniversary. Entitled, "United and Strong against Discrimination against Women," the purpose of this 1995 event was to begin the next phase of the organization's constitution by formulating MEC's objectives and a plan for achieving them as well as determining an organizational structure that would best reflect the needs of its constituency. The event was a tremendous success with some eight hundred women in attendance. An entire discussion session was devoted to "Women and Organization," and it was from this session and the larger discussion that it sparked among the participants in the event that MEC founders drew up plans for the organization's reconstitution. Organizers concluded from the session: "The women emphasized the autonomy of the Movement [MEC]…[and] the principle of a broad-based, pluralist and strong movement that brings together women from diverse social sectors without distinction of race, political [party] or religious orientation and with a multiplicity of demands" (MEC 1995).

The issue of autonomy has been a prominent organizational principle for Latin American women's movements (Jaquette 1994; Chinchilla 1992; Hellman 1992; Alvarez 1990). For the groups that make up the Latin American women's movements, autonomy "entails a recognition of the diversity of social interests, the refusal of class reductionism, and, above all, of economism" (Chinchilla 1992:47). Notwithstanding, it is important not to gloss over the complexity of the processes involved in the construction of collective definitions of autonomy within women's organizations. Shared understandings of the meaning of autonomy do not exist *a priori*, but rather emerge from the articulations of members' identities as political actors with the specific political and social conditions of the historic conjuncture. Under contemporary conditions, then, the meaning of autonomy depends upon particular interactions between global and local processes and local actors' understandings of them. In the case of MEC autonomy came to hold varied meanings for the different women of the organization, and this was in part the result of their positions within MEC as well as their experiences in the CST.

An emphasis on autonomy—both of the organization and of individuals within it—reflects another important departure from organizational strategies practiced within the mass organizations of the FSLN during the 1980s. Within these revolutionary organizations individuals within the collective were conceived of as "militant[s] committed to a collective ideal to which individuals themselves could legitimately be sacrificed. Self sacrifice was elevated to the highest moral status, to an ethical value sanctioned by superior significance of the collectivity" (Melucci 1996:184).

Other scholars have documented the rich testimonies of women who received their political socialization in the FSLN and whose commitment to the revolutionary cause often involved deep personal sacrifices—for example, the abandonment of young children and family members, undesired abortions and the loss of sons to war (Randall 1992, 1994). The women of MEC were no strangers to these kinds of sacrifices. They often recalled with great sadness being forced to leave small children in the care of mothers and grandmothers and being separated from them for months at a time. Others remembered being accused of being *burguesa* (bourgeois) for requesting time to care for a sick child. In the words of one workshop participant: "*la patria* was above all else: a mother's love, love of ourselves." Josefa from León remembered: "I felt the load here [motions to her back]...we had to give two hundred percent . . . There was never a Sunday or a Saturday with all the tasks of the Revolution."

In contrast to the demands of the militant organizations of the Revolution, the women of MEC envisioned their organization as a space in which participants could achieve personal autonomy. This vision involved a type of collective that was strengthened by individuality and difference and involved a transformed relationship between the individual and the collectivity. Sara contends:

> This Marxism-Leninism—this collectivism—*ya no me va* [it no longer suits me]...Rather, the collective oppresses the individuals within it . . . Each of us has to defend herself within her own space . . . assuming her own role within this space . . . There is the collective, but there is also individualism within the collective . . . Of these things we never speak—of the individual processes within groups.

Women's Movement(s) and Feminist Identities

Understandings of the meaning of autonomy, however, were not simply forged within the local arena of MEC's organizational space. In addition, MEC organizers' orientations regarding autonomy were closely linked with contrasting definitions and understandings of feminism that MEC organizers encountered. As Alvarez (2000:36) points out, the issue of movement autonomy has long been a key axis of debate in regional and transnational forums such as the *encuentros* of the Latin American feminist movement. More direct participation in the Nicaraguan feminist movement (a subsection of the larger autonomous women's movement) and participants' closer association with self-identified feminists led to MEC organizers' becoming more exposed to and gradually appropriating discourses from the transnational feminist movement.

Feminism offered the women of MEC a new conceptual understanding of their experiences within the FSLN as well as organizational principles that coincided with their rejection of class-reductionism and decision-making based on a revolutionary vanguard. Often MEC organizers would draw a comparison between their own experiences in the CST and those of a "battered woman" in an abusive relationship. MEC's coordinator told me in an interview:

> So we said, "Hey, this is like masochism," like staying in a masochist relationship . . . when you are adoring, idolizing the man, while the man beats you, beats you, beats you . . . One day we woke up and we said, "Enough!" And *I* was the first to wake up. I said, "Enough already!" "How long!" [emphasis in original].

Making the link between gender oppression in the home, such as in the case of domestic violence, and gendered power differentials that occurred within the mass organizations like the CST was an important consciousness-raising process for many MEC organizers. This process was experientially based, but was also supported and bolstered by MEC organizers' participation in events, workshops, and seminars organized by the feminist movement in Nicaragua and abroad. For example, in the early 1990s when MEC organizers still made up the leadership of the CST's Women's Secretariat, the Secretariat secured NGO funding to send several organizers to a feminist *encuentro* held in Cuba. It was there that some regional leaders first learned about feminism. At the national level when MEC was newly formed with virtually no financial base and still had not established an office of its own, the feminist organization, *Puntos de Encuentro*, in an act of solidarity offered MEC its conference area to hold an "internal" meeting for MEC leaders. During this retreat-like session, MEC leaders began to collectively work through the extremely painful process of their separation from the CST. Leaders from *Puntos de Encuentro* facilitated the meeting and paid for its tape-recording so that the personal testimonials given could be preserved as the institutional history of MEC. MEC leaders saw this process as having been an extremely important step in the organization's constitution.

In addition, transnationally circulating feminist discourses—particularly the "language of rights and discrimination" became effective "frames" for articulating MEC's demands and objectives. The language of human rights, which has become an important tool for framing women's issues within the transnational feminist movement, gave a name to MEC organizers' experiences within the CST (Keck and Sikkink 1998). Phrases like "gender discrimination," "gender equality" and "rights" effectively described and resonated with MEC organizers' experiences. Founders would speak of how the "*el odio machista*" [*machista* hate] of the CST leaders "violated our human rights."

The use of such language also was intimately connected with participants' construction of feminist collective identities. Jill, a *cooperante* [international volunteer] from Canada who had worked for twelve years with MEC organizers observed: "They became used to talking about defending their rights as workers. Soon they started talking about defending their rights as women . . . They started to see that being a feminist isn't being more than what they are . . . that it wasn't just an intellectual term." Indeed, many MEC organizers would define feminism as "the struggle to defend women's rights" and described MEC's principal objective as being: "to organize women to defend their rights." Thus, a language and concepts shared with the transnational women's movement played a key role, not only in framing MEC's demands, but also in constructing a vision of how the women of MEC saw themselves and the history and objectives of their organization. At a 1995 national meeting in which national and regional leaders developed the work plan and organizational strategy for the coming year, Sara declared: "We need feminism. We have to get to know it better."

The language of rights also coincided with the value that MEC participants placed on personal autonomy within the collective. Rights discourse and feminist concepts, like "the personal is political" became important idiomatic tools for developing and articulating MEC's organizational principles, mission and collective identit[ies]. In this manner globalized discourses gave participants the words to articulate their grievances in the CST as well as to describe what they sought in the local, autonomous, women-only space, which they were in the process of creating. Thus, by 1996 the Managua-based group of MEC's leadership revised its statement of purpose to describe MEC as: "A feminist, environmentalist, autonomous, pluralist movement that promotes solidarity among women . . . and contributes to the improvement of the socioeconomic situation of women" (MEC 1996).

In expressing their feminism, however, MEC organizers emphasize and clarify that they adhere to a particular interpretation of feminism, calling themselves "*feministas de base*" (grassroots feminists). In this manner, MEC participants who identify with feminism do not merely *adopt* feminist principles, but actively construct and reconfigure them, making them their own. Due to suspicions regarding the place that class issues hold within feminism, participants are reluctant to identify themselves or their organization with a predefined notion of "feminist." Their articulation of a "popular feminism" echoes that of working class and grassroots women's organizations throughout Latin America who are claiming feminism as their own in order to cope with poverty, inequality, and austerity brought about by globalization (Safa 1996). Just as Alvarez (1994, 1998) describes in the case of Brazil, MEC organizers' expression of a class-centered, feminist identity involves a criticism of *"las institucionalizadas"* who in the post-1990 context have increasingly focused efforts at political lobbying and public opinion campaigns, turning away from work centered in grassroots communities. MEC leaders would frequently lament: "No one wants to do grassroots work anymore."

The continued identification with and as "*mujeres de base*" represents one component of an articulated collective identity of MEC members. All MEC leaders come from poor or working class backgrounds, and the great majority of them continue to reside in poor *barrios*. As the Managua collective and regional coordinators secured funding for programs, they continually recruited women from the grassroots communities to administer them. This system of using grassroots "promoters" to run programs in the communities served as a mechanism to promote leadership among women from poor or working-class backgrounds. Such women were gradually incorporated into the Managua team.

This practice, which reflects MEC members' identification as grassroots women, stands in clear continuity with the Leninist-inspired, Sandinista strategy of creating cadres. As former cadres of the revolution, MEC founders were well acquainted with the idea of gradually incorporating members of the base who showed special potential. This practice, left over from their days in the FSLN, maintains and reinforces an important aspect of MEC's collective class-oriented identity, differentiating the group from other, more professionalized, autonomous women's organizations.

Just as gender-based contradictions led to the creation of the autonomous MEC, MEC organizers' identities as, not only women, but also women workers, caused their organization to hold a particular position within the *autonomous* women's movement. Their "humble" or working class backgrounds set organizers apart from many feminists in the Nicaraguan autonomous women's movement such as those active in more middle-class feminist collectives as *Las Malinches, Cenzontle,* and *Mujer y Cambio* or professional, service organizations like *S.I. Mujer* and *Ixchen.*

This would be clear at coalition or network meetings of the larger Nicaraguan women's movement that MEC members—usually members of the Managua office—would attend. Sara and the others would often speak of feeling "out of their environment" at meetings like the 1996 meeting organized by the Nicaraguan Women's Institute (INIM), at that time a government office. The purpose of the meeting was to "consolidate the coordination and cooperation between INIM and the Nicaraguan Women's Movement" (INIM 1996b:2). Participants formed working groups to draft a document specifying how INIM and the various organizations that make up the autonomous women's movement would cooperate "to accomplish greater levels of influence within the Nicaraguan state in solving the problems that affect women" (INIM 1996a:2). Representatives from twenty-nine women's organizations attended this event, held in the Intercontinental Hotel. The luxurious surroundings of the conference area gave the atmosphere a professional and business-like feel. A catered lunch was served in the hotel's dining room, and the event closed with a cocktail hour. Many well-dressed, professional women active in organizations such as *Fundación Internacional para el Desafío Económico Global* (FIDEG*), Cenzontle,* and *Colectivo Itza* were present and were among the most vocal in the discussion. Despite efforts by organizers to include all participants in the forum and the election of Sara as the moderator in one of the working groups, it was in spaces such as these that MEC leaders often felt confronted with their own class origins and in many cases limited educational backgrounds.

Even simply getting to such meetings reflected what MEC members perceived as class biases. Evelyn expressed frustration at the assumption that everyone owned her own car for transportation to and from such activities, especially at night when travel on public buses was dangerous. Some of the Managua team members often commented on the parking lots in front of certain, well-known feminist organizations, as a clear indication of the class position of the women who worked there. In contrast, at MEC only two international *cooperantes* owned their own cars—a luxury in a country where the price of gasoline is high even for those earning U.S. dollars. Members, like Laura and Josefina, most often relied on public buses if they needed to visit local communities or the FTZ. Or, they would hitchhike or ask for a ride (*pedir ray*) from the international *cooperantes* or the coordinator's spouse, who had a pickup truck.

MEC's close connection to poor communities was apparent at other events. When a group of autonomous women's organizations arranged a preparatory meeting for the 1995 Bejing conference, a leader from *Puntos de Encuentro* called Sara at home in a desperate plea to mobilize women from grassroots communities. MEC's mobilizing influence in these communities was clear when Sara and the other women from Managua immediately sent word to MEC's regional offices and filled several buses of women from local communities to participate in the event. Sara proudly sat outside the conference hall greeting the women personally, as bus after bus pulled up to the entrance.

Josefina, a MEC organizer from the Managua office, confided to me: "I'm not just saying this, Jennifer, but it's as if there has been a failure of the work at the grassroots...there is no social base." The problem, according to the women of MEC, was that much of the autonomous women's movement in Nicaragua is made up of NGOs that provide services to grassroots women. Fewer and fewer groups continued work at the grassroots as far as organizing grassroots women or working directly within the *barrios* themselves.

Diversity and Divergences within the MEC Organization

At the time of MEC's formation, participants collectively placed a high value on organizational autonomy and articulated an identity of "grassroots women"— sometimes even "grassroots feminists." Beneath the surface of these collectively voiced ideas, however, were differing views about the appropriate course that MEC should take in its development as an organization. By early 1996, these differing, sometimes conflicting ideas came to a head in a crisis that nearly brought about MEC's dissolution. As part of this crisis a number of MEC's founders left the organization, several of them returning to "mixed" organizations affiliated with the FSLN. These departures caused great upheaval and deep emotional wounds among the women who remained with MEC. Rather than merely emerging from personal disagreements, these internal conflicts reflected participants' differing notions of what the goals and organizational practices of an autonomous, women's organization should be.

As participants collectively grappled with how to structure their organization in a manner that would reflect MEC's founding principles, disagreements arose stemming from a tension between notions of autonomy versus unity. Interwoven with this tension, were differing ideas about feminism and globally circulating feminist ideals and discourses. Though it is important to recognize that any categorization is insufficient in effectively capturing the complexity embodied within individual outlooks and orientations, it is possible to identify three streams that emerged as the result of these differing orientations. These three streams were: the Managua collective (formerly the national leadership of the Women's Secretariat), the departmental or regional leaders and coordinators (most of whom were founders of MEC), and founders who continued to maintain close relations with organizations of the labor movement and/or the FSLN (some of whom eventually left MEC to return to mixed organizations).

The first of these factions—the Managua collective—gradually began to put less weight on an idea of unity among the regional offices, but instead on "local autonomy." These organizers began to call for the abandonment of a centralized national structure. Instead, they proposed an organizational structure in which each regional office worked independently, coordinating efforts with the other offices, but not hierarchically linked to Managua as a "national office." This model would be based on the work of regional teams or collectives at each office, which would form their own local strategy and plans of action. The regional office would then be horizontally linked through the coordination of a "network-like" structure and the implementation of a few national programs.

Regional leaders representing the second camp cautiously embraced this idea in varying degrees. Some were in favor of the idea of regional autonomy but feared the prospect of having to independently plan and seek funding for local programs and projects. In the words of one coordinator: "Autonomy has its pro's and con's." Others were extremely reluctant to let go of a national structure. Conflicts arose in which the regional coordinators felt abandoned by Managua—formerly the national office. Referring to the idea of the financial autonomy of the regional offices, a coordinator from Granada contended: "That's fine for her [referring to one of the regional coordinators who has secured funding for her office's operation], but what am I going to do? I don't have anything." At a national meeting another regional coordinator expressed doubts: "We're not entirely convinced of this autonomy and separation." "It would be a great loss if only Managua were able to come out well."

In turn, Sara and the Managua collective felt tired of having to "carry the big load of the departments on our backs." "They only want autonomy when it is convenient to them," they said of the regional coordinators. In addition, there were very real practical implications for an emphasis on a more diffuse, network-like organizational structure. Sara pointed out, "The international organizations are not interested in the Movement's [MEC's] national plan. They are interested in local plans and 'local empowerment.'" Thus, the Managua collective's organizational model for MEC reflected and was greatly influenced by the practical realities of financial survival in an era of transnational dependence on international donors and NGOs.

These two groups—the Managua collective and the regional leaders—also differed in their orientations towards the autonomous women's movement in Nicaragua and with it concepts and ideas connected with the larger transnational feminist movement. After MEC's formation, the women of the Managua collective began to engage in more active participation in the activities, networks, coalitions, and meetings of the autonomous women's movement. For the most part, the regional leaders did not join in this process to the same extent. Though some of the regional offices took part in isolated activities of the women's movement, most of them maintained their alliances and organizational relations with local Sandinista organizations.

Within the Nicaraguan women's movement(s), tensions among self-identifying feminists, who in the post-Sandinista context often belong to autonomous women's organizations, AMNLAE and the Women's Secretariats of the trade union federations have a long-standing history. Class-based tensions stem from the upper-class backgrounds of many of *las feministas*. The women of the mass organizations, like the leaders of the Women's Secretariats, often complain that feminists from the autonomous women's movement look down on their work in the mixed organizations and are not supportive of the "popular demands" of grassroots women (Criquillon 1995; Chinchilla 1994).

Nonetheless, in many cases the women of the Managua office discovered that they shared similar experiences with organizers from these feminist groups—especially with regard to their experiences of sexual harassment and sexism within the FSLN. For example, Evelyn and Sara attended meetings with well-known feminists like Rosa María Vargas, whose upper-class origins and feminist orientations had earned her the labels of "bourgeois" and "lesbian separatist" within the FSLN. MEC invited Rosa María to conduct a national workshop in Managua on the topic of feminism. Organizers from the Managua office as well as most of the regional offices attended the activity. Participants were riveted at Rosa María's testimonies and nodded in empathy, sometimes tearfully, when she described her experiences within the FSLN: "When I was in the Front I learned that we women have to do three times as much to receive the same recognition . . . Men who didn't do half what we did are now among the high-ranking leaders." A MEC organizer agreed emphatically:

> In the world of the trade union movement we had to demonstrate that we were just as capable as they. It was a huge survival struggle. The male militants always saw us as hardly capable . . . For us women the only thing that we lacked was to slit our wrists to prove our commitment—that was the only thing that the Revolution didn't ask of us.

As was the case for many class-based movements of the Latin American Left, in the organizations of the FSLN, the common orthodox view was to see feminism as "foreign," divisive, and even counter-revolutionary (Randall 1992, 1994; Sternbach et al. 1992). In the words of one MEC organizer, "The word 'feminist' was like the devil." Other women spoke of how Sandinista leaders would ostracize feminists by labeling them as lesbians. Though some MEC founders had been exposed to feminism before MEC's formation, and even identified as "feminists," for most, feminism was a murky area. As María Luisa expressed, "I began to get to know the word 'feminism' in 1990. I didn't know this word—I didn't know whether it was eaten with a fork or spoon." For the Managua collective, especially, the dramatic split from the CST as well as changed orientations, contacts and experiences in the broader women's movement led them to identify themselves and their work as "feminist."

Thus, the Managua collective's process of identification with feminist principles coincided with this group's view of autonomy as being more than just independence from male-dominated organizations and political parties. For this group, notions of autonomy became closely meshed with feminist organizational principles of participative democracy, gender solidarity and the personal as political. In addition, rather than just working in a separate organizational space from the men and the Sandinista party in order to better the economic situation of women workers and unemployed women, the Managua collective began to envision the aim of their struggle as the transformation of gendered power structures. In the words of one organizer, "The movement [MEC] won't advance just by finding funding for small businesses for women. We need to address the values that support this *machista* society" (quoted in Jubb 1995:23).

With some notable exceptions, regional coordinators were less inclined to define autonomy in this manner and to bring feminist language and ideals into their work. For most of the regional coordinators and leaders who made up this second camp of MEC organizers, autonomy meant little more than access to decision-making power without *"un hombre que anda atrás jodiendo"* [a man going along behind bothering or messing/screwing around]. Regional organizers viewed autonomy as the freedom to independently pursue the very same kinds of projects and programs as they had within the CST organization. Activities launched by the regional offices tended to be focused on creating income-generating activities and job training for women and girls. Most of the offices offered training in very traditional skills such as sewing, knitting, and cosmetology. Others offered credit programs for women to start micro-enterprises. Health programs and small clinics were also common in the regional offices like those in Chinandega and El Viejo. Such programs included little emphasis on gender as a system of power. In a few cases, regional coordinators professed little familiarity with feminist concepts, viewing feminism as "men and women pitted against one another."

The third camp that emerged within MEC was comprised of leaders who maintained relations with (and in many cases continued to participate in) organizations of the FSLN. Some of these women took on an orientation of what has been termed *"doble militante,"* doing their "gender work" in MEC, but continuing to participate in regional labor federations or other Sandinista organizations (Sternbach et al. 1995). For example, the coordinator of the El Viejo office continued her work with MEC, while simultaneously holding an office in a municipal post under the FSLN party banner. Many women of this group were not willing to concede the spaces that they had fought for within these "mixed" organizations. For example, Tamara refused to give up her spot within the metalworkers' federation: "We have fought for this space in the union and . . . It's not going to be easy to get rid of us" (quoted in Jubb 1995:20).

Some members of this camp eventually left MEC to return to the mixed organizational spaces of the Sandinista party and popular organizations. These resignations were the result of personal conflicts and disagreements regarding organizational strategy, depending upon the individuals involved. For example, differences arose regarding how best to serve the needs of women workers. The regional coordinator who returned to the Women's Secretariat of the CST reflected to me that truly "integral" work should be completed within the mixed "*instancias*" [instances, or organizational spaces]. "It's always easier to talk about gender among women. If we really want to transform society, then we have to make the men conscious of the importance of women's participation." To varying degrees, the women of this camp continued to see the labor movement and the FSLN party as the most appropriate organizational space for working to improve the conditions facing women workers and unemployed women.

Internal divisions and diverging orientations among MEC organizers reveal that though MEC's "official" narrative regarding the group's formation relates a story of an unequivocal break from the labor movement, a closer analysis demonstrates that this collective move involved diverse processes at the level of each participant's personal history as a political actor. The complexity lying beneath the surface of MEC's development serves as a reminder that organizations do not possess lives of their own and that it is artificial to separate an organizational analysis from that of the experiences of the individuals that comprise it. Organizations are not homogenous, but embody various orientations, identities and perspectives.

In the case of MEC each participant's view of herself as a member of the movement arises from a distinct set of experiences framed by the specifics of place and local history. For example, Maria Luisa, the coordinator of the Granada office, explained what the formation of MEC meant to her: "So on the personal level, very personal . . . the Movement [MEC] for me was a space that came to fill an aspiration that I had . . . I considered that it was my space." Locally constituted individual experiences, however, are not alone in giving rise to the formation of collective identities. These individual-level, locally constituted processes articulate with transnational ones, as concepts and ideas from the transnational feminist movement(s) resonated with MEC organizers' experiences. The organizational practices of MEC demonstrate similar transnational/local interarticulations. The tension-ridden process through which MEC organizers created an organizational structure involved a complex interplay of locally constituted political identities with transnationally flowing ideas about feminist organizational principles.

"Transnational Tensions": NGOs and MEC's Organizational Practices

MEC's changing relations with international and Northern-based NGOs reveals another example of how transnational relations of power have shaped MEC's internal, organizational processes. Reflecting newly opened political spaces within the global system, NGOs have formed complex and wide-ranging linkages with one another as well as with state agencies, social movements, and international development organizations. Such linkages often span multiple international borders in loosely coordinated transnational networks and frequently involve the transfer of material resources from NGOs in the North to those in the South. Along with material resources, these networks facilitate the transnational circulation of ideas, knowledge, and discourses, which in turn provides new possibilities for collective practices.

The case of MEC exhibits much regarding the power dynamics within relations between progressive NGOs in the North and social justice groups in the South. Like all the mass organizations of the FSLN, the Women's Secretariat of the CST relied heavily on international funding from solidarity groups in Canada, Europe and the United States for many of its projects and programs. With MEC's autonomy, however, as well as the new context of post-Sandinista Nicaragua, the organization became even more dependent upon funding sources from the North. Indeed, it is safe to say that MEC could not exist without this support.

This external dependency has affected MEC's institutionalization. For the women of MEC, then, issues of autonomy remain extremely relevant in its transnational, interorganizational relations. Aspects of neocolonialism[10] are still apparent in the dependence of popular organizations from the South upon resources from Northern-based NGOs. This is not lost on the women of the Managua collective. Though Sara and the other organizers are adamant about administering the services and programs that their organization offers, it is clear that dependency on external funds affects the kinds of programs that they implement. For example, MEC organizers are astutely conscious of what kinds of programs are "fundable" and "fashionable" for receiving international funds. As the consultations with their constituents suggests, they formulate goals and programs after conducting needs assessment with their social base. They are, however, equally aware that certain kinds of proposed programs are more attractive to donors than others. In addition, organizers who are more experienced in grant writing understand the need to represent themselves as successful agents of grassroots transformation (Mindry 2001). Thus, in seeking funds from a German church group in which many members are active in unions, MEC leaders from the Managua collective were careful not to include "anti-unionist" language in the proposal. Like any good grant writer, they are astute enough to sprinkle their proposals with fashionable "sound bytes," like "sustainable development," "participative, democratic organization," and "local autonomy."

In addition, the members of the Managua collective spend a great deal of energy and effort in maintaining public relations with international visitors and donors, often holding receptions for them or calling together program participants to *"intercambiar experiencias"* [exchange experiences] with them. Many NGO donors also require MEC to provide spaces for NGO representatives to hold private evaluation sessions with participants to assess the effectiveness of the programs.

The women of the Managua collective often expressed resentment at having to spend so much time on impression management for *los cheles* [white people]. Often there were tensions regarding NGO requirements for the use of funds, and MEC organizers had to negotiate how much autonomy they were willing to sacrifice in exchange for funding. This was particularly the case in funding for the programs for *maquila* workers. The Canadian and European organizations that funded these programs were often affiliated with or even part of labor organizations and tended to focus solidarity efforts in support of union activity. On a number of occasions Sara and the others had to defend their reasons for not cooperating with the Nicaraguan trade union movement and for not implementing unionist strategies like forming trade unions within the FTZ. Sometimes this led to conflicts with some members of international NGOs, and the women of the Managua collective felt they had to remain firm and not accept the condition of working with the labor movement. They expressed frustration at outsiders pressuring them to organize in ways that they felt did not reflect the needs or the realities of women in the maquila factories. A continual tension resulted from MEC's "can't live with 'em, can't live without 'em" relationship with international NGOs. And the women's use of *"chele/a"* [white people] as synonymous with "international donor" reflected their recognition of the neocolonial/racial aspects of this dependent relationship.

Requirements of external donors pose particular dilemmas of accountability for feminist organizations (Acker 1995; Mansbridge 1995). Such tensions become even more complicated when North/South dynamics are added to the equation (Mendez and Wolf 2001; Lebon 1996; Safa 1996). As Ferguson (1996:575) observes, problems and contradictions emerge from development projects that are "designed almost exclusively by women in the North as paternalistic gestures meant to benefit women seen as Other, as objects of relief rather than as subjects." Such problems are salient in WID (Women in Development) models that uncritically incorporate elements of the modernization paradigm in their approach to gender and development.

Despite the best intentions of donors from the North, the dependency of groups in the South on external funding limits the range of activities that they can engage in and strongly shapes their practices (Chigudu 1997; Stewart and Taylor 1997). Programs must be designed to fit funding agency requirements and to some degree must resonate with the principles and goals of international donors (Sethi 1993:234). MEC is no exception, and organizers constantly walk a tightrope between accountability to their constituents, their political principles, and accountability to international donors.

The "NGOization" or professionalization of women's organizations in Latin America has gone hand-in-hand with the transnationalization of feminism (Lebon 1996; Alvarez 1990). In Brazil, openings in the state emerging after a political transition to democracy facilitated this process, and we can see a similar trend in the explosion of autonomous women's groups after the political transition in Nicaragua (cf. Alvarez 1994). Autonomy from "mixed" organizations of the Left has meant an increasing dependence of women's groups on international NGO donors for funding. The search for autonomous funding sources has translated into the need for a "professional," more bureaucratized structure to efficiently divide labor tasks in order to effectively devise and write project proposals and reports as well as to increase attractiveness of the organization to NGO funders (Keck and Sikkink 1998). This process of professionalization has greatly affected both the practices and the internal organizational processes of MEC and is the result of MEC's connections with and participation in transnational networks—including women's networks and networks of NGOs.

As Lebon (1996) notes, as professionalized autonomous women's organizations have become increasingly involved with the transnational women's movement, they have adopted a more bureaucratized structure. In connection with the efforts of the transnational movement, the work of many women's organizations has come to revolve around externally imposed deadlines. Preparing for events, such as UN meetings and international conferences, necessitates a more rigorous work pace and time schedule, which in turn presuppose (admittedly Western) professional skills such as time management. Thus, the more "professionalized" NGO, as an organizational form has inhibited entrance of newcomers to women's movement, due to a difficult work schedule and the need for more educated participants and for newcomers to undergo a professionalization process.

The increased NGOization of the women's and feminist movement(s) has marked new boundaries and tensions within the transnational feminist movement. Some have pointed to the NGOs as facing the danger of becoming "the preserve of middle-class intellectuals" due to professionalization and the class differences that it accentuates (Lebon 1996:602). Other feminist activists and analysts have noted that feminist NGOs have access to more international development funding and that these professional, policy-oriented groups have in many cases become "privileged interlocutors with public officials, the media and bilateral and multilateral aid and development agencies" as opposed to the more informally organized, activist-oriented groups (Alvarez 1998:313).

Despite the populist-feminist collective identity of the women of MEC, the Managua collective has undergone a similar institutionalization process. The group has gradually become less "activist-oriented," relying on a core of trained, paid staff to run specific programs for women at the grassroots. In the Managua office an accountant is in charge of the bookkeeping and each team member is in charge of a different area of services to women and the programs that comprise it. Team members receive remuneration from the NGO funds that finance the programs. For example, Evelyn maintains and runs the Documentation and Research Center that is housed in the Managua office. The center was first established through a grant from an NGO based in California. Sara writes most project proposals and spends a great deal of time networking with Northern-based NGOs to seek and maintain the different program's funding. In 1996, the Managua office employed a graduate from the job-training program to work as the office's receptionist, answering the phone and completing general office work.

In the Managua collective's meetings the group has emphasized "professional work" and "rules of the game." At one meeting in which members of the collective evaluated its past performance, participants listed "activism" as a weakness of their organization. Experts at crisis resolution and handling emergencies, the women of the Managua team saw a need to develop time management skills and learn to plan and work towards future collective goals.

The team has shifted in orientation from the populist and mass-based orientations of the FSLN to emphasize professionalism in its work. A clear example of this was in the case of a report regarding the progress of the program for maquila workers. Part of the task was the responsibility of one of the program's participants who often engaged in administrative duties when funds allowed for her to be contracted. She completed a section regarding the brand names produced in the zone, gluing garment tags on white paper and drawing out a chart by hand, decorated with handmade drawings. When Sara saw the report she indicated that it had to be redone. Josefina disagreed, "Look at this. This is beautiful, *la compañera* did it with her own hands." Sara did not concur and sent the report to be typed, adding graphics from a computer program. "This is a professional job!" she said approvingly, as she looked over the computer-generated diagrams.

Many of the same tensions that are manifested in the transnational feminist movement are reflected within the MEC organization. Actors struggle with issues of accountability, representation, and tensions stemming from institutionalization. Caught in a system in which more professional, NGO-like structures are in a better position for accessing international funds, MEC organizers struggle to balance their populist and feminist principles with the very real issue of the need for material resources.

MEC's search for an organizational structure, though taking place in an extremely specific local setting, is infused with processes occurring at a transnational level. One could argue that in part reliance on international NGO funding may have influenced MEC's shift to a "network-like" structure. In the 1990s, bilateral, multilateral, and private funders have all thrown their support behind efforts at global and regional coalition building. As a Uruguayan feminist observed at the recent Bejing conference, this trend reflects changes in "cycles of fashion of the agencies of international cooperation…which went from [support for] research centers, to grassroots organizations, to NGOs, to local networks, to regional networks, and now global networks" (quoted in Alvarez 1998:308-9).

Finally MEC organizers, like those of other local organizations, are caught in an interesting bind. On the one hand, their dependency on international NGO funds means that they must strive to represent themselves as worthy recipients of funding and "authentically" local representatives of grassroots women. On the other hand, in order to represent themselves effectively in this way, they must have professional skills such as finessed grant-writing abilities and a working familiarity with a particular language used to describe successful project proposals. Thus, MEC leaders must maintain yet another balancing act of appearing "local enough," (i.e., connected to the grassroots) and being "global enough" by developing and maintaining professional skills and keeping up to date regarding the latest trends in international funding.

CONCLUSIONS

This examination of MEC's organizational practices has revealed the ways in which transnational processes occur in locally constituted sites and how local actors reconstruct and reconfigure as well as appropriate transnationally circulating ideas and discourses. Tensions in the MEC organization have stemmed from extremely localized and internal issues, such as members' different, individual experiences as political actors and varying ideas about the meaning of autonomy, as well as from transnational processes, such as the tension between reliance on international external funding and accountability to the grassroots and differing orientations towards feminist discourses and organizational strategies. Transnational connections with NGOs and engagement with globalized feminist discourses have offered MEC a series of opportunities for obtaining funding, adopting new organizational models and employing important discursive resources that helped them formulate and constitute their "women-only space" in a way that resonated with the experiences of organizers.

On the one hand, in the case of relations with NGOs, transnational linkages presented MEC with a set of very real constraints and limitations stemming from inequalities in the global system. In a context of globalization then, new spaces have opened for groups like MEC, while other relations of domination and inequality continue or are intensified. Often heralded as clear expressions of participative democracy, NGOs are seen as a solution to the top-down, modernist development strategies of previous decades. And yet, the NGO model does not escape the power dynamics stemming from North/South relations in a postcolonial context. Despite the flow of ideas and resources across national borders, a great deal of power remains in the hands of political actors in the North. In the case of international NGOs, "global agents" based in the North are able to shape both the methods and projects undertaken by groups in the South, who are dependent upon them for funding (Jelin 1998:414, n. 3). This lack of financial autonomy greatly affects projects and orientations of organizations like MEC. Organizers must learn and become skilled at the use of the language of funding agencies, underlying which is "politics of virtue," impelling funding recipients to demonstrate that they are deserving of help and that their projects are worthwhile (Mindry 2001:1193).

On the other hand, scholars have noted (and the case of MEC supports this contention) that international organizations and donors, including NGOs, have been influential in pushing organizations in the South to focus on gender issues. For example, Gay Seidman's (1999) analysis of the South African case offers striking parallels with the case of Nicaragua. Seidman describes a multi-layered process through which South African women have inserted gender issues into discussions about the democratization process. She notes how the activities of an articulate and vocal women's movement were both supported and influenced by a global discourse around gender issues espoused by international donor agencies and NGOs. Of course, this trend also reflects the influence of the transnational feminist movement, which has helped equip local women's movement organizations, like MEC and the organizations that Seidman depicts, with important material and ideological resources. MEC organizers could relate feminist ideas to their own experiences as political actors, and feminist concepts such as "unity through diversity" helped form the basis for the formulation of organizational practices that resonated with organizers' view of social change and their own changing, identities as *feministas de base*.

Finally, the case of MEC demonstrates how locally constituted identities and experiences influence the ways in which organizational actors interact with, appropriate and transform transnationally circulating discourses, ideas, and organizational models. Even within the small, local space of MEC differential experiences as political actors both within and outside organizations affiliated with the FSLN led to varying orientations towards and engagement with transnational discourses and ideas—including those related to feminism. Thus, how transnational circulating discourses and ideas are appropriated, implemented and reconfigured depends on local processes including place-based experiences and the formation of political identities. Analyses of transnational processes, including the study of the transnational feminist movement, must not gloss over the more microlevel processes and practices that occur locally. Instead, we must interrogate the complex relations between the transnational and the local by examining the struggles of particular women's groups to create organizational "spaces of their own."

NOTES

1.   This article is based on research that I conducted with support from an Inter-American Foundation fellowship, a Fulbright Study Abroad Fellowship, a

University of California Humanities Institute scholarship, and a research grant from Sigma Xi. I am grateful to Michael Lewis, Tom Linneman, Cecilia Menjívar, Gül Ozyegin, and Timmons Roberts as well as three anonymous reviewers for their comments and feedback regarding earlier drafts of this article. Finally, I am indebted to the organizers and founders of MEC, particularly the woman I call Sara Rodriguez, for teaching me important lessons about gender solidarity and social justice and for their willingness to share their lives and friendship with me. I am honored and humbled to tell their stories.

2. In many cases this separation was far from voluntary, but confrontational and violent. After a core group of leaders from the Women's Secretariat officially resigned from the CST, members of the National Executive locked the doors of the Women's Secretariat national office to the other affiliates and leaders. Subsequently, CST leaders replaced coordinators and organizers of projects and programs that had been established under the tenure of the original leadership with women who were handpicked by the CST leaders and the newly appointed director of the Women's Secretariat. For example, Reyna, the organizer of the domestic workers' union "Rigoberta Menchú," and other union members were physically thrown out of the CST office by a top ranking CST leader. The Secretariat's office was subsequently ransacked, and members of the CST's National Executive accused MEC founders of being responsible for this destruction as well as having absconded with computers and other resources that were donated by international NGOs for use in the Secretariat's activities. In February 1995, MEC leaders won an appeal of an earlier ruling and were found innocent of all charges in a court of law. See Mendez (forthcoming) for a more complete and in-depth analysis of MEC's formation, strategies, and practices.

3. Free trade zones (FTZs) are important components of the globalization of capital. A series of 1991 laws passed by the Chamorro regime in order to attract foreign investment and reactivate Nicaragua's devastated economy established the existence of free trade zones within the country's national borders. The Free Trade Zone "Las Mercedes" opened the following year with eight factories in operation (Renzi 1996). Currently, there are fifteen factories located in Nicaragua's state-owned Free Trade Zone and four privately operated zones that hold another eleven factories with another twenty-three maquila factories that enjoy FTZ status but are not located in a FTZ. Recent estimates place the number of workers in the assembly factories of the FTZ at 37, 143 (Comisión nacional de zonas francas 2002).

4. In post-revolutionary Nicaragua the "autonomous women's movement" refers to an extremely diverse, loosely coordinated (often in the form of coalitions or networks) set of women's organizations ranging from small community-based organizations to larger, more professional ones that have exerted a more nation-

al presence (Babb 1997, 2001; Criquillon 1995). The word "autonomous" is key, as it denotes independence from political parties, particularly the FSLN. Thus, AMNLAE and the women's branches or secretariats of the mass organizations are not included in this category.

5. All interviews were tape-recorded and transcribed, and translations from Spanish are my own. Quotes that are not cited are from my field notes or from the interview transcriptions. The names of organizations are unchanged, while names of individuals are pseudonyms.

6. In the early years of the Sandinista period, the six major mass organizations included the Sandinista Defense Committees (CDS), the July 19th Sandinista Youth (JS-19), National Union of Farmers and Ranchers (UNAG), the Rural Workers Association (ATC), the Association of Nicaraguan Women, Luisa Amanda Espinoza (AMNLAE), and the CST (Luciak 1995:25).

7. Vanden and Prevost (1993:55) note an inherent tension between, on the one hand, radical, participative democracy involving direct participation of the masses and on the other, vanguardism and centralized decision-making within the Sandinista party and government. This tension is also reflected within the mass organizations themselves. Vanden and Prevost (1993) attribute this tension to the multiclass composition of the coalition that overthrew the Somoza regime as well as the different variants of Marxism (Leninism but also heavily influenced by the Cuba revolution and other Latin American revolutionary thought including liberation theology and the interpretations and ideas of Che Guevara) that underlay the Sandinistas' political ideology.

8. In 1996, the IMF suspended disbursements to Nicaragua under the ESAF program due to failure to meet the conditions of the SAP (Close 1999:132).

9. Molyneux's (1986) much-cited article draws a distinction between "practical gender interests" and "strategic gender interests." The former refers to those interests derived inductively from women's position in the sexual division of labor. "Strategic gender interests" arise deductively, as women struggle to change the structural conditions under which they live.

10. Petras (1997:17) sees NGOs as fostering a new type of economic dependency and colonialism. This new type of economic dependence is a reflection of the changing nature of "post"-colonial relations in a context of globalization.

REFERENCES

ACKER, Joan.
    1995. "Feminist Goals and Organizing Processes." In *Feminist Organizations: Harvest of the New Women's Movement*, edited by Myra Marx Ferree and Patricia Yancey Martin. Philadelphia, Pennsylvania: Temple University Press.

ALVAREZ, Sonia E.
    1990. *Engendering Democracy in Brazil: Women's Movements in Transition Politics*. Princeton, New Jersey: Princeton University Press.
    ———. 1992. "Feminisms in Latin America: From Bogotá to San Bernardo." In *The Making of Social Movements in Latin America: Identity, Strategy and Democracy*, edited by Arturo Escobar and Sonia E. Alvarez. Boulder, Colorado: Westview Press.
    ———. 1994. "The (Trans)formation of Feminism(s) and Gender Politics in Democratizing Brazil." In *The Women's Movement in Latin America: Participation and Democracy*, edited by Jane S. Jaquette. San Francisco, California: Westview Press.
    ———. 1998. "Latin American Feminisms 'Go Global': Trends of the 1990s and Challenges for the New Millenium." In *Culture of Politics/Politics of Cultures: Re-visioning Latin American Social Movements*, edited by Sonia E. Alvarez, Evelina Dagnino, and Arturo Escobar. Boulder, Colorado: Westview Press.
    ———. 2000. "Translating the Global Effects of Transnational Organizing on Local Feminist Discourses and Practices in Latin America." *Meridians* 1(February):29-67.

ALVAREZ, Sonia E., Evelina Dagnino, and Arturo Escobar.
    1998. "Introduction: The Cultural and the Political in Latin American Social Movements." In *Culture of Politics/Politics of Cultures: Re-visioning Latin American Social Movements*, edited by Sonia E. Alvarez, Evelina Dagnino, and Arturo Escobar. Boulder, Colorado: Westview Press.

APPADURAI, Arjun.
    1991. "Global Ethnoscapes: Notes and Queries for a Transnational Anthropology." In *Recapturing Anthropology: Working in the Present*, edited by Richard G. Fox. Santa Fe, New Mexico: School of American Research Press.

BABB, Florence.
    1996. "After the Revolution: Neoliberal Policy and Gender in Nicaragua. *Latin American Perspectives* 23(1):27-48.
    ———. 1997. "Negotiating Spaces: Gender, Economy, and Cultural Politics in Post-Sandinista Nicaragua." *Identities* 4(1):45-70.
    ———. 2001. *After Revolution: Mapping Gender and Cultural Politics in Neoliberal Nicaragua*. Austin: University of Texas Press.

BASU, Amrita.
    1995. *The Challenge of Local Feminisms: Women's Movements in a Global Perspective*. San Francisco, California: Westview Press.
    ———. 2000. "Globalization of the Local/Localization of the Global: Mapping Transnational Women's Movements." *Meridians* 1(February):68-84.

CHIGUDU, Hope.
    1997. "Establishing a Feminist Culture: The Experience of Zimbabwe Women

Resource Centre and Network." *Gender and Development* 5(1):35-42.
CHINCHILLA, Norma Stolz.
    1992. "Marxism, Feminism and the Struggle for Democracy in Latin America." In *The Making of Social Movements in Latin America*, edited by Arturo Escobar and Sonia E. Alvarez. San Francisco, California: Westview Press.
    ———. 1994. "Feminism, Revolution, and Democratic Transitions in Nicaragua." In *The Women's Movement in Latin America: Participation and Democracy*, edited by Jane S. Jaquette. San Francisco, California: Westview Press.
CLOSE, David.
    1999. *Nicaragua: The Chamorro Years*. Boulder, Colorado: Lynne Rienner Publishers.
COMISION NACIONAL DE ZONAS FRANCAS.
    2002. Web-site. http://www.czf.com.ni
CRIQUILLÓN, Ana.
    1995. "The Nicaraguan Women's Movement: Feminist Reflections from Within." In *The New Politics of Survival: Grassroots Movements in Central America*, edited by Minor Sinclair. New York, New York: Monthly Review Press.
DESAI, Manisha.
    2002. "Transnational Solidarity: Women's Agency, Structural Adjustment, and Globalization." In *Women's Activism and Globalization: Linking Local Struggles and Transnational Politics,* edited by Nancy A. Naples and Manisha Desai. New York, New York: Routledge.
EVANS, Trevor.
    1995. "Ajuste Estructural y Sector Público en Nicaragua." In *La Transformación Neoliberal del Sector Público: Ajuste Estructural y Sector Público en Centroamérica y el Caribe*, edited by Trevor Evans. Managua, Nicaragua: Coordinadora Regional de Investigaciones Económicas y Sociales (CRIES).
FERGUSON, Ann.
    1996. "Bridge Identity Politics: An Integrative Feminist Ethics of International Development." *Organization* 3(4):571-587.
FISHER, Julie.
    1993. *The Road from Rio: Sustainable Development and the Nongovernmental Movement in the Third World*. Westport, Connecticut: Praeger.
FISHER, William.
    1997. "Doing Good?: The Politics and Antipolitics of NGO Practices." *Annual Review of Anthropology* 26:439-464.
HELLMAN, Judith Adler.
    1992. "The Study of New Social Movements in Latin America and the Question of Autonomy." In *The Making of Social Movements in Latin America: Identity, Strategy and Democracy*, edited by Arturo Escobar and Sonia E. Alvarez. San Francisco, California: Westview Press.
INSTITUTO NICARAGÜENSE DE LA MUJER.
    1996a. "Documento de Acuerdo entre el INIM y el Movimiento de Mujeres."

Managua, Nicaragua: Author.

———. 1996b. "Informe: Encuentro con las Organizaciones no Gubernamentales dentro del Proceso de Desarrollo Institucional del INIM." Managua, Nicaragua: Author, October 10.

JAQUETTE, Jane S.
  1994. *The Women's Movement in Latin America: Participation and Democracy*, 2nd ed. Boulder, Colorado: Westview Press.

JELIN, Elizabeth.
  1998. "Towards a Culture of Participation and Citizenship: Challenges for a More Equitable World." In *Culture of Politics/Politics of Cultures: Re-Visioning Latin American Social Movements*, edited by Sonia E. Alvarez, Evelina Dagnino, and Arturo Escobar. Boulder, Colorado: Westview Press.

JUBB, Nadine.
  1995. "Women Organizing for Change in Nicaragua: Setting the Agenda for Social Transformation." *Latin American Working Group Letter Series* 47:1-42.

KECK, Margaret and Kathryn Sikkink.
  1998. *Activists Without Borders: Transnational Advocacy Networks in International Politics*. Ithaca, New York: Cornell University Press.

LEBON, Nathalie.
  1996. "Professionalization of Women's Health Groups in Sao Paulo: The Troublesome Road towards Organizational Diversity." *Organization* 3:588-609.

LUCIAK, Ilja A.
  1995. *The Sandinista Legacy: Lessons for a Political Economy in Transition*. Gainesville: University Press of Florida.

MANSBRIDGE, Jane.
  1995. "What Is the Feminist Movement?" In *Feminist Organizations: Harvest of the New Women's Movement*, edited by Myra Marx Ferree and Patricia Yancey Martin. Philadelphia, Pennsylvania: Temple University Press.

MEC.
  1995. Untitled. Unpublished Report. Managua, Nicaragua: Author.

———. 1996. "Planificación Estratégica." Unpublished. Managua, Nicaragua: Author.

———. 1997. "Movimiento de Mujeres Trabajadoras y Desempleadas, María Elena Cuadra." Unpublished pamphlet.

MELUCCI, Alberto.
  1996. *Challenging Codes: Collective Action the Information Age*. New York, New York: Cambridge University Press.

MENDEZ, Jennifer Bickham.
  Forthcoming. *The Global Here and Now: Gender and the Politics of Transnationalism in Nicaragua*. Durham, NC: Duke University Press.

MENDEZ, Jennifer Bickham, and Diane L. Wolf.
  2001. "Where Feminist Theory Meets Feminist Practice: Border-Crossing in a Transnational Academic Feminist Organization." *Organization* 8(4):723-750.

METOYER, Cynthia Chavez.

2000. *Women and the State in Post-Sandinista Nicaragua*. Boulder, Colorado: Lynne Rienner Publishers.

MINDRY, Deborah.
2001. "Nongovernmental Organizations, 'Grassroots,' and the Politics of Virtue." *Signs: Journal of Women and Culture in Society* 26:1187-1211.

MOLYNEUX, Maxine.
1986. "Mobilization without Emancipation? Women's Interests, State and Revolution." In *Transition and Development: Problems of Third-world Socialism*, edited by Richard R. Fagen, Carmen Diana Deere, and José Luis Coraggio. New York, New York: Monthly Review Press.

PATKAR, Medha.
1995. "The Struggle for Participation and Justice: A Historical Narrative." In *Toward Sustainable Development? Struggling over India's Narmada River*, edited by William F. Fisher. Armonk, New York: Sharpe.

PÉREZ-ALEMÁN, Paola.
1992. "Economic Crisis and Women in Nicaragua." In *Unequal Burden: Economic Crises, Persistent Poverty, and Women's Work*, edited by Lourdes Benería and Shelley Feldman. Boulder, Colorado: Westview Press.

PETRAS, James.
1997. "Imperialism and NGOs in Latin America." *Monthly Review* 49(7):10-27.

RANDALL, Margaret.
1992. *Gathering Rage: The Failure of Twentieth Century Revolutions to Develop a Feminist Agenda*. New York, New York: Monthly Review Press.

———. 1994. *Sandino's Daughters Revisited: Feminism in Nicaragua*. New Brunswick, New Jersey: Rutgers University Press.

RENZI, María Rosa, and Sonia Agurto.
1993. *Qué Hace la Mujer Nicaragüense ante la Crisis Económica?* Managua, Nicaragua: Fundación Internacional para el Desafío Económico Global (FIDEG).

———. 1996. *La Mujer y los Hogares Urbanos Nicaraguenses: Indicadores Económicos y Sociales*. Managua, Nicaragua: Fundación Internacional para el Desafío Económico Global (FIDEG).

SAFA, Helen I.
1996. "Beijing, Diversity and Globalization: Challenges to the Women's Movement in Latin America and the Caribbean." *Organization* 3:563-570.

SEIDMAN, Gay.
1999. "Gendered Citizenship: South Africa's Democratic Transition and the Construction of a Gendered State." *Gender and Society* 13(3):287-307.

SETHI, Harsh.
1993. "Action Groups in the New Politics." In *New Social Movements in the South: Empowering the People*, edited by Ponna Wignaraja. Atlantic Highlands, New Jersey: Zed Books.

STERNBACH, Nancy Saporta, Marysa Navarro-Aranguren, Patricia Chuchryk, and

STEWART, Sheelagh and Jill Taylor.
> 1997. "Women Organizing Women: 'Doing It Backwards and in High Heels.'" In *Getting Institutions Right for Women in Development*, edited by Anne Marie Goetz. New York, New York: Zed Books.

STIENSTRA, Deborah.
> 2000. "Dancing Resistance from Rio to Beijing." In *Gender and Global Restructuring: Sightings, Sites and Resistances*, edited by Marianne H. Marchand and Anne S. Runyan. New York, New York: Routledge.

THAYER, Milllie.
> 2000. "Traveling Feminisms: From Embodied Women to Gendered Citizenship." In *Global Ethnography: Forces, Connections and Imaginations in a Transnational World*, edited by Michael Burawoy. Berkeley: University of California Press.

VANDEN, Harry E. and Gary Prevost.
> 1993. *Democracy and Socialism in Sandinista Nicaragua*. Boulder, Colorado: Lynne Rienner Publishers.

VARGAS, Virginia and Cecilia Olea Mauleon.
> 1998. "Knots in the Region." In *Roads to Beijing: Fourth World Conference on Women in Latin America and the Caribbean*. Lima, Peru: United Nations Children's Fund (UNICEF), United Nations Development Fund for Women (UNIFEM).

WIGNARAJA, Ponna.
> 1993. *New Social Movements in the South: Empowering the People*. Atlantic Highlands, New Jersey: Zed Books.

MAKING FEMINIST SENSE OF NEOLIBERALISM: THE INSTITUTIONALIZATION OF WOMEN'S STRUGGLES FOR SURVIVAL IN ECUADOR AND BOLIVIA[1]

Amy Lind*

ABSTRACT

Since the early 1980s, community-based women's organizations have emerged throughout Ecuador and Bolivia in response to persistent poverty, economic crisis, neoliberal-development policies and related political and cultural crises. In Ecuador, women and men currently face an unprecedented financial crisis, the "dollarization," and the new 1998 Constitution. In Bolivia, various sectors of women have addressed the harsh economic measures implemented since 1985, growing tensions surrounding migration, rising homelessness and poverty rates, and the "War on Drugs." In both countries, women have been among the first to make connections among everyday life and development policies. In this article I examine the contradictions organized women face as they struggle for economic and political empowerment in the context of neoliberal development. I argue that development policies that rely upon women's unpaid labor sometimes contribute to institutionalizing women's struggles for survival rather than merely empowering them, as they hope to do, through their community participation.

INTRODUCTION

It remains a challenge to find a language to speak about, and rethink, neoliberal development in an era of globalization. As Chilean feminist Raquel Olea so aptly puts it, "There is a dominant discourse and too often we speak from inside that discourse" (quoted in Alvarez 2000:53). In the past fifteen years, we have witnessed enormous changes affecting community women's organizations throughout Latin America. In Ecuador and Bolivia, urban poor and rural women's community organizations—numbering in the several hundreds and begun initially as temporary responses to the economic crisis—often have become institutionalized. Now their participants view their work as longer-term and necessary for their survival, particularly since the inception of neoliberal-development policies (including structural adjustment, privatization, economic liberalization, state retrenchment and related decentralization measures).[2] At the local level, many poor women continue to face severe economic hardship, even those who have acquired significant political and economic advances for themselves and their communities. In this context, women struggle not only for their daily lives, but also to change economic, political, and social inequalities in their societies. Yet the irony is that neoliberal-development policies "target" poor women and tend to

---

* Women's Studies Program, Arizona State University, Tempe, AZ 85287, U.S.A.

reinforce and institutionalize their participation in community-development projects and organizations, rather than easing their burdens. While broader women's movements—including middle-class nongovernmental organizations (NGOs)—have gained important political advances, the poorest of women today have higher economic burdens than ever before. Thus, finding a language to speak about development policies that benefit poor sectors of women is difficult in this historical period. It is an issue we continue to face today as researchers, policymakers, and activists, along with members of women's organizations and poor sectors themselves.

Much feminist research on globalization and neoliberal development focuses on the effects of specific neoliberal policies on women's work and daily lives. Importantly, researchers have revealed the hidden male biases of neoclassical-economic models, including macroeconomic structural adjustment frameworks (Elson 1992 and 1998) and gross domestic product (GDP) measures (Benería 1995), as well as their concrete effects on daily lives and so-called reproductive, productive, and community-management roles in households and communities (Moser 1989). Both individual- and collective-survival strategies have been addressed as a way to understand the hidden gender dimensions of development policies as they shape family structure, household and community survival (Dwyer and Bruce 1988; Benería and Feldman 1992). Along with broader restructuring of societies around the world that some have pointed out, we have witnessed a restructuring of daily life (Benería 1992) that includes changes in consumption patterns, cultural practices, community and family networks and household expenditures. In addition, some researchers have addressed the symbolic, as well as the material effects, in terms of how women are culturally (mis-)represented in western gender and development discourse (Mohanty 1991) and in terms of how cultural representations can lead to material inequalities amongst neoliberal-development policy recipients—"poor women" (Schild 1998).

In this article I address how community-based women's organizations and poor sectors of women have been affected by neoliberal-development policies, including structural adjustment, social welfare redistribution and privatization and decentralization measures. I address these policy effects on two aspects of women's individual and collective survival strategies: (1) women's household and community labor, and (2) women's political responses to neoliberal reform. I utilize examples from my ethnographic research in Ecuador and Bolivia to address the ways in which women's survival strategies have been institutionalized through neoliberal-development policies, often leading to privatization of women's struggles along with the broader neoliberal-inspired privatization of goods and services (Benería 1992). Through their institutionalization or privatization, I argue, poor women increasingly have been viewed as the "answer" to a weak welfare state as well as a source of cheap labor. This has led to their disempowerment rather than empowerment or "integration into the development process," as earlier Women in Development (WID) scholars and contemporary proponents have claimed.[3]

In this article I refer to "institutionalization" of women's struggles for survival in three important senses. First, women's temporary involvement in development initiatives, or their spontaneous organization of community networks, often have become long-term solutions to the deteriorating standard of living in Ecuador and Bolivia. Although many observers in the international-financial community spoke of an economic turnaround following Latin America's "lost decade" in the 1980s, the effects of economic crisis continue to affect the majority of Latin Americans today. Women's collective survival strategies—including community organizations and networks—tend to become necessary on a permanent basis, despite women's desires to work elsewhere. The second sense is the way that women's organizations, which developed autonomously, have become the "targets" of neoliberal-development policies; policies that assume women have endless amounts of time and flexibility to participate in development projects. In this way, women's "invisible" reproductive work is exacerbated and extended to the realm of the community, rather than decreased and made more equitable with men's work. The assumption that women have time to spare is also based on the idea that women's roles in social reproduction (e.g., childbearing and childrearing, household management and community activism) are extensions of their "natural" maternal roles and responsibilities and that they are "naturally" better at this than men. In development studies, not only have scholars drawn from essentialist frameworks, but also social constructionists have made this type of hypothesis by assuming that women, and not men, should participate in these projects, thus, burdening women with improving their daily living situation and changing societal values about gender. Third, and related to my previous point, the "institutionalization" of women's struggles for survival is sometimes related to their privatization, particularly in neoliberal contexts. By "privatization" I am referring to how women's organizations have lost state support and have had to rely increasingly on private support for their survival, in financial as well as in ideological terms. In this sense, the institutionalization of women's struggles for survival is commonly related to the broader privatization process, a term originally conceptualized by Lourdes Benería in her research on women's survival strategies in Mexico City (1992).

My general argument is that neoliberal-development policies differentially affect specific sectors of women. This differential impact depends largely upon women's class, racial, ethnic and geographical locations, as well as upon their political locations and strategies. What we see is a series of gendered contradictions, arising both from within neoliberal-development-policy frameworks themselves as well as from the types of survival strategies and political responses women have created.[4] Through this process specific sectors of poor women have tended to lose out, particularly urban and rural poor or indigenous women. Interestingly, it is also true that some women have gained as a result of neoliberal-privatization policies, state-civil society restructuring and decentralization.

I conducted fieldwork for this research project over the last ten years, specifically in Ecuador in 1992-1993, 1998, and 2001. There I interviewed over one hundred women in various political, governmental, nonprofit and community organizations and at research institutes and universities. In Bolivia, I interviewed over fifty women in 1995, 1999, and 2001. I conducted individual interviews, group interviews, focus groups, and I participated regularly in meetings and activities of approximately ten women's organizations. In each research location, my general focus has been on the effects of neoliberal reform, including structural-adjustment policies, women's work and women's collective-survival strategies. In this article, I discuss contrasting aspects of this process in each country, emphasizing the policies or issues that I find most relevant and interesting for this discussion—hence the different emphases in each study.

Neoliberal Development, Globalization, and Women's Struggles for Survival

"Neoliberalism" is not easy to define. This is so, I have found, because neoliberalism does not refer only to a set of economic policies—as some might believe—but rather to a political strategy which relies upon an ideology of the market and implementing a certain set of policies. Neoliberal-economic policies themselves are not new: International trade and comparative advantage, for example, have been theorized and practiced for centuries (see Benería and Lind 1995); privatization and economic liberalization are strategies that have been used in many countries and regions well before the 1980s; and modernization theory (including the notion that economic growth will "trickle down" to the poorest sectors of society) has provided the conceptual foundation of the development field since its inception in the 1950s and 1960s (Escobar 1995; Phillips 1998; Boserup 1970). Indeed, as Lynne Phillips (1998:xii) points out, "the objectives of many aspects of neoliberalism have been around for some time under guises."

Many speak of the homogenizing effects and globalizing tendencies of neoliberalism (Fisher and Kling 1993; Phillips 1998). Indeed, a defining feature of neoliberalism is the push to introduce a specific set of policies (e.g., privatization, economic-liberalization measures and regional-trade initiatives—such as Mercosur and the Pacto Andino—and decreasing state spending) in order to integrate (and "globalize") national economies, cultures, communication, and ideas at a historically unprecedented pace. With the advent of information and communication technologies (ICTs)—including the fact that television stations such as CNN can now bring us stories live from towns and rural villages on the other side of the world—the neoliberal push toward market integration, coupled with a new global, multi-language, consumer culture, is occurring more rapidly than ever. Neoliberal policies help to crystallize what George Ritzer (1996) has called the "McDonaldization" of third-world countries and what Manuel Castells views as the totalizing hegemonic effects of globalization in poor regions such as the Andes (Castells 1998). Some argue that neoliberalism is a clear example of postmodernity in Latin America because the neoliberal context reflects a further fragmentation of political and cultural identities (Fernández-Alemany 2000) and a wider gap between rich and poor. Others argue that since the region has barely reached modernity, it can hardly be postmodern.[5] Still others argue that Latin America should not be viewed in western terms, as "premodern, modern or postmodern," but rather in its own terms, as eclectic, nonlinear and hybrid (Klor de Alva 1995).

Despite one's ideological perspective on neoliberalism, it can hardly be viewed as homogenous. Neoliberalism represents much more than just a standard set of policies with a standard set of economic and social outcomes. Policies introduced by states or international financial institutions (including the World Bank and IMF) are challenged, contested, ideologically supported or dismissed and negotiated. Their cultural effects are widespread, yet they vary geographically, historically, and politically from country to country, region to region. Neoliberal policies are "subject to transformation" and, therefore, are fluid, changeable, and negotiable (Phillips 1998:xii).

In addition, different neoliberalisms invoke different political responses. I found that women's political responses to neoliberal policies in Ecuador and Bolivia hold some interesting similarities yet are also context specific. Women strategize how to respond to their government based on the political environment at that specific time in that specific state space. Yet because women of poor and working-class backgrounds in countries around the world share similar perspectives on the daily effects of neoliberal-development policies (Basu 1995), they often choose similar survival and protest strategies.

For example, neoliberalism has led to locally organized protests against McDonald's and other businesses, which represent U.S. cultural and economic hegemony, being established in the region. In many cases, women are the first to protest against these establishments, such as in Brazil on International Women's Day (March 8, 2001), where approximately 100 women in Porto Alegre occupied a local McDonald's and called the Brazilian government a "vassal of world neoliberalism" (*Arizona Republic* 2001). Similar protests against McDonald's have occurred in Bolivia, Peru, and other Latin American countries, in which women commonly have initiated the protests or played protagonist roles.

Women have also protested foreign banks, the IMF, and the World Bank, as well as local supermarkets, by so-called food riots (Walton and Seddon 1994; Daines and Seddon 1994). These protests have resulted from spontaneous, unplanned forms of resistance and organized, collective political strategies. In Ecuador, women have protested against foreign banks, such as Citibank, in order to challenge the bank's policies on lending to Ecuador.[6] Similarly, indigenous or poor women in Bolivia have mobilized against foreign banks, corruption, cocaine dollars, increased poverty and inflation and the foreign-debt crisis.[7] Yet many others have not responded publicly but rather through individual means or social networks, by restructuring their household budgets and lowering their daily expenses, sharing costs with neighbors and collectively working together in local planning initiatives—such as the construction of a local church, community center or road (McFarren 1992).[8]

Another example concerns the historical emergence and institutionalization of women's community-based struggles. In Ecuador, one study estimates that 500 to 800 informal women's organizations emerged throughout the country in the 1980s, primarily in response to the inception of structural-adjustment policies (Centro María Quilla 1990). Many of these organizations have formed the basis for what both the state and NGOs now perceive as available volunteer or low-paid labor for community-development projects. Bolivia's food-for-work projects in El Alto are another example. These projects, established in the 1990s, were designed to provide food to volunteer laborers and their families in exchange for work (e.g., construction, clean-up, food distribution—see Ochsendorf 1998). The well-known soup-kitchen movement in Lima, Peru, in which thousands of women have volunteered to provide more than 40,000 men, women, and children with meals on a daily basis (see Sara-Lafosse 1984; Delpino 1991; Barrig 1996; Lind 1997) is yet another example of how women's struggles for survival—in this case, literally putting bread and butter on the table—has been institutionalized through time, often as a result of state- and international-development policies which sustain and reinforce women as volunteer or undervalued labor through their funding and institutional practices.

Through these grassroots struggles and development initiatives, supporters have pointed out that local women have benefited from their collective participation in these community endeavors. Indeed, it is true that many women have gained political visibility through the organizing process, beginning in the local arena (IULA/CELCADEL/USAID 1992, 1996, 1997). Increasingly, more and more women with roots in community activism are participating in the official political arena both at local and national levels (Zabala 1999; Arboleda 1994). Additionally, many women have become trained as policymakers and advisors on issues pertaining to gender and public policy (Alvarez 2000). Yet at the same time, the poorest women—those who would most benefit from collective, community-based initiatives, such as daycare centers and food-for-work programs—have not gained any economic power. Rather, we have witnessed poor women's increased burdens as household managers and caretakers, community organizers, and now volunteers in neoliberal-inspired-development projects. In this sense, although poor women may be gaining political visibility, I argue that their economic burdens have tended to increase rather than decrease since the inception of neoliberal-development policies in the early 1980s. This is a product not only of the ongoing economic crisis in each country, but also of the ways in which traditional welfare responsibilities have been shifted to local communities and poor women themselves, rather than being supported by the state or even the for-profit and nonprofit private sector.

Being the first region to systematically undergo World Bank and IMF-inspired "structural-adjustment" policies (SAPs), debt-ridden Latin American countries were in many ways forced to introduce neoliberal measures as a prerequisite for receiving additional loans—namely through SAPs. In this sense, structural-adjustment and neoliberal policies are deeply connected, unlike in industrialized countries where governments are not bound by their debts.[9] In 2000 to 2001, Bolivia's total external debt was over U.S.$6 billion and Ecuador's was over U.S.$16 billion (World Bank 2001; BIS/IMF/OECD/World Bank 2002) and both countries rely upon additional loans and debt renegotiation to make their payments and project future economic growth.

Since the return to formal democracy in 1980, the Ecuadorian state has negotiated over 20 loans and its current foreign debt of U.S.$16 billion is the highest per capita debt in Latin America. While governments in Ecuador have varied in their ideological and political approaches, there has been a general tendency to prioritize the market and decrease state intervention in the economy as well as state power. This situation has only been exacerbated by the recent dollarization of Ecuador's economy, a plan adopted by the Ecuadorian government in September 1999 and initiated in early 2000 (North 1999; Acosta 2001).

With the U.S. dollar as Ecuador's official currency, thousands of people have fallen below (or further below) the poverty line and many people have been left without their savings and social security due to the bankruptcy of over twenty major banks. In addition, the Central Bank has virtually no cash reserve that has important ripple effects amongst state ministries. Although the government promised that the cost of living would not increase, it in fact has risen due to inflation and to a lack of change in the country, forcing people to round up to the nearest dollar for their everyday transactions with taxi drivers, street vendors, store clerks, and so on. The Bolivian government's foreign debt also presents an extremely high burden for its citizens, which number just under 8.5 million. Bolivia recently qualified as a recipient of the World Bank/IMF "highly indebted poor country" (HIPC) initiative, a worldwide initiative designed "to reduce the external debt of the world's poorest, most heavily indebted countries" (World Bank 2001).[10]

In each of these countries, implementing neoliberal reforms typically has been coupled with political reforms of decentralization and popular participation measures. Bolivia, for example, is known for its radical and successful decentralization project, in which over 300 new municipalities have been created since the mid-1990s (Albó 1996). On one hand, decentralization measures have transferred more decision-making power to local municipalities and civic groups, sometimes giving a political voice to women of various classes and ethnic and regional backgrounds. On the other hand, the new restructuring of state-local political institutions has led to the further integration of local communities into the nation-state, a process that homogenizes and appropriates local cultures and political structures rather than strengthening them. This process does not necessarily include a transfer of power to women, as I will show in the Bolivian case. Through these measures, women's and men's daily lives (including their household and community labor) are intimately linked to broader macroeconomic and political decision-making processes.

Institutionalizing Women's Struggles for Survival in Ecuador and Bolivia

In this section, I discuss the gender dimensions of neoliberal policies in Ecuador and Bolivia during the late 1980s and 1990s, focusing in particular on the emergence and institutionalization of women's struggles for survival in each country. In the case of Ecuador, I focus on the institutionalization of women's survival struggles through one specific governmental policy, the Community Network for Child Development. This led to the establishment of daycare centers run by already-existing women's organizations in local communities in the late 1980s and early 1990s. In the case of Bolivia, I focus on the more recent effects of decentralization upon sectors of women already impacted by structural-adjustment measures and the foreign-debt crisis—particularly women's community organizations that participate in the new local political structures put into place through decentralization. In each instance, things that once were viewed as spontaneous, temporary struggles have now become necessary, long-term strategies for household and community survival.

Ecuador

Since the early 1980s, community women's organizations have emerged throughout Ecuador, largely in response to emerging economic crisis. Along with middle-class feminist groups and the broader move towards the "NGOization" of the women's movement (Alvarez 1998), many community-based groups requested legal status (personería jurídica) in order to acquire funding and other forms of support from the government and international-development organizations. By the late 1980s, approximately 50 to 60 women's organizations of this type, out of the estimated 500 to 800 groups that existed in the country, had acquired their legal status. Although these formal and informal organizations have played important roles in their communities (and nation) during the 1980s to the present, they have received little formal support from the state—with the important exception of educational campaigns, including domestic-violence programs, voting workshops, literacy campaigns and community development teach-ins. One could say that they have received attention, but not adequate economic support. Besides these activities, often implemented through state women's agencies[11] or women's NGOs, they have been targeted primarily in their capacity as volunteer cheap laborers.

One example of this concerns the Community Network for Child Development (Red Comunitaria para el Desarollo Infantil), a program established by Ecuadorian President Rodrigo Borja (1988-1992). This program targeted young children and their mothers and was influenced by the United Nations Children's Fund's (UNICEF's) widely adopted framework to address "adjustment with a human face" (UNICEF 1987; Cornia, Jolly, and Stewart 1987). The program addressed sectors of children under the age of six and their mothers—

women who had been most severely affected by the negative consequences of structural adjustment and the foreign-debt burden. In 1990 it was estimated that from a total population of 12,000,000, there were 1,900,000 children under the age of six, with an estimated 1,400,000 of those children, along with their families, in need of direct social assistance. Based on average figures, the typical poor family had two children under the age of six, in which case the program targeted approximately 570,000 poor households (Ojeda Segovia 1993).

Implicit in this program was the belief that all projects should be self-sustaining in the long term. Importantly, this included capitalizing on already existing community practices, such as the groups established by women. The program's main objective was to organize daycare networks, with participation from local communities in both urban and rural areas. At its peak, it reached approximately between 140,000 and 200,000 children daily, in both rural and urban areas, through contracts between the state and over 300 community-based organizations.[12] The concept of "child development" was central to the program's philosophy: it emphasized not only "evolutionary development," but also the "influences from community, environment and family" that affect children's development in poor sectors (Delgado Ribadeneira 1992b:1-2). The program was intended not only to improve direct living conditions for poor children, based on indicators of health and nutrition, but also to "initiate interinstitutional activities oriented to improve the economic and social bases of the children's families" (Delgado Ribadeneira 1992b:2). Central to the program's success was the assumption that social development requires a collaborative effort by the state and popular sectors:

> The [Community] Network presupposes . . . an innovative conception of social development, in a coordinated effort between the state and popular sectors. It is innovative in the sense that services are organized in an integral, interrelated way; popular and community participation are articulated as the crux of development; and, it views community development in relation to the [broader] economic and social environment. (Ojeda Segovia 1993:197, translation mine)

This project, therefore, relied upon existing women's organizations and the parents in the communities to provide the labor for the daycare centers. This included not only the small percentage of women's organization members who were employed by the centers but also the parents, who were asked to voluntarily participate in community meetings to organize and oversee the centers' maintenance and management. Their participation, it was assumed, would help to generate the "participation of civil society"—by asking people to actively participate in their own welfare—that the Borja administration was looking for in its goal to overcome paternalistic, or top-down, ways of providing welfare.

In practice, however, many problems arose. In terms of reaching its goal of targeting 570,000 households, even the ex-director of the program, Ernesto Delgado Ribadeneira, claims that by 1992, the program probably only reached about 120,000 households (Delgado Ribadeneira 1992a). And, despite the rise in the fiscal budget share of the Ministry of Social Welfare (from 1.0 percent in previous governments to 3.3 percent during the Borja government), a World Bank report claims that the redistribution had "limited effects" and that the sectors who benefited most were not the poorest, but rather were "middle class" (quoted in Ojeda Segovia 1993:199). There are ideological disparities between the World Bank's and the Borja administration's perspective on this policy and, therefore, the validity of the report is uncertain. It nevertheless raises important questions about the extent to which Borja's social policies successfully reached sectors of society that had not been reached in the past or who had been most severely affected by the economic crisis.

Problems arose as well with the implementation of the daycare centers. In particular, it was assumed that women—targeted as mothers of the preschool children—would play central roles both in the centers' productive work and in the voluntary parents' associations that served as informal "boards" for the centers in the respective neighborhoods. Several issues arise from this situation. On one hand, the centers provided employment for some women, but only a small percentage. At a center that provided daycare for fifty children, for example, five or six women were employed on either a full-time or part-time basis. Typically, two women worked on a full-time basis and the rest worked on a part-time basis. This depended largely on decisions made within the popular organization that was locally responsible for the daycare center's success. Furthermore, the women employees were paid little ("not enough for the vital minimum"), and they lost "their rights in terms of stable employment, work promotion, salary raises, and participation in unions" (Costales, quoted in Ojeda Segovia 1993:209).

On several occasions in 1992 and 1993, I visited one of these daycare centers. It was located in a district that was previously a *hacienda* of ex-President Velasco Ibarra, a ranch where primarily indigenous Ecuadorians had worked in a semi-feudal fashion as *huasipungeros*, for the owner(s). The ranch was abandoned decades ago, following Ecuador's agrarian reforms in the 1960s and 1970s.[13] By the time I visited this district, it had become an incorporated district on the southern outskirts of the Quito metropolitan area. Interestingly, the city's official name is Cooperativa de vendedores ambulantes (Cooperative of Street Vendors), reflecting local residents' background in this cooperative movement to establish rights for street vendors, many of which came from families who once worked on ex-President Velasco Ibarra's ranch. Today, many of the approximately 200-plus houses are without running water and electricity and only portions of roads are paved. It is a poor neighborhood; the average monthly household income of the women I interviewed in this district was S/119,500 (U.S.$66.00 per month) and the average spent on household purchases per month was S/95,000, or U.S$53.00. Their exposure to state agencies and NGOs was significantly less than other regions, as well as their exposure to North Americans or Europeans.

This particular women's organization had received funding from the

Community Network of Child Development and established a daycare center in 1992. The Center itself, located in a building made of cement blocks and mortar, was a very austere building with basic supplies and sleeping arrangements for approximately 40 to 50 young babies and children. Bunk beds for eight children were crammed into one small room. Often, at least two children shared one mattress. There were two long, low tables in the dining room where the children sat to eat soup or bread for lunch. The floors were primarily made of dirt. The 5 to 6 women who worked there were members of the local women's organization, one of the three groups organized by the Cotopaxi women's organization. Those who received a wage for their work got minimal salaries (approximately S/5,000 or U.S.$2.80 per week) that were not designed to promote self-sustainability among the women workers. The fund provided small salaries but generally were based on the assumption that women's volunteerism is "extra" or a "second salary" and does not require compensation as other forms of "male" employment do.

According to results of the Pilot Project evaluated by the Consejo Nacional del Desarrollo (CONADE),[14] the project was viewed differently by state bureaucrats than by the mothers and community residents who participated in it. On one hand, the project was designed as a strategy for "integral child development." The mothers who participated in it, however, viewed it as an "alternative form of assistance for immediate subsistence, given the critical situation in which they live" (Ojeda Segovia 1993:208). Neighborhood women's organizations that provided local support for the daycare centers, therefore, took advantage of the government's support and spent exhaustive amounts of time and energy to make the centers a success—mainly because they and their families needed it. In this sense, establishing the daycare centers had both positive and negative effects for the neighborhood organizations that supported them, as well as for local families who relied upon this service. The local communities and the neighborhood organizations themselves were in desperate need not only of daycare but also of forms of subsistence and, more generally, of funds that would give further meaning and life to the organizations in an era when state funding was extremely limited. Thus, during this period, many neighborhood organizations were enthusiastic about establishing daycare centers in their neighborhoods—many of which had no such service beforehand.

On the other hand, many observers questioned the project's legitimacy in enhancing civil society participation. Some critics (Ojeda Segovia 1993; Delgado Ribadeneira 1992b) questioned the extent to which Borja's social-policy reforms—which included, under the banner of "democratization through decentralization," popular sectors and local governments in the national-development process—did more than rely upon the voluntary or cheap labor of sectors of poor people to carry out the administration's proposed projects. In this way, Borja's program helped to institutionalize poverty and women's struggles for survival. Furthermore, it set the stage for later administrations to continue state reliance on women's labor and to transfer more responsibilities to the private sector—both formally, through privatizing state enterprises, and informally, by adding to the realm of women's daily work. This program was based on the assumption that poor people, and especially women, have endless time to participate in local development projects. It also assumed that women would automatically benefit from their participation, which is not always the case, since many women complain of working too much (Lind 1990), getting "burned out" (Moser 1989) or losing their funding. This resonates with the general trend in Latin America to seek women's political support by providing them (typically volunteer) opportunities to participate in development initiatives, offering them food or a small remuneration, in exchange for their support (Barrig 1996).

Ultimately, the Community Network of Child Development was short-lived. In 1992, upon President Sixto Durán-Ballén's (1992-1996) entry into office, the Community Network was left inactive and Borja's Social Front was dismantled and replaced by the World Bank- and IMF-inspired emergency social investment fund (ESIF or Fondo de Inversión Social de Emergencia). The initial impacts of putting this program "on hold" (which ended up being indefinite) were devastating for the daycare centers and community women's organizations involved in the centers. Some daycare centers were closed and those centers that continued to exist did so since women's, parents' and children's advocacy groups pushed for these centers to remain active, even when no funding was available. They, therefore, have operated through voluntary labor and primarily parents' efforts to raise funds. Needless to say, they have extremely limited funding (if any) to continue the centers' main tasks of caring for approximately fifty children per day five days a week; providing the children with lunches; and providing salaries (however limited they may be) for the women who manage the centers. In this way, women's struggles for survival—in this case, providing daycare—became institutionalized. In addition, the struggle of women to maintain the daycare centers has been privatized, along with the broader privatization of former businesses. Here privatization occurs "invisibly," along with the invisible transfer of responsibilities to the private realm, the realm of women's work. The privatization of women's struggles occurs as they are institutionalized and, in addition, lose funding for their activities. Unlike NGOs, which increasingly have been subcontracted by the state as a result of the new public-private partnerships, community women's organizations do not have access to this relationship with the state, other than through entirely paternalistic means. They have been forced to operate more out of their own pockets than out of state-funded programs, because they are small and informal and many are not eligible or prepared to apply for funding from foreign agencies. In this way, poor sectors of Ecuadorian women play significant, yet often invisible, roles in buffering the economic crisis and supporting the economy.

Bolivia

As in Ecuador, urban poor and rural women's organizations in Bolivia have both benefited from and been affected negatively by neoliberal-development policies. This is particularly true since 1985, when the Bolivian government implemented a historically and globally unprecedented set of economic-restructuring measures. Commonly known in Bolivia as Decree 21060, the World Bank and the IMF supported this structural-adjustment plan designed by economist Jeffrey Sachs. At the time, inflation was as high as 20,000 percent and many workers brought their devalued salaries home in flour sacks, only to give most of it away again for a loaf of bread and a few other basic food items. Decree 21060 allowed the government to undergo a series of measures—including privatization of state-owned enterprises (most importantly, the mining sector), economic liberalization and state retrenchment. While inflation was curbed, most people were in dire economic straits, victims of Latin America's "lost decade," as the international financial community labeled it.

Prior to the adjustment period, women's organizations were established throughout the country, through both "bottom-up," grassroots-initiated groups and networks and "top-down" government-initiated groups. The now globally recognized Bolivian tin miners' wives,[15] who became particularly active following the privatization of Bolivia's mining sector, originally participated in state-organized *clubes de madres* (mothers' clubs) created by the military government of Hugo Banzer in the 1970s. Organizing women in their communities was a way to garner women's support for the government (see Salinas Mulder et al. 1994).[16] Despite the tin miners' wives' origins in this state-sponsored initiative, they negotiated the state's proposal in ways which permitted them to define their organizational agendas and identities in more autonomous terms. State agendas may have influenced women involved with the *clubes de madres,* but many women also learned to rearticulate and appropriate the state's masculinist, Eurocentric interests so as to better address their own needs and identities. The tin miners' wives struggled publicly against privatizing the tin-mining sector and against the World Bank and IMF—two institutions that helped to draft Decree 21060 (Barrios de Chungara, personal interview, April 1999; McFarren 1992). In this historical sense, the Bolivian state can be seen paradoxically both as repressive toward as well as creative of contemporary women's organizations. This is so although, of course, the Bolivian state—like other Latin American states—has "organized women to demobilize them" rather than organizing them to create an autonomous social movement (see Salinas Mulder et al. 1994; Paulsen and Calla 2000).[17]

The Food-for-Work project, initiated in El Alto in the mid-1990s, is a more recent example of a development initiative relying on women's cheap labor and transferring welfare-provision responsibility (e.g., providing food to the poor) to the community itself, especially to women. State planners that initiated this project relied upon the historical fact that El Alto is a newly established city of migrant tin-mining families and others displaced by the economic crisis. Just as its grassroots origins lie in informal, collective forms of community development and planning, so too do contemporary projects implemented in this city of over one million settlers. Although the Food-for-Work program did not rely explicitly on women's organizations, it did rely on local women's labor. Furthermore, informal women's groups in El Alto, in desperate need of basic provisions, did play important roles in the project more out of necessity than choice. This project lasted only a few years, as new Bolivian governments prioritized other policies and programs (Ochsendorf 1998).

Perhaps part of this program's perceived "success" lies in the fact that it converges nicely with the state's broader process of neoliberal restructuring and, most concretely, with urban planners' and politicians' perceptions of how communities should participate in community-development initiatives. Like Ecuadorian President Borja's philosophy, in Bolivia many politicians and planners believed during this recent period that communities should "help themselves," rather than merely "be helped." While debates on social welfare and community participation characterized most Latin American states in the twentieth century, in the 1990s the political rhetoric of neoliberalism reinforced this by encouraging communities to "pull themselves up by their own bootstraps" as a way to "sacrifice" on behalf of the country (Alvarez, Dagnino, and Escobar 1998) and "pay their dues" for the national budget deficit. Often, at the individual level, women themselves are unaware of their economic burden until they have worked in the project or learned about gender roles and family responsibilities in their organizations or through informal conversations with their neighbors.

Bolivia's decentralization measures, the most radical and successful of their kind in Latin America, have converged with neoliberal reform as well. Although decentralization measures themselves are not considered "neoliberal," their emphasis on local participation blends well with state-retrenchment and institutional-restructuring strategies. In 1993, Gonzalo Sanchez de Lozada's administration (1993-1997) implemented this innovative set of measures to accompany the structural-adjustment and stabilization measures stemming from Decree 21060. At the time, international and governmental development agencies, such as the United Nations and U.S. Agency for International Development (USAID), were pushing for decentralization as well, with a strong gender perspective (IULA/CELCADEL/US AID 1992, 1996, 1997). Sanchez de Lozada's decentralization measures catalyzed an intense shift from centralized-state power to decentralized power in local municipalities and provinces. His so-called popular participation measures were designed to democratize political participation by (1) creating new political structures, (2) seeking a wider representation of people and interests within the new political structures, and (3) providing more democratic "checks-and-balances" among state and civil-society organizations—in order to avoid political corruption and opportunism. To do this, he set up a tripartite system of local decision-making—including local municipalities, *organizaciones territoriales de base* (OTBs, or territorial-based organizations), and *comités de vigilancia* (vigilance committees). In theory, supporters of these measures claim that they have been designed to incorporate previously marginalized voices into the formal political system and to strengthen democracy by increasing local participation, viewed as the foundation of democracy.

To some degree, women's community organizations and local women activists have successfully gained new visibility and, perhaps, "power" as a result of decentralization and popular participation measures.[18] There have been several attempts to incorporate women into local politics and municipalities and to include women's organizations in municipal planning (Urioste, personal interview April 1999; Uriona, personal interview April 1999). For example, women who previously participated in an informal organization may now be on the board of an *organización territorial de base* or a *comite de vigilancia*, two groups established through the decentralization measures designed to enhance citizen participation and provide a checks-and-balances system for the new local political structures. Preliminary studies show that despite the popular belief that "more women are participating," the percentage of women politicians has decreased rather than increased, since the popular participation measures were first implemented and since the new quota system for female political candidates was introduced in 1997 (Zabala, personal interview April 1999; also see Zabala 1999). In some cases, women's organizational participation has actually decreased rather than increased (Zabala, personal interview April 1999; Urioste, personal interview April 1999). In addition, as some have pointed out (Arboleda, personal communication October 1995; Zabala, personal interview April 1999), even when women's organizations participate in these new structures, they may gain visibility but they do not necessarily gain political or economic power.

An unintended consequence of decentralization is that some women's organizations have lost out or been left without funding or support. Successful women's organizations have collaborated with their local municipalities to prepare plans and strategize long-term development. Some even receive state contracts to do this, transforming grassroots activists into professional consultants or advisors. Other women's groups have not been so fortunate. One reason for this is political clientelism between women's organizations and governments in power: the age-old situation in that "whom you know" makes all the difference. Another is the fact that some organizations are more prepared to deal with market-oriented development than others, an issue that affects them most directly in their grant-writing and management skills. Organizations without political support of some kind, whether it be from middle-class feminist NGOs, church groups or political parties, are less apt to benefit than those who already had contact with the new municipal political leaders. It is not surprising then that women's organizations themselves are sharply divided over the meaning of decentralization and popular participation. Some women's NGOs, such as Cochabamba-based *Instituto Femenino para la Formación Integral* (IFFI), believe that the reforms are opening spaces for more women to participate politically. Perhaps they hold this perspective because IFFI has been intimately involved in local planning and development, particularly by mobilizing poor sectors of women to participate more actively in local decision-making. Others, such as La Paz-based *Centro de Desarrollo de la Mujer Aymara* (CDIMA), believe that the reforms are violent impositions on cultural practices and everyday lives (Abya Yala, n.d.): they prefer to focus on other efforts rather than on working within the new neoliberal political and economic structures. To some degree, both are correct: neoliberal policies have brought new opportunities to women's community organizations, yet they have also contributed to the economic hardship and cultural/racial/ethnic degradation that many poor women continue to face.

The Gendered Contradictions of Neoliberalism

Neoliberal reforms tend to exacerbate women's workloads, institutionalize their struggles for survival and produce new inequalities among rich and poor, women and men. This is so despite the fact that these reforms have contributed to the growth of contemporary women's movements. Most positively, neoliberal reforms have contributed to strengthening some women's NGOs, particularly those that have had the appropriate skills and knowledge to lobby or to work within the new public-private arrangements. Until recently, most women activists did not participate in lobbying activities (Alvarez 2000), yet the presence of global feminist organizing, United Nations' legislation, and the Latin American feminists' own turn toward "working with the boys," indeed have changed this trend. These are a few of the ways in which neoliberalism has perhaps benefited some sectors of women.

Yet this is just one side of the contradictory balancing act that women policy-makers, politicians, and NGO activists have negotiated: on one hand, women have become more visible through their political and economic participation; on the other hand, they continue to maintain their second-class status within the private realm of the family, household, and informal economy. Particularly, urban and rural poor women—poor women from indigenous and *mestiza* backgrounds as well as African, Asian, Middle Eastern, and European backgrounds—continue to lack economic and political power and to be displaced from the most important national debates. Peruvian scholar Maruja Barrig (1986) pointed out in the 1980s that urban poor women in Lima, Peru often struggle to transition from their status as "neighbors" to full "citizens."[19] Her observation resonates well with the reality of community women's organizations in Latin America at the turn of the century. In a sense, neoliberal policies have institutionalized poor women's second-class "neighbor" status, despite rhetorical claims to the contrary. These contradictions raise a series of questions about the sustainability of community women's organizations and their ability to affect broader social change. To what extent can small, community-based groups of women, acting in traditional roles, gain access to material resources and acquire full citizenship? To what extent can they challenge broader economic and social policies? Can the (often invisible) welfare-responsibility transfer to local communities and decentralization measures really help women? Observers have addressed this question on two levels. Indeed, we must acknowledge the broad historical, economic, social, and political systems in Latin America (and globally), which pit women against each other in their struggles to survive, acquire full citizenship status and gain access to limited resources. More specifically, we need to address how community women's organizations themselves have been conceptualized in economic-development discourse and practice, as this has serious implications for the women's lives, families, and communities affected by these initiatives. It is this second level upon which I address my abovementioned questions.

First, although women's community organizations have become institutionalized, they have not become self-sustainable. Many development initiatives, both preceding and during the contemporary neoliberal period, have been designed, at least rhetorically, with long-term self-sustainability in mind. Yet rather than contribute to the ongoing success of poor communities planning and developing themselves and participating in the formal-political process, in some cases, state initiatives tend to create economic dependence rather than sustainability. This is true even in cases where women have changed their political consciousness and have acquired political empowerment. Specific governments may announce their development projects, but they do not have any control over what happens to the projects after they leave office. In addition, states tend to extend their support to specific sectors at different times: one sector may receive funding one year, while other sectors receive the same funding the following year. Thus, a community may begin the project but once they lose funding the only way they can continue it is to do so on a volunteer basis. The international-development field creates this dependence as well, since development funding, after all, is never permanent; it is always temporary. Communities cannot assume that funding will always be there. When organizations prepare grant proposals with development agency guidelines in mind, it is not necessarily with their own vision in mind. This is the name of the game in seeking funding. For organizations that are offered funding, they cannot expect a long-term commitment on behalf of the state or a particular development agency. Both the Community Network for Child Development in Ecuador and the Food-for-Work program in Bolivia, as well as numerous communal/soup kitchens throughout the central Andes illustrate this point. Sustainability requires an examination of the root of the problem, not merely a focus on how to "fix" the immediate situation. In this sense, state and development institutions sometimes participate more so in the long-term, institutional "failure" of women's organizations rather than in their success. Additionally, to the extent that women's organizations have learned how to negotiate state and development contracts, in some ways they have learned how to become more dependent, rather than less dependent, on these entities. At the very least, when the state is asking them to "help themselves," some organizations continue to be in dire need of external support. This contradiction besets the neoliberal-development context and suggests that gender biases in development practices can be exacerbated in neoliberal contexts to the extent that women are viewed as willing, passive "absorbers" of economic crisis and restructuring.

Along with the lack of sustainability among women's organizations, women have not necessarily acquired more citizen rights.[20] Beginning with the fact that they are "targeted" and represented as "poor" and "in need" by development experts, they are set at a distance from, and lower on the hierarchy than, the very experts who design the policies and name the "problem" (Fraser and Gordon 1994; Escobar 1995; Schild 1998). It is easy to overgeneralize when implementing national policies, but more could be done to address the complexity of women's experiences—examining the intersection of political, economic, cultural, and social factors in shaping women's lives and survival strategies and critiquing how traditional notions of family, women's responsibility to the welfare system and religious and cultural expectations of motherhood and childbearing contribute to gender and heterosexist biases in contemporary development policies.[21] In many studies of survival strategies, for example, it is assumed that all women are married and fit the traditionally-defined family unit (e.g., nuclear or extended families and heterosexual marriages or partnerships, see Lind and Share forthcoming). One might ask, instead, which women participate in community organizations and which do not? Where are the most marginalized women, such as women who do not fit within acceptable gender and family norms? In addition, many development projects focus primarily—if not exclusively—on women's economic roles, without considering important factors such as gender, ethnicity/race, religion or geographic location. This perspective is narrowed because it assumes that women's conditions are related to poverty and to the modern economy and the tendency is to ignore the complexity of the intersection between economic, political, and social constructs. This renders women as "victims" rather than as active, conscientious participants in the so-called development process. These examples demonstrate how poor sectors of women are affected both by the development policies themselves as well as the cultural representations of gender and poverty that underlie those development-policy frameworks. This targets women primarily in their roles as producers or consumers of the modern economy. Because development policies are, in fact, primarily economically based, feminist policymakers and NGO activists have found it more difficult to address women's needs more broadly. This also requires a great deal of work, funding and initiative on behalf of national- and global-development institutions.

Middle-class feminists have, in fact, gained—to some degree—from neoliberal policies. One contradiction of women's activism within neoliberal contexts is that women's state agencies throughout Latin America are stronger (i.e., have higher institutional status within the state) than ever before.[22] This has occurred at the same time that the women's survival struggles have been institutionalized and poor women's work often has been exacerbated rather than alleviated. To the extent that the state—with pressure from international organizations such as the United Nations Development Fund for Women (UNIFEM) and

UNICEF—has extended more responsibilities to the women's agencies, middle-class feminists have acquired some power within the state and within the public decision-making processes. In addition, some women's NGOs that are subcontracted by the state have also benefited to a large degree, in political as well as financial terms. Such is the case of IFFI in Cochabamba, Bolivia. This perceived power is not necessarily permanent, it depends on future political relationships and policies and IFFI may or may not retain this power. In this sense, social-movement organizations' power is uncertain, at best, even though some do successfully acquire relatively permanent leadership roles. Historically speaking, the relationships among women's organizations and nation-states have always fluctuated. That is, some women have power during one administration while others gain power later. Women's perceived political/economic power depends on clientelism and the ideological bent of national-development plans.

Even more complicated is the fact that nation-states also are dependent on international finance and development communities. Thus, while NGOs and community organizations may criticize the state for representing the interests of domestic or foreign capital, the state is also bound by its foreign debt obligations and the international-development funding that flows into the country. Some women's groups have responded to the contradictory position of nation-states in creative ways. In the Citibank protest in Quito, Ecuador, for example, women protested against Citibank for having frozen the Ecuadorian government's assets, while they also protested the government's mismanagement of the national budget. In this context, the Ecuadorian state had to contend both with its own dependence upon foreign loans as well as its powerful role as manager of national development. States contend with both sides and women's political responses tend to address these arenas (e.g., state and international development) as well. Poor women have, after all, been among the first to make connections between their daily lives and global-economic change.

CONCLUSION: MAKING FEMINIST SENSE OF NEOLIBERALISM

Where, then, do we turn our attention? This article shows that women's struggles for survival in Ecuador and Bolivia have been institutionalized through neoliberal-development policies in the 1980s and 1990s. Many communities' women's organizations are busy responding to ongoing crises, rather than proactively shaping a different kind of future. While there has been a vast amount of research on the emergence and importance of women's community action (see Lind 1997), much could be done to address the gender biases in neoliberal social- and economic-development policies and their mid- to long-term consequences for women's work and survival strategies. What kind of research, strategies or projects can be supported to foster this process? The following are some suggestions:

1) *Redefine the Gender and Development Research Agenda*: Researchers could propose concrete alternatives to the neoliberal model, at both macro- and microlevels. This includes, among others, additional gender analysis of the effects of the invisible transfer of welfare responsibilities to the community and household realms. This type of research is needed to address how neoliberal restructuring and institutionalizing survival strategies affect women negatively and usually in invisible ways. It is also needed to show how neoliberal reforms and related measures may propel women to activism, political leadership, and economic empowerment. Additionally, and perhaps most importantly, this research agenda could also include understanding the hidden "male biases" in seemingly gender-neutral frameworks—such as macroeconomic growth (Elson 1998). This would allow researchers to develop more complex frameworks for understanding how gender shapes, and is shaped by, economic change. Many studies of decentralization and social policy currently focus on how communities respond to this restructuring process, yet little has been done to understand how women continue to be viewed as the "absorbers" of economic restructuring. Although much feminist research has been conducted to analyze household survival strategies in the context of structural adjustment (Moser 1989; Elson 1992; Benería and Feldman 1992), much more could be done to address women's work in the context of specific community-development initiatives resulting from restructuring and decentralization.

2) *Rethink Women's Community Participation*: A broader understanding of women's community participation and development could be fostered, to better comprehend how development policies frequently have negative effects on women's lives if they do not take into consideration multiple economic, social, political, and cultural factors. In addition, women could be encouraged to create their own visions of quality of life, work, culture, and development. Among others things, this would include further education about women's roles in the "private" realm of the economy as well as a continued focus on how women's unpaid labor supports the local and global economy. This would include rethinking the process by which development projects and planners tend to define the boundaries of women's participation, rather than women themselves. In the current scenario of institutionalization, women tend to work within the neoliberal arrangements rather than work toward an alternative.

3) *Denaturalizing Gender*: Policymakers, politicians, and activists could work together to create more viable strategies for community development and daily survival. This should include ones that do not rely exclusively on women's labor nor assume that (1) women have endless time and energy to participate, and (2) women are secondary breadwinners and, therefore, do not need comparable

salaries. Because women are viewed as mothers and caretakers, their community involvement has become naturalized along with their domestic labor; their collective participation is not considered "work" (Folbre 1994).

4) *"Talk to the Boys"*: Feminist economists and other social scientists could examine systematically gender dimensions of macroeconomic and social-policy frameworks, particularly those associated with neoliberal development. This would be a better way to account for women's contributions to the local and global economy and it would reveal the hidden gender biases. Initial research has been conducted in this area, including studies that examine economic growth and trade from a gender perspective (Jackson and Pearson 1998). Feminist economist Diane Elson (1998) speaks about this in terms of learning how to "talk to the boys." UNIFEM commissioned a paper, "The Gender Dimensions of the Financing for Development Agenda" (Floro 2001), to be presented at the first international conference on Financing for Development, scheduled for Fall 2002. As the foundational document for this discussion, this report addresses the gender dimensions of the five main topics of the conference: mobilizing domestic resources, mobilizing international resources, international trade, international-financial cooperation, and external debt. It is crucial that global discussions such as these be engender. Importantly, this includes the need for male policymakers and researchers to "talk to the girls." After all, as of now, it has been primarily women, not men, who have addressed these gender issues in policy design and implementation—issues affecting resource distribution, daily survival and the quality of life of men and women around the world.

These suggestions address the current situation but not the root of the problem. To do that, we need to rethink the neoliberal-development model, economic, political, and cultural globalization, and the history of colonialism in Latin America, along with the cultural biases in understanding "gender" and "women" in cross-cultural perspective. This article reveals some of the ways in which women and their local communities are affected by broad structural change—including economic and political restructuring. Perhaps most importantly, we (and the international-financial community) need to consider more seriously debt-forgiveness in highly indebted countries such as Bolivia and Ecuador. Only through broader measures such as this will we truly see women's struggles for survival de-institutionalized and long-term changes made in global economic, political, and social inequalities.

NOTES

1. A Fulbright-Hayes Dissertation Fellowship (1992-1993), an Inter-American Foundation Dissertation Fellowship (1992-1993) in Ecuador, and a Fulbright

2. Senior Scholar Grant (1999) in Bolivia supported the research for this paper. I also thank the Women's Studies Program and the Center for Latin American Studies at Arizona State University for their support. In Ecuador, I thank Gioconda Herrera at Facultad Latinoamericano de Ciencias Sociales (FLACSO), Rocío Rosero, Lilia Rodríguez, Susana Wappenstein and numerous other individuals who generously shared their time and thoughts with me for this project. In Bolivia, I extend warm thanks to Vivian Arteaga. I also thank Pamela Calla, Tom Kruse, and María Esther Pozo for their support, along with the many representatives of women's NGOs their time to conduct interviews. I thank Stephanie Brzuzy for her comments on an earlier version of this article. Finally, I owe many thanks to Cecilia Menjívar and four anonymous reviewers for their invaluable comments on this paper. While many people have provided their insight into this paper, all opinions expressed are my own.

2. There is much debate on whether decentralization measures themselves are considered "neoliberal." Most researchers and policymakers I have spoken with in Bolivia and Ecuador make the distinction between neoliberal-development policies (especially structural-adjustment measures) and other measures that, they argue, may converge with, yet remain institutionally separate from, SAPs themselves. Others argue that to the extent that neoliberal reforms also include issues of good governance and notions of trying to increase public accountability of administration and government—namely through decentralization, health care and educational reforms—decentralization measures can be considered "neoliberal." I thank an anonymous reviewer for articulating this debate for me.

3. For background information on the historical development of the Women in Development (WID) field, see Tinker 1990; Rathgeber 1990.

4. By "gendered contradictions" I am referring to the ways in which seemingly gender-neutral economic policies—which rarely posit individuals as gendered (i.e., "male" or "female")—actually have "male biases" (Elson 1991) which tend to render women's work in the private sphere invisible and which tend to impact sectors of women in negative ways. I am also referring to how women themselves (ourselves, as this is true everywhere) work within the context of neoliberal reform in contradictory ways, typically due to our need to work within the given context while also being critical of it.

5. For an excellent overview of the debates on postmodernism in Latin America, see Beverley, Oviedo, and Arrona 1995.

6. The most widely cited example concerns a women's protest against Citibank in May 1992. Within a twenty-four-hour period, over 100 women mobilized to protest Quito-based Citibank's freeze on U.S.$80 million from the Ecuadorian

Central Bank's account. Following a dispute regarding loan repayment guidelines, Citibank-New York, the bank that headed the group of foreign lenders, had frozen the Central Bank's assets because it claimed that the Ecuadorian government had defaulted on its loan payments. The following day, a group of approximately 100 women gathered outside Citibank's office to protest which, at the time, was unprecedented in Ecuadorian history. Several anti-debt protests have occurred since then, attended by members of women's organizations as well as by participants in other political sectors, such as the indigenous movement, labor, peasants, and the urban poor. Other protests of this kind, led by women, have occurred throughout Latin America as well—such as the so-called IMF riots in Argentina and Venezuela and the food riots in Brazil and Argentina. See Daines and Seddon (1994) for a comparative analysis of women's roles in food riots and protests against the IMF and World Bank.

7. The video, *Hell to Pay* (Anderson and Cottringer 1988), illustrates how indigenous and peasant women in Bolivia articulated their political stance against debt-related corruption and poverty during the 1980s.

8. Numerous studies document the household-level effects of economic restructuring, including anthologies edited by Dwyer and Bruce (1988) and Benería and Feldman (1992).

9. The United States, for example, has the largest debt in the world yet, for political and economic reasons, it is not bound to paying back the debt nor restricted from applying for additional forms of finance.

10. Bolivia is one of only four countries in the region to qualify. The other countries are Nicaragua, Honduras, and Guyana. In contrast, thirty-three African countries have qualified thus far, as well as three Asian and one Middle Eastern country (World Bank 2001).

11. In the late 1980s, the Ecuadorian state women's agency was named Dirección Nacional de la Mujer (DINAMU). Later, in the mid-1990s, the agency acquired higher institutional status within the state and its current name is Consejo Nacional de la Mujer (CONAMU). In Bolivia, the state women's agency is the Direccion General de Asuntos de Género (DGAG), located in the Ministry of Gender and Generational Affairs.

12. This number has been disputed. Official reports of the Community Network for Child Development, based on information provided by the participant organizations, estimates that 200,000 children were served daily. Ernesto Delgado Ribadeneira (1992a), however, contends that the figures used to arrive at this estimate were probably conflated and, in his own estimation, the Program sup-

ported 140,000 children on a daily basis. In terms of the number of community organizations involved, unfortunately I do not have specific figures, besides the figure of "300 organizations" that Delgado himself relies upon.

13. See Lynne Phillips (1987) for a discussion of the gender dimensions of agrarian reforms of a redistributive nature in Ecuador, including the abolishment of the *huasipungo* system.

14. The Pilot Project took place in two locations: in a rural village in the Pichincha Province, and in a poor neighborhood in Guayaquil. The results of this study were published in 1991, see the Consejo Nacional del Desarrollo/Programme des Nations Unies pour le Développement/United Nations Educational, Scientific and Cultural Organization/United Nations Children's Fund/Ministry of Social Welfare (CONADE/PNUD/UNESCO/UNICEF/Ministerio de Bienestar Social 1991; also see Ojeda Segovia 1993).

15. Perhaps the most well known testimony of the tin-mining wives' movement is that of movement leader Domitila Barrios de Chungara in the publication, *Si me Permiten Hablar*, translated in English as *Let Me Speak*! (Barrios de Chungara 1978).

16. Hugo Banzer again held power in the 1990s, when he was democratically elected as President of Bolivia in 1997. When he resigned in August 2001, following major cancer surgery, then Vice President Jorge Quiroga (August 2001-present) was sworn in as the new President.

17. This is true for both military authoritarian as well as formally democratic states.

18. I put the term "power" in parentheses as a way to highlight the ambiguity and vagueness of this term. "Power" has been defined in numerous ways, including in modernization, liberal, Marxian, and Foucauldian theory. Here I refer to women's "power" as including their access to material resources and economic-class status, their level of participation in formal and informal political processes and the more intangible ways in which contemporary women's movements have influenced popular culture and women's and men's daily lives.

19. By making the distinction between "neighbor" and "citizen," Barrig is referring to the fact that many women have been protagonists in neighborhood-based struggles, yet historically their participation has been ignored because it is not considered part of the formal political system.

20. Some Latin American feminist scholars have pointed out that the meaning of citizenship in the neoliberal era draws from a "free-market" notion of individuality,

growth and competition. Furthermore, it has been argued, contemporary forms of violence (including territorial, state-inspired, cultural or symbolic) stem directly from this notion of citizenship. This idea that women's and men's citizen status in the neoliberal period is based upon a broad definition of citizenship, includes political as well as economic, cultural, and social rights (see Schild 2000).

21. By "heterosexist biases" I am referring to the ways in which the naturalized, social institution of heterosexuality shapes and affects women's (and men's) lives such that women who do not fit within a traditional family model (e.g., the western, nuclear family, the extended family, a two-parent male-female marriage and household) are often viewed as "lesser than" the cultural norm. Development policies reproduce these norms when assumptions are made about what a "family" is; some feminist scholars have addressed this in their research, in terms of how women lose out economically and politically if they do not marry (Mohanty 1991) and in terms of how single mothers, "inappropriate" women and lesbians are not included in some family-oriented development initiatives (Lind and Share forthcoming).

22. I discuss the position of state women's agencies in Latin American neoliberal contexts at length in my book-length manuscript, tentatively titled: *The Paradoxes of Survival and Struggle: Women's Organizations and the Cultural Politics of Neoliberalism in Ecuador* (Lind 2002, see especially Chapter 6).

REFERENCES

ABYA YALA.
   n.d. "Alicia Canaviri Habla con SAIIC sobre la Mujer, los Jovenes y la Globalización en las Comunidades Indígenas de Bolivia." *Abya-Yala* 10(4):22-24.

ACOSTA, Alberto.
   2001. "El Falso Dilema de la Dolarizacion." *Nueva Sociedad* 172(marzo-abril):66-84.

ALBÓ, Xavier.
   1996. "Making the Leap from Local Mobilization to National Politics." *NACLA Report on the Americas* 29:15-20.

ALVAREZ, Sonia E.
   1998. "Latin American Feminisms 'Go Global': Trends of the 1990s and Challenges for the New Millennium." In *Cultures of Politics/Politics of Cultures: Revisioning Latin American Social Movements*, edited by Sonia E. Alvarez, Evelina Dagnino, and Arturo Escobar. Boulder, Colorado: Westview Press.

———. 2000. "Translating the Global: Effects of Transnational Organizing on Local Feminist Discourses and Practices in Latin America." *Meridians* 1(1):29-67.

ALVAREZ, Sonia, Evelina Dagnino, and Arturo Escobar.

1998. "Introduction: The Cultural and the Political in Latin American Social Movements." In *Cultures of Politics/Politics of Cultures: Re-visioning Latin American Social Movements*, edited by Sonia Alvarez, Evelina Dagnino, and Arturo Escobar, Boulder: Westview Press.

ANDERSON, Alexandra and Anne Cottringer.
1988. *Hell to Pay.* VHS, 52 minutes, color. London, England: Channel Four Television.

ARBOLEDA, María.
1994. "Mujeres en el Poder Local en el Ecuador." In *Jaque al Rey: Memorias del Taller "Participación Politica de la Mujer,"* edited by the Red de Educación Popular entre Mujeres (REPEM). Quito, Ecuador: REPEM/CIUDAD.
_____. 1995. Personal communication, 2 October.

ARIZONA REPUBLIC.
2001. "Women's Protest in Brazil." 9 March, p. A12.

BANK FOR INTERNATIONAL SETTLEMENTS (BIS), International Monetary Fund (IMF), Organization for Economic Cooperation and Development (OECD), and World Bank.
2002. "Joint BIS-IMF-OECD-World Bank Statistics on External Debt" [online]. Washington, D.C.: International Monetary Fund. Retrieved August 6, 2002 (http://www1.oecd.org/dac/debt/htm/jt_ecu.htm).

BARRIG, Maruja.
1986. *De Vecinas a Ciudadanas.* Lima, Peru: Servicios Urbanos para Mujeres de Bajos Ingresos (SUMBI).
———. 1996. "Women, Collective Kitchens and the Crisis of the State in Peru." In *Emergences: Women's Struggles for Livelihood in Latin America,* edited by John Friedmann, Rebecca Abers, and Lilian Autler. Los Angeles: University of California-Los Angeles, Latin American Center Publications.

BARRIOS DE CHUNGARA, Domitila with Moema Viezzer.
1978. *Let Me Speak!* New York: Monthly Review Press.
_____. 1999 Personal interview, 15 April.

BASU, Amrita, ed.
1995. *The Challenge of Local Feminisms: Women's Movements in Global Perspective.* Boulder, Colorado: Westview Press.

BENERÍA, Lourdes.
1992 "The Mexican Debt Crisis: Restructuring the Economy and the Household." In *Unequal Burden: Economic Crisis, Persistent Poverty and Women's Work,* edited by Lourdes Benería and Shelley Feldman. Boulder, Colorado: Westview Press.
———. 1995. "Toward a Greater Integration of Gender in Economics." *World Development* 23(11):1839-1850.

BENERÍA, Lourdes and Shelley Feldman, ed.
1992 *Unequal Burden: Economic Crisis, Persistent Poverty and Women's Work.* Boulder, Colorado: Westview Press.

BENERÍA, Lourdes and Amy Lind.
    1995 "Engendering International Trade: Concepts, Policy, Action." In *A Commitment to the World's Women: Perspectives on Development for Beijing and Beyond,* edited by Noeleen Heyzer. New York, New York: United Nations Development Fund for Women (UNIFEM).

BEVERLEY, John, José Oviedo, and Michael Arrona, eds.
    1995. *The Postmodernism Debate in Latin America.* Duke University Press.

BOSERUP, Ester.
    1970. *Woman's Role in Economic Development.* New York, New York: St. Martin's Press.

CASTELLS, Manuel.
    1998. *End of Millennium.* Malden, Massachusetts: Blackwell Publishers.

CENTRO MARÍA QUILLA, Consejo de Educación de Adultos de América Latina (CEAAL).
    1990. *Mujeres, Educación y Conciencia de Género en Ecuador.* Quito, Ecuador: Centro María Quilla, Consejo de Educación de Adultos de América Latina (CEAAL).

CONSEJO NACIONAL DEL DESARROLLO (CONADE), Programme des Nations Unies pour le Développement (PNUD), United Nations Educational, Scientific and Cultural Organization (UNESCO), United Nations Children's Fund (UNICEF), Ministry of Social Welfare (Ministerio de Bienestar Social).
    1991. *Informe General, Prueba Piloto de Evaluación de Impacto de los Proyectos de Acción del Ministerio de Bienestar Social en el Programa "Red Comunitaria para el Desarrollo Infantil."* Quito, Ecuador: Consejo Nacional del Desarrollo (CONADE) and United Nations (UN).

CORNIA, Giovanni Andrea, Richard Jolly, and Frances Stewart.
    1987. *Adjustment with a Human Face.* Oxford, Oxfordshire, England: Clarendon Press.

DAINES, Victoria and David Seddon.
    1994. "Fighting for Survival: Women's Responses to Austerity Programs." In *Free Markets and Food Riots: The Politics of Global Adjustment,* edited by John Walton and David Seddon. Oxford, United Kingdom: Blackwell.

DELGADO RIBADENEIRA, Ernesto.
    1992a. Ecuador: Balance de las Políticas para Pagar la Deuda Social 1987-1990, Programa "Red Comunitaria" para el Desarrollo Infantil. Unpublished paper.
    ———. 1992b. "Programa Red Comunitaria para el Desarollo Infantil 1987-1990." In. *Ecuador: Los Costos Sociales del Ajuste, 1980-1990,* edited by Latin American Employment Programme of the International Labour Office (PREALC), vol. II: *Informe de los Consultores.* Santiago de Chile: Latin American Employment Programme of the International Labour Office (PREALC).

DELPINO, Nena.
    1991. "Las Organizaciones Femeninas por la Alimentación: Un Menú Sazonado." In *La Otra Cara de la Luna: Nuevos Actores Sociales en el Perú,* edit-

ed by Luis Pásara. Buenos Aires, Argentina: Manantial/Centro de Estudios de Derecho y Sociedad (CEDYS).

DWYER, Daisy and Judith Bruce, ed.
    1988. *A Home Divided: Women and Income in the Third World.* Stanford, California: Stanford University Press.

ELSON, Diane, ed.
    1991. *Male Bias in the Development Process.* Manchester, England: Manchester University Press.

———. 1992. "From Survival Strategies to Transformation Strategies: Women's Needs and Structural Adjustment." In *Unequal Burden: Economic Crisis, Persistent Poverty and Women's Work*, edited by Lourdes Benería and Shelley Feldman. Boulder, Colorado: Westview Press.

———. 1998. "Talking to the Boys: Gender and Economic Growth Models." In *Feminist Visions of Development: Gender Analysis and Policy,* edited by Cecile Jackson and Ruth Pearson. London, England: Routledge.

ESCOBAR, Arturo.
    1995. *Encountering Development.* Princeton, New Jersey: Princeton University Press.

FERNÁNDEZ-ALEMANY, Manuel.
    2000. "Negotiating Gay Identities: The Neoliberalization of Sexual Politics in Honduras." Paper presented at the XXIInd International Congress of the Latin American Studies Association, March 16-18.

FISHER, Robert and Joseph Kling, ed.
    1993. *Mobilizing the Community: Local Politics in the Era of the Global City.* Urban Affairs Annual Review No. 41. Beverley Hills, California: Sage Publications.

FLORO, Maria.
    2001. "The Gender Dimensions of the Financing for Development Agenda." Paper commissioned by United Nations Development Fund for Women (UNIFEM)-New York, April.

FOLBRE, Nancy.
    1994. *Who Pays for the Kids? Gender and the Structures of Constraint.* London, England: Routledge.

FRASER, Nancy and Linda Gordon.
    1994. "A Genealogy of Dependency: Tracing a Keyword of the U.S. Welfare State." *Signs* 19(2):303-337.

INTERNATIONAL UNION OF LOCAL AUTHORITIES (IULA), Centro Latinoamericano de Capacitación y Desarrollo de los Gobiernos Locales (CELCADEL), U.S. Agency for International Development (USAID).
    1992. *De la Mujer al Género: Democratización Municipal y Nuevas Perspectives de Desarrollo Local.* Quito, Ecuador: U.S. Agency for International Development (USAID).

———. 1996. *Local Governments and Gender Equity: New Perspectives and*

Responsibilities. Quito, Ecuador: U.S. Agency for International Development (USAID).

———. 1997. *Los Procesos de Reforma del Estado a la Luz de las Teorías de Género.* Quito, Ecuador: U.S. Agency for International Development (USAID).

JACKSON, Cecile and Ruth Pearson, ed.
    1998. *Feminist Visions of Development.* London, England: Routledge.

KLOR DE ALVA, J. Jorge.
    1995. "The Postcolonization of the (Latin) American Experience: A Reconsideration of 'Colonialism,' 'Postcolonialism,' and 'Mestizaje.'" In *After Colonialism: Imperial Histories and Postcolonial Displacements*, edited by Gyan Prakash. Princeton: Princeton University Press.

LIND, Amy.
    1990. "Economic Crisis, Women's Work and the Reproduction of Gender Ideology: Popular Women's Organizations in Quito, Ecuador." Unpublished master's thesis, Cornell University.

———. 1997 "Gender, Development and Urban Social Change: Women's Community Action in Global Cities." *World Development* 25(8):1205-1223.

———. 1998 "Negotiating Boundaries: Women's Organizations and the Politics of Restructuring in Ecuador." In *Gender and Global Restructuring: Sightings, Sites and Resistances*, edited by Marianne H. Marchand and Anne Sissan Runyan. New York, New York: Routledge.

———. 2002 "The Paradoxes of Survival and Struggle: Women's Organizations and the Cultural Politics of Neoliberalism in Ecuador." Unpublished manuscript.

LIND, Amy and Jessica Share.
    In Press. "Queering Development: Institutionalized Heterosexuality in Development Theory, Practice and Politics in Latin America." In *Feminist Futures: Re-imagining Women, Culture and Development*, edited by Kum-Kum Bhavnani, John Foran, and Priya A. Kurian. London, England: Zed Press.

MCFARREN, Wendy.
    1992. "The Politics of Bolivia's Economic Crisis: Survival Strategies of Displaced Tin-mining Households." In *Unequal Burden: Economic Crisis, Persistent Poverty and Women's Work,* edited by Lourdes Benería and Shelley Feldman. Boulder, Colorado: Westview Press.

MOHANTY, Chandra Talpade.
    1991. "Under Western Eyes: Feminist Scholarship and Colonial Discourses." In *Third World Women and the Politics of Feminism,* edited by Chandra T. Mohanty, Ann Russo, and Lourdes Torres. Bloomington: Indiana University Press.

MOSER, Caroline.
    1989. "The Impact of Recession and Structural Adjustment Policies at the Micro-level: Low-income Women and Their Households in Guayaquil, Ecuador." Paper prepared for United Nations Children's Fund (UNICEF), Ecuador.

NORTH, Liisa.
    1999. "Austerity and Disorder in the Andes." *NACLA Report on the Americas* 33(1):6-9.

OCHSENDORF, A.
 1998. Constructing Power Through Food-for-Work Projects in El Alto, Bolivia. Undergraduate honors thesis, Wellesley College, Wellesley Massachusetts.

OJEDA SEGOVIA, Lautaro.
 1993. *El Descrédito de lo Social: Las Políticas Sociales en el Ecuador.* Quito, Ecuador: Centro para el Desarrollo Social (CDS).

PAULSEN, Susan and Pamela Calla.
 2000. "Gender and Ethnicity in Bolivian Politics: Transformation or Paternalism?" *Journal of Latin American Anthropology* 5(2):112-149.

PHILLIPS, Lynne.
 1987. "Women, Development and the State in Rural Ecuador." In *Rural Women and State Policy: Feminist Perspectives on Latin American Agricultural Development,* edited by Carmen Diana Deere and Magdalena León. Boulder: Westview Press.

———, ed. 1998. *The Third Wave of Modernization in Latin America: Cultural Perspectives on Neoliberalism.* Wilmington, Delaware: Scholarly Resources Books.

RATHGEBER, Eva.
 1990. "WID, WAD, GAD: Trends in Research and Practice." *Journal of Developing Areas* 24(July):489-502.

RITZER, George.
 1996. *The McDonaldization of Society: An Investigation into the Changing Character of Contemporary Social Life.* Thousand Oaks, California: Pine Ridge Press.

SALINAS MULDER, S. et al.
 1994. "Una Protesta sin Propuesta: Situación de la Mujer en Bolivia: 1976-1994." La Paz, Bolivia. Unpublished paper.

SARA-LAFOSSE, Violeta.
 1984. *Comedores Comunales: La Mujer Frente a la Crisis.* Lima, Peru: Servicios Urbanos para Mujeres de Bajos Ingresos (SUMBI).

SCHILD, Verónica.
 1998. "New Subjects of Rights?: Women's Movements and the Construction of Citizenship in the 'New Democracies.'" In *Cultures of Politics/Politics of Cultures: Revisioning Latin American Social Movements,* edited by Sonia Alvarez, Evelina Dagnino, and Arturo Escobar. Boulder, Colorado: Westview Press.

———. 2000. "Neo-liberalism's New Gendered Market Citizens: The 'Civilizing' Dimension of Social Programmes in Chile." *Citizenship Studies* 4(3):275-305.

TINKER, Irene.
 1990. "The Making of a Field: Advocates, Practitioners, and Scholars." In *Persistent Inequalities: Women and World Development,* edited by Irene Tinker. New York, New York: Oxford University Press.

UNITED NATIONS CHILDREN'S FUND (UNICEF).
    1987. *The Invisible Adjustment: Poor Women and the Economic Crisis.* Santiago, Chile: United Nations Children's Fund (UNICEF), The Americas and the Caribbean Regional Office.

URIONA, Catriona.
    1999. Personal interview, 14 April.

URIOSTE, Diana.
    1999. Personal interview, 21 April.

WALTON, John and David Seddon.
    1994. *Free Markets and Food Riots: The Politics of Global Adjustment.* Oxford, United Kingdom; Cambridge, Massachusetts: Blackwell.

WORLD BANK.
    2001. "The HIPC Debt Initiative" [online]. The World Bank Group, Washington, D.C. Retrieved July 18, 2002
    (http://www.worldbank.org/hipc/about/hipcbr/hipcbr.htm).

ZABALA, María Lourdes.
    1999a. *Mujeres, Cuotas y Ciudadania en Bolivia.* La Paz, Bolivia: Coordinadora de la Mujer and United Nations Children's Fund (UNICEF).

———. 1999b. Personal interview, 23 April.

COMPETITION AND COOPERATION AMONG WORKING WOMEN IN THE CONTEXT OF STRUCTURAL ADJUSTMENT: THE CASE OF STREET VENDORS IN LA PAZ-EL ALTO, BOLIVIA

Victor Agadjanian*

ABSTRACT

This case study of women street vendors in La Paz-El Alto, Bolivia, examines the dynamics of competition and cooperation among this group of poor working women in the context of economic structural adjustment and political pluralization. It is argued that the economic and political reforms not only increase street vendors' insecurities, but may also undermine the potential for their broad-based solidarity and collective actions. Extreme competition in the overcrowded street commerce, diminishing returns, and disillusionment with traditional forms of workers' organization hinder cooperation among street vendors and fragment the social body of the street marketplace, often by further reinforcing its gender, class, ethnoracial, and religious fault lines.

INTRODUCTION

Like many Latin American countries in the late twentieth century, Bolivia in the early twenty-first century has lived through an onslaught of neoliberal economic reforms. A comprehensive structural adjustment package, named the *Nueva Política Económica*, was introduced in 1985 after years of economic and fiscal instability. As elsewhere, Bolivia's structural adjustment was hailed by its proponents as a strong and sure medicine for the country's economic woes—hyperinflation, a large external debt, and pervasive poverty—but was chastised by its critics as a misguided policy serving the interests of big national and transnational capital (Sanabria 1999). Almost two decades later, the results of the structural adjustment reforms offer no clear support to either side of the argument. Thus, while macroeconomic stabilization has been achieved, the foreign debt reduced, and inflation brought under control, the expectation of a steady and rapid economic growth has not materialized (van Dijck 1998). The effects of structural adjustment on poverty alleviation in Bolivia remain the subject of heated debates (Gill 1994, 2000; Kohl 2002; Sanabria 1999; Thiele 2001; van Dijck 1998).

What is beyond doubt, however, is that the reforms have greatly altered the poor's livelihood options and strategies. The macroeconomic gains have come at the expense of dramatic social dislocations resulting from the shrinking of the state apparatus and closure of numerous industrial enterprises. Among the most obvious and universal trends spurred by structural adjustment in Bolivia, as

---

* Department of Sociology, Arizona State University, Tempe, AZ 85287-2101, U.S.A.

throughout most of Latin America, has been a rapid increase in informal employment, especially in urban areas. Already a prominent part of urban economy in Bolivia and other Latin American countries prior to the structural adjustment reforms (Doria Medina 1986), the informal sector has grown rapidly following the onset of the reforms, absorbing a considerable portion of workers, mainly men, who were laid off from the closing formal sector enterprises, but also large numbers of women who have often been forced to enter the labor force to make up for the incomes lost by their laid-off husbands and other male members of their households (Cerrutti 2000; Chant 1991, 1996; Gilbert 1994; Parrado and Zenteno 2001). Women's entry into the informal sector, far from providing a magic solution to the problems of unemployment and poverty, has exacerbated their own and their families' economic and social insecurities. While it remains widely contested whether the feminization of the informal labor has actually increased poverty, available data show that women working in the informal economy, like those in the formal sector, have consistently lower earnings than men (Psacharopoulos and Tzannatos 1992).

The explosion of urban street commerce has been, perhaps, the most conspicuous outcome of the informalization of Latin American economies. In La Paz, Bolivia's largest city and economic capital and in its satellite city of El Alto, this explosive proliferation of street commerce, condoned and even encouraged by authorities as a quick fix to unemployment problems, has been particularly visible. As the traditional enclosed markets have declined in commercial importance, large areas of the two cities have been transformed into open marketplaces often accommodating several shifts of vendors during a single day. Street commerce, unlike many other segments of the informal labor market, has been historically a mainly female occupation: migrant women, who would typically start their urban labor force careers as domestic workers, would move to petty trade as they aged, married, and had children (Arteaga and Larrazábal 1988; Centro de Estudios para el Desarrollobr Laboral y Agrario/Facultad Latinoamericano de Ciencias Sociales 1987; Gill 1994). Although the economic crisis of the 1980s and subsequent structural reforms have brought an increasing number of men into street trade, even a casual observation of street vendors in any open-air market in the La Paz-El Alto area proves that women vendors still greatly outnumber men.

A large body of literature has looked at informal workers' (including street vendors') occupational choices, livelihood strategies, and gender identities in the context of the economic crisis and ensuing structural adjustment in Latin America and beyond (e.g., Arteaga and Larrazábal 1988; Blanc 1998; Cross 1998; Cross and Balkin 2000; Espinal and Grasmuck 1997; Hays-Mitchell 1994; Portes, Castells, and Benton 1989; Seligman 2001). Studies have emphasized the crucial importance of informal workers' social networks for their economic survival (Lomnitz 1991, 1994; Rivera Cusicanqui 1996; Schroeder 2000). Other literature has examined instances of workers' successful mobilization to achieve legal and political recognition and defend their interests against the hostile state (Clark

1988; Cross 1998; Staudt 1996). A large group of studies has focused specifically on poor working women's collective struggles (e.g., Berger and Buvinic 1989; Friedmann, Abers, and Autler 1996; Hays-Mitchell 1995; Lind 1997, 2000; Ray and Korteweg 1999). However, while acknowledging the symbolic and practical importance of workers' collective actions, it is also important to recognize that such instances have been relatively few and, as a rule, have enjoyed only limited success. Their relatively modest social impact becomes particularly puzzling when we consider that the economic liberalization has unfolded in parallel with the political pluralization of society, which in a country like Bolivia, with its long tradition of authoritarian rule, held a no less radical promise of unleashing popular activism and participation in government.

This article sets out to investigate this paradox by looking at informal sector women workers' social interactions. Whereas much academic literature is concerned with the causes and mechanisms of workers' collective actions and these actions' impact on workers' livelihood, the fundamental concern underlying this study is why the increasingly disenfranchised workers are unable to translate their common plight and interests into concerted political action. I address this concern by investigating the dialectics of competition and cooperation among women street vendors in La Paz-El Alto. While not dealing with the nature, forms, and outcomes of workers' political actions per se, I argue that increased competition in the swollen marketplace, combined with a sanctification of private initiative and self-reliance by the dominant class ideology, undermines workers' collective strategies both by alienating them individually and by reinforcing compartmentalistic small-scale solidarities and alliances within various subgroups of workers. In women's case specifically, these processes are circumscribed by gender ideology that both reflects and distorts the social-class ideological constraints. Finally, these processes occur against the backdrop of a generalized disenchantment with democracy and political pluralism, thus, further eroding a potential basis of workers' collective actions.

This study is based on quantitative and qualitative data collected in the La Paz-El Alto area in 1999 and 2001. The quantitative data includes a survey of 440 women street vendors (excluding vendors in enclosed markets) conducted in 1999. In order to maximize the representativeness of the survey sample, respondents were selected using a systematic sample of vendors selling in the main commercial areas of both cities. In the resulting sample the share of respondents selling in El Alto was slightly larger than that of those selling in La Paz. In addition to collecting information on respondents' sociodemographic, economic, and cultural characteristics, the survey addressed vendors' interactions with one other, including conversations, mutual help, and tensions and conflicts occurring among them.

The qualitative data, consisting of 36 semi-structured interviews and observations carried out in 1999 and 2001, thematically paralleles the survey but is focused more on the dynamics of women vendors' mutual attitudes, interactions, and assistance, as well as on tensions and conflicts among them. In the following text, I first present and discuss the results of the survey and then summarize and assess the evidence gleaned from the qualitative interviews and field observations.

SURVEY OF WOMEN STREET VENDORS IN LA PAZ AND EL ALTO

The Social Profile of Street Vendors

Although the survey sample cannot be considered representative in a strict statistical sense, the data it generated nonetheless allow for a credible demographic and sociocultural portrayal of women street vendors in the La Paz-El Alto area and for a general assessment of the dynamics of cooperation and competition in their midst. Table 1 presents selected characteristics of the survey sample. As we can see, slightly less than half of the respondents were natives of La Paz-El Alto, and among the rest more than two-thirds were born in the La Paz department (the administrative unit in which both cities are located) overwhelmingly in rural areas. There were relatively few recent migrants among non-native respondents: about ten percent of the total sample had lived in the city for less then five years, while about forty percent had lived there at least 20 years. About sixty percent resided in the city of La Paz, while the rest lived in El Alto and (a tiny fraction) in nearby towns.

Respondents' age range from 17 to 70, with a median age of 35, and about one-half are clustered between ages 29 and 42. Over two-thirds of women are in marital unions (formal or informal). The average educational level is 5.7 years, and respondents display a variety of educational attainment. One in ten had not attended school and one in five could not read at all or could read with difficulty (respondents' reading ability was self-reported and was not tested). At the same time, almost a quarter of the respondents had more than seven years of schooling and about fifteen percent had twelve years or more. This wide range of educational attainment demonstrates that street vendors, while generally poor and disadvantaged, come from diverse socioeconomic backgrounds.

It proved impossible to obtain consistent and credible information about respondents' income. Therefore, I approximate vendors' economic conditions by the ownership status of the residence (whether owned or rented) and by ownership of certain durable goods such as refrigerator. Thus, 45 percent of women lived in residences they owned (solely or with their husbands) and only fourteen percent had a functioning refrigerator in their residences.

Several survey questions dealt with respondents' ethnocultural characteristics.[1] Almost forty percent of respondents spoke only Spanish at home; the rest spoke Spanish and Aymara, Spanish and Quechua, or just Aymara or Quechua (Bolivia's main indigenous languages). The type of clothes—either a traditional ensemble consisting of a gathered skirt (*pollera*), a derby hat, an embroidered

Table 1. Main Characteristics of Survey Respondents: Survey of Women Street Vendors in La Paz-El Alto, 1999

Age in years (median)	35
Years of education (mean)	5.7
Years is street commerce (mean)	11.8
Place of work (percent)	
La Paz	48
El Alto	52
Type of business (percent)	
Puesto fijo	63
Ambulante	37
Type of products sold (percent)	
Foodstuffs	41
Clothes and shoes	26
Other	33
Participation in a vendors' association (percent)	
Participates	46
Does not participate	54
Place of birth (percent)	
La Paz-El Alto	44
Other	56
Language spoken at home (percent)	
Only Spanish	39
Aymara/Quechua or Aymara/Quechua and Spanish	61
Type of dress (percent)	
De pollera	62
De vestido	38
Religious affiliation (percent)	
Catholic	73
Evangelical or other Protestant	27
Ownership of a refrigerator (percent)	
Household has a refrigerator	14
Household has no refrigerator	86
Ownership of residence (percent)	
Owns or co-owns	45
Does not own	55

blouse, a shawl, and often shoes of a certain type or western-type dress—is an important ethnocultural marker. Although women *de pollera* (as they are called) are thought to dominate petty commerce, western-clad women, who are usually referred to as *de vestido* (lit. wearing [western-type] dress) or *de pantalon* (lit. wearing pants), constituted forty percent of the sample.[2] In another sociocultural dimension, slightly over one-fourth of women belonged to Protestant, primarily Evangelical (*Cristiana*) churches, while the rest considered themselves Catholics.

The survey highlighted a variety of vending experiences. The average duration of selling career, 11.8 years, conceals considerable differences among the surveyed vendors: while about a quarter had been selling in the streets for three years or less, another quarter were veterans having spent twenty years or more in the business. The work trajectories that had brought these women into street commerce also differed. While for just under half of them street commerce was their first labor market experience, others moved into that niche after trying other options, primarily domestic work and employment in formal commerce. Over ninety percent of the respondents owned or co-owned their businesses, and for almost all of the women, street trade was their only income-generating occupation. Almost two-thirds of respondents were selling from a permanent stall, or *puesto fijo* (lit. fixed stall), while the rest were mobile, or *ambulantes*.[3] When broken down by the type of product sold, vendors of foodstuffs (produce, meat, or processed food) constituted the largest group—over forty percent of the sample; those selling clothes and shoes made up another quarter. Forty-seven percent were members of a vendors' association (*asociación* or *sindicato*)—practically all of them *puesto-fijo* vendors.

A series of survey questions dealt with respondents' interactions with other vendors. Some of the statistics derived from these questions are presented in Table 2. When asked whether they knew others who were selling in the area (i.e., whether they regularly greeted them or knew their names), most respondents claimed good acquaintance with other vendors: only six percent of them said they did not know anyone, fourteen percent said they knew them "more or less," and the remainder gave an unqualified affirmative answer.

Much of vendors' interaction is limited to conversations. Vendors' conversations are common: more than nine out of ten respondents said they chatted with other vendors, and almost sixty percent did so regularly or frequently. Such conversations rarely involved men; in fact, among women reporting such conversations one-third chatted solely with women. Business-related conversations were most frequent, but conversations regarding family matters or children were not unusual either. Other conversation topics were much less common. Most of the vendors' interactions occur in the work settings: less than ten percent of respondents reported engaging in joint leisure activities with other vendors, and only twelve percent reported having visited another vendor's home.

A quarter of respondents said they would trust a secret to a fellow vendor, but relatives generally enjoyed a higher degree of trust. Respondents were also more likely to turn to relatives for advice or to share their problems with them. Finally, relatives were much more likely to be called upon in the case of an emergency. In general, this conforms to findings of previous research on the importance of kin support in women's survival strategies in the face of structural adjustment reforms (Schroeder 2000).

The pattern of responses to the question on whether women vendors helped one another closely followed that of the question on knowing other vendors. Similarly, eighty percent of the respondents who acknowledged mutual help among women vendors said that such help involved only or mainly women, and practically none said it involved mainly or only men. Changing large bills and watching another vendor's business while she stepped away were the most commonly mentioned forms of help.

Despite the obvious risks entailed, vendors' cooperation involving money was not uncommon. Thus, 46 percent of respondents reported having lent money to other vendors or having participated with them in rotating credit schemes.

However, more sophisticated forms of cooperation were less often practiced. For example, only fifteen percent of respondents said they had teamed up with other vendors to buy products in bulk at wholesale prices and less than one-third had ever coordinated prices with other vendors.

The survey respondents were also asked about problems, misunderstandings, or fights occurring among vendors (because of the sensitivity of the subject, respondents were not asked about their personal involvement in any of such prob-

Table 2. Knowledge, Help, and Problems among Vendors: Survey of Women Street Vendors in La Paz-El Alto, 1999 (Percent)

	Total	Class of business		Association membership		Type of dress		Religious denomination	
		P.Fijo	Ambul.	Yes	No	Pollera	Vestido	Catholic	Protestant
Knows other vendors in the area									
Does not know	6	2	14	2	11	6	7	6	8
Knows "more or less"	14	8	23	6	20	17	9	14	14
Knows well	80	90	63	92	69	77	84	80	79
Talks with other vendors									
Does not talk	8	8	9	8	8	8	9	9	6
Talks occasionally	33	31	37	32	34	36	29	33	33
Talks frequently/regularly	58	61	55	60	57	56	63	58	61
Talks about business									
Does not talk	16	13	22	9	23	20	10	16	17
Talks occasionally	19	18	20	6	30	28	5	17	24
Talks frequently/regularly	65	68	58	85	47	52	85	67	60
Talks about family and children									
Does not talk	44	42	49	34	54	52	33	45	45
Talks occasionally	14	14	14	10	18	15	12	12	21
Talks frequently/regularly	41	43	37	55	29	32	55	44	34
Can trust a secret to a vendor									
No	75	71	81	77	73	75	75	73	78
Yes	25	29	19	23	27	25	25	27	22
Reporting help among vendors									
No help	6	3	11	2	10	7	5	6	7
Occasional help	19	15	26	10	27	26	8	17	23
Frequent/regular help	75	82	63	89	63	68	87	77	70
Type of help reported									
Exchange money	82	84	79	80	84	81	83	83	80
Watch over business	75	77	71	85	66	85	69	75	75
Childcare	32	34	27	39	25	28	37	32	30
Reporting problems among vendors									
Observed frequently	27	29	25	36	19	19	40	29	23
Observed occasionally	29	27	32	31	27	28	30	28	32
Rarely or almost never observed	44	44	43	32	54	53	29	43	44

Note: Statistically significant associations ($p<.05$) are in **boldface**.

lems and conflicts). Over a quarter said that such problems occurred often and another 29 percent said they happened occasionally. This being a sensitive matter, it is possible that respondents underreported the occurrence of such problems.

Table 2 also presents the bivariate associations between the social interaction variables and four variables describing respondents' occupational and ethnocultural characteristics. Associations that are statistically significant (chi-square statistic significant at $p<.05$) are in boldface. As we can see, the more established *puesto-fijo* vendors were significantly more likely than *ambulantes* to know other vendors, to trust them, to talk to them about business, and to report help among vendors. Membership in a vendors' association, which is correlated with the previous variable (very few *ambulantes* are affiliated) appears to increase vendors' interactions, such as business and family-related conversations and help. Interestingly, affiliated women also seem more likely than nonaffiliated ones to report problems among vendors. Women d*e pollera* were less inclined than ones *de vestido* to regularly talk with others about business or family matters. They were also less likely to report regular help among vendors in general, but were more likely to mention watching others' business. Women d*e pollera* were also less likely to report problems among vendors. Regarding religious division, the only statistically noticeable association was in conversations of family matters: *hermanas* ("sisters," as members of Evangelical congregations are called) seemed less willing to talk about such matters with other vendors (presumably because of their primarily Catholic surroundings).

Multivariate Analyses

To examine the net effects of vendors' individual characteristics on relations with other vendors I carry out multivariate tests for three dependent variables: 1) Whether or not a respondent knew well other vendors in the area; 2) Whether or not she reported regular help among vendors; and 3) Whether or not she reported problems among vendors (regardless of frequency of occurrence). Because all three dependent variables are dichotomous, I use logistic regression for these analyses. The results of these analyses are presented in Table 3.

The model that predicts the likelihood of knowing other vendors selling in the vicinity includes the following covariates: type of business combined with union affiliation—*puesto-fijo* vendors affiliated with a workers' association, *puesto-fijo* vendors not affiliated with an association (which may also include those who were members but did not participate in any way in their associations' activities), and *ambulantes* (practically none of them was affiliated with an association); type of dress (a proxy for ethnocultural identity)—*de vestido* vs. *de pollera*; vending location—La Paz vs. El Alto; length of time vending in the street—three years or less vs. more than three years; type of merchandised sold classified into three categories—garments and shoes, food (reference category), and miscellaneous; ownership of a refrigerator (a proxy for material status); religious denomination—Protestant (in most cases Evangelical) vs. Roman Catholic; age, broken down into three groups—30 and younger (reference), 31-40, and 41 and older; educational level (completed years of schooling, a continuous variable); and marital status—married, including cohabiting vs. not married. The asterisk indicates that the effect of the predictor on the outcome variable is statistically significant at the $p<.05$ level.

As we can see from the first column of Table 3, several predictors exert

**Table 3. Logistic Regression Analyses:
Survey of Women Street Vendors in La Paz-El Alto, 1999**

	Knows others		Reports help		Reports problems	
	Coef.	SE	Coef.	SE	Coef.	SE
Age						
[30 or younger]	—	—	—	—	—	—
31-40	-0.20	0.34	-0.50	0.32	0.28	0.27
41 or older	0.84*	0.44	0.35	0.39	0.05	0.31
Years of education (continuous)	0.11*	0.05	0.16*	0.05	0.04	0.04
Marital status						
Married or cohabiting	-0.15	0.32	0.07	0.28	0.00	0.24
[Not married]	—	—	—	—	—	—
Place of business						
Sells in La Paz	1.39*	0.33	0.65*	0.29	0.22	0.24
[Sells in El Alto]	—	—	—	—	—	—
Years in street commerce						
Three years or less	-0.25	0.33	-0.76*	0.31	-0.28	0.27
[More than three years]	—	—	—	—	—	—
Category of vendor						
[Affiliated *puesto fijo*]	—	—	—	—	—	—
Not affliated *puesto fijo*	-0.20	0.46	-0.78*	0.38	-1.29 *	0.34
Ambulante	-1.62*	0.34	-1.16*	0.31	-0.19	0.26
Type of merchandise						
[Foodstuffs]	—	—	—	—	—	—
Clothes	0.66	0.40	0.52	0.36	0.54	0.29
Other	0.08	0.31	0.37	0.29	0.20	0.25
Ownership of a refrigerator						
Household has a refrigerator	0.32	0.51	-0.20	0.46	-0.42	0.33
[Household has no refrigerator]	—	—	—	—	—	—
Ethnocultural identity						
De pollera	0.49	0.35	-0.55	0.33	-0.61 *	0.26
[*De vestido*]	—	—	—	—	—	—
Religion						
[Catholic]	—	—	—	—	—	—
Evangelical and other Protestant	-0.04	0.30	-0.15	0.28	0.14	0.24
Reporting of help among vendors						
Reported help	n/a	n/a	n/a	n/a	0.58 *	0.27
[Reported no help]	n/a	n/a	n/a	n/a	—	—
Likelihood ratio chi-square	78*		79*		67*	
Number of cases	421		418		418	

Note: SE = standard error; reference categories in brackets; n/a = not applicable; * significant at $p<.05$.

statistically significant effects on the odds of knowing other vendors. Thus, conforming to the earlier detected bivariate pattern, being an *ambulante* (as opposed to affiliated *puesto fijo*) decreases the odds, which probably has to do with *ambulante* vendors' lack of a strong attachment to the areas where they sell and therefore fewer ties to other women who sell there. The oldest women (over forty) are more likely to know other vendors: these women may enjoy greater respect among vendors and patronize younger ones through advice or reprimand. Education also has a significant positive effect on the likelihood of knowing other vendors, as education may render people more sociable and widen their social networks. Finally, women selling in La Paz are significantly more likely than those selling in El Alto to know other vendors, net of other characteristics. La Paz street vendors are generally more established than those in El Alto, a relatively new community with a largely migrant population (Gill 2000), where the continuing demographic expansion and influx of rural migrants in the street marketplace may hinder the development of personal ties among vendors.

The model predicting the odds of reporting assistance among vendors produces somewhat similar results. One distinction is that the effect of age is no longer statistically significant. While the disadvantage of *ambulantes* remains statistically potent (even if decreasing in magnitude), the difference between affiliated and nonaffiliated *puesto-fijo* vendors also becomes statistically significant, pointing to the importance of association-based mutual aid mechanisms and channels. The effect of education increases relative to the "knows-others" model. In contrast, the importance of trade location decreases in magnitude but remains statistically significant, indicating that La Paz vendors are more likely to help one another (or at least report such help) than El Alto vendors. Finally, unlike the previous model, women with shorter vending careers (three years or less) are significantly less likely to report help among vendors than are women with longer selling records.

The last model predicts the odds of reporting problems (conflicts) among vendors. It uses the same set of predictors as in the previous two models but in addition includes reporting assistance to other vendors. Remarkably, reporting help is positively associated with reporting problems. Although no causal relationship can be implied here, this association is illustrative of how help and conflict among vendors go hand-in-hand. Also notably, while *ambulante* vendors are not significantly different from affiliated *puesto-fijo* vendors, the nonaffiliated *puesto-fijo* vendors are, showing a much lower likelihood of reporting problems. Longer vending experience now does not have any statistically significant impact, nor do age and education. But curiously, women *de pollera*, as in the bivariate test, are significantly less likely than women *de vestido* to report such problems— because they are less likely to witness them, less willing to report them, or may simply have a different notion of what constitutes a "problem" among vendors.

The above explorations and statistical analyses depict only a general pattern of vendors' social interactions. While such characteristics as type and duration of selling experience, age, education, and ethnocultural identity proved relevant, even if to varying degrees, others, such as the type of merchandise, material conditions, marital status, and religious denomination displayed no influence on vendors' social interactions. These relationships, however, may be too complex and subtle for a standardized survey to capture. Qualitative data helps to bring these and other nuanced relationships into greater relief as these relationships are embedded in the dialectical amalgamation of cooperation and competition in women vendors' daily lives. The remainder of this article presents findings from the qualitative interviews. In addition, the following presentation is injected with some insights generated by an open-ended question dealing with problems and conflicts among vendors that was also included in the survey. The survey respondents who had reported being aware of or having witnessed problems were asked to identify them and their causes. Because of the already mentioned sensitive nature of the matter, many respondents refused to elaborate and even those who did identify specific problems tried to downplay their importance. Some, however, did talk about them, and their descriptions provide a valuable support to this discussion and will be mentioned whenever appropriate.

INSIGHTS FROM QUALITATIVE DATA

Vendors' Assessment of the State of the Trade

The interviews were permeated with complaints about the decreased profitability of street trade. The interviewees typically described the state of their business with such epithets as "completely collapsed" and "totally dead." Although such extreme negative judgments may be due to the fact and circumstances of the interview and to a distorted view of the past, the dissatisfaction with the current business environment was too unanimous to be dismissed as an artifact of the interview setting. Women also showed a clear understanding of what was wrong, pointing to an increased number of vendors and intensified competition. Some, like Clara, saw more fundamental, structural causes of this predicament. "Before, sales were going well, there weren't enough hands to sell," she reminisced about the bygone times, "But now, because of privatization, because they have thrown out [workers] from factories, there are no more sales."

The interviewees complained not only about the worsening economic conditions, increased competition, and diminished sales, but also about a decline of work ethics and a deterioration of the moral and social environment within their trade. Valeria shared her memories of better days and her assessment of the current reality:

> It wasn't like this before, everything was done honestly, everyone was concerned: "Let's pay the tax, let's keep the place clean." The leader [of the vendors' association] would say "garbage shouldn't be strewn around because it's ugly, parents

shouldn't let their children urinate in the street. We have to educate ourselves, to better ourselves, because people who come here look at us. We have to treat our customers with care, good manners and respect" . . . It used to be like that, but now it's all gone. No one notices if the street is filthy and if people, children, pardon the expression, relieve themselves in the street.

Interestingly, when asked about the causes of this decline, Valeria put the blame on corrupt leaders at all echelons of political power, and ultimately, on the multiparty democracy. "[It is because of] the politics. So many parties were born in this small country, and all they care about is money, how they can fill their pockets . . . It all begins with the government and ends with lowest-level leaders."

It may be argued that the idealization of the past and the denigration of the present that Valeria and other interviewees demonstrated is a universal human tendency which may not accurately reflect real changes in urban society. What is unquestionable, however, is that street vendors do perceive the decline in morals and ethics as real, and such attitudes contribute to enhancing the alienation and tensions among vendors.

Although amplified by perceptions of the deterioration of the economic and social environment, these tensions have deeper roots—in class and gender ideologies and in the stereotypes of street vendors these ideologies produce and legitimize. Street commerce is commonly viewed as a low-prestige female activity (despite a growing involvement of men in it), delimiting both the economic role and social status of women vendors. Street vendors are well aware of these stereotypes and occasionally even hear them expressed by their customers. As Marcela explained: "Sometimes our customers pretend that they are superior to us . . . [They] think that all of us who sell are ignorant, that we haven't gone to high school. But for economic reasons one has to go out and sell, because salaries are so low . . . And that's what people don't understand." Interestingly, she also felt that women customers are more likely to demonstrate such attitudes and in general treat vendors worse than do men, reflecting how a fusion of social class and gender ideologies distort gender inequality into inter-women antagonism.

In addition to justifying women vendors' socioeconomic subordination, the dominant gender and class ideologies promote the negative moral stereotypes that often equate women selling in the streets with "street women." These stereotypes prevent some women from entering street commerce or at least cause their marital partners to oppose it. Alicia talked about her husband's resistance to letting her sell in the street: "[My husband said that] women who sell behave badly, that they aren't good wives, that women who sell cheat on their husbands, and that's why [he said] no." Notably, Alicia herself did not think that her husband's fears were unfounded. When asked whether cases of street vendors' cheating on their husbands were common, she replied:

Yes, very much so. They go with other men. Even now that my husband already knows me well, he always tells me about it . . . that women who are selling in the street are unfaithful, that his friends' wives who sell drink with other men, that their husbands have seen them with other men.

Alicia's remarks exemplify how the notions of female propriety imposed and enshrined by the dominant gender ideology are manipulated to control women (Gill 1993). Although men's infidelity is more widespread, it is also more tolerated. In contrast, women are expected to remain faithful to their husbands, and just the type and circumstances of their work—let alone any interactions with unrelated men—may give rise to suspicions and *chismes* (gossip). Importantly, however, even though largely controlled by men and the gender ideology that affirm men's dominance, these *chismes* are spread and reinforced by women themselves. Paradoxically, the predominantly female environment of street commerce further exacerbates women's fears of becoming objects of gossip or badmouthing and, therefore, further alienate them, as the near absence of men in women vendors' social interaction circles deprives women of points of reference upon which a sense of gender solidarity can be constructed.

Chismes about other women's improper behavior, therefore, become important weapons of inter-women competition. Successful sales may be attributed to some indecent interactions with male customers or suppliers—flirting or even offering sex in order to gain their preference. The fear of becoming an object of such *chismes* (and as a likely result, a victim of the husband's fury and violence) constrains women street vendors' interactions both with their customers or suppliers and one another. This fear limits the vendors' mutual trust, their ability and willingness to discuss sensitive matters with fellow vendors, or seek advice or psychological and emotional support in any matters that are somehow related to their private lives, and by extension, in business matters. The reluctance to talk with other vendors about private matters, despite the numerous opportunities that a long and slow working day may offer, is, of course, part of a general atmosphere of distrust created by fierce competition, dire economic insecurity, and sociocultural fault lines that cut through street commerce society. "No, we don't do that," said Claudia referring to conversations on private matters, "It's better not to talk about personal things. Because later you'll see people will puff it up." And she elaborated further on why she does not like talking about personal things: "Because I want to have good relations with my neighbors [i.e., vendors selling in the area]. Sometimes if you talk and tell them something, then you hear a *chisme* ... I've seen that and have had experience, and I don't like it." Paradoxically, then, maintaining distance (and avoiding *chismes* and problems) is more important for "good relations" with fellow vendors than actively interacting with them. Keeping private matters private is helped by vendors' minimal interaction outside the work places. Supporting the survey findings, the qualitative interviews showed that joint leisure activities and home visits among street vendors were extremely rare.

Of course, personal conversations, as the earlier discussed survey results also showed, do happen. The interviews suggest that these are more likely to occur with select, especially trusted vendors. A few of the interviewed vendors saw benefits in such interactions, even if they concerned touchy personal matters. For some, like Guillermina, conversations on personal topics even helped build trust among vendors and, therefore, foster cooperation. Still, most conversations, as it also transpired from the survey, revolve around the difficulties of doing business—sluggish sales, high costs of merchandise, obnoxious customers, omnipresent thieves, exorbitant taxes, abusive municipal police, etc. These conversations take place during frequent lulls in long business days; when sales are slow, vendors from neighboring stalls may get together to chat, share a meal or a cup of *mate*, or play a game of cards. Although most such conversations involve women who sell near one another, they may also involve other women vendors and customers, and occasionally even men.

Help and Conflicts among Vendors

The commonalities of social identity and economic (mis)fortune, as well as shared daily challenges, ranging from endemic pilferage to customers' rudeness to police abuse, not only furnish topics for vendors' conversations but also promote their solidarity and mutual help. Yet, at the same time, these very commonalities impose limits on such solidarity and help. The most common area of women's cooperation—financial—is also the riskiest. As suggested by the survey, women tend to limit their help in this area to changing large denomination bills and, much less frequently, short-term loans of small amounts of money. Larger and longer-term personal loans are practically unheard of—both because of a lack of cash to lend and because of perceived degrees of risk. For the same two reasons women rarely cooperate to purchase merchandise in bulk at a discount for wholesalers. The interviews did not provide any evidence that vendors selling similar goods in the same area might try to coordinate their prices, but as can be recalled, even in the much larger survey sample such evidence was scant. Finally, echoing the survey results, fellow vendors almost never figure among those to whom one would turn in cases of financial emergency—kin are much more likely to be asked for help in such cases (although for some women even their relatives were not an option).

    Two types of joint financial operations are illustrative of the nature and limits of women vendors' cooperation. The first one is group loans that women can obtain from banks, especially the *Banco Solidario*, popularly known as *Bancosol* that specializes in microcredit (Rivera Cusicanqui 1996). Such collective bank loans are not uncommon, but they often go sour as some participants of these loans fail to make their share of monthly payments and the others have to pick up their debt. This happened to Julia, for example, who once took a loan from the *Bancosol* with two other vendors. One of those women soon was unable to make her payments, and Julia and the other woman had to pay for her. Julia never again considered getting a collective bank loan. This kind of scenario deterred other interviewed women from participating in such ventures. The women did realize, however, that failures to pay one's share of debt result not from personal irresponsibility but rather from the precarious nature of street commerce. "This business is not certain—one day you have [money], another day you don't," summed up Cecilia, "and when you take a loan, you have to fulfill [your payment obligations]." Cecilia herself had never applied for a bank loan.

Another common type of financial cooperation among street vendors (and poor urbanites in general) is a kind of informal rotating credit known as *pasanacu*. This scheme involves fixed daily or weekly contributions of several participants to a common pot of money managed by a trusted person (who typically collects a commission for her service) and periodic disbursements of larger amounts to the individual participants. Although *pasanacu* presents an alternative to bank loans, it implies similar rules of regular contributions and, therefore, comparable risks. Juana explained why she stopped "playing" *pasanacu*: "We used to play before, but not these days—there are no sales, nothing . . . When things were selling, it was working out, but nowadays because there are no sales, we have no money to pay." The fear that the *pasanacu* manager will disappear with the participants' money further discourages women from engaging in such schemes.

The failure to pay one's loan share or to make a *pasanacu* contribution is one of many factors that may lead to tensions among vendors. Tensions and *miramiento* (envy, envious looks) occasionally erupt into overt confrontations. These confrontations usually take form of verbal arguments over the size or the state of the vending stalls or vendors' identity and behavior. The interviewees considered them frequent occurrences but were reluctant to provide details. Most were concerned about asserting the properness of their own behavior by distancing themselves from the stereotype of *mala educación* (bad manners, offensive talk, lack of tact and politeness, and so on) associated with such confrontations. Interestingly, again, what becomes apparent if we look at the matter through the lens of class-gender stereotypes is that the interviewees, having been socialized into those stereotypes, typically saw women as especially prone to manifesting *mala educación* by arguing and quarreling with others, compared to their assessments of men as more reasonable, calmer, compromise-seeking.

Alignments, rifts, and confrontations within street society, as frequent and complex as they are, do not emerge at random. The street marketplace is crisscrossed with social boundaries that enhance solidarities within them and foment tensions across them. I now focus on four interrelated dimensions along which the borders of street societies are drawn and solidarities and competition are articulated: membership in occupational-territorial associations (*sindicatos*), the *puesto fijo* vs. *ambulante* dimension, the ethnocultural dimension manifested in the *de pollera* vs. *de vestido* divide, and the growing religious split—between Roman Catholics and Protestants (Evangelicals).

Membership in Vendors' Associations

Bolivia has a long tradition of active syndicalism. Although not as sophisticated and militant as unions of the formal sector workers, street vendors' associations are an important element of the street commerce social organization, especially of its *puesto-fijo* segment. Acquiring a *puesto* is practically impossible without membership in an association that "controls" the area where the aspiring vendor intends to sell. Participation in associations' regular meetings is often enforced and nonparticipation may lead to fines and even the loss of the *puesto*. (Curiously, as the field observations suggest, female leaders of vendors' associations tend to be harsher on nonparticipating women members than nonparticipating men members.) City authorities still see vendors' associations as their legitimate representatives, and vendors' grievances aimed at the city hall or the municipal police have to be channeled through these associations. When collective complaints cannot be resolved by negotiation, association leaders may organize *marchas* (demonstrations) to build up pressure; *marchas* may also be called for to protest the government's intentions and decisions perceived to be threatening members' interests. Association leaders are expected to confront the city police who periodically raid the streets and confiscate merchandise for alleged city ordinance violations. Association leaders are also expected to help members in disputes with customers, rival *sindicatos*, suppliers, and the competition from *ambulantes*, as well as to help resolve frictions and conflicts among association members (in fact, some associations have "secretaries for conflicts" on their staff). Finally, an association still functions as an emergency safety net, and it is common among association members to collect money for assisting members in distress. As Julia described:

> When, for example, a *compañera* is ill and can't work—and you know money is everything—the secretary-general calls an emergency meeting and ask us to collaborate [i.e., contribute money]. They don't say how much money one must give, it depends on an individual's will. That's how we collaborate.

Members' allegiance to their associations is symbolically reinforced by social gatherings that associations organize regularly, even if rarely. The most important annual event is typically the celebration of the association's anniversary. Irene described what her association does for the occasion:

> We collect money, rent a place for the date we agree upon, and all of us go there to have a party. Sometimes they hire a music band, with amplifiers.

Although *sindicatos* continue to command respect and even awe in the eyes of their members and of the political establishment alike, the effectiveness of their self-regulating mechanisms is undermined by the very competition that they are meant to help alleviate. The interviewed association members expressed their discontent with the lack of financial transparency, the corruption of association leaders, and their inability and unwillingness to stand up for members' interests. Valeria's words represent these attitudes:

> They collect monthly fees and other fees, and all goes to their pockets. No one says for what purpose [the money is collected], not even [the families of] those who died get help, not even the sick. Before we used to help... the leaders would pick up the general list of members and would suggest that every member gives a certain amount, and the members would approve... So we had trust that we were making collections to help. But now we've lost trust in our leaders. They say, give us money, give us money [for the sick], collect, say, one *boliviano* [Bolivian currency] per person, from five hundred members of our association, and then give two hundred [to the sick] and keep the rest for themselves.

Her words were echoed by Gloria, who did not want to join an association (and preferred to remain *ambulante*) "because in a *sindicato* they call assemblies and meetings to get money [from members], and no one knows where that money goes ... they never give an account." These women's remarks convey vendors' growing discontent with their associations, reflecting the general decline of organized labor in Bolivia and other parts of Latin America after the introduction of structural adjustment and pluralistic political systems (Sanabria 1999).

Despite pervasive concerns about transparency and corruption, however, members are often afraid to speak out. Rosa, for instance, although very critical about leaders' financial practices, refused to elaborate because: "It's prohibited. If we don't give [money], they may throw us out. We have to always give them." Vendors' associations, then, continue to be gatekeepers in street commerce, claiming to protect the interests of the members in their frequent confrontations with city authorities, and, as the street market is being flooded with more and more vendors and merchandise, in defending the association's "turf" against other associations or unaffiliated, mainly *ambulante* intruders, and finally in quelling disagreements within the association's ranks. However, vendors' associations are increasingly unable to live up to these mounting tasks and the growing perception of ineffectiveness and corruption of the associations' leadership breeds new tensions within them, derailing their members' attempts to find and articulate a common ground.

Puesto fijo vs. *Ambulante*

The distinction between *puesto fijo* and *ambulante* vendors is among the most pervasive in the street market. It is essentially a socioeconomic divide: *ambulantes* are generally poorer and have a lower social status in street commerce society (even if they are not necessarily less educated) than *puesto-fijo* vendors.

Ambulantes' relative poverty stems from the circumstances of their entry into street trade: most are not career vendors, take up selling in the streets against their will, and lack capital or credit record to expand their businesses. Their disadvantage is perpetuated through their social and organizational vulnerability. The mobile nature of their trade and the dearth of resources inhibit any meaningful and enduring articulation of solidarity. Very few *ambulante* women are affiliated with vendors' associations, and the lack of the powerful *sindicato* backing makes them susceptible to abuse from both the authorities and *puesto-fijo* vendors. The latter are particularly inimical if *ambulantes* sell the same or similar type of merchandise or if they are thought to affect the sales indirectly—by blocking customers' traffic or the view of the stalls, distracting potential customers' attention, etc. In such cases, *puesto-fijo* women try to expel the *ambulantes*, often enlisting the authority, temper, and even physical force of their associations' leaders. Sara, an *ambulante* with a university degree and a nurse by training and previous occupation, recounted how *puesto-fijo* vendors and their *sindicato* leaders often harass her:

> Yes, there is a problem [with being *ambulante*]. You have to move all the time, they turn you out. You have to be courageous, get up and move to another place . . . The ladies are bad, they come and yell at you, call you names. And you don't know anyone [to ask for help] and have to move . . . They have their leaders, presidents, whatever. They are sometimes very aggressive and tell you all that, "get out" they say . . . And I sometimes move out before they even come, to avoid problems.

Whereas *ambulante* vendors complain about harassment on the part of *puesto-fijo* vendors, the latter often grumble about unfair competition from their mobile counterparts. The resulting bitterness permeates the relations and mutual perceptions of the two groups. This bitterness is somewhat countervailed by women's understanding of others' need to earn a living, but the corporate culture of *puesto-fijo* associations works to prevent any compromise. A compromise, however, can be achieved at the individual level, often in the form of patron-client arrangements that reflect *ambulante* vendors' disadvantage: an *ambulante* woman can perform some minor "favors" such as cleaning or watching the merchandise for a *puesto-fijo* vendor in exchange for the right to sell in the latter's space.

The Ethnocultural Divide

Race-ethnicity is a major delimiter of the urban social space. Although clear ethnoracial distinctions among women vendors are difficult to establish, these distinctions are present in any street setting and situation. The distinctions, however, are articulated not just through ethnoracial categories (such as *india* or *chola*) or language (Spanish, Aymara, or Quechua) but also through related sociocultural identifiers—dress, *educación*, and behavioral patterns in general. The common term *chola* (and its diminutive form *cholita*) is widely used to designate a woman who is different from white, middle- and upper-class urban women and Indian women of the countryside. The term has come to be almost synonymous with female market or street vendors in urban Bolivia as well as other parts of the Andean region (Peredo Beltrán 1993; Seligman 1989). Practically all street vendors are between the white and Indian ends of the ethnoracial spectrum, but the amalgamation of the dominant social class and ethnoracial ideologies imposes racial and cultural whiteness as a superior standard, and any Indian elements in speech, appearance or behavior—which is what the term *chola* implies—connote inferiority.

First, *chola* connotes the use of Aymara (and to a lesser extent, Quechua, which has a relatively small presence in the La Paz/El Alto area). Aymara is widely used in street markets, especially in El Alto. However, most women vendors, except perhaps some of those who do not live in La Paz-El Alto and come there just to sell their products, can communicate in Spanish reasonably well, and practically no study participants spoke Aymara to their children. Clothing style conveys a more obvious sociocultural distinction—between women *de pollera* and women *de vestido* (or *de pantalon*). The "inferiority" of *chola*/Aymara/*pollera* is, of course, in the eye of the beholder: some *chola*/*pollera* vendors who have achieved relative affluence look down at generally poorer *de vestido* vendors, especially those they refer to as *birlochas*, for instance, *cholas* who have traded their *polleras* for western-style garb in an attempt to blend into white society. Thus, Irene, an *ambulante de vestido* confided:

> They [*de pollera* vendors] have yelled at me, "These *birlochas* must go. What do the come here for? This street is for *cholas*" . . . That's why people get angry. Well, I say nothing to them. Just look at them, laugh to myself, and that's it. What else can I do?" She added later: "There is always this discrimination. They say, "You, *señorita*, have to go work in an office, or work in some other place. This place [i.e., street market] is not for you."

Notably, in Irene's case, the ethnocultural divide was compounded by the earlier discussed antagonism between *puesto-fijo* and *ambulante* vendors.

As much as these ethnocultural differences are visually noticeable, however, so much they are concealed in social interaction. Women *de pollera* and *de vestido* seamlessly mix and interact in the streets. The differences in clothing styles are not generational: for example, one interviewed woman *de vestido* had her sister, a woman *de pollera*, selling next to her. Most of the interviewees did not see much difference between the two types of women, considering individual qualities more important. Still, the clothing style and related ethnocultural stereotypes express a pervasive social rift in street commerce society. *Vestido* or *pantalon* are symbols of greater urbanism and women *de pollera* are, therefore, deemed less integrated into the urban culture. Women *de vestido*, who typically end up selling in the streets by vicissitudes of life rather than by choice and who are often disadvantaged economically, tend to construe their cultural advantage in terms of higher levels of education and greater urbaneness. Thus, when the woman *de vestido* whose sister *de pollera* was selling nearby explained the reason for the difference in their clothes, she quickly pointed to her higher educational level. When asked whether, in general, women with more schooling are more likely to use *vestido*, she was not as certain, and then rephrased her personal choice of wardrobe in terms of lower costs of *vestido*.

The *pollera* ensemble may indeed be quite expensive, but while some women *de vestido* may view it as an irrational waste of money, women *de pollera* see it as status symbol and often invest heavily in it trying to outstrip others in the splendor and quality of their attire. In fact, women *de vestido* see the competition among *de pollera* vendors about their clothes as a major cause of envy and conflicts among *de pollera* vendors. For example, a *de vestido* respondent commented: "They come, look at what others are wearing: if the shawl is expensive or cheap, if the colors of the *pollera* are in fashion, if the hat is domestic-made or Brazilian." She added: "For us, women *de vestido*, those things don't matter because we are of advanced age and come here to work." This woman's view may be an exaggeration (and contradicts the age difference between women *de pollera* and *de vestido* in the survey sample), but it illustrates the disjunction between the two categories of women that, although expressed culturally, is rooted in their competition in the marketplace. Women *de pollera*, who have traditionally dominated street markets, try to hold on to their domination not only by economic but also cultural means—by asserting their dress code and their *chola* identity in general—whereas women *de vestido*, relative newcomers to street trade with much more limited economic assets, attempt to compensate for their economic disadvantage with claims to cultural superiority. The ethnocultural discourse then shifts into a sociocultural plane—that of differences in *educación*, which, as mentioned earlier, defines not just (and not even so much) the level of formal schooling, but also urbaneness, good manners, and soft and polite speech, that is, all the external attributes of the dominant white cultural behavioral model. Here is how Rosa, a woman *de vestido*, clarified these nuances:

> There are some women *de pollera* who are *educadas* . . . Sometimes women *de vestido* are bullies . . . Their mouth is worse than that of *cholas*. They behave worse than *cholas*. The same thing, when they say "*birlocha*," it's ignorance that causes them to say so . . . It's lack of culture, of *educación*. They are people who haven't studied. Also, they don't have *educación* because their mothers didn't teach them. When a person has studied, has morals, has *educación*, she knows how to treat others.

Inocencia, a woman *de pollera*, expressed her vision of the matter: "We [women *de pollera* and *de vestido*] are equal. Those *de vestido* are also good, kind, and gentle. We, women *de pollera*, sometimes speak loudly and get angry. Some of us haven't studied, so they don't see it [i.e., that such behavior is wrong]. Others, who've studied, know how to speak, how to treat others." Obviously, women vendors of all types want to dissociate themselves from the commonly held stereotype of uncultured and raucous street vendors. From this perspective, women *de pollera*'s lower likelihood of "noticing" problems among vendors detected in the multivariate analysis of the survey data can be interpreted as their attempt to fight the label of troublemakers that the general public so readily attaches to them.

A distinction related to race-ethnicity arises from a person's origin. Women born in the city see themselves as more cultured than migrants, especially those coming from rural areas. At the same time, migrants, regardless of their ethnocultural roots, scorn city women's individualism and lack of mutual support, as did Sara, herself a migrant from a distant provincial town:

> In my town, I can say, people are rather supportive. People know others' lives, who needs what, all these things, and they help one another . . . In contrast, here it is different. Here everyone does his things differently. Everyone's on his own.

And within the migrant population, as it is typical everywhere in the developing world, common provenance is a basis for selective socializing and greater trust, even though the mixed urban environment diminishes its importance.

The Religious Schism

As in much of Latin America (Martin 1990; Stoll 1990), Bolivia has seen an explosive growth of Evangelical churches, a trend catalyzed by uncertainties and insecurities arising from the economic crisis and subsequent structural adjustment reforms (Aguirre, Rosazza, and Diaz de Zalles 1996; Gill 1990). The religious schism between Roman Catholics and a growing number of adherents of Protestant, primarily Evangelical and Pentecostal, churches is omnipresent in the streets of La Paz and El Alto. Owing to the powerful position of the Catholic church in Bolivian society, religious conversion remains a very sensitive topic: suffice it to say that no question on religion has been included in the national census and in many large surveys conducted in Bolivia.

As can be recalled, the survey failed to detect any appreciable differences between Catholic and *Cristiana* vendors with respect to social interactions (with a possible exception of family-related conversations). These differences are not easy to expose even with a more flexible and powerful qualitative lens. Direct religious and religion-colored frictions or confrontations in the street market are indeed very rare, but conversion to Protestantism is typically accompanied by behavioral changes and rearrangement of social networks that affect the converts' social positions and interactions. Evangelical women, especially recent converts are more likely to socialize with members of the same church and other *hermanas*. Conversation partners tend to be selected on the basis of religious affinity (including both men and women), and conversation topics are often faith-related. Sharing the same faith becomes for *Cristianas* an important source of trust both in business and personal matters. Conversion also affects women's socializing outside of the workplace, as *Cristianas* tend to shy away from association-led and other celebrations that involve worship of Catholic saints, consumption of alcohol, or dancing. The incompatibility of these activities with their new faith poses a difficult dilemma for converts—to affirm their loyalty to their associations by compromising their beliefs or to uphold their beliefs and alienate non-converted association members. (They have a similar, and even more dramatic dilemma in relations with their non-converted kin.) Simmering Catholic-Evangelical tensions may surface in women's conversations that, although rarely focusing in on theological differences, nonetheless may foment mutual negative stereotypes between Catholics and Evangelicals. Julia, a convert, said: "Sometimes we have these discussions [with Catholics]. Sometimes they say that *hermanas* are bad . . . they criticize. I also criticized *hermanas* before, but now I know what's right."

For converted women religious solidarity may help overcome or at least attenuate the *puesto fijo-ambulante* antagonism. Thus, one of the *ambulante* survey respondents said that any *hermana* with a *puesto fijo* would let her sit in her space and sell, while Catholic vendors normally would not. She also said that she had taken a loan from the *Bancosol* with three other *Cristianas*, and their group never had any problems with payment defaults. Finally, conversion is a psychological shield to help withstand the hostile environment of the street market competition. Francisca explained:

> There are problems [among vendors], but because I am *Cristiana*, I say nothing, keep quiet, just look and that's it. I just say to God: "My God, give patience to the heart of this lady [who causes problems] because it's no good" . . . If I get involved in these problems, what kind of *Cristiana* am I? [To be a *Cristiana*] is not to envy others, not to criticize them, not to tell them "You do good, you do bad."

As Francisca's words also illustrate, the psychological protection of Evangelical conversion comes in the typical form of individual-centered acquiescence, which hinders women's ability to articulate and promote common goals and strategies.

CONCLUSION

Women carry a disproportionate burden of structural adjustment reforms, as they are increasingly forced into the double shift of paid and unpaid labor, their economic contributions remain undervalued, and their male partners' financial input into the household declines (Alarcon-Gonzalez and McKinley 1999, Benéria and

Feldman 1992; Friedmann, Abers, and Autler 1996; Tanski 1994). Yet despite this rising burden, poor Latin American women's collective attempts to defend their interests and improve their lot have been relatively few, relative small-scale, and, in the long-run, unsuccessful.

In the foregoing analysis I have used the case of street vendors in La Paz-El Alto to examine some of the underlying causes of the limited scope and success of women's collective actions aimed at improving their lot. I have argued that among women street vendors the perennial balancing act of competition and cooperation is increasingly tilted in favor of the former due to extreme overcrowding and low and unpredictable profits that characterize this market niche, combined with an increasing entrenchment of individualism and the decline of "common cause" ideological paradigms and of political forms that used to sustain them. Even though women vendors are fully aware of the commonalities of their woes and of the potential benefits of sharing and cooperating, the overwhelming competition leaves opportunities for cooperation underrated and underutilized.

Although the cross-sectional data at hand did not allow me to test directly for a possible causal link between Bolivia's neoliberal reforms and the patterns of women vendors' social interactions, such a link can be suggested. The economic and sociopolitical climate of structural adjustment exacerbates class, race, ethnic, and gender ideologies that fracture the street commerce social body by cementing the compartmentalization of its constituent parts. Instead of nurturing a sense of solidarity, then, vendors engage in symbolic rivalries and sometimes in overt and violent group or individual confrontations with one another.

As Latin American societies grow increasingly disenchanted with the overall outcome of neoliberal reforms, a rise of social tension and conflict seems inevitable. Yet one should not expect an easy and substantial triumph for labor. While increasing insecurities and stirring discontent among the poor, economic structural adjustment, the retreat of the state, and political pluralization have divided the poor, diluted the image of the state as their common enemy, and discredited traditional forms of their political organization, which together undermine the poor's ability to articulate and pursue their common interests. These debilitating effects of economic and political liberalization appear particularly strong among poor working women. The imminent social battles will require a reinvention of ideological and organizational frameworks allowing the poor to sort out their class, ethnic, race, and gender diversity into inclusive, flexible, and viable political agendas.

ACKNOWLEDGEMENTS

I am grateful to Juana Huañapaco, Juana Irene Coronel, and Sophia Hinojosa for their participation in data collection.

NOTES

1. The meanings of terms race, ethnicity, and ethnic culture and their derivatives in the Andean context have been the topic of endless debates, at it is not my objective to engage in these terminological polemics. In general, I use these terms interchangeably but prefer "ethnocultural" and "ethnoracial" as most inclusive and, therefore, most accurate.

2. The survey sample may have somewhat underrepresented women *de pollera*, as those were more likely to decline being interviewed.

3. The term *puesto fijo*, although referring to a physical structure, means primarily the officially sanctioned right of the vendor to sell in a particular lot on a street/sidewalk designed for vending. Selling from a *puesto fijo*, however, does not automatically imply the seller's ownership of the *puesto*. In few cases, a *puesto* can be owned by a relative or even rented from an unrelated person. Vendors selling under these arrangements are still considered *puesto-fijo* vendors in this study. Also, for the sake of simplicity, I include a small number of vendors who co-owned their *puestos* and sold half time (*a medio tiempo*) into the *puesto-fijo* category.

REFERENCES

AGUIRRE, Marta U. de, Teresa Rosazza, and Elisa Diaz de Zalles.
    1996. *El Fenómeno Religioso No Católico en Bolivia: Una Primera Aproximación*. La Paz, Bolivia: Ministerio de Relaciones Exteriores y Culto, Subsecretaria de Culto.

ALARCON-GONZALEZ, Diana and Terry McKinley.
    1999. "The Adverse Effects of Structural Adjustment on Working Women in Mexico." *Latin American Perspectives* 26(3):103-117.

ARTEAGA, Vivian and Noemí Larrazábal.
    1988. *La Mujer Pobre en la Crisis Económica: Las Vendedoras Ambulantes de La Paz*. La Paz, Bolivia: Facultad Latinoamericano de Ciencias Sociales (FLACSO).

BENERÍA, Lourdes and Shelley Feldman, ed.
    1992. *Unequal Burden: Economic Crises, Persistent Poverty, and Women's Work*. Boulder, Colorado: Westview Press, Inc.

BERGER, Marguerite and Mayra Buvinic, ed.
    1989. *Women's Ventures: Assistance to the Informal Sector in Latin America*. West Hartford, Connecticut: Kumarian Press.

BLANC, Bernadette.
    1998. "Women Vendors' Work Histories in Port-au-Prince: What Lessons Can Be Learned for Research and Action?" *Environment and Urbanization* 10(1):187-199.

CENTRO DE ESTUDIOS PARA EL DESARROLLOBR LABORAL Y AGRARIO (CEDLA)/Facultad Latinoamericano de Ciencias Sociales (FLASCO).
    1987. *El Sector Informal Urbano en Bolivia.* La Paz, Bolivia: CEDLA/ FLASCO.

CERRUTTI, Marcela.
    2000. "Economic Reform, Structural Adjustment and Female Labor Force Participation in Buenos Aires, Argentina." *World Development* 28(5):879-891.

CHANT, Sylvia.
    1991. *Women and Survival in Mexican Cities: Perspectives on Gender, Labour Markets, and Low-income Households.* Manchester, England: Manchester University Press.
    ———. 1996. "Women's Roles in Recession and Economic Restructuring in Mexico and the Philippines." *Geoforum* 27(3):297-327.

CLARK, Gracia, ed.
    1988. *Traders vs. the State: Anthropological Approaches to Unofficial Economies.* Boulder, Colorado: Westview Press.

CROSS, John.
    1998. *Informal Politics: Street Vendors and the State in Mexico City.* Stanford, California: Stanford University Press.

CROSS, John and Steve Balkin, ed.
    2000. Special Issue on Street Vending in the Modern World. *International Journal of Sociology and Social Policy* 21(3/4).

DORIA MEDINA, Samuel.
    1986. *La Economia Informal en Bolivia.* La Paz, Bolivia: EDOBOL.

ESPINAL, Rosario and Sherri Grasmuck.
    1997. "Gender, Households and Informal Entrepreneurship in the Dominican Republic." *Journal of Comparative Family Studies* 28(1):103-128.

FRIEDMANN, John, Rebecca Abers, and Lilian Autler.
    1996. *Emergences: Women's Struggle of Livelihood in Latin America.* Los Angeles: University of California-Los Angeles, Latin American Center Publications.

GILBERT, Alan.
    1994. "Third World Cities: Poverty, Employment, Gender Roles and the Environment during a Time of Restructuring." *Urban Studies* 31(4/5):605-634.

GILL, Lesley.
    1990. "'Like a Veil to Cover Them': Women and the Pentecostal Movement in La Paz." *American Ethnologist* 17(4):708-721.
    ———. 1993. "'Proper Women' and City Pleasures: Gender, Class, and Contested Meanings in La Paz." *American Ethnologist* 20(1):72-88.
    ———. 1994. *Precarious Dependencies: Gender, Class, and Domestic Service in Bolivia.* New York, New York: Columbia University Press.
    ———. 2000. *Teetering on the Rim: Global Restructuring, Daily Life, and the Armed Retreat of the Bolivian State.* New York, New York: Columbia University Press.

HAYS-MITCHELL, Maureen.
    1994. "Street Vending in Peruvian Cities: The Spatiotemporal Behavior of Ambulantes." *Professional Geographer* 46(4):425-438.
    ———. 1995. "Voices and Visions from the Streets: Gender Interests and Political Participation among Women Informal Traders in Latin America." *Environment and Planning D: Society and Space* 13(4):445-469.

KOHL, Benjamin.
    2002. "Stabilizing Neoliberalism in Bolivia: Popular Participation and Privatization." *Political Geography* 21(4):449-472.

LIND, Amy C.
    1997. "Gender Development and Urban Social Change: Women's Community Action in Global Cities." *World Development* 25(8):1205-1223.
    ———. 2000. "Negotiating Boundaries: Women's Organizations and the Politics of Restructuring in Ecuador." In *Gender and Global Restructuring*, edited by Marianne H. Marchand and Anne Sisson Runyan. New York, New York: Routledge.

LOMNITZ, Larissa A.
    1991. *Como Soberviven los Marginados*, 11th ed. Mexico-City: Siglo XXI.
    ———. 1994. *Redes Sociales, Cultura, y Poder: Ensayos de Antropología Latinoamericana*. México City, México D.F.: Facultad Latinoamericano de Ciencias Sociales (FLACSO); MA Porrúa.

MARTIN, David.
    1990. *Tongues of Fire: The Explosion of Protestantism in Latin America*. Oxford, United Kingdom; Cambridge, Massachusetts: Blackwell.

PARRADO, Emilio A. and René M. Zenteno.
    2001. "Economic Restructuring, Financial Crises, and Women's Work in Mexico." *Social Problems* 48(4):456-77.

PEREDO BELTRÁN, Elizabeth.
    1993. *Recoveras de los Andes: La Identidad de la Chola del Mercado: Una Aproximación Psicosocial*. La Paz, Bolivia: Instituto Latinoamericano de Investigaciones Sociales (ILDIS-TAHIPAMU).

PORTES, Alejandro, Manuel Castells, and Lauren A. Benton, ed.
    1989. *The Informal Economy: Studies in Advanced and Less Developed Countries*. Baltimore, Maryland: The Johns Hopkins University Press.

PSACHAROPOULOS, George and Zafiris Tzannatos.
    1992. *Women's Employment and Pay in Latin America: Overview and Methodology*. The World Bank Regional and Sectoral Studies. Washington, D.C.: The World Bank.

RAY, Raka and Anna C. Korteweg.
    1999. "Women's Movements in the Third World: Identity, Mobilization, and Autonomy." *Annual Review of Sociology* 25:47-71.

RIVERA CUSICANQUI, Silvia.
    1996. "Trabajo de Mujer: Explotación Capitalista y Opresión Colonial." In *Ser*

Mujer Indígena, Chola o Birlocha en la Bolivia Postcolonial de los Años 90, edited by Silvia Rivera Cusicanqui. La Paz, Bolivia: Ministerio de Desarrollo Humano, Subsecretaría de Asuntos de Género.

SANABRIA, Harry.
    1999. "Consolidating States, Restructuring Economies, and Confronting Workers and Peasants: The Antinomies of Bolivian Neoliberalism." *Comparative Studies in Society and History* 41(3):535-561.

SCHROEDER, Kathleen.
    2000. "Spatial Constraints on Women's Work in Tarija, Bolivia." *Geographical Review* 90(2):191-205.

SELIGMANN, Linda J.
    1989. "To Be in Between: The Cholas as Market Women in Peru." *Comparative Studies in Society and History* 31(4):694-721.

———. 2001. *Women Traders in Cross-cultural Perspective: Mediating Identities, Marketing Wares*. Stanford, California: Stanford University Press.

STAUDT, Kathleen.
    1996. "Struggles in Urban Spaces: Street Vendors in El Paso and Ciudad Juárez." *Urban Affairs Review* 31(4):435-454.

STOLL, David.
    1990. *Is Latin America Turning Protestant? The Politics of Evangelical Growth*. Berkeley: University of California Press.

TANSKI, Joseph M.
    1994. "The Impact of Crisis, Stabilization, and Structural Adjustment on Women in Lima, Peru." *World Development* 22(11):1627-1642.

THIELE, Rainer.
    2001. The Social Impact of Structural Adjustment in Bolivia. Working Paper No. 1056. Kiel, Germany: Kiel Institute of World Economics.

VAN DIJCK, Pitou, ed.
    1998. *The Bolivian Experiment: Structural Adjustment and Poverty Alleviation*. Amsterdam, The Netherlands: Centro de Estudios para el Desarrollo Laboral y Agrario (CEDLA), Latin American Studies.

ABOUT THE AUTHORS

Victor Agadjanian is an Associate Professor of sociology at Arizona State University. His recent research deals with gender, work, and reproduction in various Third World settings. He focuses in particular on how informal social interactions reflect and alter the socioeconomic, cultural, and reproductive realities in developing societies. His recent publications include "Men Doing 'Women's Work': Masculinity and Gender Relations among Street Vendors in Maputo," *Journal of Men's Studies* 2002; "Men's Talk about 'Women's Matters': Gender, Communication, and Contraception in Mozambique," *Gender & Society*; "Religion, Social Milieu, and the Contraceptive Revolution," *Population Studies* 2002; (with Alex Chika Ezeh) "Polygyny, Gender Relations, and Reproduction in Ghana," *Journal of Comparative Family Studies* 2000; "Women's Work and Fertility in a Sub-Saharan Urban Setting: A Social Environment Approach," *Journal of Biosocial Science* 2000.

Jennifer Bickham Mendez is an Assistant Professor in the Department of Sociology at the College of William and Mary. Her research interests include gender and globalization, social movements, and transnational migration. She has published articles in the journals: *Identities, Organization, Social Problems* and *Mobilization* (forthcoming). Her book *The Global Here and Now: Gender and the Politics of Transnationalism* is forthcoming with Duke University Press.

Sylvia Chant holds a Chair in Geography at the London School of Economics. She has worked in Costa Rica, Mexico, and the Philippines on a range of issues relating to gender and development, including migration, poverty, employment, household survival strategies, lone parenthood, and men and masculinities. Recent publications include *Women-headed Households: Diversity and Dynamics in the Developing World* (Macmillan/St Martins 1997), *Three Generations, Two Genders, One World: Women and Men in a Changing Century* (with Cathy McIlwaine) (Zed 1998), *Mainstreaming Men into Gender and Development: Debates, Reflections and Experiences* (with Matthew Gutmann) (Oxfam 2000), and *Gender in Latin America* (in association with Nikki Craske) (Latin America Bureau/Rutgers University Press 2003).

Rocío Enríquez Rosas, a social anthropologist, is a Research Professor at the Jesuit University ITESO (Instituto Tecnológico y de Estudios Superiores de Occidente), Guadalajara, México. Her research interests include gender, households and poverty, the sociocultural construction of emotions in contexts of exclusion, and social networks and urban poverty. Some of her recent publications include "Voces de la Pobreza: malestar emocional femenino y redes sociales. Un estudio comparativo sobre jefaturas de hogar pobres, AVANCES, ITESO (1998); "Pobreza y hogares de jefatura femenina en México". En: Los rostros de la pobreza: el debate, ITESO-UIA (1998); "Conformación y funcionamiento de los hogares pobres urbanos," Revista de Trabajo Social (1999); "Características de los hogares pobres urbanos," in Hogar, pobreza y bienestar en México, ITESO (with Paola Aldrete) 1999.

Elisa Facio is an Associate Professor in the Department of Ethnic Studies at the University of Colorado at Boulder. Her research interests include racial/ethnic women, for example, her recent book, *Understanding Older Chicanas: Sociological and Policy Perspective* (Sage 1996). More recently research interest have turned toward understanding the relationship between socialism, nationalism, and feminism in Cuba. Currently she is working on an anthology on Cuba with scholars from the University of Havana.

Cristina Gomes, a physician and demographer, is a professor and researcher at FLACSO-México, and aconsultant to The Ford Foundation in Mexico. She has worked as an associated researcher at the *Escola Nacional de Saude Publica—Fundacao Oswaldo Cruz*, in Rio de Janeiro, and has been consultant to health and pensions programs in banks and in labor associations in Brazil. Recent publications include "Households Income Structure and Social Policy in Brazil, México and Colombia," in *Exclusion and Engagement: Social Policy in Latin America* (London, Institute of Latin American Studies, University of London 2002); *México - un país de jóvenes, en rápido proceso de envejecimiento, Participación Laboral, Pensiones, Discapacidad y Uso de Servicios de Salud, in Políticas Públicas en América Latina* (UNAM 2002); Life Course, Households and Institutions, in the *Journal of Comparative Family Studies* 2002; *Hogares e Ingresos en tres generaciones de jefes y jefas en diferentes contextos institucionales*, in Revista de Estudios Demográficos y Urbanos 2001.

Amy Lind is Assistant Professor of Women's Studies at Arizona State University. Her research focuses on gender and development, women's movements, Third World feminisms, and the international politics of sexuality. Her book manuscript, *Development Engendered: Women's Movements and the Cultural Politics of Neoliberalism in the Andes*, is currently under review. She has published articles in journals such as *World Development* and *Latin American Perspec*tives as well as in numerous anthologies.

Silvia López Estrada, a sociologist, is an Assistant Professor in the Department of Population Studies, El Colegio de la Frontera Norte, Tijuana, México. Her research interests include family and work, gender and space, and women's political participation. Her recent publications include: "Uso y significado de la casa como lugar de trabajo." *Esto es cosa de hombres? Trabajo, Género y Cambio Social*. México: PUEG-UNAM, 2001; and "Women, Urban Life, and City Images in Tijuana, Mexico," *Historical Geography* 1998.

ABOUT THE AUTHORS

Susana Masseroni, a sociologist, is an Adjunct Professor of research methods in Sociology at the University of Buenos Aires. She is also a researcher at the Gino Germani Institute of the School of Social Sciences at the University of Buenos Aires. Her areas of specialization include social stratification, family and women's work. Among her current publications are: "La transformación del trabajo femenino en la ciudad de Buenos Aires. Evaluaciones y Perspectivas sobre el futuro laboral," in R. Sautu (ed), *Las mujeres hablan: Consecuencias del ajuste económico en familias de sectores pobres y medios en la Argentina*, La Plata, Ediciones Al Margen.(2000), and "Ocupación y género: Las consecuencias del ajuste económico sobre los sectores medios del área metropolitana de Buenos Aires, Buenos Aires." Instituto Gino Germani, Facultad de Ciencias Sociales, UBA (2002)

Cecilia Menjívar, a sociologist, is Associate Professor in the School of Justice Studies at Arizona State University. She has written on the social processes of migration—social networks, gender relations, family dynamics, transnational spaces, and religious communities—among Central Americans in the United States, including the book "*Fragmented Ties: Salvadoran Immigrant Networks in America*" (UC Press 2000). She is co-editing a book (with Néstor Rodriguez) on state terror in Latin America and writing a monograph that examines comparatively the social networks of indigenous and ladina women in Guatemala.

Helen I. Safa is Professor Emerita of Anthropology and Latin American Studies at the University of Florida. She was formerly Director of the Center for Latin American Studies at UF and President of the Latin American Studies Association. Her research has focused on gender, race, development and globalization, particularly in the Hispanic Caribbean. Her book, *The Myth of the Male Breadwinner: Women and Industrialization in the Caribbean* (Westview 1995), analyzes women industrial workers in Puerto Rico, Cuba, and the Dominican Republic. She received her Ph.D. in anthropology from Columbia University in 1962.

Susana Sauane is a doctoral student in Psychology at the University of Buenos Aires and an adjunct professor of psychosomatic illnesses among children. She is also a researcher at the Research Institute of the Psychology Department at the University of Buenos Aires. Her areas of specialization include psychosomatic disorders among adults and children. Among her recent publications are "Estados depresivos y angustias específicas en niños psicosomáticos." Buenos Aires, Revista de Investigaciones en Psicología, Facultad de Psicología, UBA (1999), and "Incidencias de las fallas paraexitatorias parentales en la vulnerabilidad psíquica y somática infantil," Buenos Aires, Revista de Investigaciones en Psicología, Facultad de Psicología, UBA (2000).

Anne R. Roschelle is Associate Professor of Sociology at the State University of New York at New Paltz and the former Director of Women's Studies at the University of San Francisco. She has written extensively on race, class, and gender with a focus on extended kinship networks and family poverty. Her publications include *No More Kin: Exploring Race, Class, and Gender in Family Networks* (Sage), "The Tattered Web of Kinship: Black White Differences in Social Support in A Puerto Rican Community," In *The New Politics of Race: From DuBois to the 21st Century*, edited by Marlese Durr. CT: Praeger, 2002; "Shaping the Future City Through Gentrification and Social Exclusion: Spatial Policing and Homeless Activist Responses in the San Francisco Bay Area." (Co-authored with Talmdage Wright). In *Urban Fortunes*, edited by Tim Hall and Malcolm Miles. London: Routledge. (Forthcoming). She is currently writing a book about homeless and formerly homeless families in the San Francisco Bay Area based on a four-year ethnographic study.

Maura I. Toro Morn is Associate Professor of Sociology at Illinois State University. She has written extensively on the gender and class dimensions of Puerto Rican migration to the United States, and has conducted cross-cultural research in Spain, China, Cuba, and Puerto Rico. Her most recent publications include "A Study of Men and Women from Different Sides of Earth to Determine if Men are from Mars and Women are from Venus in their Beliefs about Love and Romantic Relationships," *Sex Roles* 2002, (co-authored with Sue Sprecher); "'Yo era muy arriesgada': A Historical Overview of the Work Experiences of Puerto Rican Women in Chicago," *Centro: Journal of the Center for Puerto Rican Studies* 2001; and "Gendered Geographies of Home: Mapping Second and Third Generation Puerto Ricans' Sense of Home," (co-authored with Marixsa Alicea), forthcoming in *Gender and U.S. Immigration: Contemporary Trends*, edited by Pierrette Hondagneu-Sotelo. Berkely: University of California Press. She is currently working on a book manuscript to examine the gendered nature of international migration. She teaches about race, class, and gender inequality in the United States.

INDEX

Abers, R., 264, 284
Acker, J., 219
Acosta, A., 237
Agadjanian, V,. 9, 262, 289
Aguirre, M.U., 282
Agurto, S., 204
Ahrentzen, S., 191
Alarcon-Gonzalez, D., 283
Albó, X., 237
Alvarez, S.E., 199, 201-203, 208-209, 211, 220, 222, 231, 236, 238, 244, 246
Appadurai, A., 201
Arboleda, M., 236, 245
Argentina, 5, 61-62, 65, 67-70, 72, 75, 80, 118, 141, 253, 291
Arias, D., 120
ARIAS, O., 144
Arriagada, I., 112
Arteaga, V., 263
Asia, 32, 55, 246, 253
Aulagnier, P., 64
Autler, L., 264, 284

Babb, F., 204-205, 225
Badilla, A.E., 115
Báez, C., 13, 27
Balkin, S., 263
Barba, C., 91
Barrig, M., 236, 242, 246, 254
Basu, A., 202, 235
Bazán, L., 88
Beach, B., 175, 188
Bearak, B., 27
Beccaría, L., 63
Belanger, C., 32
Beltrão, K.I., 154, 166
Beneria, 32
Benería, L., 1, 25, 32, 112, 174, 176-177, 191, 232-234, 250, 253
Bengelsdorf, C., 34
Benton, L.A., 263
Berger, M., 264
Berheide, C.W., 32, 50
Bertone, A.M., 47, 55
Blanc, B., 263
Blanco, L., 115
Blanco, M., 177
Blasco, M., 156-157, 165
Blomqvist, H.C., 32
Bolivia, 8-9, 231-238, 242-244, 247, 249, 251-254, 262-265, 277-278, 280, 282, 284

Boris, E., 174
Bose, C.E., 32
Boserup, E., 234
Bradshaw, S., 115
Brazil, 6-7, 118, 130, 143, 152-167, 211, 220, 235, 253, 290
Brea, R., 25, 28
Bruce, J., 3, 232, 253
Budowski, M., 113-114, 140, 142, 144
Buvinic, M., 264

Calla, P., 243, 252
Campbell, Al., 37-39
Canada, 43, 47, 210, 218
Carazo, R., 115
Caribbean, 1-4, 9, 12-14, 20, 24, 26, 32, 40, 42-43, 50, 53, 118, 291
Castells, M., 112, 234, 263
Castro, Fidel, 35, 39
Catasus Cervera, S.I., 37
Central America, 12, 24, 27, 291
Centro María Quilla, 236
Cerrutti, M., 112, 263
Chant, S., 4, 6, 26, 88-89, 98, 102, 112-120, 122-124, 126, 128-130, 132, 134, 136-138, 140, 142-144, 146, 148, 150, 156, 175-177, 194, 263, 289
Chayovan, N., 155
Chiarello, F., 89
Chigudu, H., 219
Child Protection, 125
Chile, 118, 231
China, 12, 24, 27, 33, 292
Chinchilla, N.S., 207-208, 215
Chow, E.N., 32, 50
Christensen, K., 175, 180, 184, 189-191
Cicerchia, R., 141
Clark, G., 263
Cole, J., 34, 37
Colombia, 6-7, 123, 152-161, 163-167, 290
Concepción, M.B., 156
Cordera, R., 176
Cornia, G.A., 238
Cortés, F., 165
Cortés, R., 63
Costa Rica, 6, 14, 112-115, 117-120, 126-129, 132, 138-144, 289
Cotman, J., 43-44
Coverman, S., 49
Cranford, C., 32
Craske, N., 112, 115, 289
Criquillón, A., 203, 205, 215

Cross, J., 263-264
Cuba, 4-5, 12, 32-55, 225, 290-292

Dagnino, E., 199
Daines, V., 235, 253
Datta, K., 112
de Oliveira, O., 85, 105, 132
Deere, C.D., 24
Delgado Ribadeneira, E., 239-241, 253
Delpino, N., 236
Desai, M., 200, 202
Developed Countries, 12, 155, 174
Developing Countries, 11-12, 27, 52, 155, 166, 204
Diaz de Zalles, E., 282
Díaz González, E., 39
Divorce, 112, 114, 117, 134
Dobles Oropeza, I., 124, 126, 130, 143
Doezema, J., 47
Dominican Republic, 3, 11-15, 21-28, 50, 130, 291
Dore, E., 141
Doria Medina, S., 263
Duarte, I., 19, 25, 28
Dwyer, D., 3, 232, 253
Dyck, I., 190

East Asia, 12
East Germany, 32
Economies
    Capitalist, 4, 32, 36, 53-54
    Industrial, 4, 55
    Underground, 4, 33, 39
Ecuador, 8, 231-238, 240, 242, 247, 249, 251-252, 254-255
Elson, D., 21, 139, 232, 250-252
England, 14
English, 38, 44, 52, 254
Enríquez, R., 1, 5-7, 84, 86, 88, 90, 92, 94, 96, 98, 100, 102, 104, 106, 108, 110, 165, 289
Escobar, A., 199, 234, 244, 248
Escobar, S., 173
Espinal, R., 24, 263
Esteinou, R., 89
Estrada, M., 88
Estrada, S.L., 7, 172, 180-181, 188-189, 191, 290
Europe, 12, 44, 47, 173, 218
Evans, T., 204

Facio, E., 4-5, 32, 43, 49, 290

Family Breakdown, 117-118, 128-129, 131-132, 135, 137
Family Change, 119-120, 126, 135-137, 140
Family Perspectives, 155
Family Relations, 32, 50, 85, 90, 101, 125, 136
Fauné, M.A., 113-114
Federation of Cuban Women, 35, 54
Feldman, S., 232, 250, 253, 284
Female Housewife, 113
Feminism, 200-202, 209-211, 214-216, 220, 223, 290
Feminist, 36-37, 49-50, 53-55, 112, 139, 174-175, 190, 199-202, 205, 209-218, 231-233, 235, 237-239, 241, 243, 245-251, 253-255, 257, 259, 261
Ferguson, A., 219
Fernández-Alemany, M., 235
Fernandez-Kelly, M.P., 32
Filgueira, C., 86-90, 97, 99, 101-102, 104
Fine, G.A., 64
Fisher, J., 201
Fisher, R., 234
Fisher, W., 201
Fleites-Lear, M., 34, 37
Flores, C.E., 156
Folbre, N., 112, 251
Follari, R., 1
Fonseca, C., 20
France, 14
Freeman, C., 32
Freud, S., 64, 72, 75, 81
Friedmann, J., 264, 284
Fundapec, 21

García, B., 85, 105, 132, 173-176, 189-190, 194
Geldstein, R., 112
Gender Equity, 4, 32-34, 54-55
Gender Perspectives, 155
Gender Relations, 1, 3, 7, 12-13, 18, 34, 50, 54, 172, 175, 188, 193, 289, 291
Gendreau, M., 106
Germany, 42
Ghorayshi, P., 32
Gilbert, A., 263
Gill, L., 262-263, 271, 274, 282
Glenn, E.N., 50
Global Capitalism, 4, 34, 54
Global Economy, 3-4, 32-33, 40, 47, 49, 54-55, 250
Global Sex Market, 47, 55
Globalization, 3-4, 11-14, 19, 21, 23, 25-28, 32, 34, 43, 112, 118, 200-202, 211, 222, 224-225, 231-232, 234, 251, 289, 291
Goldani, A.M., 154, 165

Gomáriz, E., 138
Gomes da Conceição, M.C., 6, 152-153, 166, 290
González de la Rocha, 2, 26, 85-90, 92, 94, 98, 100, 104, 106, 112, 174, 175, 189
González Tiburcio, E. 176
Goody, J., 155-156
Grasmuck, S., 263
Gubrium, J.F., 37
Gudmundson, L., 141
Guinnane, T.W., 155
Gutiérrez Castillo, O., 37
Guzmán, L., 113

Hageman, A., 34
Hanson, S., 174-175
Harris, R., 1
Hartmann, H., 49-50
Hays-Mitchell, M., 263-264
Henthorne, T.L., 37, 55
Heyl, B., 37
Hispanic, 14, 291
Hodge, D.G., 47, 49
Höhn, C., 156
Holstein, J.A., 37
Homosexuality, 117
Hondagneu-Sotelo, P., 32, 292
Household Conflict, 181, 183-186, 188, 190
Household Economy, 17
Huberman, A., 66
Human Rights, 12, 73, 118, 210
Hungary, 32

Ibáñez, J., 66
India, 27, 279
International Monetary Fund, 11, 204
Itzigsohn, J., 14, 17

Jackson, C., 251
Japan, 11, 55
Jaquette, J.S., 208
Jaramillo, H., 154
Jatar-Hausmann, A., 37
Jelin, E., 112, 175, 223
Jennissen, T., 33-36, 55
Jineteras, 48-49
Jineterismo, 33, 46-48, 54
Jolly, R., 238
Jubb, N., 216-217

Kahn, J., 12
Kamo, M., 11
Kaztman, R., 86-90, 97, 99, 101-102, 104, 112
Keck, M., 220
Kempadoo, K., 47
Kim, C., 23
Kling, J., 234
Klor de Alva, J.J., 235
Knodel, J., 155-156
Kohl, B., 262
Kono, S., 156
Korteweg, A.C., 264
Kuijsten, A.C., 155
Kuznesof, E.A., 141, 167

La Búsqueda, 33, 46, 54
Labor Rights, 21-22
Lara, J.B., 37, 141
Larrazábal, N., 263
Laslett, P., 155-156
Latin America, 1-3, 9, 11, 20, 27-28, 32, 43-44, 49, 112, 115, 117-118, 138-141, 143, 152, 154, 156, 165-166, 189, 201-202, 208-209, 211, 215, 220, 225, 231, 233-237, 242-244, 246-248, 251-255, 262-263, 278, 282, 284, 289-291
Leacock, E., 32
Lebon, N., 201-202, 219-220
Lind, A., 1, 8-9, 231, 234, 236, 242, 248-249, 255, 264, 290
Lindon, A., 175, 189
Lomnitz, L.A., 263
López, N., 63
Lozano, C., 62-63
Luciak, I.A., 203, 225
Lundy, C., 33-36, 55
Lutjens, S.L., 34-37

Mackenzie, S., 174-175, 180
Madrigal, J., 117
Male Breadwinner, 113, 144, 291
Mansbridge, J., 219
Marchand, M.H., 32
Marenco, L., 116
Marriage, 112, 114-115, 117, 120, 129, 134, 140-142, 144, 248, 255
Martin, D., 282
Masseroni, S., 5-7, 61, 80-81, 291
McCallum, C., 130, 143
McClenaghan, S.O., 17
McDowell, L., 174-175
McFarren, W., 236, 243

McIlwaine, C., 112, 123, 289
McKinley, T., 283
Meléndez, E., 24
Melucci, A., 208
Méndez Main, S., 178
Mendez, J.B., 7-9, 199, 219, 224, 289
Menjívar, C., 1-2, 173, 224, 252, 291
Metoyer, C.C., 204
Mexico, 24, 26-27, 43, 47, 84, 90, 92-93, 104-107, 118, 132, 142, 154, 172-173, 176-178, 182, 185, 188-189, 193-194, 233, 290
Mexico, Economic Crisis, 176-177, 185, 194
Miles, M., 292
Miles, M.B., 66
Mindry, D., 218, 223
Mingione, E., 89
Miraftab, F., 194
Moghadam, V., 32, 50
Mogrovejo, N., 104
Mohanty, C.T., 232, 255
Molyneux, M., 205, 225
Moore, H., 113
Moreno, W., 118, 120, 139, 140
Morgan, D.I., 66
Morioka, K., 155
Moser, C., 84, 86-90, 97-98, 100-102, 104, 106, 123, 232, 242, 250
Muñoz, H., 174-175

Nash, J., 32
Neoliberalism, 231, 233-235, 237, 239, 241, 243-247, 249, 251, 253, 255, 257, 259, 261
Nicaragua, 202-205, 207, 209-210, 212-213, 215, 218-220, 223-225, 253
Nicaraguan Women's Organization, 199
North, L., 237

Oberhauser, A.M., 173-174, 177, 180
Ochsendorf, A., 236, 244
Ojeda Segovia, L., 239-241, 254
Olea Mauleon, C., 202
Oliveira, O de, 173-177, 189, 190, 194
Oswald, S., 37, 55

Pacheco, E., 177
Padula, A., 34-36, 39, 50
Palomar, J., 104
Parker, D., 34, 37
Parpart, J.L., 32
Parrado, E.A., 177, 263
Passinato, M., 154, 166

Pastor, M., 37
Patkar, M., 201
Paulsen, S., 243
Pearson, R., 21, 251
Peredo Beltrán, E., 280
Pereira García, 113, 143
Pérez Sáinz, J.P., 173
Pérez Villanueva, O.E., 37
Pérez-Alemán, P., 204
Peru, 235-236, 246
Philippines, 47, 289
Phillips, L., 234-235, 254
Pinheiro, S., 154, 166
Poland, 32
Portes, A., 263
Posadas, C., 9
Poverty, 5-6, 9, 25-26, 63, 74, 84-94, 96-107, 116, 119, 139-141, 153-154, 165-166, 174, 176, 211, 231, 235, 237, 241, 248, 253, 262-263, 279, 289, 292
Pozos, F., 91
Pratt, G., 174-175
Prevost, G., 203, 225
Prostitution, 4, 33, 35, 47, 53, 55, 117, 123, 125, 131
Prugl, E., 174
Psacharopoulos, G., 263
Puerto Rico, 12, 14, 17, 47, 50, 291, 292

Randall, M., 203, 205, 209, 216
Ray, R., 264
Raynolds, L., 21
Reinharz, S., 37
Renzi, M.R., 204, 224
Rivera Cusicanqui, S., 263, 275
Roberts, B., 2, 86, 88-90, 100, 102, 104, 173-174
Robinson, W.I., 1, 27
Rodríguez, E., 140
Roldán, M., 25, 174, 191
Román, I., 84
Romero, R.R., 66, 100
Rosazza, T., 282
Roschelle, A.R., 4-5, 32, 292
Roy, K.C., 32
Ruezga Barba, A., 154
Ruiz, E.V., 37
Runyan, A.S., 32

Saegert, S., 190
Safa, H.I., 2-4, 11-13, 20, 22-23, 32-34, 37, 50, 52, 112, 115, 130, 201-202, 211, 219,

Sagot, M., 117
Salas, J.M., 128, 144
Salinas Mulder, S., 243
Salmi, M., 175, 179, 184
Sanabria, H., 262, 278
Sánchez Egozcue, J.M., 37
Sandoval García, C., 115
Sara-Lafosse, V,. 236
Sauane, S., 5-7, 61, 66, 291
Sautu, R., 61-63, 291
Scheper-Hughes, N., 105
Schifter, J., 117
Schild, V., 232, 248, 255
Schmink, M., 174
Schroeder, K., 263, 267
Schteingart, M., 104
Schwartz, R., 47
Seddon, D., 235, 253
Selby, H., 86-89, 94, 97
Seligmann, L.J., 263, 280
Sennett, R., 70
Sethi, H., 220
Sex Workers, 33
Sexual Relations, 120
Sheley, J., 49
Sikkink, K., 220
Siriboon, S., 155
Slavery, 14
Smith, L.M., 34-36, 39, 50
Socialism, 33-35, 39, 50, 290
Socioeconomic Development, 5
Sokoloff, N.J., 50
Sources of Income, 161
South Africa, 42, 223
Soviet Union, 4, 32, 38, 53
Spain, 47, 49, 292
Spanish, 38, 225, 265, 279-280
Standing, G., 12, 173
Staudt, K., 264
Sternbach, N., 216-217
Stewart, F., 238
Stewart, S., 219
Stienstra, D., 202
Stimpson, C.R., 32
Stoll, D., 282
Stone, E., 34-35
Structural Changes, 1, 61-62, 85, 156

Tanski, J.M., 284
Taylor, J., 219
Tejada Holguín, R., 19
the Netherlands, 14
Thiele, R., 262
Thorp, R., 153, 166
Tiffer, C., 118
Tisdell, C.A., 32
Toro-Morn, M.I., 4-5, 32, 292
Torres, M., 100
Tourism, 14, 17, 32-33, 40, 42-45, 47, 49, 53, 55, 119, 121, 177
Trejos, 141
Triana, J.C., 37
True, J., 34
Tuirán, R., 156, 158, 167
Tzannatos, Z., 263

Uhlenberg, P., 155
Unemployment, 4-5, 7, 12, 15, 19-20, 53, 62-63, 68, 70-72, 79-80, 90-91, 104, 114, 119-120, 127, 141, 165, 174, 263
Unemployment, Male, 177
Unemployment, Rate, 80, 84, 177
UNICEF, 138, 143, 238, 249, 254
United Nations, 11-12, 21, 112, 115-116, 118, 154, 166, 238, 244, 246, 248, 254
United States, 1, 11-12, 14-15, 17-18, 21-26, 32, 37-38, 43, 47, 143, 173, 177, 189, 200, 203, 218, 253, 291, 292
Uruguay, 118, 221

van Dijck, P., 262
Vanden, H.E., 203, 225
Vargas, V., 202, 215
Varley, A., 156-157, 165
Vasallo Barrueta, N., 37
Vasilachis Degialdino, I., 63
Vega, I., 139
Velasco, L., 190

Wall, R., 155-156
Walton, J., 235
Ward, K., 32
Watson, S., 181, 190
Weeks, J., 1
Western Europe, 49
Wignaraja, P., 201
Williams, K., 9
Winkel, G., 190
Wolf, D.L., 86, 94, 219

Wolfberg, E., 65
Women Workers, 18, 22, 28, 32-33, 35, 40, 54-55, 127, 174, 179, 181, 193, 199-200, 204-205, 212, 216-217, 241, 264
Women
    Baking, 178, 180, 182, 187
    Childcare, 178, 180, 185, 189
    Cuban, 4, 33-39, 42, 47-50, 53-55
    Dentistry, 178, 185
    Divorced, 157
    Hairstyling, 178
    Home-Based Work, 172-174, 176-179, 181-194
    Middle-class, 61-62, 72, 177-178, 180, 185, 189-192
    Poor, 84, 181, 185, 189, 205, 231-233, 235-236, 246, 248-249
    Professional, 33, 42, 61, 65-68, 178, 190, 212
    Sales, 178
    Sewing, 38, 173, 178, 180-181
    Street Vendors, 262-265, 271, 273-274, 276-277, 280, 282, 284
    Survival Strategies, 86-88, 97, 173, 232-234, 248-249, 289
Women's Movement, 12, 25, 199-201, 205-206, 208-209, 211-213, 215-216, 220, 223-224, 232, 238, 246, 254, 290
Women's Perceptions, 188
Women's Rights, 12, 36, 127, 211
World Bank, 11-12, 14, 25, 80, 118, 153, 166, 235-237, 240, 242-243, 253
World Trade Organization, 11

Young, C.M., 155

Zabala, M.L., 236, 245
Zaffaroni, C., 86, 88-90, 99, 104
Zenteno, R.M., 112, 177, 263